Recognition and Difference

edited by
Scott Lash
and Mike Featherstone

SAGE Publications
London • Thousand Oaks • New Delhi

First published 2002

SAGE Publications Ltd
6 Bonhill Street
London EC2A 4PU

SAGE Publications Inc
2455 Teller Road
Thousand Oaks, California 91320

SAGE Publications India Pvt Ltd
32, M-Block Market
Greater Kailash – I
New Delhi 110 048

British Library Cataloguing in Publication data

A catalogue record for this book is
available from the British Library

ISBN 0 7619 4987 9

Library of Congress control number is available

Typeset by Type Study, Scarborough, UK
Printed on acid-free paper by the Alden Press, Oxford

Contents

Theory, Culture & Society

Theory, Culture & Society caters for the resurgence of interest in culture within contemporary social science and the humanities. Building on the heritage of classical social theory, the book series examines ways in which this tradition has been reshaped by a new generation of theorists. It also publishes theoretically informed analyses of everyday life, popular culture, and new intellectual movements.

EDITOR: Mike Featherstone, *Nottingham Trent University*

THE TCS CENTRE
The Theory, Culture & Society book series, the journals *Theory, Culture & Society* and *Body & Society*, and related conference, seminar and postgraduate programmes operate from the TCS Centre at Nottingham Trent University. For further details of the TCS Centre's activities please contact:

Centre Administrator
The TCS Centre, Room 175
Faculty of Humanities
Nottingham Trent University
Clifton Lane, Nottingham, NG11 8NS, UK
e-mail: tcs@ntu.ac.uk
web: http: //tcs.ntu.ac.uk

Recent volumes include:

Individualization
Ulrich Beck and E. Beck-Gernsheim

Virilio Live
John Armitage

The Sociological Ambition
Chris Shilling and Philip A. Mellor

The Tourist Gaze
John Urry

Critique of Information
Scott Lash

Recognition and Difference
Politics, Identity, Multiculture

Scott Lash and Mike Featherstone

Recognition

THIS VOLUME in some respects has its origins in Charles Taylor's
Multiculturalism and 'The Politics of Recognition', published by
Princeton University Press in 1992. The context of that book was
Taylor's lecture inaugurating the founding of Princeton University's Center
for Human Values in 1990. Laurance S. Rockefeller has largely funded the
Princeton Center. Indeed, Steven C. Rockefeller was a contributor to the
volume. Center Director Amy Gutmann was editor of the book and its
second, 1994 edition. The context was largely that of the challenge of multiculturalism to the presumed universalism of human values. More precisely,
the theme of the book was how can we re-think human values in the context
of particular cultures. The theme was the implications for human values in
the context of the attribution of institutional recognition, not just to the
human dignity of all individuals qua individuals, but also the public recognition of *particular cultures*. This meant also the evaluation of societies in
terms of their performance, as it were, in regard to human values. The
method was to evaluate society's public institutions, regarding delivery of
the 'primary goods' of human values (Gutmann, 1994: 4). These are goods
shared by all citizens: income, health care, education, freedom of conscience, speech, press and association, the right to vote and to hold office.
The goal is to understand the challenge of multiculturalism and identity
politics to this – and multiculturalism is expanded here to include the
cultures of women and sexual minorities. The authors asked themselves
should there not be another primary good, that is, 'a secure cultural context
to give meaning and guidance to choices in life' (Gutmann, 1994: 5). The
starting point in the Princeton volume is value universalism. And Professor
Taylor's seminal essay as well as multiculturalism is contextualized in terms
of a shared value universalism.

■ *Theory, Culture & Society* 2001 (SAGE, London, Thousand Oaks and New Delhi),
   Vol. 18(2–3): 1–19
   [0263-2764(200104)18:2–3;1–19;017478]

The context of this volume, *Recognition and Difference*, is rather another story. The location is no longer the lofty and hallowed halls of Princeton, but the gritty streets of south London. Indeed, in the London borough of Lewisham, one of the poorest and highest minority composition councils in all of Britain, home for example to Gary Oldman's *Nil by Mouth*. The event was a two-day colloquium held in May 1999 at Goldsmiths College. It was the first conference held by the newly funded Centre for Cultural Studies at Goldsmiths. The inspiration for cultural studies, as distinct from human values, is less the universalist political philosophy – as in the Princeton case – of Rawls, Habermas and Ronald Dworkin, than the cultural studies tradition incorporated in the work of Stuart Hall. Its background less the Kantian ethics of the US Ivy League than the shock-aesthetics of conceptual art of the Goldsmiths Young British Artists that has produced the likes of Damien Hirst and Steve McQueen and so upset New York's mayor Rudy Giuliani. The Princeton setting for the human-values volume was overwhelmingly American, while the setting of this cultural studies volume was quite European. Participating, apart from the volume's contributors, were Stuart Hall, Angela McRobbie, Hermann Schwengel, Eli Zaretsky, Werner Fricke of the Ebert Stiftung, Robert Boyer and Michel Wiewiorka. Also participating were figures with a more practical or critical input into British New Labour politics such as Charles Leadbeater, Ben Pimlott, Mark Leonard and Will Hutton. The colloquium was funded in large part by the Anglo-German Foundation for the Study of Industrial Society, with contributions from Goldsmiths and *Theory, Culture & Society*.

In comparison with the original volume, the starting point of this one is not universalism but difference. It is more how difference and multi-culturalism take on the arguments of universalist humanism than the inverse. The conference held at Goldsmiths was titled 'The Future of Political Culture'. There has been an intervening debate, after Princeton and before the Goldsmiths event. In this debate the opposition has been between a politics not of liberal humanism, but socialist redistribution versus multi-culturalism and difference. Here the key figure has been Nancy Fraser in a benchmark article published in 1995 in *New Left Review*, followed by contributions from inter alia Richard Rorty, Axel Honneth and Judith Butler (Fraser and Honneth, 2001). This also strongly informed the present meeting, with Fraser's contribution pivotal. But, in contrast to both the Princeton and NLR/Verso publications, the mainstream of this volume is not political philosophy but cultural studies and cultural sociology. It is also practical politics. Its starting point is perhaps less constitutions and political ideas than popular culture and street politics. Finally, the colloquium was taking place at the height of the Kosovo War: the struggle of group rights versus individual rights was in highest relief. All of which has heightened significance today in the aftermath of September 11th.

The volume starts with a contribution from Fraser on 'Recognition without Ethics?'. Fraser notes that the rise of identity politics has turned attention from 'economic harms' to 'cultural harms' and this has put the question of recognition at centre stage. Both economic harms and human rights come under the heading of 'justice'. It is such a politics of justice that she contrasts to a politics of recognition. Here under justice would be Kant, under recognition Hegel's *Sittlichkeit* (community); under justice the principle of right, under recognition that of 'good' or 'the good life'. Justice speaks the language of redistribution, recognition the language of community. Justice is a question of morality, recognition of ethics; justice of respect, recognition of esteem. What Fraser attempts to do in this opening chapter is to recuperate the problematique of recognition under the heading of justice. She wants to remove the question of recognition from *Sittlichkeit* and ethics and address it under *morality*, as deontological. Deontological ethics are abstract ethics. Thus Hegel addressed Kantian *Moralität* in the *Philosophy of Right*. Deontological ethics focuses on acts are morally obligatory regardless of consequences. For Kant and deontological ethics the only properly *moral* motivation would be neither the likes of prudence nor benevolence, but only respect for the moral law. Deontological ethics are purely universalist.

Fraser wants the theory of justice to extend beyond the distribution of rights and goods to examine institutionalized patterns of cultural value. The way to do this she argues is through addressing the question of recognition, not along the lines of identity but instead in terms of *status*. At issue are recognition-claims. If we think of recognition claims in terms of identity then we are in the thorny position of evaluating and comparing different versions of the good life. If we look at recognition claims instead in terms of *status*, by which Fraser means 'parity of participation in social life', then we avoid such difficult evaluation. Thus Fraser disagrees with the identity-based notion of recognition in Taylor (1994) and Axel Honneth (1995). For Honneth, as we see in the second article, claims for recognition are based in a psychological theory of intersubjective conditions for 'undistorted identity formation'. Taylor too understands mis-recognition or non-recognition primarily in terms of damaged self-identity, and the sort of stunted subjectivity limiting the capacity of achieving the good life. Fraser will bring these questions back under Kant's banner and avoid questions of the good life, by looking instead at status. For example, she considers the case of French policy prohibiting Muslim girls from wearing headscarves in state schools. On the grounds of status as parity of participation – that is not evaluating Muslim tradition – Fraser can oppose these policies. Fraser's recognition based on status rather than evaluative judgements of culture is indeed a case for recognition based on morality, indeed a case for recognition without ethics.

Fraser's view has virtues if at stake is the recognition by public bodies – if it is public institutions that are doing the recognizing. Yet in some ways recognition is irreducibly *cultural*, indeed at the same time irreducibly private and immediate. It must be more than the recognition by public institutions; it has to do with everyday intersubjectivity as well. What Fraser rather brilliantly does is to take recognition out of the realm of culture, of particularity, of indeed ethics in the sense that ethics are grounded in particular forms of life and attempt to bring it under the heading of morality, of justice. What Fraser has done is to treat cultural claims as if they were a question of morality, of justice. Claims for recognition are in this sense different from claims for respect or dignity. Respect and dignity can easily be handled under the universalist rubric of individual rights. Fraser does recognize the importance – indeed the particular contemporary pertinence – of cultural claims. These are indeed not redistribution but recognition claims. But the best way our institutions can treat them is as if they were instead claims for respect and dignity.

Axel Honneth's chapter, 'Recognition or Redistribution? Changing Perspectives on the Moral Order of Society', does at least implicitly address the cultural dimension of recognition claims. Fraser is concerned with public institutions in regard to recognition claims. The distinction, of course, is of recognition claims from redistribution and other universalist claims (such as the right to vote). Fraser's bringing recognition under the very non-recognition ethos of deontology and morality may be the best solution for thinking of recognition vis-a-vis public institutions. Honneth is more concerned with more immediate intersubjectivity. Honneth bases this starting from the young Hegel, in the psychology of George Herbert Mead. Honneth gives us a Meadean (hence psychological) reading of Hegel's theory of needs. Here the human subject has two types of needs in regard to our intersubjective relations: we need both respect and recognition. Respect has to do with dignity. In regard to respect, we want to be treated like any other subject – that is, given space for autonomy, have certain universal rights and the like. In terms of recognition, I need to be understood in my singularity: as the particular subject that is 'me'. In the *Phenomenology*, Hegel spoke not just in terms of the universal and particular, but the universal, the particular and *the singular* (*Das Einzelne*). The dialectic of master and slave has been variously read in terms of either universal subjectivity or singular subjectivity, or as the universal grounded in the singular. For his part, Honneth clearly defines universality in terms of respect or dignity – much like Fraser's deontology – and recognition in terms of singularity. Honneth also speaks the language of recognition claims. But for him these are based, not in principles of universalist justice but in a psychology of needs, As stakes are the main dimensions of the human personality: what Charles Taylor has understood as the two 'sources' of the modern 'self'.

Honneth notes that redistributive politics and universalist justice is connected with dignity-needs or respect-needs – this is so from Kant to Marx to Rawls. But recognition per se is based in 'affective needs and the reciprocation of social esteem from concrete others'. This is the basis of our self-trust, Honneth continues. In this sense we can understand the pain caused by mis-recognition. If we thus are called a 'dirty Jew' or an 'Irish bastard', we suffer on two counts, in terms of both these dimensions of the self. First, to be treated negatively as a Jew or an Irishman is to be treated as less than a universalist subject in terms of our respect and dignity. Second, we are also dis-esteemed in our particularity as Irishman or Jew. So, (a) we are not treated as individuals, and (b) our (collective) culture is abused. We suffer in both our universalist and singular subjectivity. Honneth harks back to the young Hegel's (prior to the *Phenomenology*) writings on three types, or stages of recognition: the first 'legal', the second of 'love' and the third of 'the state'. In legal recognition we are accorded respect and dignity by abstract laws. In love we are recognized in our singularity. There are reverberations of this in today's feminist ethics of care (Benhabib, 1992). The state, as the con-crete-universal should, recognizes us in both our universality and singular-ity. Honneth argues that in today's politics of social movements and multiculturalism, a purely universalist moral order is not enough. It is not enough in terms of justice and it is no longer an adequate basis for solidarity. What is needed is a principle of solidarity based on recognition as much as on redistribution (respect, dignity). Recognition, too, must be incorporated into the changing moral order of society.

Majid Yar takes his starting point from the logic of Honneth's argu-ment. Yar's assumptions are not so much from Meadean psychology, but more Hegel's own transcendental framework. Here even singular subjectivity is not any one individual concrete psychological subject, but is an ontological dimension of meaningful subjectivity. Yar starts from Hegel's notions of desire. He looks at this in the context of a critique of poststructuralism's notion of 'the other'. Taylor's original Princeton essay criticized what he called the 'neo-Nietzscheans' for what he saw as their reduction of the debate between the discourses of difference and of universalism to mere questions of power. Yar's critique is of poststructuralist assumptions of the impossi-bility of recognition. In particular, he takes to task Emmanuel Levinas's ethics, which is based on a non-recognizable alterity. Poststructuralists – e.g. Lacan and Levinas – begin where Hegel began, with a differentiation of human subjectivity from the world. This differentiation is what constitutes 'lack' at the very centre of the subject. This lack is our fundamental dis-turbance, its filling – or fulfilling – our fundamental motivator. For Hegel this is a matter of a struggle to attain self-consciousness. Hegel's subject achieves self-consciousness through the recognition of the other. For post-structuralism it is radically different. Yar in this context compares the con-trast between Levinas and Jean-Paul Sartre. This originary lack constitutes the subject and also the subject's desire. For Sartre this desire, this exist-ence within the lack is what constitutes our 'nothingness' and, at the same time, our freedom. This 'nothingness' is also a 'becoming' that is under con-stant threat indeed from recognition, from being annihilated by 'being'. Here it is the 'specular face' of the recognizing other that turns the subject into an object. Here the 'other's gaze solidifies my possibilities'. Thus in *Huis Clos*, 'hell is other people' or recognition is hell. Levinas, in this sense, merely reverses the roles of same and other. Sartre is afraid of the specular gaze of the other on the same: Levinas by the gaze of the same on the other. Most primordial for Levinas is the ethical relationship with the other. This is a relationship of non-recognition. Once we need or desire the other we attempt to enter into a not ethical but instead cognitive relation. We attempt to know or recognize the other, which violates the first, ethical principle.

Yar circumvents poststructuralism by a return to Hegel via Alexander Kojève. Hegel almost invariably begins the tale of his dialectic in nature, in a philosophy of nature. Nature, he presumes, is the place from which consciousness is differentiated as desire, or 'need'. Hegel's idea of nature is dependent on Hobbes and on Kant's first Critique, *The Critique of Pure Reason*. Nature is thus about the relation of consciousness to objects, to things. In the Hobbesian war of all against all consciousness encounters such objects only via the potential satisfaction of his desire. Knowledge of nature through Kant's logical categories was just the way that we humans set about appropriating these things. Kant understood this knowledge as integrally connected with instrumental reason. Kojève in this context, however, wants to make a distinction between the instrumental *need* for the object and 'desire' proper which for him is a matter of intersubjectivity. In Hegel's nature, the place of our Hobbesian and (first-critique) Kantian appropriation of the object, we do not become fully human or self-conscious. This only happens via the 'desire for recognition', that is, for 'someone to take us in the terms in which we wish to be taken'. This takes us out of nature, out of Hobbes and into the space of Kant's ethics. The difference from Kant is a disagreement with the abstraction of his ethics. For Kojève and Hegel the 'value' a subject attributes to himself only becomes a 'truth' when intersubjectively mediated.

Yar, like Taylor and Honneth, wants to make the step from intersubjective recognition to solidarity, to community, to what Hegel called *Sittlichkeit* and Wittgenstein 'forms of life'. He wants to make the step from the recognition of the subject as singular to the culture that enables this singularity. Taylor here notes that a subject can only be esteemed for his particular 'virtues' (say use of language, images, ethical activities, thought, bodily expression, and so on), if he draws on the resources – the forms of life – of a particular culture. Thus recognition of the singular subject (that a matter of esteem, not dignity/respect) also entails esteem for a culture. Yar, himself, moves from intersubjectivity to culture or community via a shift (that Hegel really does not make) from the specular to an intersubjectivity of language, or dialogue as in the work of Hans-Georg Gadamer. Here persuasion and interpretative dialogue are possible, with in the constitution of community, of culture and intercultural understanding.

John O'Neill begins in a similar way, but works back from interculturalism to the sort of universalism we saw in Fraser. O'Neill gives us a very strong set of social-theoretical arguments for redistribution. Again there is stringent critique of poststructuralism and the impossibility of recognition and shared values, but instead 'value-contingency' in Levinas and Derrida. This, he argues, winds up taking us back into Hegel's and Hobbes's originary state of nature, which itself is not a lot different than today's neo-liberal global markets. Radical multiculturalism, similarly, O'Neill argues, provides an inadequate basis or a politics of recognition. What is needed is a 'middle'

(Rose, 1992), a mediated and 'civic' intersubjectivity that translates the *desire* of the quasi-natural laws of the market into *value*. This mediated intersubjectivity is Hegelian *Sittlichkeit* that, following from the recognition of master and slave, opens the way to reason and freedom. This was *Hegel's* critique (of the natural laws of) political economy. O'Neill understands these intersubjective natural rights, in terms of the reciprocity of Marcel Mauss's gift. It is Mauss that he juxtaposes to Hobbesian possessive individualism. Like Mauss, O'Neill calls for a 'civic covenant', for a new 'civic cohesion' on which the welfare state can be revived. This communal reciprocity of recognition can be the basis for redistribution. Like Fraser, O'Neill finishes with a strong case for an a-cultural politics of redistribution. Legal, political and social citizenship rights are individual rights come under the heading not of recognition or cultural demands, but are universalistic. They are not asking that we esteem any particular culture or form of the good life. This said, Fraser uses redistribution arguments, universalistic arguments to extend also to a politics of recognition. O'Neill does the reverse. He starts with the contemporary ('post-socialist') ethos of recognition. And he uses this, as did Mauss, to make the case for redistribution.

Ruth Lister's contribution takes the debate into an empirical exploration of the concrete politics of the welfare state. Lister is clearly in the universalist camp. She argues that not just Fraser's 'cultural justice', but also 'socio-economic justice' is central to any meaningful politics of recognition. She challenges third-way discourses of 'active modernization' and the 'active welfare state'. These arguments have been used in Britain to move from a Continental, universalist model of comprehensive and inclusive social insurance to an American model of 'residual poverty relief'. The assumption is that in contemporary post-Fordism, economic risk-taking is discouraged by universal benefits. Lister shows that in concrete cases, there is rather another scenario. A universalist safety net is necessary for risk-taking because there is something to fall back on in case of failure. Thus a large measure of redistribution is necessary for the singularity of innovation that accompanies risk-taking. Risk-taking and redistribution are two of what Lister calls the '3 Rs' of welfare reform. The third R is recognition. Here Lister, like Will Hutton (1998) in *The Stakeholding Society*, argues that unless there is sufficient redistribution there will be no recognition. Today's extreme inequalities have produced exclusion from both ends of the spectrum: both underclass exclusion and the 'overclass' (self-) exclusion of global elites. In this context there can be no cultural basis for reciprocity and recognition between classes in a nation. Thus the importance of an extended rights agenda for Lister, one redefining 'active modernization' and active welfare state via the active participation of the poor in welfare decision-making.

Sylvia Walby casts an eye on to the concrete reality of politics. She argues that claims in mundane political struggles are typically neither universalist (re-distributive) nor particular (of recognition). They are instead claims with reference to some middle ground between universal and

particular. They instead have to do with *reference groups*. Walby uses reference group theory to understand 'why social groups choose some standards
rather than others as constitutive of their interests and as focus of their aspirations'. Reference-group claims typically are neither universalist – they do
not refer to any sort of abstract subject; nor are they particularist – they do
not correspond to communities or forms of life. She gives the example of
political claims that have gender as reference group. Gender, while not
universalist is also not per se a community, a culture, a form of life in the
extent that say, the Sikh community in London is. The same is true for class
groupings in trade union politics. Walby notes that even in political campaigns for universalist claims like global human rights, that coalitions
invoke particular cases like the Holocaust – and in many ways Jews are not
exactly a community or culture, but a group that is somehow in between
Gemeinschaft of culture and universalist *Gesellschaft*. Again the justice-
claims are grounded in reference groups rather than abstract arguments for
universal morality. In practice she notes further that universalist individual-
rights discourse has been used as a basis for arguing for collective or *group
rights* such as trade union immunities. In the context of trade union group
rights it is not easy to understand how Jürgen Habermas and Claus Offe have
taken such strong stands against group rights (Habermas, 1994). What
Walby is saying is that perhaps we should not be making such a fetish of
'community' in a context in which politically engaged social groupings
may indeed be closer to 'coalitions'. She is arguing further that the contemporary ethos of recognition, the ideology of recognition may be used as a
'handmaiden for struggles for *equality*' in today's global era.

Difference

If the first half of this volume, like Charles Taylor's seminal piece, stressed
the theme of recognition, the second half focuses on the problem of difference. In the remaining the contributions they go back to rethink the problem
of recognition, having started from the viewpoint of difference. By difference,
we are not referring to the poststructuralists like Levinas, whose assumptions of a same who cannot at all the non-recognizability of an absolute other,
that is of absolute difference. Nor do we refer primarily to Derrida's idea of
'differance'. In which differance is the third space between same and other.
For Derrida this difference is primordial in that it is the condition of possibility of both same and other. Difference in the context of this volume refers
instead to *flux*, to *movement*, to *becoming*, to *indeterminacy*, indeed to the
flows of the global information order. This is a notion of difference, not so
much indebted to Derrida and Levinas, but instead much more comfortable
with the assumptions of Henri Bergson or Georg Simmel.

Thus Zygmunt Bauman writes of today's 'great war of recognition'. In
what is for Bauman a previous regime of 'solid modernity', Hegel's
master–slave dialectic was valid, and power was a question of domination.
In contemporary 'liquid modernity', it is no longer domination but mobility
and the ability to 'dis-engage' that decides who has power. Power no longer

resides in the frame of master and slave, but is instead in the hands of the 'frame-breakers'. Charles Taylor argued that recognition was unalterably modern, that it was connected with modern expressive individualism. He maintained that ancien-regime status arrangements had to disappear before recognition could become the hegemonic idiom. Now, Bauman contends, we are living in a post-recognition age or at least an age in which the master–slave type of recognition no longer predominates. Recognition is predominant in territorialized regimes of power. Now we live in a de-territorialized economy and a still territorialized polity, which itself is in the process of de-territorialization. Hence recognition in liquid modernity is a great war, not so much of master and slave but of all against all, consisting of almost chronic 'reconnaissance battles'. Solid modernity's distribution claims were for social justice, and were 'substantive' and 'comprehensive'. This stands in contrast to the 'open ended' and 'formal' human-rights (and rights of nations) claims in liquid modernity. No longer is the focus on the 'good society' but instead on human rights as entitlements to have one's difference recognized. Thus the wars of liberation associated with the 'positive recognition' of solid modernity are displaced by wars of difference associated with liquid modernity's 'negative recognition'.

Richard Rorty's argument about a shift from 'movement politics' to 'campaign politics' makes sense. In liquid modernity we have neither Taylor and Honneth's recognition via 'self-realization' nor Fraser's recognition as social justice. We have instead negative recognition as pure difference, as the social bond itself comes under threat. The social bond linking the master–slave tension of recognition comes unstuck in a certain atomism of a neo-Hobbesian all against all of recognition. This is not Hobbesian but *neo*-Hobbesian in that it is not utilitarian interests that are at stake but, instead, esteem struggles. Indeed there seems to be 'a standing invitation' in liquid modernity to register these recognition claims: claims cannot be decided in advance. There is a veritable 'accumulation of difference' in liquid modernity, as compared to solid modernity's accumulation of the same. Never were there more claims, 'never were there more identities', yet we are free to 'break' these identities 'tomorrow'. The implications are for Bauman pessimistic. On the one hand those making recognition claims tend increasingly to put absolute value on their own form of life. Global elites, on the other, tend to take on the attitude of negative recognition. This does not involve giving esteem to others, but only a let-them-be attitude of toleration. Recognition claims are thus fine for global elites, so long as they do not involve redistribution.

It is starting from the problematique of difference that Paul Gilroy scrutinizes contemporary British 'third way' politics. Blairism gives itself off as modernizing, but for Gilroy it is still promoting Bauman's territorialized polity in the context of a de-territorialized society. Their hope for a 'joined-up politics' in an era of general value meltdown is anachronistic (Whimster, 2001). Gilroy thus understands British comic Ali G as iconic of the 'decay of Englishness': of the 'dwindling fund of common values' in an 'era of post-colonial melancholia'. Yet, third-way political elites are still living in the ether of a territorialized imaginary of the colonial past. For them, 'multiculturalism' represents a 'fixed mosaic' in which 'race thinking remains' while at the same time they try to keep 'race' out of politics. While there is a 'disavowed subscription to racial codes', in New Labour's fixed mosaic there is effective 'dis-recognition' and 'no opening for black belonging'. What is disavowed at the same time is that English-ness and indeed 'white belonging' is under threat. For Gilroy 'culture' no longer should to be understood as 'property' but instead as 'process'. If culture is thus process then recognition must be a question no longer of being but of becoming. Recognition must move out of the register of representation and emerge as a matter of mobility, of flows, of movement. In the context of the chronic movement and displacement of Gilroy's (1993) Black Atlantic, multiculture is no longer a mosaic but 'a dialectic of recognition', comprising movement, wars and negotiations of recognition.

The McPherson Report in the wake of the Stephen Lawrence case found institutional racism in the police force, attesting to the still territorialized, anachronistic nature of political institutions: to race-thinking not just in the police but in 'the economy, Whitehall and the Inns of Court'. Gilroy contrasts the fixed mosaic of third way multiculturalism from above to a 'surreptitious multiculture' from below: a multiculture of the street, a process-based and 'agonistic humanism' in the context of contemporary value meltdown. This would open possibilities for the reconstitution of values. This 'planetary humanism' is not perhaps primarily a question of rights. Rights are 'properties' of 'beings'. We must look to other idioms for such a process-based multiculture of becoming. In any event, any chance of registering such a cultural change in a transformed public sphere depends on renouncing the possibility of both 'joined up politics' and 'post-colonial melancholia'.

Francoise Vergès takes a parallel tack in understanding creole intellectuals in the French-speaking Caribbean and Africa. Like Gilroy, Vergès is not making any claims for absolute other-ness, or any return to roots. Her notion of difference is also a question of movement. She notes how the construction of 'home' itself produces a certain vertigo among intellectuals in Martinique, Réunion, Malagache and Senegal. Hegel's and Franz Fanon's politics of recognition promised self-realization as a result of emancipation. But instead the result is 'vertigo', as witnessed in *Cahier d'un retour au pays natal* by Antaillais surrealist poet and statesman Aimé Césaire. The question that poses itself is how do you recognize flux? How do you recognize movement? The notion of the creole is pivotal to Vergès's argument. The term's etymology is Haitian, really only fully applicable to the French speaking Caribbean, in which creole was understood in counterposition to 'bossale'. Edouard Glissant, Martiniquais poet and dramatist, developed the theory of 'creolization' in which the creole was 'absolutely original', yet at the same time, rhizomatic, growing like a rhizome without fixed roots. Born in 1928, 15–20 years the junior of Césaire and Leopold Senghor, his notion of the creole stood in contrast to their ideas of 'negritude'. Glissant indeed made a distinction between creole cultures such as those of the Caribbean and 'cultures ataviques' such as in Europe and Africa.

Indeed the movement of ideas and people across Paris and the Black Francophone world in the 1920s and 1930s was little short of extraordinary. In what Vergès labels 'circuits of mimicry and anthropophagy' – in salons and Parisian revues like the *Revue du monde Nègre* – debates on metissage abounded. Metissage and creolization are questions of process, movement and not of property or being. Vergès (1999) addressed metissage in great depth in her *Monsters and Revolutionaries*. In the present volume she understands creole cosmopolitanism in opposition to, and as a refusal of, French Republican politics, with its human rights discourse and 'assimilative programme'. This assimilative Republicanism would seem to converge with the consensual human rights notions of cosmopolitanism in the work of Martha Nussbaum (1997) and David Held (1996). Opposed to this stands the sort of creole cosmopolitanism she advocates of 'circuits of trans-local political culture'. Opposed to the fixed mosaic multiculturalism of human rights on a world scale, here again multiculture is process and movement: there is a necessary and fundamental dissensus.

Boaventura de Sousa Santos takes further this problematique of metissage, anthropophagy and a cosmopolitanism of not consensus but difference into the Latin American realm. For Santos there are three stages of Westernization: (1) the Crusades, (2) the European world system of nation-states expansion from 1500 through most of the 20th century and, finally, what he calls (3) millennial Americanization. The last of these proffers a consensual and hegemonic globalization as embodied in neo-liberalism and third way politics. Santos advocates a counter-hegemonic globalization under the heading of 'Nuestra America'. Nuestra America, that is, another, non-Eurocentric America, 'our America', was the name of an essay by Cuban poet and political exile Jose Marti in 1891. The American of 'nuestra America' was Marti's American mestiza. This metissage, proceeded through a sort of 'anthropophagy' intoned in the *Anthropophagous Manifesto* by Brazilian poet and avant-garde publicist Oswald de Andrade. His 'Caribbean Revolution' proceeded via the subaltern's cannibalization of European ideas to create difference: this theme of cannibalization repeated in the 1998 Biennale in São Paulo. This 'centrifugal', 'baroque ethos', notes Santos, was possible only in chains of imperial dependency where there was a 'weak centre', as in Portuguese and Spanish colonialisms. Thus a cohesive set of symbolic structures, or a symbolic was unable to be imposed on these peripheries, making such *mestizaje* possible. Santos proposes here a new natural law: a centrifugal, 'baroque cosmopolitan law'. Baroque subjectivity emerges with the exhaustion of canons, working in a problematique of neither utopia, nor 'orthotopia', but instead 'heterotopia'. Early 20th-century German art historian Heinrich Wölfflin contrasted the permanence of the Renaissance with the movement of the baroque. The baroque, noted Jose Antonio Maravall (1986), comprises a temporality of interruption, a spatiality that is at once formless and an 'etremism of form'. Baroque painting blurred outlines and colours, like *mestizaje*, creating new forms. On the political realm the slave faced with the non-recognizing master has two choices. Like Fanon he can kill the master and obtain emancipation. Or he can symbolically eat the master, swallow the master's symbolic and open up this sort of heterotopia.

The volume concludes with contributions by Jan Nederveen Pieterse, Sallie Westwood and Abram de Swann. Pieterse takes further the above themes in extended discussions of hybridity. Westwood warns us of extending the notion of 'difference' too far into into third world politics, which is still largely a territorialized politics of master and slave. De Swann emphasizes the continued importance of recognition and dis-recognition even in our global information society. De Swann understands the 'mass exterminism' of the Third Reich and other genocidal and quasi-genocidal regmes in terms of a 'dyscivilizing process'. Here recognition is identified with civilization. What Third Reich mis-recognition involved was the 'withdrawal of identificatory affect'. Here identification with an other entails the investment of affect. And the perpetrators of genocide were involved in a massive disinvestment of such affect with their victims. Taylor and Honneth gave us a dialectics of recognition from the psychological standpoint of the recognized ('slave'). De Swann looks instead at the 'recognizer' (master), whose mis-recognition (and exterminism) comes from such a 'compartmentalization of emotions'.

Communications and the Social Bond

Let us return for a moment to Charles Taylor's original argument before we make a bit of a statement of our own in regard to how recognition and difference might work in the global information age. Taylor was not particularly concerned with redistribution in his benchmark essay: but only with the tensions between universalism and multiculturalism. Taylor spoke thus of two poles of recognition: a pole of 'dignity and a pole of 'authenticity'. The pole of dignity has Kant as one of its earliest advocates. It relates to our status as self-directing rational agents. That is we are to be recognized by institutions and others as self-directing rational agents. For Taylor Hegel's dialectic of master and slave was primarily about dignity and less about authenticity. The assumption is that master and slave are deserving of equal recognition as rational agents: they deserve to be equally respected and accorded equal dignity. They are to be accorded, in short, equal rights as individuals. In Rousseau's *Contrat social*, Taylor notes there is also this idea of a collectivity of rational self-directing agents. Hegel, he continues, took his master–slave dialectic from Rousseau. For Rousseau here all are the same: there is no space for difference. The pole of dignity is evoked, notes Taylor, in the 1982 Canadian Charter of individual rights. As in other nations' bills of rights – for example in the US or the *Grundrechte* of the Federal German constitution – these are schedules mainly of individual rights providing a basis for judicial review. Judicial review allows courts to challenge the actions of public authorities, including those actions deriving authority from laws passed by parliaments on the basis of constitutional texts. Judicial review provides a counterweight to the 'ordinary political process of majority building with a view to legislative action' (Taylor, 1994: 58). These individual rights, as noted by Rawls, Dworkin and Habermas, are by definition not substantive, but *procedural* rights. Substantive rights address the 'good life' for an individual or culture. Substantive rights presume 'the goal of legislation is to make people virtuous in one way or another' (Taylor, 1994: 57). The Canadian Charter does not allow that a goal of legislation is to make people virtuous. Its rights protect 'dignity, not associated with any particular understanding of the good life', but instead with individuals powers 'to consider and espouse for oneself some view or other' (1994: 57).

Taylor's second pole of recognition is 'authenticity'. Authenticity stands opposed to the abstract individualism of both Kantian justice and utilitarianism. It was evoked by Rousseau who was a source of not just modernity's dignity, but also its 'subjectivist turn' in his *'sentiment de l'existence'*. This is alluded to in Herder's idea that 'we each have an *original* way of being human'. It is evoked in moral-sense theory. Dignity is at the basis of citizenship: authenticity is instead somehow about *culture*. If dignity is somehow a public phenomenon, authenticity is fundamentally also private. As authentic, I am not recognized as an equal-rights-bearing person to be exchanged with any other: I am recognized in my particularity as 'me'. Authenticity is central to the 'love relation', which is a 'crucible of self-affirmation and discovery'. In a politics of equal dignity we each have the same basket of rights and immunities. In authenticity's politics of difference, we want to be recognized as unique, in terms of our identities. Authenticity, though particular, is the subject of universalist arguments. We use 'universalist arguments' here to support claims that 'we need to give acknowledgement to what is not universally shared' (Taylor, 1994: 39). The principle of dignity requires our (and public institutions') respect for the potential of individuals. Authenticity, in contrast, is not about esteem or recognition for potential at all but for individuals as they are and for 'actually evolved cultures'. For Taylor, recognition of authenticity is as important a source of the self as dignity-recognition: cultural justice as central as universalist justice. The cultural dimension must not be conceived monologically, as defenders of the Western canon like Bloom (1988) and Bloom (1999) would have it. For Taylor multiculturalism is necessarily the dialogical. The pole of authenticity and identity is about esteem: about our esteeming other cultures. And we can only judge other cultures if we fuse horizons with them. He thus suggests

> . . . the study and fusion of horizons with other cultures that have provided a horizon of meaning for large numbers of human beings over a long period of time – that have articulated their sense of the holy, the good and the admirable. (1994: 72)

Taylor discusses specific authenticity-recognition claims such as the teaching of French in Canada, the language of signage, the language of business, the powers of a Quebec parliament. Habermas (1994) takes a position against group rights. Taylor says the answer is 'not to ask whether these things are something that others can demand from us as a right'. He wants, however, to distinguish fundamental liberties from these 'privileges and immunities that can be revoked or restricted for reasons of public policy', 'though one would need a strong reason to do so' (1994: 72).

We think Taylor is at his most poignant when he is being sociological, in particular his understanding of recognition – both poles of dignity and authenticity – as part and parcel of the Weltanschauung of *modernity*. For Taylor recognition (both poles) is the source of the *modern* self. In the *ancien regime*, the source of the self came from God or the good (1994: 28): our identities from a sort of regime of 'honour'. Only with modernity's detachment of identity from the feudal *Stände* does it become tied to recognition. Honour was a system of 'preferential esteem'. Rousseau in his letter to D'Alembert saw this in terms of a theatre where some were on the stage and others in the audience. Rousseau's modern vision – and this was also a sort of return to Classical antiquity – was that all actors and speakers are a part of the drama and that each be furnished with spectacles to regard one another. Rousseau here was as concerned with esteem. He would not have understood modern esteem as tied up with positional goods (Taylor, 1994: 45). He wanted equality of esteem. He wanted esteem in which all virtuous citizens were equally honoured.

Rousseau also understood here that 'esteem works through reciprocity and unity of purpose'. Reciprocity and unity of purpose are thus at the heart of *the social bond. Recognition, grounded in reciprocity and unity of purpose, is thus not only the source of the self, but also the source of modernity's social bond.* It is likely, we think, that the social bond and the entire problematic of recognition are under threat from today's processes of globalization and informationalization. The problematic of intersubjective recognition (though perhaps not other types of recognition) is under pressure from a globalization that it entails not homogeneity but a genuine cosmopolitanism as evoked in this volume by Gilroy, Vergès, Santos and Bauman. To repeat, recognition is not just the source of the self and the system of justice for modernity, it is also the source of the *social bond*. This is true for the abstract bond of the dignity pole of recognition. It is even more the case for the particular bond of the identity pole, in which I am recognized not just as one 'I' among a universe of 'I's but as 'me'. The identity pole came from Romanticism argued Taylor (1992) in his magnum opus, *Sources of the Self*. The dignity pole was about Zivilisation in the sense described in de Swann's contribution, the identity pole about *Kultur*. Authenticity or identity means drawing on the resources, the language of a particular culture. The Romantics developed this pole of identity and Kultur of recognition. Hegel's was always a dialectic of the two, a grounding of *zivilisatorische* dignity in particularist Kultur. Here the Kultur dimension – a bit like Bloom's (1999) canonical monoculture – was not in any sense multiculture and difference. The Romantics were of course first concerned with the singularity (not the universality) of the individual, which always presumed the particularity of culture. This again was a quintessentially *modern* question. Its assumption is that this sharing of culture under conditions of modern individualization is the basis of the social bond. This entailed the above mentioned Rousseauan reciprocity and common purpose. It entailed a sentiment of the nation as imagined community, in which the willingness to die for one another in battle was not explicable by the dignity or Zivilisation dimension of recognition, but only by the particular bond of collective identity and Kultur.

The question is then what happens when the social bond breaks down. The authors in the first half of this volume tend more or less to address the dignity and justice pole of Taylor's recognition continuum, and those in the second half tend to address the pole of identity and culture. All authors understand the social bond as under severe strain in our contemporary order of global communications. [1] Now in Rousseau's context Marcel Mauss understood the social bond, the *lien social*, in terms of reciprocity in *The Gift*. O'Neill comments on this in his piece in this volume. Mauss and his uncle Emile Durkheim understood our systems of classification as based on the social bond. This metamorphosed in the transition from 'primitive classifications' to 'modern classifications' (Durkheim and Mauss, 1963). Mauss's (1990) *Gift* looked at the circulation of gifts among tribes in the South Sea islands. This gift exchange and circulation were themselves mediated by structures. These structures were very much the same as the structures of Durkheim's (1947) *Elementary Forms of Religious Life*, in which cosmology, ritual and magic and indeed structures of classification mediated the flows of gifts and other symbolic flows and exchanges. We see these again in Levi-Strauss's structures of kinship and myth, again mediating the flows and exchanges of gifts, women and money between lineages. Durkheim of course was virtually obsessed with what would happen to the social bond – the basis of the Durkheimian *conscience collective* and of the symbolic structures – with the transition to modernity. The disruption to the social bond indeed is anomie. Durkheim however saw room for optimism in a sort of reconstituted and individualized bond, of which Taylor too is of course aware. Thus the emergence of new structures, new institutions mediating different, and longer-distance flows – of food, migrants, commodities, disease, language – in modernity (De Landa, 1997). All this gives new resources for recognition, for common purpose (*volonté générale*) and a conscience collective. All this has to do with nation, which makes some sense of Durkheim's endorsement of the French entry into the First World War. After transitional anomie, thus there took place a more or less successful individualization and nationalization of the social bond.

But what happens with the global information society? Now the social bond is not about the emergence and consolidation of recognition-based national Kultur, but about the claims for recognition by a multiplicity of cultures. Hence the recognition question is reconstituted from the recognition of the same to one of difference. Here is where Fanon displaces Hegel. Hegel's singularity was grounded in the same: Fanon's in difference. Hence we have a continuum – with recognition on one pole and difference on the other. Here Taylor is located towards the recognition pole, himself not recognizing how far the social bond has fragmented. The question is how much we are in an era of post-industrial, informational anomie, corresponding to that of the older anomie of the emerging national, industrial and individual order. This is much more than the fusion of horizons Taylor recommends with say, Chinese and Indian civilizations. That is because even these horizons are de-traditionalized, transformed and fragmented from the emergence of the communications order. *The question is how can we pose the question of recognition in an era of the breakdown of the social bond.* Let us continue. Now Durkheim and Mauss's most important opponent was Georges Bataille. Bataille gives us perhaps the key to information anomie, of social-bond breakdown and value meltdown in the information order. Bataille's notion of excess was grounded in Mauss's *Gift*. But whereas Mauss spoke of reciprocity, Bataille was interested in agons, in contests of gift-giving. Whereas Mauss was interested in reproduction, Bataille was interested in waste, in 'expenditure'. Bataille's gift has nothing to do with the social bond: his gift-giving agons take place in the space of excess in what he called the *économie générale*: the space in which the social bond had broken down[2]. This was a space outside of modernity's linear institutions, in excess of Durkheim's symbolic; a space of what today we would call 'the real' (Deleuze and Guattari, 1984, Žižek, 1989). The real here has nothing to do with realism of representations, but has a materiality, a tactility that is non-representable and avoids completely the question of representation.

Now this was not a general problem when excess had mainly to do with a surrealist avant garde. But what seems to be emerging now is a veritable institutionalization, or routinization of excess. This is what is at issue when the social bond comes more and more to resemble the *communication*. The communication stands in radical contradistinction to everyday social relations – between ego and alter – in modernity's linear institutions. The communication is compressed, faster, more intense than Taylor's social relations of intersubjective recognition, and often takes place at a distance. The communication is also, perhaps typically, machine-mediated: whether these machines are transportation, communication or other information machines. The communication takes place – outside of symbolic structures – in the real (Hardt and Negri, 2000). Flows of communications are channelled, mediated by, now *non*-linear socio-technical and psycho-technical assemblages and systems (Lash, 2001). Not just desire and economic value, but all sorts of plural values flow in this communications space (Boltanski and Thevenot, 1991). With the fragmentation of the symbolic and institutional meltdown, values disengage themselves from structures and are set free into the general flows. Machine mediated communication deals typically with signals: often, digital signals. Its environment is not so much the reality it seeks to mirror, but instead is constituted by noise (Luhmann, 1997), which escapes the whole problematic of mirroring. Does it also entail a fundamental rethinking of the issue of classical recognition? How we make sense of the world must intimately be related to how we recognize others. If sense-making decreasingly putting an (analogue) mirror to nature and is increasingly a question of selecting from a world of noise, then making sense, or recognizing others would seem also to change.

The implications of this would seem to be that political power is increasingly nomadic as Bauman argues in his contribution. If so, power would no longer primarily be exercised through the symbolic, or through the symbolic violence of ideology. This puts the problem of hegemony into question. With the symbolic in fragments is it possible to speak any more of hegemony? Are we living in what is increasingly a post-hegemonic age? To the extent that the global information society escapes the above logic of the symbolic, power increasingly is a phenomenon of the real. For Žižek, for example, power is a question of the symbolic, resistance is from the real. But Žižek understands the real in terms of excess, wastage and the death drive. The point is that global communications themselves are coming increasingly to inhabit the real. Power becomes communicational. Recognition becomes also pattern recognition (Hayles, 1999). Recognition becomes making sense of the information and communitational flows. The implications for inter-subjectivity are major. We make sense of the world and of others increasingly through more or less non-linear socio-technical institutions and systems. We are human beings, but our psychology is also mediated by communication machines, channelling, accelerating, blocking, re-routing the flows. Intersubjectivity and recognition become machine mediated and communicational. There is perhaps not just a disappearance of the social bond and value meltdown, but perhaps also by value re-composition and an eventual communicational bond.

We don't want to push this line of argument too far in the present context. We are developing it elsewhere. We just want to push a bit further the arguments of the contributors to this book, all of whom are aware that both social bond and recognition are in some danger. The irony is that the issue of recognition has been posed by social and cultural theory precisely at the point in time that recognition is in decline, precisely when the nation-state, the human (as we know it) and the social bond are in perhaps terminal decline. In a further irony for a volume in which Hegel figures so prominently, at issue is a classic reprise of the master's dictum regarding 'philosophy painting its grey on grey'. In the Preface to the *Philosophy of Right*, 'the owl of Minerva spreads its wings only with the falling of dusk'. Recognition, as stability, becomes problematized only as the flows, the flux of becoming or difference are emerging as pervasive. It is in this context that the present volume finds its significance.

Notes

1. This is true even of Jürgen Habermas, who in terms of this volume is at the end of the dignity pole. In *Stukturwandel der Offentlichkeit* (1962) Habermas thought that modern media and communications were destroying the socio-political bond of the public sphere. Subsequently Habermas broke with the philosophy of

consciousness that is at the heart of Hegel's recognition for a philosophy of language and communication. Can his communicative rationality provide a new basis for such a bond? In his theory this is unlikely due to the abstract procedural nature of the bond.

2. We are grateful to David Le Breton for this point.

References

Benhabib, S. (1992) *Situating the Self*. Cambridge: Polity.

Bloom, A. (1988) *The Closing of the American Mind*. New York: Touchstone Books.

Bloom, H. (1999) *Shakespeare: The Invention of the Human*. New York: Fourth Estate.

Boltanski, L. and L. Thevenot (1991) *De la justification. Les économies de la grandeur*. Paris: Gallimard.

De Landa, D. (1997) *A Thousand Years of Nonlinear History*. New York: Swerve Editions.

Deleuze, G. and F. Guattari (1984) *Anti-Oedipus*. London: Routledge.

Durkheim, E. (1947) *Elementary Forms of the Religious Life*. London: Allen & Unwin.

Durkheim, E. and M. Mauss (1963) *Primitive Classification*. London: Cohen & West.

Fraser, N. and A. Honneth (2001) *Redistribution or Recognition?: A Philosophical Exchange*, trans. J. Golb. London: Verso.

Gilroy, Paul (1993) *The Black Atlantic*. London: Verso.

Gutmann, A. (1994) 'Introduction', pp. 3–24 in A. Gutmann (ed.) *Multiculturalism: Examining the Politics of Recognition*. Princeton, NJ: Princeton University Press.

Habermas, J. (1962) *Stukturwandel der Offentlichkeit*. Neueid: Luchterhand.

Habermas, J. (1994) 'Struggles for Recognition in the Democratic Constitutional State', pp. 107–48 in A. Gutmann (ed.) *Multiculturalism: Examining the Politics of Recognition*. Princeton, NJ: Princeton University Press.

Hardt, M. and A. Negri (2000) *Empire*. Cambridge, MA: Harvard University Press.

Hayles, N.K. (1999) *How We Became Posthuman*. Chicago, IL: University of Chicago Press.

Held, D. (1996) *Democracy and the Global Order: From the Modern State to Cosmopolitan Governance*. Cambridge: Polity Press.

Honneth, A. (1995) *The Struggle for Recognition: The Moral Grammar of Social Conflicts*. Cambridge: Polity Press.

Hutton, W. (1998) *The Stakeholding Society*. Cambridge: Polity Press.

Lash, S. (2002) *Critique of Information*. London: Sage.

Luhmann, N. (1997) *Die Gesellschaft der Gesellschaft*. Frankfurt: Suhrkamp.

Maravall, J.A. (1986) *Culture of the Baroque: Analysis of a Historical Structure*. Minneapolis: University of Minnesota Press.

Mauss, M. (1990) *The Gift: The Form and Reason for Exchange in Archaic Societies*. London: Routledge.

Nussbaum, M. (1997) *Cultivating Humanity: A Classical Defence of Reform in Liberal Education*. Cambridge, MA: Harvard University Press.

Rose, G. (1992) *The Broken Middle: Out of our Ancient Society*. Oxford: Blackwell.

Taylor, C. (1992) *Sources of the Self*. Cambridge: Cambridge University Press.

Taylor, C. (1994) 'The Politics of Recognition', pp. 25–74 in A. Gutmann (ed.) *Multiculturalism: Examining the Politics of Recognition*. Princeton, NJ: Princeton University Press.

Vergès, F. (1999) *Monsters and Revolutionaries*. Durham, NC: Duke University Press.

Whimster, M.S. (2001) 'Fields of Vision: Arts and Regeneration in the New East End', Conference Report, London Guildhall University.

Žižek, S. (1989) *The Sublime Object of Ideology*. London: Verso.

Recognition without Ethics?

Nancy Fraser

FOR SOME time now, the forces of progressive politics have been divided into two camps. On one side stand the proponents of 'redistribution'. Drawing on long traditions of egalitarian, labor and socialist organizing, political actors aligned with this orientation seek a more just allocation of resources and goods. On the other side stand the proponents of 'recognition'. Drawing on newer visions of a 'difference-friendly' society, they seek a world where assimilation to majority or dominant cultural norms is no longer the price of equal respect. Members of the first camp hope to redistribute wealth from the rich to the poor, from the North to the South, and from the owners to the workers. Members of the second, in contrast, seek recognition of the distinctive perspectives of ethnic, 'racial', and sexual minorities, as well as of gender difference. The redistribution orientation has a distinguished philosophical pedigree, as egalitarian redistributive claims have supplied the paradigm case for most theorizing about social justice for the past 150 years. The recognition orientation has recently attracted the interest of political philosophers, however, some of whom are seeking to develop a new normative paradigm that puts recognition at its center.

At present, unfortunately, relations between the two camps are quite strained. In many cases, struggles for recognition are dissociated from struggles for redistribution. Within social movements such as feminism, for example, activist tendencies that look to redistribution as the remedy for male domination are increasingly dissociated from tendencies that look instead to recognition of gender difference. And the same is largely true in the intellectual sphere. In the academy, to continue with feminism, scholars who understand gender as a social relation maintain an uneasy arm's-length coexistence with those who construe it as an identity or a cultural code. This situation exemplifies a broader phenomenon: the widespread decoupling of cultural politics from social politics, of the politics of difference from the politics of equality.

■ *Theory, Culture & Society* 2001 (SAGE, London, Thousand Oaks and New Delhi),
   Vol. 18(2–3): 21–42
   [0263-2764(200104/06)18:2–3;21–42;017479]

In some cases, moreover, the dissociation has become a polarization. Some proponents of redistribution see claims for the recognition of difference as 'false consciousness', a hindrance to the pursuit of social justice. Conversely, some proponents of recognition reject distributive politics as part and parcel of an outmoded materialism that can neither articulate nor challenge key experiences of injustice. In such cases, we are effectively presented with an either/or choice: redistribution or recognition? class politics or identity politics? multiculturalism or social equality?

These, I have argued elsewhere, are false antitheses (Fraser, 1995, forthcoming a, forthcoming b). Justice today requires *both* redistribution *and* recognition; neither alone is sufficient. As soon as one embraces this thesis, however, the question of how to combine them becomes pressing. I maintain that the emancipatory aspects of the two problematics need to be integrated in a single, comprehensive framework. The task, in part, is to devise an expanded conception of justice that can accommodate both defensible claims for social equality and defensible claims for the recognition of difference.

Morality or Ethics?

Integrating redistribution and recognition is no easy matter, however. On the contrary, to contemplate this project is to become immediately embroiled in a nexus of difficult philosophical questions. Some of the thorniest of these concern the relation between morality and ethics, the right and the good, justice and the good life. A key issue is whether paradigms of justice usually aligned with 'morality' can handle claims for the recognition of difference – or whether it is necessary, on the contrary, to turn to 'ethics'.

Let me explain. It is now standard practice in moral philosophy to distinguish questions of justice from questions of the good life. Construing the first as a matter of 'the right' and the second as a matter of 'the good', most philosophers align distributive justice with Kantian *Moralität* (morality) and recognition with Hegelian *Sittlichkeit* (ethics). In part this contrast is a matter of scope. Norms of justice are thought to be universally binding; they hold independently of actors' commitments to specific values. Claims for the recognition of difference, in contrast, are more restricted. Involving qualitative assessments of the relative worth of various cultural practices, traits and identities, they depend on historically specific horizons of value, which cannot be universalized.

Much of recent moral philosophy turns on disputes over the relative standing of these two different orders of normativity. Liberal political theorists and deontological moral philosophers insist that the right take priority over the good. For them, accordingly, the demands of justice trump the claims of ethics. Communitarians and teleologists rejoin that the notion of a universally binding morality independent of any idea of the good is conceptually incoherent. Preferring 'thick' accounts of moral experience to 'thin' ones, they rank the substantive claims of culturally specific community values above abstract appeals to Reason or Humanity.

Partisans of the right, moreover, often subscribe to distributive models of justice. Viewing justice as a matter of fairness, they seek to eliminate unjustified disparities between the life-chances of social actors. To identify these disparities, they invoke standards of fairness that do not prejudge those actors' own (varying) views of the good. Partisans of the good, in contrast, reject the 'empty formalism' of distributive approaches. Viewing ethics as a matter of the good life, they seek to promote the qualitative conditions of human flourishing (as they understand them), rather than fidelity to abstract requirements of equal treatment.

These philosophical alignments complicate the problem of integrating redistribution and recognition. Distribution evidently belongs on the morality side of the divide. Recognition, however, seems at first sight to belong to ethics, as it seems to require judgments about the value of various practices, traits and identities. It is not surprising, therefore, that many deontological theorists simply reject claims for the recognition of difference as violations of liberal neutrality, while concluding that distributive justice exhausts the whole of political morality. It is also unsurprising, conversely, that many theorists of recognition align themselves with ethics against morality; following the same reasoning as their liberal counterparts, they conclude that recognition requires qualitative value judgments that exceed the capacities of distributive models.

In these standard alignments, both sides agree that distribution belongs to morality, recognition belongs to ethics, and never the twain shall meet. Thus, each assumes that its paradigm excludes the other's. If they are right, then the claims of redistribution and the claims of recognition cannot be coherently combined. On the contrary, whoever wishes to endorse claims of both types courts the risk of philosophical schizophrenia.

It is precisely this presumption of incompatibility that I aim to dispel. *Contra* the received wisdom, I shall argue that one *can* integrate redistribution and recognition without succumbing to schizophrenia. My strategy will be to construe the politics of recognition in a way that does not deliver it prematurely to ethics. Rather, I shall account for claims for recognition as *justice claims* within an expanded understanding of justice. The initial effect will be to recuperate the politics of recognition for *Moralität* and thus to resist the turn to ethics. But that is not precisely where I shall end up. Rather, I shall concede that there may be cases when ethical evaluation is unavoidable. Yet because such evaluation is problematic, I shall suggest ways of deferring it as long as possible.

Identity or Status?

The key to my strategy is to break with the standard 'identity' model of recognition. On this model, what requires recognition is group-specific cultural identity. Misrecognition consists in the depreciation of such identity by the dominant culture and the consequent damage to group members' sense of self. Redressing this harm means demanding 'recognition'. This in turn requires that group members join together to refashion their collective identity by producing a self-affirming culture of their own. Thus, on the identity model of recognition, the politics of recognition means 'identity politics'.[1]

This identity model is deeply problematic. Construing misrecognition as damaged identity, it emphasizes psychic structure over social institutions and social interaction. Thus, it risks substituting intrusive forms of consciousness engineering for social change. The model compounds these risks by positing *group* identity as the object of recognition. Enjoining the elaboration and display of an authentic, self-affirming and self-generated collective identity, it puts moral pressure on individual members to conform to group culture. The result is often to impose a single, drastically simplified group identity, which denies the complexity of people's lives, the multiplicity of their identifications and the cross-pulls of their various affiliations. In addition, the model reifies culture. Ignoring transcultural flows, it treats cultures as sharply bounded, neatly separated and non-interacting, as if it were obvious where one stops and another starts. As a result, it tends to promote separatism and group enclaving in lieu of transgroup interaction. Denying internal heterogeneity, moreover, the identity model obscures the struggles *within* social groups for the authority, and indeed for the power, to represent them. Consequently, it masks the power of dominant fractions and reinforces intragroup domination. In general, then, the identity model lends itself all too easily to repressive forms of communitarianism.[2]

For these reasons, I shall propose an alternative analysis of recognition. My proposal is to treat recognition as a question of *social status*. From this perspective – I shall call it *the status model* – what requires recognition is not group-specific identity but rather the status of group members as full partners in social interaction. Misrecognition, accordingly, does not mean the depreciation and deformation of group identity. Rather, it means *social subordination* in the sense of being prevented from *participating as a peer* in social life. To redress the injustice requires a politics of recognition, to be sure, but this no longer means identity politics. In the status model, rather, it means a politics aimed at overcoming subordination by establishing the misrecognized party as a full member of society, capable of participating on a par with other members.[3]

Let me elaborate. To view recognition as a matter of status is to examine institutionalized patterns of cultural value for their effects on the relative standing of social actors. If and when such patterns constitute actors as *peers*, capable of participating on a par with one another in social life, then we can speak of *reciprocal recognition* and *status equality*. When, in contrast, institutionalized patterns of cultural value constitute some actors as inferior, excluded, wholly other or simply invisible, hence as less than full partners in social interaction, then we should speak of *misrecognition* and *status subordination*.

On the status model, then, misrecognition arises when institutions structure interaction according to cultural norms that impede parity of participation. Examples include marriage laws that exclude same-sex partnerships as illegitimate and perverse, social-welfare policies that stigmatize single mothers as sexually irresponsible scroungers, and policing practices such as 'racial profiling' that associate racialized persons with criminality. In each of these cases, interaction is regulated by an institutionalized pattern of cultural value that constitutes some categories of social actors as normative and others as deficient or inferior: straight is normal, gay is perverse; 'male-headed households' are proper, 'female-headed households' are not; 'whites' are law-abiding, 'blacks' are dangerous. In each case, the result is to deny some members of society the status of full partners in interaction, capable of participating on a par with the rest.

In each case, accordingly, a claim for recognition is in order. But note precisely what this means: aimed not at valorizing group identity, but rather at overcoming subordination, claims for recognition in the status model seek to establish the subordinated party as a full partner in social life, able to interact with others as a peer. They aim, that is, *to de-institutionalize patterns of cultural value that impede parity of participation and to replace them with patterns that foster it.*

This status model avoids many difficulties of the identity model. First, by rejecting the view of recognition as valorization of group identity, it avoids essentializing such identities. Second, by focusing on the effects of institutionalized norms on capacities for interaction, it resists the temptation to substitute the re-engineering of consciousness for social change. Third, by enjoining status equality in the sense of parity of participation, it valorizes cross-group interaction, as opposed to separatism and group enclaving. Fourth, the status model avoids reifying culture – without denying culture's political importance. Aware that institutionalized patterns of cultural value can be vehicles of subordination, it seeks to de-institutionalize patterns that impede parity of participation and to replace them with patterns that foster it.

Finally, the status model possesses another major advantage. Unlike the identity model, it construes recognition in a way that does not assign that category to ethics. Conceiving recognition as a matter of status equality, defined in turn as participatory parity, it provides a deontological account of recognition. Thus, it frees recognition claims' normative force from direct dependence on a specific substantive horizon of value. Unlike the identity model, then, the status model is compatible with the priority of the right over the good. Refusing the traditional alignment of recognition with ethics, it aligns it with morality instead. Thus, the status model permits one to combine recognition with redistribution – without succumbing to philosophical schizophrenia. Or so I shall argue next.

Justice or the Good Life?

Any attempt to integrate redistribution and recognition in a comprehensive framework must address four crucial philosophical questions. First, is recognition a matter of justice, or is it a matter of self-realization? Second, do distributive justice and recognition constitute two distinct, *sui generis,* normative paradigms, or can either of them be subsumed within the other? Third, does justice require the recognition of what is distinctive about individuals or groups, or is recognition of our common humanity sufficient? And, fourth, how can we distinguish those claims for recognition that are justified from those that are not?

How one answers these questions depends on the conception of recognition one assumes. In what follows, I will employ the status model in order to provide a deontological account. Drawing on that model, I shall expand the standard conception of justice to accommodate claims for recognition. By stretching the notion of morality, then, I shall avoid turning prematurely to ethics.

I begin with the question, Is recognition an issue of justice, and thus of morality, or one of the good life, and thus of ethics? Usually, recognition is understood as an issue of the good life. This is the view of both Charles Taylor and Axel Honneth, the two most prominent contemporary theorists of recognition. For both Taylor and Honneth, being recognized by another subject is a necessary condition for attaining full, undistorted subjectivity. To deny someone recognition is to deprive her or him of a basic prerequisite for human flourishing. For Taylor, for example:

> . . . nonrecognition or misrecognition . . . can be a form of oppression, imprisoning someone in a false, distorted, reduced mode of being. Beyond simple lack of respect, it can inflict a grievous wound, saddling people with crippling self-hatred. Due recognition is not just a courtesy but a vital human need. (Taylor, 1994: 25)

For Honneth, similarly, 'we owe our integrity . . . to the receipt of approval or recognition from other persons. [D]enial of recognition . . . is injurious because it impairs . . . persons in their positive understanding of self – an understanding acquired by intersubjective means' (1992: 188–9). Thus, both these theorists construe misrecognition in terms of impaired subjectivity and damaged self-identity. And both understand the injury in ethical terms, as stunting the subject's capacity for achieving a good life. For Taylor and Honneth, therefore, recognition is an issue of ethics.

Unlike Taylor and Honneth, I propose to conceive recognition as an issue of justice. Thus, one should not answer the question 'What's wrong with misrecognition?' by saying that it impedes human flourishing by distorting the subject's 'practical relation-to-self' (Honneth, 1992, 1995). One should say, rather, that it is unjust that some individuals and groups are denied the status of full partners in social interaction simply as a consequence of institutionalized patterns of cultural value in whose construction they have not equally participated and which disparage their distinctive characteristics or the distinctive characteristics assigned to them. One should say, that is, that misrecognition is wrong because it constitutes a form of institutionalized subordination – and thus, a serious violation of justice.

This approach offers several important advantages. First, by appealing to a deontological standard, it permits one to justify claims for recognition as morally binding under modern conditions of value pluralism.[4] Under these conditions, there is no single conception of the good life that is universally shared, nor any that can be established as authoritative. Thus, any attempt to justify claims for recognition that appeals to an account of the good life must necessarily be sectarian. No approach of this sort can establish such claims as normatively binding on those who do not share the theorist's horizon of ethical value.

Unlike such approaches, the status model of recognition is deontological and nonsectarian. Embracing the spirit of 'subjective freedom' that is the hallmark of modernity, it assumes that it is up to individuals and groups to define for themselves what counts as a good life and to devise for themselves an approach to pursuing it, within limits that ensure a like liberty for others. Thus, the status model does not appeal to a conception of the good life. It appeals, rather, to a conception of justice that can – and should – be accepted by those with divergent conceptions of the good life. What makes misrecognition morally wrong, in this view, is that it denies some individuals and groups the possibility of participating on a par with others in social interaction. The norm of *participatory parity* invoked here is nonsectarian in the required sense. It can justify claims for recognition as normatively binding on all who agree to abide by fair terms of interaction under conditions of value pluralism.

Treating recognition as a matter of justice has a second advantage as well. Conceiving misrecognition as status subordination, it locates the wrong in social relations, not in individual or interpersonal psychology. To be misrecognized, in this view, is not simply to be thought ill of, looked down on, or devalued in others' conscious attitudes or mental beliefs. It is rather to be denied the status of a full partner in social interaction and prevented from participating as a peer in social life as a consequence of institutionalized patterns of cultural value that constitute one as comparatively unworthy of respect or esteem. When such patterns of disrespect and disesteem are institutionalized, they impede parity of participation, just as surely as do distributive inequities.

Eschewing psychologization, then, this approach escapes difficulties that plague rival approaches. When misrecognition is identified with internal distortions in the structure of self-consciousness of the oppressed, it is but a short step to blaming the victim, as imputing psychic damage to those subject to racism, for example, seems to add insult to injury. Conversely, when misrecognition is equated with prejudice in the minds of the oppressors, overcoming it seems to require policing their beliefs, an approach that is illiberal and authoritarian. For the status model, in contrast, misrecognition is a matter of externally manifest and publicly verifiable impediments to some people's standing as full members of society. And such arrangements are morally indefensible *whether or not they distort the subjectivity of the oppressed*.[5]

Finally, by aligning recognition with justice instead of the good life, one avoids the view that everyone has an equal right to social esteem. That view is patently untenable, of course, because it renders meaningless the notion of esteem.[6] Yet it seems to follow from at least one prominent rival account. In Axel Honneth's theory, social esteem is among the 'intersubjective conditions for undistorted identity formation' which morality is supposed to protect. It follows that everyone is morally entitled to social esteem (Honneth, 1995). The account of recognition proposed here, in contrast, entails no such *reductio ad absurdum*. What it *does* entail is that everyone has an equal right to pursue social esteem under fair conditions of equal opportunity.[7] And such conditions do not obtain when, for example, institutionalized patterns of cultural value pervasively downgrade femininity, 'nonwhiteness', homosexuality and everything culturally associated with them. When that is the case, women and/or people of color and/or gays and lesbians face obstacles in the quest for esteem that are not encountered by others. And everyone, including straight white men, faces further obstacles if they opt to pursue projects and cultivate traits that are culturally coded as feminine, homosexual, or 'nonwhite'.

For all these reasons, recognition is better treated as a matter of justice, and thus of morality, than as a matter of the good life, and thus of ethics. And construing recognition on the model of status permits us to treat it as a matter of justice.

But what follows for the theory of justice?

Expanding the Paradigm of Justice

Supposing that recognition is a matter of justice, what is its relation to distribution? Does it follow, turning now to our second question, that distribution and recognition constitute two distinct, *sui generis* conceptions of justice? Or can either of them be reduced to the other?

The question of reduction must be considered from two different sides. From one side, the issue is whether existing theories of distributive justice can adequately subsume problems of recognition. In my view, the answer is no. To be sure, many distributive theorists appreciate the importance of status over and above the allocation of resources and seek to accommodate it in their accounts.[8] But the results are not wholly satisfactory. Most such theorists assume a reductive economistic-cum-legalistic view of status, supposing that a just distribution of resources and rights is sufficient to preclude misrecognition. In fact, however, not all misrecognition is a byproduct of maldistribution, nor of maldistribution plus legal discrimination. Witness the case of the African-American Wall Street banker who cannot get a taxi to pick him up. To handle such cases, a theory of justice must reach beyond the distribution of rights and goods to examine institutionalized patterns of cultural value. It must consider whether such patterns impede parity of participation in social life.[9]

What, then, of the other side of the question? Can existing theories of recognition adequately subsume problems of distribution? Here, too, I contend the answer is no. To be sure, some theorists of recognition appreciate the importance of economic equality and seek to accommodate it in their accounts. But once again the results are not wholly satisfactory. Axel Honneth, for example, assumes a reductive culturalist view of distribution. Supposing that all economic inequalities are rooted in a cultural order that privileges some kinds of labor over others, he believes that changing that cultural order is sufficient to preclude all maldistribution (Honneth, 1995). In fact, however, not all maldistribution is a byproduct of misrecognition. Witness the case of the skilled white male industrial worker who becomes unemployed due to a factory closing resulting from a speculative corporate merger. In that case, the injustice of maldistribution has little to do with mis-recognition. It is rather a consequence of imperatives intrinsic to an order of specialized economic relations whose *raison d'être* is the accumulation of profits. To handle such cases, a theory of justice must reach beyond cultural value patterns to examine the structure of capitalism. It must consider whether economic mechanisms that are relatively decoupled from structures of prestige and that operate in a relatively impersonal way impede parity of participation in social life.

In general then, neither distribution theorists nor recognition theorists have so far succeeded in adequately subsuming the concerns of the other.[10] Thus, instead of endorsing one of their conceptions to the exclusion of the other, I propose to develop an expanded conception of justice. My conception treats distribution and recognition as distinct perspectives on, and dimensions of, justice. Without reducing either perspective to the other, it encompasses both dimensions within a broader, overarching framework.

As already noted, the normative core of my conception is the notion of *parity of participation*.[11] According to this norm, justice requires social arrangements that permit all (adult) members of society to interact with one another as peers. For participatory parity to be possible, I claim, at least two conditions must be satisfied.[12] First, the distribution of material resources must be such as to ensure participants' independence and voice. This I call the *objective condition* of participatory parity. It precludes forms and levels of material inequality and economic dependence that impede parity of participation. Precluded, therefore, are social arrangements that institutional-ize deprivation, exploitation and gross disparities in wealth, income and leisure time, thereby denying some people the means and opportunities to interact with others as peers.[13]

In contrast, the second condition requires that institutionalized pat-terns of cultural value express equal respect for all participants and ensure equal opportunity for achieving social esteem. This I call the *intersubjective condition* of participatory parity. It precludes institutionalized norms that systematically depreciate some categories of people and the qualities associ-ated with them. Precluded, therefore, are institutionalized value patterns that deny some people the status of full partners in interaction – whether by burdening them with excessive ascribed 'difference' or by failing to acknow-ledge their distinctiveness.

Both the objective condition and the intersubjective condition are necessary for participatory parity. Neither alone is sufficient. The objective condition brings into focus concerns traditionally associated with the theory of distributive justice, especially concerns pertaining to the economic structure of society and to economically defined class differentials. The intersubjective condition brings into focus concerns recently highlighted in the philosophy of recognition, especially concerns pertaining to the status order of society and to culturally defined hierarchies of status. Thus, an expanded conception of justice oriented to the norm of participatory parity encompasses both redistribution and recognition, without reducing either one to the other.

This approach goes a considerable way toward resolving the problem with which we began. By construing redistribution and recognition as two mutually irreducible dimensions of justice, and by submitting both of them to the deontological norm of participatory parity, it positions them both on the common terrain of *Moralität*. Avoiding turning prematurely to ethics, then, it seems to promise an escape route from philosophical schizophrenia.

Recognizing Distinctiveness?

Before proclaiming success, however, we must take up our third philosophical question: does justice require the recognition of what is distinctive about individuals or groups, over and above the recognition of our common humanity? If the answer proves to be yes, we will have to revisit the question of ethics.

Let us begin by noting that participatory parity is a universalist norm in two senses. First, it encompasses all (adult) partners to interaction. And, second, it presupposes the equal moral worth of human beings. But moral universalism in these senses still leaves open the question whether recognition of individual or group distinctiveness could be required by justice as one element among others of the intersubjective condition for participatory parity.

This question cannot be answered, I contend, by an *a priori* account of the kinds of recognition that everyone always needs. It needs rather to be approached in the spirit of a pragmatism informed by the insights of social theory. From this perspective, recognition is a remedy for social injustice, not the satisfaction of a generic human need. Thus, the form(s) of recognition justice requires in any given case depend(s) on the form(s) of *mis*recognition to be redressed. In cases where misrecognition involves denying the common humanity of some participants, the remedy is universalist recognition; thus, the first and most fundamental redress for South African apartheid was universal 'non-racial' citizenship. Where, in contrast, misrecognition involves denying some participants' distinctiveness, the remedy could be recognition of specificity; thus, many feminists claim that overcoming gender subordination requires recognizing women's unique and distinctive capacity to give birth. In every case, the remedy should be tailored to the harm.[14]

This pragmatist approach overcomes the liabilities of two other, mirror-opposite views. First, it rejects the claim, espoused by some distributive theorists, that justice requires limiting public recognition to those capacities all humans share. Favored by opponents of affirmative action, that approach dogmatically forecloses recognition of what distinguishes people from one another, without considering whether such recognition might be necessary in some cases to overcome obstacles to participatory parity. Second, the pragmatist approach rejects the opposite claim, equally decontextualized, that everyone always needs their distinctiveness recognized.[15] Often favored by recognition theorists, this second approach cannot explain why it is that not all, but only some, social differences generate claims for recognition – nor why only some of those claims, but not others, are morally justified. More specifically, it cannot explain why those occupying advantaged positions in the status order, such as men and heterosexuals, usually shun recognition of their (gender and sexual) distinctiveness, claiming not specificity but universality (Nicholson, 1996). Nor why, on those occasions when they do seek such recognition, their claims are usually spurious. By contrast, the approach proposed here sees claims for the recognition of difference pragmatically and contextually – as remedial responses to specific pre-existing injustices. Putting questions of justice at the center, it appreciates that the recognition needs of subordinated actors differ from those of dominant actors and that *only those claims that promote parity of participation are morally justified.*

For the pragmatist, accordingly, everything depends on what precisely currently misrecognized people need in order to be able to participate as peers in social life. And there is no reason to assume that all of them need the same thing in every context. In some cases, they may need to be unburdened of excessive ascribed or constructed distinctiveness. In other cases, they may need to have hitherto underacknowledged distinctiveness taken into account. In still other cases, they may need to shift the focus onto dominant or advantaged groups, outing the latter's distinctiveness, which has been falsely parading as universal. Alternatively, they may need to deconstruct the very terms in which attributed differences are currently elaborated. Finally, they may need all of the above, or several of the above, in combination with one another and in combination with redistribution. Which people need which kind(s) of recognition in which contexts depends on the nature of the obstacles they face with regard to participatory parity.

We cannot rule out in advance, therefore, the possibility that justice may require recognizing distinctiveness in some cases.

Justifying Claims for Recognition

Up to this point, I have managed to answer three major philosophical questions about recognition while remaining on the terrain of *Moralität*. By construing recognition on the model of status, I have given it a deontological interpretation. And by expanding the standard paradigm of justice, I have treated redistribution and recognition as two mutually irreducible dimensions of, and perspectives on, justice, both of which can be brought under the common norm of participatory parity. Thus, I have so far avoided the turn to ethics and escaped philosophical schizophrenia.

At this point, however, the question of ethics threatens to return. Once we accept that justice *could*, under certain circumstances, require recognition of distinctiveness, then we must consider the problem of justification. We must ask: what justifies a claim for the recognition of difference? How can one distinguish justified from unjustified claims of this sort? The crucial issue is whether a purely deontological standard will suffice – or whether, on the contrary, ethical evaluation of various practices, traits and identities is required. In the latter event, one will have to turn to ethics after all.

Let us begin by noting that not every claim for recognition is warranted, just as not every claim for redistribution is. In both cases, one needs an account of criteria and/or procedures for distinguishing warranted from unwarranted claims. Theorists of distributive justice have long sought to provide such accounts, whether by appealing to objectivistic criteria, such as utility maximization, or to procedural norms, such as those of discourse ethics. Theorists of recognition, in contrast, have been slower to confront this question. They have yet to provide any principled basis for distinguishing justified from unjustified claims.

This issue poses grave difficulties for those who treat recognition as an issue of ethics. Theorists who justify recognition as a means to self-realization are especially vulnerable to objections on this point. According to Axel Honneth, for example, everyone needs their distinctiveness recognized in order to develop self-esteem, which (along with self-confidence and self-respect) is an essential ingredient of an undistorted identity (Honneth, 1995). It seems to follow that claims for recognition that enhance the claimant's self-esteem are justified, while those that diminish it are not. On this hypothesis, however, racist identities would seem to merit some recognition, as they enable some poor Europeans and Euroamericans to maintain their sense of self-worth by contrasting themselves with their supposed inferiors. Antiracist claims would confront an obstacle, in contrast, as they threaten the self-esteem of poor whites. Unfortunately, cases like this one, in which prejudice conveys psychological benefits, are by no means rare. They suffice to disconfirm the view that enhanced self-esteem can supply a justificatory standard for recognition claims.

How, then, *should* recognition claims be judged? What constitutes an adequate criterion for assessing their merits? The approach proposed here appeals to participatory parity as an evaluative standard. As we saw, this norm overarches both dimensions of justice, distribution and recognition. Thus, for both dimensions the same general criterion serves to distinguish warranted from unwarranted claims. Whether the issue is distribution or recognition, claimants must show that current arrangements prevent them from participating on a par with others in social life. Redistribution claimants must show that existing economic arrangements deny them the necessary objective conditions for participatory parity. Recognition claimants must show that institutionalized patterns of cultural value deny them the necessary intersubjective conditions. In both cases, therefore, the norm of participatory parity is the standard for warranting claims.

In both cases, too, participatory parity serves to evaluate proposed remedies for injustice. Whether they are demanding redistribution or recognition, claimants must show that the social changes they seek will in fact promote parity of participation. Redistribution claimants must show that the economic reforms they advocate will supply the objective conditions for full participation to those currently denied them – without significantly exacerbating other disparities. Similarly, recognition claimants must show that the sociocultural institutional changes they seek will supply the needed intersubjective conditions – again, without substantially worsening other disparities. In both cases, once again, participatory parity is the standard for warranting proposals for reform.

This represents a considerable improvement over the 'self-realization' standard just discussed. Focusing on capacities for participation, the status model condemns the institutionalization of racist values even in cases where the latter provide psychological benefits to those who subscribe to them. Nevertheless, it remains to be seen whether the norm of participatory parity is by itself sufficient to distinguish justified from unjustified claims for the recognition of difference.

Same-Sex Marriage, Cultural Minorities and the Double Requirement

The problem is that not all disparities are *per se* unjust. Theorists of distributive justice have long appreciated this point with respect to economic inequalities. Seeking to distinguish just from unjust economic disparities, some of them have drawn the line between those inequalities that arise as a result of individuals' choices on the one hand, and those that arise as a result of circumstances beyond individuals' control on the other, arguing that only the second, and not the first, are unjust (see, for example, Dworkin, 1981). Analogous issues arise with respect to recognition. Here, too, not all disparities are unjust – because not all institutionalized value hierarchies are unjust. What is needed, consequently, is a way of distinguishing just from unjust disparities in participation. The key question here, once again, is whether the deontological norm of parity of participation is sufficient for this purpose – and whether, if not, one must turn to ethics.

To answer this question, let us apply the standard of participatory parity to some current controversies. Consider, first, the example of same-sex marriage. In this case, as we saw, the institutionalization in marital law of a heterosexist cultural norm denies parity of participation to gays and lesbians. For the status model, therefore, this situation is patently unjust, and a recognition claim is in principle warranted. Such a claim seeks to remedy the injustice by de-institutionalizing the heteronormative value pattern and replacing it with an alternative that promotes parity. This, however, can be done in more than one way. One way would be to grant the same recognition to homosexual partnerships that heterosexual partnerships currently enjoy by legalizing same-sex marriage. Another would be to de-institutionalize heterosexual marriage, decoupling entitlements such as health insurance from marital status and assigning them on some other basis, such as citizenship and/or territorial residency. Although there may be good reasons for preferring one of these approaches to the other, both of them would serve to foster participatory parity between gays and straights; hence both are justified in principle – assuming that neither would exacerbate other disparities. What would not be warranted, in contrast, is an approach, like the French PACS[16] or the 'civil union' law in the US state of Vermont, that establishes a second, parallel legal status of domestic partnership that fails to confer all the symbolic or material benefits of marriage, while reserving the latter, privileged status exclusively for heterosexual couples. Although such reforms represent a clear advance over existing laws, and may command support on tactical grounds as transitional measures, they do not fulfil the requirements of justice as understood via the status model.

Such tactical considerations aside, the case of same-sex marriage presents no difficulties for the status model. On the contrary, it illustrates a previously discussed advantage of that model: here, the norm of participatory parity warrants gay and lesbian claims deontologically, without recourse to ethical evaluation – without, that is, assuming the substantive judgment that homosexual unions are ethically valuable. The self-realization approach, in contrast, cannot avoid presupposing that judgment, and thus is vulnerable to counter-judgments that deny it.[17] Thus, the status model is superior in handling this case.

Perhaps, however, this example is too easy. Let us consider some presumptively harder cases involving cultural and religious practices. In such cases, the question arises whether participatory parity can really pass muster as a justificatory standard, whether, that is, it can serve to warrant claims deontologically, without recourse to ethical evaluation of the cultural and religious practices at issue. In fact, as we shall see, participatory parity proves adequate here as well – provided it is correctly applied.

What is crucial here is that participatory parity enters the picture at two different levels. First, at the *intergroup* level, it supplies the standard for assessing the effects of institutionalized patterns of cultural value on the relative standing of *minorities* vis-à-vis *majorities*. Thus, one invokes it when considering, for example, whether erstwhile Canadian rules mandating uniform headgear for Mounted Police constituted an unjust *majority communitarianism*, which effectively closed that occupation to Sikh men. Second, at the *intragroup* level, participatory parity also serves to assess the *internal effects of minority practices* for which recognition is claimed – that is, the effects on the groups' own members. At this level, one invokes it when considering, for example, whether Orthodox Jewish practices of sex segregation in education unjustly marginalize Orthodox girls and whether those practices should be denied recognition in the form of tax exemptions or school subsidies.

Taken together, these two levels constitute a double requirement for

claims for cultural recognition. Claimants must show, first, that the institutionalization of majority cultural norms denies them participatory parity
and, second, that the practices whose recognition they seek do not themselves deny participatory parity – to some group members as well as to non-
members. For the status model, both requirements are necessary; neither
alone is sufficient. Only claims that meet both of them are deserving of
public recognition.

To apply this double requirement, consider the French controversy
over the *foulard*. Here the issue is whether policies forbidding Muslim girls
to wear headscarves in state schools constitute unjust treatment of a religious
minority. In this case, those claiming recognition for the *foulard* must establish two points: they must show, first, that the ban on the scarf constitutes
an unjust majority communitarianism, which denies educational parity to
Muslim girls; and, second, that an alternative policy permitting the *foulard*
would not exacerbate female subordination – in Muslim communities or in
society-at-large. Only by establishing both points can they justify their
claim. The first point, concerning French majority communitarianism, can
be established without difficulty, it seems, as no analogous prohibition bars
the wearing of Christian crosses in state schools; thus, the current policy
denies equal standing to Muslim citizens. The second point, concerning the
non-exacerbation of female subordination, has proved controversial, in contrast, as some French republicans have argued that the *foulard* is itself a
marker of such subordination and must therefore be denied recognition.
Disputing this interpretation, however, some multiculturalists have rejoined
that the scarf's meaning is highly contested in French Muslim communities
today, as are gender relations more generally; thus, instead of construing it
as univocally patriarchal, which effectively accords male supremacists sole
authority to interpret Islam, the state should treat the *foulard* as a symbol of
Muslim identity in transition, one whose meaning is contested, as is French
identity itself, as a result of transcultural interactions in a multicultural
society. From this perspective, permitting the *foulard* in state schools could
be a step toward, not away from, gender parity.[18]

In my view, the multiculturalists have the stronger argument here.
(This is *not* the case, incidentally, for those who would recognize what they
call 'female circumcision' – actually, genital mutilation, which clearly
denies parity in sexual pleasure and in health to women and girls.) But that
is not the point I wish to stress here. The point, rather, is that the argument
is rightly cast in terms of parity of participation. For the status model, this
is precisely where the controversy should be joined. As in the case of same-
sex marriage, so in the case of cultural and religious claims: participatory
parity is the proper standard for warranting claims. Differences in its
interpretation notwithstanding, the norm of participatory parity serves to
evaluate such recognition claims deontologically, without any need for
ethical evaluation of the cultural or religious practices in question.[19]

In general, then, the status model sets a stringent standard for justify-
ing claims for the recognition of cultural difference. Yet it remains wholly

deontological. Applied in this double way, the norm of participatory parity suffices to rule out unwarranted claims, without any recourse to ethical evaluation.

Ecology without Ethics?

The question remains, however, whether participatory parity suffices in every case, or whether it must be supplemented by ethical considerations in some. In the latter event, not all claims that passed the deontological test would be justified. Rather, only those that survived a further round of ethical examination would be deemed worthy of public recognition. On this hypothesis, participatory parity would be a necessary but not sufficient condition of justification. While serving to filter out claims that are unacceptable on deontological grounds, it would be incapable of supplying the final step, namely, assessing the *ethical value* of contested practices. Thus, it would be necessary, in the end, to turn to ethics.

This prospect arises when we consider cases that are not amenable to pluralist solutions. These would be cases, unlike same-sex marriage or *l'affaire foulard*, that cannot be handled by institutionalizing toleration. In those two cases, people with different ethical views of the good life could agree to disagree and opt for a regime of live-and-let-live. Suppose, however, we encountered a case in which people's ethical visions were so directly antithetical, so mutually undermining, that peaceful coexistence was an impossiblity. In that event, the society would be forced to choose between them, and parity of participation would cease to be a relevant goal. With that deontological standard no longer applicable, it would be necessary to evaluate the alternatives ethically. Citizens would have to assess the relative worth of two competing views of the good life.

Certainly, such cases are in principle possible. But they are not as common as those who assign recognition to ethics believe. Consider the hypothetical case of a society committed to ensuring the integrity and sustainability of the natural environment. Let us suppose that the social arrangements in this society institutionalize eco-friendly patterns of cultural value. Let us also suppose that the effect is to disadvantage a minority of members who identify with eco-exploitative cultural orientations. Suppose, too, that those members mobilized as a cultural minority and demanded equal recognition of their cultural difference. Suppose, that is, that they demanded the institutionalization of a new pattern of cultural value that ensured parity for eco-friendly and eco-exploitative cultural practices.

Clearly, this is a case that is not amenable to a pluralist solution. It makes no sense to institutionalize parity between eco-friendly and eco-exploitative orientations within a single society, as the latter would undermine the former. Thus, society is effectively constrained to opt for one orientation or the other. The question is what can justify the choice. Proponents of ethics assume that the grounds must be ethical. As they see it, citizens must decide which orientation to nature better conduces to a good form of life; and they must justify their choice on such ethical grounds. If citizens opt for enviromentalism, for example, they must appeal to value judgments rooted in an ecological world-view; if they opt for anti-environmentalism, on the contrary, they must appeal to anti-ecological values. Such appeals are problematic, however, for reasons we have already noted. Both invoke justifications internal to a world-view that the other side explicitly rejects. Thus, neither side can justify its position in terms that the other could in principle accept. And so neither can avoid casting the other outside the circle of those entitled to such justification.[20] Yet that is itself a failure of recognition – of one's fellow citizens *qua* citizens. In general, then, if no other – non-ethical – justification is available, misrecognition, and therefore injustice, cannot be avoided.

Fortunately, the difficulty is less intractable than first appears. In fact, a non-ethical resolution is available, as the anti-ecologists' claim violates the deontological standard of participatory parity – well before ethical evalu-ation has to kick in. Specifically, it violates the second prong of the double requirement, which holds that proposed reforms must not exacerbate one disparity of participation in the course of remedying another. In this case, the anti-ecologists seek to remedy their own disparity vis-à-vis their eco-friendly fellow citizens – but they would do so at the expense of future gener-ations. By instituting parity now for practices that would worsen global warming, they would deny their successors the material prerequisites for a viable form of life – thereby violating intergenerational justice. Thus, the anti-ecologists' claim fails the test of participatory parity. And so this case, too, like same-sex marriage and *l'affaire foulard*, can be adjudicated on deontological grounds. No recourse to ethics is necessary.

The moral here is that one should proceed cautiously before turning to ethics. Ethical evelution, after all, is problematic. Always contextually embedded, it is subject to dispute whenever divergent evaluative horizons come into contact. Thus, one should take care to exhaust the full resources of deontological reasoning before taking that step. In fact, as this example shows, cases that initially seem to require ethics can often be resolved by deontological means. This is not to say that cases requiring ethical evalu-ation are impossible in principle. But one can only determine whether or not one is really facing such a case by going through a long chain of moral reasoning, aimed first at finding a deontological resolution. To fail to com-plete that chain is to turn prematurely to ethics. In that event, one embarks on a dubious enterprise. Appealing to substantive horizons of value that are not shared by everyone concerned, one sacrifices the chance to adjudicate recognition claims definitively – in ways that are binding on all.

Conclusion

For this reason, as well as the others I have offered here, one should postpone the turn to ethics as long as possible. Alternative approaches, favored, alas, by most recognition theorists, turn prematurely to ethics. Foreclosing the option of developing a deontological interpretation of recognition, they miss the chance to reconcile claims for the recognition of difference with claims for egalitarian redistribution. Thus, they miss the chance to restructure the conceptual terrain that is currently fostering philosophical schizophrenia.

Given that unpalatable alternative, it is reassuring to see just how far one can get with a deontological interpretation of recognition. And we *did* get remarkably far here. By employing the status model, with its principle of participatory parity, it was possible to handle apparently ethical questions, such as the recognition of same-sex marriage on the one hand, and of minority religious and cultural practices on the other, without in fact turning to ethics. Even the seemingly harder case of environmental ethics proved susceptible to deontological resolution.

In general, then, the argument pursued here supports a rather heartening conclusion: there is no need to pose an either/or choice between the politics of redistribution and the politics of recognition. It is possible, on the contrary, to construct a comprehensive framework that can accommodate both – by following the path pursued here. First, one must construe recognition as a matter of justice, as opposed to 'the good life'. This, in turn, requires replacing the standard identity model of recognition with the alternative status model sketched here. Next, one must expand one's conception of justice to encompass distribution and recognition as two mutually irreducible dimensions. This involves bringing both dimensions under the deontological norm of participatory parity. Finally, after acknowledging that justice could in some cases require recognizing distinctiveness over and above common humanity, one must subject claims for recognition to the justificatory standard of participatory parity. This, as we saw, means scrutinizing institutionalized patterns of cultural value, and proposals for changing them, for their impact on social interaction – both across and within social groups. Only then, after all these steps, *might* one encounter a situation in which it *could* prove necessary to turn to ethics. Apart from such cases, one will succeed in remaining on the terrain of *Moralität* and in avoiding the ethical turn.

It is possible, I conclude, to endorse both redistribution and recognition while avoiding philosophical schizophrenia. In this way, one can prepare some of the conceptual groundwork for tackling what I take to be the central political question of the day: how can we develop a coherent orientation that integrates redistribution and recognition? How can we develop a framework that integrates what remains cogent and unsurpassable in the socialist vision with what is cogent and irrefutable in the new, apparently 'postsocialist' vision of multiculturalism? If we fail to ask this question, if we cling instead to false antitheses and misleading either/or dichotomies, we will miss the chance to envision social arrangements that can redress both economic and cultural injustices. Only by looking to integrative approaches that unite redistribution and recognition can we meet the requirements of justice for all.

Notes

Portions of this article are adapted and excerpted from my essay, 'Social Justice in the Age of Identity Politics: Redistribution, Recognition and Participation' (Fraser, forthcoming a). I am grateful to the Tanner Foundation for Human Values for support of this work, an earlier version of which was presented as the Tanner Lecture on Human Values at Stanford University, 30 April–2 May 1996. I thank Elizabeth Anderson and Axel Honneth for their thoughtful responses to the lecture and Rainer Forst for his probing comments on a previous draft of the present article.

1. For a fuller discussion of the identity model of recognition, see Fraser (2000).

2. For a fuller critique of the identity model, see Fraser (2000).

3. For fuller accounts of the status model of recognition, see Fraser (2000, forthcoming a).

4. I am grateful to Rainer Forst for help in formulating this point.

5. As I noted, the status model eschews psychologization. What this means, however, requires some clarification. The model does not suppose that misrecognition never has the sort of psychological effects described by Taylor and Honneth. But it maintains that the wrongness of misrecognition does not depend on the presence of such effects. Thus, the status model decouples the normativity of recognition claims from psychology, thereby strengthening their normative force. When claims for recognition are premised on a psychological theory of 'the intersubjective conditions for undistorted identity formation', as in Honneth's (1995) model, they are made vulnerable to the vicissitudes of that theory; their moral bindingness evaporates in case the theory turns out to be false. By treating recognition as a matter of status, in contrast, the model I am proposing avoids mortgaging normative claims to matters of psychological fact. One can show that a society whose institutionalized norms impede parity of participation is unjust even if it does not inflict psychic damage on those it subordinates.

6. Here I am assuming the distinction, now fairly standard in moral philosophy, between respect and esteem. According to this distinction, respect is owed universally to every person in virtue of shared humanity; esteem, in contrast, is accorded differentially on the basis of persons' specific traits, accomplishments or contributions. Thus, while the injunction to respect everyone equally is perfectly sensible, the injunction to esteem everyone equally is oxymoronic.

7. This point can be restated as follows: although no one has a right to equal social esteem in the positive sense, everyone has a right not to be *dis*esteemed on the basis of institutionalized group classifications that undermine her or his standing as a full partner in social interaction. I owe this formulation to Rainer Forst (personal conversation).

8. John Rawls, for example, at times conceives primary goods such as income and jobs as social bases of self-respect, while also speaking of self-respect itself as an especially important primary good whose distribution is a matter of justice (see Rawls, 1971: §67, §82; 1993: 82, 181, 318 ff.). Ronald Dworkin, likewise, defends the idea of equality of resources as the distributive expression of the equal moral worth of persons (1981). Amartya Sen (1985), finally, considers both a sense of self and the capacity to appear in public without shame as relevant to the capability to function, hence as falling within the scope of an account of justice that enjoins the equal distribution of basic capabilities.

9. The outstanding exception of a theorist who has sought to encompass issues of culture within a distributive framework is Will Kymlicka. Kymlicka proposes to treat access to an 'intact cultural structure' as a primary good to be fairly distributed. This

approach was tailored for multinational polities, such as Canada, as opposed to poly-ethnic polities, such as the United States. It becomes problematic, however, in cases where mobilized claimants for recognition do not divide neatly (or even not so neatly) into groups with distinct and relatively bounded cultures. It also has diffi-culty dealing with cases in which claims for recognition do not take the form of demands for (some level of) sovereignty but aim rather at parity of participation within a polity that is crosscut by multiple, intersecting lines of difference and inequality. For the argument that an intact cultural structure is a primary good, see Kymlicka (1989). For the distinction between multinational and polyethnic politics, see Kymlicka (1996).

10. Absent a substantive reduction, moreover, purely verbal subsumptions are of little use. There is little to be gained by insisting as a point of semantics that, for example, recognition, too, is a good to be distributed; nor, conversely, by maintain-ing as a matter of definition that every distributive pattern expresses an underlying matrix of recognition. In both cases, the result is a tautology. The first makes all recognition distribution by definition, while the second merely asserts the reverse. In neither case have the substantive problems of conceptual integration been addressed. In fact, such purely definitional 'reductions' could actually serve to impede progress in solving these problems. By creating the misleading appearance of reduction, such approaches could make it difficult to see, let alone address, poss-ible tensions and conflicts between claims for redistribution and claims for recog-nition.

11. Since I coined this phrase in 1995, the term 'parity' has come to play a central role in feminist politics in France. There, it signifies the demand that women occupy a full 50 percent of seats in Parliament and other representative bodies. 'Parity' in France, accordingly, means strict numerical gender equality in political represen-tation. For me, in contrast, 'parity' means the condition of being a *peer*, of being on a *par* with others, of standing on an equal footing. I leave the question open exactly as to what degree or level of equality is necessary to ensure such parity. In my formu-lation, moreover, the moral requirement is that members of society be ensured the *possibility* of parity, if and when they choose to participate in a given activity or inter-action. There is no requirement that everyone actually participate in any such activity.

12. I say '*at least* two conditions must be satisfied' in order to allow for the possi-bility of more than two. I have in mind specifically a possible third class of obstacles to participatory parity that could be called 'political', as opposed to economic or cultural. 'Political' obstacles to participatory parity would include decision-making procedures that systematically marginalize some people even in the absence of maldistribution and misrecognition, for example, single-member district winner-takes-all electoral rules that deny voice to quasi-permanent minorities. The corre-sponding injustice would be 'political marginalization' or 'exclusion', the corresponding remedy, 'democratization'. For a more extended discussion of this 'third' dimension of justice, see Fraser (forthcoming a). For an insightful account of single-member district winner-takes-all electoral rules, see Guinier (1994.)

13. It is an open question how much economic inequality is consistent with parity of participation. Some such inequality is inevitable and unobjectionable. But there is a threshold at which resource disparities become so gross as to impede partici-patory parity. Where exactly that threshold lies is a matter for further investigation.

14. I say the remedy *could* be recognition of difference, not that it must be. In fact,

there are other possible remedies for the denial of distinctiveness – including deconstruction of the very terms in which differences are currently elaborated. For a discussion of such alternatives, see Fraser (forthcoming a).

15. Both Taylor and Honneth hold this view. See Taylor (1994) and Honneth (1995).

16. This is a law permitting non-married couples (gay or straight) to register as
cohabiting partners entitled to many of the benefits previously reserved for married
couples. Although it was intended to benefit gays and lesbians, most registrants have
been straight couples who don't wish to marry.

17. Let me forestall any possible misunderstanding: I myself have no quarrel with
the view that attributes ethical value to homosexual relationships. But I still insist
that it cannot adequately ground the claim for recognition in societies where citizens hold divergent views of the good life and disagree among themselves as to the
ethical value of same-sex unions.

18. Certainly, there is room for disagreement as to the effects of the *foulard* on the
status of girls. Those effects cannot be calculated by an algorithmic metric or
method. On the contrary, they can only be determined dialogically, by the give-and-
take of argument, in which conflicting judgments are sifted and rival interpretations
are weighed.

19. In general, the standard of participatory parity cannot be applied monologically,
in the manner of a decision procedure. Rather, it must be applied dialogically and
discursively, through democratic processes of public debate. In such debates, participants argue about whether existing institutionalized patterns of cultural value
impede parity of participation and about whether proposed alternatives would foster
it – without exacerbating other disparities. For the status model, then, participatory
parity serves as an idiom of public contestation and deliberation about questions of
justice. More strongly, it represents *the principal idiom of public reason*, the preferred language for conducting democratic political argumentation on issues of both
distribution and recognition. For a fuller account of this dialogical approach, see
Fraser (forthcoming a).

20. For the argument for a basic right to justification in terms one could in principle accept, see Forst (1999).

References

Dworkin, Ronald (1981) 'What is Equality? Part 2: Equality of Resources', *Philosophy and Public Affairs* 10(4): 283–345.

Forst, Rainer (1999) 'The Basic Right to Justification: Toward a Constructivist Conception of Human Rights', *Constellations: An International Journal of Critical and
Democratic Theory* 6: 35–60.

Fraser, Nancy (1995) 'From Redistribution to Recognition? Dilemmas of Justice in
a "Postsocialist" Age', *New Left Review* 212 (July/August): 68–93; reprinted in
Nancy Fraser, *Justice Interruptus: Critical Reflections on the 'Postsocialist' Condition*. London: Routledge (1997).

Fraser, Nancy (2000) 'Rethinking Recognition: Overcoming Displacement and
Reification in Cultural Politics', *New Left Review* 3 (May/June): 107–20.

Fraser, Nancy (forthcoming a) 'Social Justice in the Age of Identity Politics:
Redistribution, Recognition and Participation', in Nancy Fraser and Axel
Honneth, *Redistribution or Recognition? A Political-Philosophical Exchange*.
London: Verso.

Fraser, Nancy (forthcoming b) *Adding Insult to Injury: Social Justice and the Politics of Recognition*, ed. Kevin Olson. London: Verso.

Guinier, Lani (1994) *The Tyranny of the Majority*. New York: The Free Press.

Honneth, Axel (1992) 'Integrity and Disrespect: Principles of a Conception of Morality Based on the Theory of Recognition', *Political Theory* 20(2): 188–9.

Honneth, Axel (1995) *The Struggle for Recognition: The Moral Grammar of Social Conflicts*, trans. Joel Anderson. Cambridge: Polity Press.

Kymlicka, Will (1989) *Liberalism, Community and Culture*. Oxford: Oxford University Press.

Kymlicka, Will (1996) 'Three Forms of Group-Differentiated Citizenship in Canada', in Seyla Benhabib (ed.) *Democracy and Difference*. Princeton, NJ: Princeton University Press.

Nicholson, Linda (1996) 'To Be or Not to Be: Charles Taylor and the Politics of Recognition', *Constellations: An International Journal of Critical and Democratic Theory* 3(1): 1–16.

Rawls, John (1971) *A Theory of Justice*. Cambridge, MA: Harvard University Press.

Rawls, John (1993) *Political Liberalism*. New York: Columbia University Press.

Sen, Amartya (1985) *Commodities and Capabilities*. Amsterdam: North-Holland.

Taylor, Charles (1994) 'The Politics of Recognition', in Charles Taylor, *Multiculturalism: Examining the Politics of Recognition*, ed. Amy Gutmann. Princeton, NJ: Princeton University Press.

Nancy Fraser is the Henry and Louise A. Loeb Professor of Politics and Philosophy at the Graduate Faculty of the New School for Social Research. She is also co-editor of *Constellations: An International Journal of Critical and Democratic Theory*. Her books include *Unruly Practices: Power, Discourse, and Gender in Contemporary Social Theory* (English edition: University of Minnesota Press and Polity Press, 1989; German edition: Suhrkamp Verlag, 1994); *Justice Interruptus: Critical Reflections on the 'Postsocialist' Condition* (English edition: Routledge, 1997; Spanish edition: Siglo del Hombres, 1997; German edition: Suhrkamp Verlag, forthcoming in 2001; Japanese edition: Jokyo Press, forthcoming in 2001); and *Adding Insult to Injury: Social Justice and the Politics of Recognition*, ed. Kevin Olson (English edition: Verso, forthcoming in 2001.) Professor Fraser is also a co-author of two books: with Seyla Benhabib, Judith Butler and Drucilla Cornell, *Feminist Contentions: A Philosophical Exchange* (English edition: Routledge, 1994; German edition: *Streit um Differenz*, Fischer Verlag, 1993) and with Axel Honneth, *Redistribution or Recognition? A Political-Philosophical Exchange* (English edition: Verso, forthcoming in 2001; German edition: Suhrkamp Verlag, forthcoming in 2001). She is a co-editor of *Revaluing French Feminism: Critical Essays on Difference, Agency, and Culture* (Indiana University Press, 1992). Her current research is on globalization.

Recognition or Redistribution?
Changing Perspectives on the Moral Order of Society

Axel Honneth

A NYONE WHO has been following developments in political philosophy over the last few years could not have failed to notice the emergence of one of those processes in theorizing in which conceptual
changes go hand in hand with changes in normative orientation. Well into
the late 1980s, the dominance of Marxism in Europe, and the widespread
influence of Rawls in the USA, ensured that there could be no doubt as to
the guiding principle of a normative theory of the political order. Irrespec-
tive of differences in the detail, they were in agreement on the imperative to
remove any form of social or economic inequality that could not be justified
on rational grounds.

In place of this influential idea of justice, which can be seen in political
terms as a manifestation of the era of social democracy, there seems to have
arisen a novel idea, that, initially, seems politically a good deal less unequivocal. Its normative aim no longer appears to be the elimination of inequality, but the avoidance of degradation and disrespect; its core categories are
no longer 'equal distribution' or 'economic equality', but 'dignity' and
'respect'. Nancy Fraser provided a succinct formula, when she referred to
this transition as one from 'redistribution' to 'recognition'. While the former
concept is tied to a vision of justice, which aims to achieve social equality
through a redistribution of the material necessities for an existence as free
subjects, in the latter concept, the conditions for a just society come to be
defined as the recognition of the personal dignity of all individuals (Fraser,
1995).

Albert O. Hirschman has something similar in mind, when he proposes
a categorial distinction in order to pinpoint a fundamental tendency in the

■ *Theory, Culture & Society* 2001 (SAGE, London, Thousand Oaks and New Delhi),
Vol. 18(2–3): 43–55
[0263-2764(200104/06)18:2–3;43–55;017480]

political culture of the present. In his view, social strife increasingly takes the form of conflicts over 'non-distributable' goods, the nature of which, in contrast to conflicts over 'distributable' goods, precludes their distribution in accordance with the tenet of equality (Hirschman, 1994).

To account for this change in normative orientation, there are two alternative interpretations available, which in a way derive from two contrasting observations. One position allows us to consider concepts such as 'dignity' or 'recognition' as the result of political disillusionment; citing as an example the series of victories by conservative parties in a substantial number of countries, which led to the dismantling of the welfare state and signalled the end of any hopes for greater social equality. From within this thesis, it is argued that, once the demands for economic redistribution appeared as an unachievable long-term goal, there emerged in their place the more concessive idea of eliminating degradation and disrespect. There is, however, an alternative interpretation possible: namely, one that considers the growing inclination towards such ideas not as the result of political disillusionment, but quite the reverse, as the consequence of an increase in moral sensibility. According to the second thesis, a range of new social movements drew our attention to the political significance of the experience of social or cultural disrespect. As a result, we have come to realize that the recognition of the dignity of individuals and groups forms a vital part of our concept of justice. It is this second thesis I would like to support in this article, and I intend to proceed as follows.

As a first step, I will introduce the processes in which, over the last three years, the concept of recognition has acquired its political-moral prominence (section I). Next, I would like to add more historical depth to this current issue by offering a few remarks directed at recalling the programme of social philosophy in which Hegel, for the first time presumably, developed the normative idea of reciprocal recognition (section II). From here, as a third step, I wish to attempt to outline the normative content of 'recognition', by differentiating between various types of recognition, with the help of a distinction between various forms of moral injury (section III).

It is only after these conceptual clarifications that I can offer, as a final step, a proposal for coming to understand conflicts of distribution, in a meaningful and adequate way, as struggles for recognition.

I

It is, of course, the case, that the concept of 'recognition' has, in one form or another, always played a central role in moral-practical philosophy. The idea that only people whose actions find social acceptance within the *polis* can lead a good life played a dominant role in the ethics of ancient Greece; Scottish moral philosophy was guided by the idea that public recognition or disapproval constitutes a social mechanism which guides the individual towards the acquisition of desirable virtues; and with Kant, finally, the concept of 'respect' even attains the function of the highest principle of all morality, in that it contains the core of the categorical imperative, to treat an

other person only as an end in itself. However, none of the clas
with the important exception of Hegel, who in this conte
initiator, placed the principle of recognition at the core o
Nonetheless, whatever indirect significance the concept m
accorded, it always remained in the shadow of other deter
were considered more fundamental.

This situation only began to change with the emergence, over the last
two decades, of a series of political debates and social movements, which,
in their own right, demanded a more pronounced consideration of the idea
of recognition. Whether in discussions about multiculturalism, or in the
theoretical self-clarification of feminism, there quickly emerged as a shared
ideal the normative view, that individuals or social groups have to be
accepted and respected in their difference. From here, it was a small step
to the generalized realization, that the moral quality of social relations
cannot be measured solely in terms of a fair or just distribution of material
goods.

In addition, our idea of justice is essentially connected with a conception as to how, and in what way, individuals recognize one another
reciprocally. In this way, political concerns gradually provided the subject-
matter for debates in moral philosophy, which issued from the consideration
that the normative content of morality has to be determined with reference
to particular forms of reciprocal recognition. When we speak of the 'moral
point of view', we refer primarily to desirable or enforceable attributes of
relationships existing between subjects. Such a suggestion, however, can
only be the starting point for the attempt to derive the normative principles
of a theory of society directly from the moral implications of the concept of
recognition. As soon as one embarks on this path, one can see very quickly
the range of problems associated with the formulation of such an approach.
Current discussions concerning the morality of recognition are, in the main,
concerned with delineating these difficulties in a systematic kind of way. The
first problem raised by such an approach has to do with the range of meanings attached to the key category.

In contrast to the concept of 'respect', which, since Kant, possesses
relatively clear moral-philosophical contours, the concept of 'recognition'
has not acquired a clear determination, whether in everyday language or in
philosophy. In the context of the formulation of a feminist ethics, this concept
is used, above all, to characterize the kind of loving attention and caring
exemplified in the mother–child relationship. In an ethics of discourse, by
contrast, 'recognition' refers to a reciprocal respect for both the unique and
equal status of all others; here, the conduct expected of participants in a discourse serves as a paradigmatic model. Finally, within the framework of
efforts directed at further developing Communitarian ideas, the category of
recognition is employed today to characterize the forms in which other ways
of life come to be esteemed, as exemplified most typically in the case of
social solidarity.

This plurality of usage gives rise to the second problem, namely that, together with its underlying semantic meaning, the moral content of the concept of recognition also appears to undergo a change. This is to say that it may be meaningful to speak of universal rights and obligations in respect of the recognition of the moral autonomy of all human beings, but that such a mode of speech would hardly be appropriate in respect of the kinds of recognition associated with loving care or social esteem. All this leads us to assume that the various meanings given to 'recognition' are in each case tied to a specific moral perspective. Out of this pluralism arises the question as to whether the various aspects of the moral order refer us to a common root, in the sense that they can all share one normative justification. Here, we touch upon the problem of a justification of those moral implications which underpin the various forms of recognition.

It is, of course, not possible to provide a wholly satisfactory answer to those complex questions in such a preliminary sketch of a full theoretical programme. A helpful approach to this problem, however, is available through the differentiations of the concept of 'recognition' to be found in Hegel's early work. They offer some insight into the various meanings of the phenomenon of recognition still evident, even today, in discussions within social philosophy.

II

At the turn of the 19th century, Hegel set out to reconstruct the historical development of human ethics with the aid of the concept of 'recognition'. At that point in time, he was already able to draw on a wide range of philosophical projects in which closely related concepts had taken on a prominent role. Hobbes, under the influence of Machiavelli, started out from the anthropological tenet that human beings are governed, first and foremost, by the desire to acquire a steadily increasing amount of 'respect' and 'honour'. Rousseau, in his critique of the process of civilization, went so far as to postulate, that only with their striving for social esteem, did people start to lose that calm self-assurance which had secured for them a peaceable life in the state of nature. Finally, Fichte strongly opposed such a negative notion in his foundation of natural law, and he came to be convinced that subjects can only acquire an awareness of their capacity for freedom in relation to the extent to which they are encouraged to make use of their autonomy and accept one another as free individuals.

However heterogeneous, even contradictory, these philosophical fragments may appear, taken together they nevertheless could lead, in the early work of Hegel, to the idea that one's self-awareness is dependent upon the experience of social recognition. There is, of course, a strong pessimistic strand apparent in the philosophical anthropology of Hobbes and Rousseau, in that they presumed that the striving for recognition entailed a threat, either to the political order, or to individual authenticity. It would also be possible, however, to draw the indirect conclusion from these views that subjects are dependent upon the respect or esteem of their fellows in the conduct of their lives.

For the concerns Hegel pursued in his early writings, the mere assertion of a necessary link between self-awareness and intersubjective recognition could not suffice, however. In order to explain how the experience of recognition could lead to progress in the sphere of ethics, an additional explanation was required of the dynamic interrelationship, which had to exist between the intersubjective acquisition of self-awareness and the moral progress of a whole society. The answers to these complex questions, which Hegel arrived at while developing his earlier ideas, represent the core of his version of a 'struggle for recognition'. It contains the daring and challenging idea that ethical progress takes place along a series of steps, with increasingly demanding patterns of recognition, which are mediated by intersubjective struggles, in which subjects try to gain acceptance for claims regarding their own identity.

The most significant aspect in Hegel's approach consists in the thesis, which points well beyond Fichte, that we need to distinguish between three forms of reciprocal recognition, as soon as we have come to an understanding of the intersubjective preconditions for the emergence of self-awareness. The mechanism involved in the reciprocal granting of a sphere of individual freedom, which Fichte had in mind in his foundation of natural law, does indeed explain the formation of a subject's awareness of the legal order. Fichte, however, falls short of a full account of the positive self-understanding characteristic of a free individual. Hegel consequently provides two further forms of reciprocal recognition, in addition to that of legal recognition – which is more or less congruent with Kant's notion of moral respect – that also have to correspond to specific stages in the self-understanding of the individual.

The first of these is love. Hegel, in his early work, still follows the emphatic notion he finds in Hölderlin's philosophy, in which two subjects reciprocally accept their specific sets of needs, so that they can attain emotional security in the articulation of their physical drives. Ethics, on the level of the state, furthermore, contains a form of recognition that allows subjects to value in each other those qualities which contribute to the reproduction of the social order. Hegel, in his early work, appears to have been convinced that the transition between these various realms of recognition is achieved through a struggle, waged between subjects, over the acceptance of their gradually developing self-perception. The claim to have more and more dimensions of one's personality recognized, in a sense leads to intersubjective conflict, which can only be resolved through establishing progressively wider realms of recognition.

Taken together, the spheres of recognition thus established form the network of normative presuppositions that has to underpin modern liberal societies, in order to facilitate the emergence of involved citizens conscious of their civil liberty. Hegel is, of course, not quite enough of a social theorist to conceive of this process as the actual constitution of modern society. Still, caught within the boundaries of German Idealism, he saw it instead as the sum total of mental achievements required by all subjects, acting in concert in order to be able to construct the common world of the 'objective spirit'. His earlier conception of a struggle for recognition is, nevertheless, complex and multi-layered enough to have stimulated a wide range of developments in the fields of moral philosophy and social theory. It is the case that Hegel – in *The Phenomenology of Spirit* – had already replaced his initial programme with a conception that laid the foundation for his later work. From then on, the constitution of social reality is no longer explained in terms of an intersubjective process of conflict generation, but rather as the result of a dialectical self-progression of Spirit. However, in *The Philosophy of Right*, Hegel established a differentiation between family, civil society and state, which once again reflects the earlier distinction between the three forms of recognition. It is this tripartite division that allows us today to develop further Hegel's mature system in the form of a moral-practical philosophy.

III

When one draws on the concept of 'recognition' today, in order to establish a conception of the moral order of society, then the starting-point tends to be a phenomenological analysis of moral injury. In this negativistic approach, a central role is played by the idea that the events experienced as an 'injustice', may provide the appropriate key for an initial explication of the internal connection between morality and recognition. On the basis of criteria used by the individuals concerned to differentiate between a moral offence and mere misfortune or force, it is not difficult to demonstrate that, in the former case, there has to be an element of recognition denied or refused, while in the latter such references naturally have no place. Thus, a physical injury becomes a moral injustice, if victims are led to view it as an action that intentionally disregarded a central aspect of their personal well-being. It is not just the inflicting of physical pain as such which constitutes a moral injury, but the additional awareness of not having one's understanding of oneself recognized and accepted.

I use as the starting-point for my differentiations the kind of disrespect that is involved in physical humiliations, such as torture or rape. These can be considered as the most fundamental kinds of humiliation, because they deprive human beings of the bodily manifestation of their autonomy in relation to themselves and, therefore, of a part of their elementary trust in their world. The relationship of recognition that corresponds to this form of disrespect, in that it leads the individual to develop such a bodily self-assurance, is that of emotional attentiveness in the way that Hegel, as a Romantic philosopher, attempted to capture in the idea of 'love'.

Because physical and affective needs can, in a way, only be 'validated' through being satisfied or answered directly, recognition in this case has to possess the character of affective acceptance and encouragement. Thus, the relationship of recognition is tied to the bodily existence of concrete Others who reciprocate their feelings of special esteem. The positive attitude to oneself that arises from such affective recognition is that of trust in oneself. It refers to the fundamental layer of emotional and bodily self-assurance in the expression of one's needs and feelings, which forms the psychological preconditions for the development of all the other aspects of self-respect. This mode of reciprocal recognition cannot be generalized beyond the circle of primary social relationships, apparent in affective ties such as family, friendship or love. Because such attitudes of emotional acceptance are tied to preconditions outside the control of individuals, such as sympathy and attraction, they cannot be transferred at will to a wider circle of interacting members. It is for this reason that this kind of relationship of recognition contains a moral particularism that cannot be dissolved into any attempts at generalizing.

It is possible to distinguish a second form of disrespect, from that of physical maltreatment, with its positive correspondence, the emotional attention in primary relationships. We are here dealing with the denial of rights and with social exclusion, where human beings suffer in their dignity through not being granted the moral rights and responsibilities of a full legal person within their own community. Accordingly, this type of disrespect has to have, as its corresponding relation, the reciprocal recognition through which individuals come to regard themselves as equal bearers of rights from the perspective of their fellows.

Mead considered the mechanism involved here as a process of taking the perspective of a 'generalized Other' in which, together with the normatively governed imposition of certain duties, the self is also granted the satisfaction of certain demands.

The positive attitude subjects can take towards themselves, when they acquire such legal recognition, is that of an elementary self-respect. They become able to consider themselves as sharing, with all the other members of their community, the attributes of a morally competent actor. Legally grounded relations, in contrast to the relations of recognition within primary relationships, allow the generalization of its characteristic medium of recognition, in the two directions of the material and social extension of rights. In the former case, material content accrues to the legal order, so that differences in the opportunities available to individuals to realize their intersubjectively guaranteed freedoms, can be given legal consideration. In the second case, legal relations are universalized, in the sense that a growing circle of hitherto excluded or disadvantaged groups within a community are granted the same rights as all other members. For this reason, the relationship of recognition apparent in the legal order contains, at its core, a universalizing dynamic that comes to the fore through historic struggles.

The third type of disrespect I would finally like to distinguish, concerns the depreciation of the social value of forms of self-realization. Such a pattern of devaluing particular achievements or forms of life has the result of not allowing the subjects concerned to relate to abilities acquired in the course of their lives, along the lines of social esteem. This form of disrespect thus corresponds to a positive relationship of recognition, one which enables individuals to acquire a measure of self-esteem, that can be found in the solidaristic acceptance and social regard of an individual's abilities and way

of life. Within such a relationship, individuals would be able to find acceptance and mutual encouragement of their individuality, as individuals formed
by their very life experiences. Mead provides the following argument concerning such a relationship of recognition: because subjects, in their practical self-understanding, have to reassure themselves of their status, as
autonomous as well as individuated beings, they must, furthermore, be able
to take the perspective of a 'generalized Other', who provides the intersubjective approval of their claim to be regarded as unique persons. Such
ethical self-assurance becomes possible on account of a relationship of
reciprocal recognition, in which Ego and Alter come to share the same sets
of values and aims, and which indicate to one another the indispensable
importance their abilities and activities possess for the other. To the extent
to which this form of recognition has to presuppose the crucial experience
of shared duties and responsibilities, it includes, in addition to the cognitive element related to ethical concerns, the affective dimension associated
with solidarity.

The positive attitude a subject can take towards itself, when recognized
in this way, is that of self-esteem: finding itself appreciated for its specific
qualities, the subject is able to identify itself wholly with its specific attributes and achievements. The unique aspect of such an ethical relationship of
recognition for Mead, consists in the fact that it contains within itself increasing scope for self-realization. The ethical norms that allow individuals
reciprocally to recognize their individuality, are open to the process of de-
traditionalization, in the course of which they shed their hierarchic and
prescriptive character, as they come to be more and more generalized. For
this reason, the relationship of recognition associated with solidarity incorporates the principle of egalitarian difference, which, as a result of pressure coming from individualized subjects, can develop more fully.

These three patterns of recognition: love, legal order and solidarity,
appear to provide the formal conditions for interaction, within which human
beings can be sure of their 'dignity' and integrity. 'Integrity' is here only
meant to indicate that subjects are able to rest secure in the knowledge that
the whole range of their practical self-orientation finds support within their
society. Whenever they participate in a social lifeworld in which they
encounter those three patterns of recognition, in whatever form, they can
then relate to themselves in the positive modes of self-confidence, self-
respect and self-esteem. This line of argument leads to some normative
implications that would require us to widen our familiar concept of social
morality, since the normative aim of undistorted recognition cannot be
encompassed fully by the concept of 'justice' without having to be reconstructed from within the framework of a formal conception of the good life.

Again, a negative line of argumentation may here provide an initial
form of reasoning. That is, that without the assumption of a certain measure
of self-confidence, of legally enshrined autonomy and of a belief in one's
ability, it is impossible to imagine a successful process of self-realization,
meaning here the unforced pursuit of freely chosen aims in life. 'Unforced'

and 'free' in such a context cannot just mean the mere absence of external pressure or influence, but also has to imply the absence of internal blockages, psychological inhibitions and anxiety. Rendered positively, this second version of freedom comes to be seen as a kind of trust turned inward, which gives individuals the assurance required to articulate their needs and to put their talents to good use. As seen above, such self-assurance, or anxiety-free modes of relating to one's self form aspects of a positive relation to one's self, which can only be achieved through the experience of recognition. In this way, the scope for self-realization is dependent upon preconditions not available to subjects themselves, since they can be acquired only with the cooperation of their fellows. These different patterns of recognition represent intersubjective prerequisites, which we have to add in our minds when we try to describe the general structures of a successful life.

Here we come upon a central difficulty, namely, that two of the three patterns of recognition introduced above, contain within themselves the potential for further normative development. As has been shown, both the legal order and the community based on shared values, are open to processes of transformation in the direction of a higher degree of universality or equality. Through this potential for development, a historical variable enters the normative conditions of self-realization, which requires us to limit the reach of our formal concept of ethics: what may be considered as an intersubjective precondition of a good life turns into a historically variable factor, determined by the actual level of development of the patterns of recognition. The formal concept loses its timelessness as it, hermeneutically, becomes dependent upon a given present that cannot be transcended.

A formal concept of ethics contains the qualitative conditions for self-realization and they differ from the plurality of all specific forms of life in that they constitute the general preconditions for the personal integrity of subjects. Because such conditions are themselves open to the possibility of normative progress, such a formal concept cannot be detached from historical change but is, rather, tied to the specific situation of its own period of origin.

This realization requires my argumentation to introduce the three patterns of recognition in such a way that only their highest available degree of development can be considered as components of an ethics. What these intersubjective preconditions of the possibility of self-realization must be like can only be seen from the historical conditions of a present, which itself has already pointed ahead towards normative progress in the conditions for recognition. The idea of a post-traditional democratic ethics, that would follow from such a line of argument, was first explored by the young Hegel, and was later developed by Mead on the basis of post-metaphysical premises. Despite all the differences between them, they both envisaged the same ideal society, in which the universalistic achievements of equality and individualism had penetrated patterns of interaction to such an extent that all subjects could find recognition both as autonomous yet individualized, as equal yet unique, persons. In addition, both these thinkers conceived of these specifically modern patterns of interaction in the form of a network of differing conditions of recognition, in which individuals can find reassurance for particular dimensions of their self-realization. In this way, both Hegel and Mead came very close to the normative idea I am trying to outline with a historically grounded, yet formal, concept of ethics.

IV

In the last few years, a number of reservations have been voiced against such an epistemological conception of the moral order of society. They amount to the view that this conception does not enable us to examine, let alone justify, reasonable demands for material redistribution. In the face of growing economic inequality, it would both be dangerous and risky to suggest that the recognition of personal or collective identity alone could form the goal of a just society, since, in this way, it would be impossible to draw attention to the material prerequisites for a just society. This challenge found its most prominent formulation in Nancy Fraser's (1995) article, which quickly achieved great resonance. In her view, a theory of the moral order revolving around recognition can only account for the current phenomenon of a 'politics of identity', and traditional forms of a politics of redistribution can no longer find expression within this framework. In my opinion, this critique is based on a grave misunderstanding, although one that is nevertheless understandable, given a particular tendency within current political-philosophical writing. There is a noticeable inclination in the debates concerned with a 'politics of recognition' to reduce the social recognition of persons to the single aspect of the cultural recognition or acceptance of their differing forms of life. 'Recognition' is here treated as a normative category, which corresponds to all those political demands raised today under the banner of a 'politics of identity'. I seem to detect a crucial misunderstanding here, which is, in the main, attributable to Charles Taylor's book on the 'politics of identity' (Taylor, 1992). I would like to outline the problems arising from such a narrowing of the paradigm of recognition in two brief steps.

(1) In his work, which achieved rapid fame and which introduced a wider public to the 'politics of recognition', Charles Taylor insinuated a highly misleading chronology. His central thesis suggests that the history of liberal capitalist societies has been accompanied by struggles for legal equality, while today we find in their place, to a large extent, struggles conducted by groups who wish to claim recognition for their culturally defined difference. I am here not concerned with the fact that Taylor employs much too narrow a concept of legal recognition, which he allows to shrink to something of a homogenizing kind of equality of treatment. What is of interest in Taylor's thesis are the historical stylizations and simplifications that lead to such a chronology. Just as he, from the outset, fails to consider all aspects of a legal nature within current struggles for recognition; so must he also, in return, strip all the cultural elements of a 'politics of identity' from the law-oriented struggles of the past, in order to arrive at the assertion of a historical sequence of the two differing types of social movements. The thesis that we

are today confronted, in the main, with struggles over the recognition of cultural difference, tacitly assumes a particular image of traditional social movements; as though, in their focus on legal equality, they had remained completely unfamiliar with goals such as the demand for the social recognition of their own value orientations or ways of life. It does not require a detailed knowledge of history, to realize how misleading and, indeed, false such a depiction, in fact, is.

The notion that identity politics is a new phenomenon is, in sum, clearly false. The women's movement has roots at least 200 years old. The founding of communes was as important in the early 1800s as in the 1960s. Were not the European nationalisms of the 19th century instances of identity politics? What of the struggles of African-Americans in the wake of slavery? What of anti-colonial resistance? Neither is identity politics limited to the relatively affluent (the 'post-materialists' as Inglehart calls them), as though there were some clear hierarchy of needs, in which clearly defined material interests precede culture and struggles over the constitution of the nature of interests – both material and spiritual (Calhoun, 1995: 215).

Just as it is impossible to reduce today's movements inspired by a 'politics of identity' to just cultural aims, so the traditional resistance movements of the late 19th and early 20th centuries cannot be reduced to mere material or legal demands. After all, the labour movement, to mention another example not cited by Craig Calhoun, was in important ways directed at the aim of gaining recognition for people's own traditions and ways of life, within the ambit of capitalist values. For this reason, the historical sequence employed by Taylor in his diagnosis is misleading, by suggesting two phases in the history of social movements when we are, in fact, only dealing with differences in nuances and the weighting of aspects. Insofar as Nancy Fraser sets out with this suggestive periodization, she inevitably takes on board the false premise of a historical opposition: between a politics of material interests and legal concerns, and a 'politics of identity'. In short, as a result of the misleading periodization of the aims of social movements, the struggle for recognition comes to be understood as a demand that has arisen as a moral issue only very recently; thus it can be reduced to the single aspect of cultural recognition so that all other dimensions of the struggle for recognition remain ignored.

(2) Demands for material redistribution arise out of the epistemological conception of a democratic ethics that I am proposing here from two sources. On the one hand, from the normative implications of equality before the law, that promises equal treatment by the law, for all members of a democratic polity. This shows that the granting of social rights, and the accompanying redistribution, fulfil the normative function of giving each citizen the opportunity to participate in the democratic process of the public formation of a community based on the law. Demands for redistribution arise also from the normative idea, that each member of a democratic society must have the chance to be socially esteemed for his or her individual achievements.

It seems to me that this pattern of social esteem corresponds largely to what Nancy Fraser calls 'just distribution' – that is, the rules organizing the distribution of material goods derive from the degree of social esteem enjoyed by social groups, in accordance with institutionalized hierarchies of value, or a normative order. Just as Marx did not feel able to consider distribution as an ultimate, so I, too, think that considerations of material distribution cannot be regarded as the ultimate point of reference for an analysis. This leads to the question as to how these rules of distribution can be accounted for, if they are to be regarded as something secondary and derivative. Marx' s idea, as we know, was to suggest that we come to understand the rules of distribution as an institutional expression of the relations of production in a society. The amount of economic reward a social group can justifiably lay claim to in a capitalist economic order is determined by their position in the process of production; that is, whether they are wage labourers or hold a managerial role, or even own the means of production. However, debates in social theory over the last two decades have shown that Marx himself committed the mistake of drawing on unclarified premises.

His category of socially necessary labour, abstracted, almost as a matter of course, from the fact that the raising of children or housework, for example, or other activities, also represent activities or social contributions which are indispensable for the everyday reproduction of capitalist society. This circumstance, in my view, shows that rules of distribution cannot simply be derived from the relations of production, but are rather to be seen as the institutional expression of a sociocultural dispositive that determines in what esteem particular activities are held at a specific point in time. Conflicts over distribution, as long as they are not merely concerned with just the application of institutionalized rules, are always symbolic struggles over the legitimacy of the sociocultural dispositive that determines the value of activities, attributes and contributions. In this way, struggles over distribution, contrary to Nancy Fraser's assumption, are themselves locked into a struggle for recognition. The latter represents a conflict over the institutionalized hierarchy of values that govern which social groups, on the basis of their status and their esteem, have legitimate claim to a particular amount of material goods. In short, it is a struggle over the cultural definition of what it is that renders an activity socially necessary and valuable. Once we are aware of this meaning of the struggle for recognition, then a pressing challenge to developed Western democracies becomes immediately apparent. Because of unemployment, which is no longer merely linked to economic cycles but is now also structural, a growing number of people do not have the opportunity to gain the kind of recognition for their acquired abilities that I refer to as social esteem. Because of this, they can hardly consider themselves as contributing members of a democratic polity, since that presupposes the experience of cooperation, that is, the socially recognized contribution to social reproduction.

For this reason, we can expect a growing number of struggles for recognition, directed at the institutionalized definitions and measures of social esteem that govern which activities and abilities may achieve symbolic or material recognition. Without a radical extension of the meaning of 'labour', and what can sensibly and justifiably be included within that, this approaching struggle for recognition cannot readily be resolved.

References

Calhoun, Craig (1995) 'The Politics of Identity and Recognition', pp. 193–215 in C. Calhoun, *Critical Social Theory*. Oxford and Cambridge, MA.

Fraser, Nancy (1995) 'From Redistribution to Recognition? Dilemmas of Justice in a "Post-Socialist" Age', *New Left Review* 212: 68–93.

Hirschman, Albert O. (1994) 'Wieviel Gemeinschaft braucht die liberale Gesellschaft?', *Leviathan* 2.

Taylor, Charles (1992) *Multiculturalism and the Politics of Recognition*. Princeton, NJ: Princeton University Press.

Recognition and the Politics of Human(e) Desire

Majid Yar

T HIS IS an article dealing with the 'politics of recognition'. By this I refer not only to 'recognition' as a form, axis, structure or subvention for political life, but also to the different 'political' renditions of 'recognition' which (for and against, implicitly or explicitly) figure the contemporary theoretical landscape. My main concern will be with those positions associated with 'post-structuralist' cultural criticism, 'postmodernism' and 'deconstructive' ethics, which reject the Hegelian model of intersubjectivity as necessarily complicit with a logic of violent appropriation. Recognition is taken as the instantiation of an economy of power which produces objectified and subjugated subjects (subjection), and/or as the *sine qua non* of an ontology which reduces alterity, otherness and difference to the identarian totality of the same (see Levinas, 1969; Foucault, 1984; Butler, 1997: 1–30). Such understandings are recuperated into the field of cultural studies, and clearly have come to inform analyses of the objectifying 'gaze' and its operation of domination with respect to gendered, ethnicized and 'queered' Others (see Mulvey, 1989; Said, 1991; Gilroy, 1993; Crossley, 1996: 31, 61, 66–7). Equally, the equation of recognition with a morally problematic identarian reduction has led to a search for alternative models of ethical engagement and communality which refuse recognition in the name of a non-cognizable alterity (see Bauman, 1993; Lingis, 1994; Derrida, 1997). The generalized suspicion of a politically progressive or emancipatory role for intersubjective recognition can be seen as part of what Martin Jay has identified as the 'anti-ocularist' tendency which has dominated much of 20th century French thought (Jay, 1994), and has in recent decades won a widespread adherence in various 'postmodern' guises. Here I wish to critically examine two of the 'pessimistic' readings of Hegelian intersubjectivity which have laid the foundations for refusing a politically meaningful role for the

■ *Theory, Culture & Society* 2001 (SAGE, London, Thousand Oaks and New Delhi),
Vol. 18(2–3): 57–76
[0263-2764(200104/06)18:2–3;57–76;017483]

recognition-theoretic approach. In the phenomenologies of Sartre and Levinas I discern an unwarranted 'pathologization' of the dynamic of Hegel's formulation, which in both readings results in the equation of recognition with an annihilative intersubjective hostility. By turning to Kojève's creative 'strong reading' of the 'master–slave' dialectic, I contend that a reconsideration of the complexities of *desire* can allow us to reclaim theoretically the positive political potentialities inherent in the concept of recognition. Approaching intersubjective recognition through the dynamic of 'human desire' can offer a resource for theorizing political relations, and the mediations of political culture, in a 'humane' manner which is simultaneously sensitive to the demands not only of *solidarity*, but also of *singularity*. As such, the openness to difference or alterity can be seen as a moment integral to, and necessary for recognition, rather than standing as its antithesis.

Sartre: The Problem of Others

In *Being and Nothingness* (1969) Sartre offers an excursus on the relation between self and others which draws extensively on the recognition relation as theorized in Hegel's 'master–slave' dialectic and, indeed, upon Hegel's account of the emergence of human self-consciousness as a whole. For Hegel, the subject can only emerge through its differentiation of itself from the world which is other than itself, outside. This awareness is only possible because of the actuality of desire, the experience of a founding *lack* which seeks its *satisfaction*. It is this lack which generates the distinction between a desiring being, a subject and a world of objects of which it is becomes *conscious* as it requires them for its satisfaction (Kojève, 1969: 2–3). Thus, from the beginning, Hegel refuses the notion of a self-subsistent, *a priori* ontologically differentiated, monadological consciousness, seeing it as instead depending upon exteriority for its existence. This relational understanding of the origins of conscious being is recuperated in Sartre's early engagements with Husserlian phenomenology, wherein a determinate intentional relation to the noema (object of intentionality) simultaneously generates the distinction and difference between consciousness and world (Sartre, 1970: 4). Moreover, consciousness comes to be seen as coextensive with desire itself, since the intentional relation is nothing other than the human desire to overcome its own lack ('negativity' for Hegel,[1] 'Nothingness' for Sartre) by appropriating the world of external objects ('Being'). Human being, as a 'Nothingness' or fundamental lack, is directionally oriented to its world in attempt to satisfy its 'desire to be' (Sartre, 1969: 3–21; Butler, 1999: 102–5).

    However, in order to apprehend the being of humans, it is necessary to account not simply for consciousness, but for *self-consciousness*. This is where, for Hegel, other subjects enter the picture. The achievement of self-consciousness, the capacity to have a reflexive self-relation in which I become the object of my own intending activity, is dependent upon an 'alienation' (*Entfremdung*) wherein I come to see myself as others see me, as the object of *their* intending activity. In other words, the achievement of self-consciousness requires a *mediation* via the consciousness of another subject (or subjects). I am dependent upon the *recognition* of myself by another conscious being in order to constitute myself as a self-conscious being, to become aware of myself in terms of my specificity, objective characteristics, and so on. It is only by seeing how others see me that I can come to apprehend and 'take possession' of myself. As Hegel puts it, 'Self-consciousness exists in and for itself when, and by the fact that, it so exists for another; that is, it only exists in being acknowledged' (Hegel, 1977: 111). Sartre reproduces this relational dependence on others as the constitutive condition for the transition from 'pre-reflective' to 'reflective' consciousness (i.e. from consciousness to self-consciousness):

> ... *being for the Other* is a necessary stage of the development of self-consciousness; the road of interiority passes through the Other. ... I must necessarily be an object for myself only over there in the Other, I must obtain from the Other the *recognition* of my being. But if another consciousness must mediate between my consciousness *for itself* and itself, then the being-for-itself of my consciousness – and consequently its being in general – depends on the Other. (Sartre, 1969: 236–7)

Thus we come to the first and crucial claim of the dialectic of intersubjective recognition, namely that the formation of one's being as a human being with particular characteristics, traits, qualities and features, in short the establishment of one's self-understanding (one's 'idea-of-self' or 'subjective self-certainty') is inextricably dependent on recognition or affirmation on the part of others (Kojève, 1969: 11). This fundamental insight founds a whole host of theorizations of intersubjectivity. For example, this relation is replayed in Lacan's analysis of the 'mirror stage' whereby the child achieves its sense of its self, its place in the symbolic and social order, via the acquisition of an external viewpoint upon itself (Lacan, 1977: 1–7). Likewise, in Merleau-Ponty's theory of intersubjectivity the 'mirror stage' corresponds to that necessary experience of 'alienation' wherein the capacity to see oneself from the viewpoint of the other is the precondition for achieving a public identity (Merleau-Ponty, 1968: 136). Similarly, in Mead's social psychology (an 'empirical naturalization' of Hegel's initial metaphysically ordered phenomenology) recognition on the part of others becomes internalized as a stock of shared social understandings (the 'me') which gives the 'I' a sense of its own publicly validated status (Honneth, 1996: 66–91).

   However, Sartre's rendition of the recognition-relation develops into a profoundly 'pessimistic' or 'pathological' vision of intersubjectivity, one which militates against any sustainable role for recognition as a means for pursuing the ends of political solidarity, autonomy, or emancipation. This reconceptualization is especially important as it has exercised a profound influence upon the formation of those 'anti-ocularist' theories adduced in my introductory remarks. It can be seen to subvene in the first instance upon the distinction between human consciousness as *pour soi* (for-itself) and the world of external objects it encounters as merely *en soi* (in-itself). The essence of the human, as *pour soi*, is that it is a constitutive absence or lack, a 'Nothingness' as opposed to the 'Being' of the world of objects (*en soi*). This 'Nothingness' is for Sartre the basis for human freedom, since it is its essence *qua* absence or lack which frees human existence from any predetermined configuration, and opens up the possibility of *choosing* one's existence (Sartre, 1969: 21–45, 95–102). Yet the subject's dependence on others for the achievement of its being as self-consciousness throws precisely this freedom, this capacity for autonomy or self-determination, into crisis. Mediation via another consciousness surrenders my being-for-itself to dependence upon something outside myself, and with it surrenders my freedom. The recognition conferred by the other determines me, fixes and reifies my being into a determinate figuration, an object, *en soi* – my dependence upon the other represents the 'death of my possibilities' (Honneth, 1995a: 161). Thus 'alienation' comes to function implicitly for Sartre not only as an analytical category, but also as a *normative* one.

Sartre, in one of the most frequently discussed sections of *Being and Nothingness*, elaborates this notion of recognition as expropriation, violation and loss of freedom through the concept of the 'look' or 'gaze'. The intersubjective encounter is rendered in richly specular terms, in which the mutual visual apprehension between subjects becomes the instrument by which the mortification of freedom and the objectification of human being take place (Jay, 1994: 275–93). It is in the look of the other, in being-seen-by-the-other, that 'I am possessed by the Other. . . . By virtue of consciousness the Other is for me simultaneously the one who has stolen my being from me and the one who causes "there to be" a being which is my being' (Sartre, 1969: 364). 'I grasp the Other's look at the very centre of . . . [the] solidification and alienation of my own possibilities . . . the look alienates me from them' (Sartre, 1969: 263). In short, while the other is necessary for my being a being, for my being objectively recognized and constituted as this being, I at the same time experience this as a profound violation, my subjection to 'the absolute look' (*le regard absolu*) which makes me into a being-for-the-other (Jay, 1994: 277, 287–9). As an example of such recognition Sartre discusses negative experiences such as shame, wherein I become aware that 'I *am* indeed that object that the Other is looking at and judging' and in which 'my freedom escapes me in order to become a *given* object' (Sartre, 1969: 261).

Sartre argues that one cannot simultaneously be the subject and object of such a look – one is either 'Being-seen-by-the-Other' and is so an object (*en soi*), or is the one 'seeing-the-Other' and so a subject (*pour soi*) (Sartre, 1969: 257). Hence the only escape from the situation of expropriation, the only way to reclaim my freedom, is to 'turn tables' on the other, and make *her* into the object of *my* own look, thereby depriving her of her own freedom via my definitional, judging act, and so reclaiming my own. This is the heart of Sartre's 'pessimistic' theorization of intersubjectivity, that the relation of recognition is a constant unending conflict between subjects who seek to make each other objects of the gaze as the pre-condition of reclaiming their inner freedom as pure possibility: 'While I attempt to free myself from the hold of the Other, the Other is trying to free himself from mine; while I seek to enslave the Other, the Other seeks to enslave me. . . . *Conflict is the original meaning of being-for-others*' (Sartre, 1969: 364, emphasis added) (it is here we can apprehend the philosophical underpinnings for Garcin's famous declamation in *In Camera* that '*L'enfer c'est les autres*' – 'hell is other people'). This leads us to 'the conclusion that the social world is constituted out of subjects' relations of mutual objectification . . . as modes of mutual subjugation and instrumentalization' (Honneth, 1995a: 161). This extends to relations such as love which, far from being seen as a structure of mutual affirmation, in fact oscillates between the poles of 'sadism' and 'masochism' – with the former I attempt to claim my freedom by exercising brutal domination over the other, while in the latter I lapse into passivity and make myself the object of the other's desires, thereby attempting to appropriate the other's freedom by seducing and so entrapping him (Sartre, 1969: 374–9, 399–406). In such a dynamic of specular recogntion, the *mutuative* realization of freedom, autonomy, self-assertion or authenticity becomes an impossibility.

This 'pathological' rendition of the recognition-relation has exercised a widespread influence over a range of post-war French theorists. Despite many divergences from Sartre, and from each other, the shared assumption of the objectifying and alienating character of specular intersubjectivity can be clearly discerned in the work of Lacan, Foucault, Althusser and others. Indeed, one recent commentator has gone so far as to contend that 'Sartre is not merely a forerunner but a real originator of much of what Deconstruction has to say on the subject' (Howells, 1992: 349). Be this as it may, the Sartrean rendition of the recognition-relation can be seen at work in Lacan's theorization, wherein the subject only ever experiences identification but never approaches self-identity in its mediated encounter with itself. It remains in a constant mire of misrecognition, as the ego constituted via definition by the other always misses the pre-reflective interiority of the subject, and the ego is thus ultimately exposed as an imaginary construct, an illusory representation (Sarup, 1992: 36; Butler, 1999: xx, 175, 185). In Althusser's work the logic of the subject's coercive objectification reappears via the interpellative insertion of the individual into trans-subjective structures of meaning by the 'big other' of ideological apparatuses (Althusser, 1994: 128–32). And Foucault, who seldom mentions either Sartre or Hegel, can nonetheless be said to replay the moment of objectifying recognition, one in which the subject comes into its self-consciousness via the constitutive and positioning gaze (be it that of medical expertise, scientific knowledge, penal and corrective institutions, the calculative rationality of the state or the anonymous 'agentless' apparatus of panoptic technology) (Barnett, 1998: 23–4). Indeed for Foucault, as for many like-minded thinkers, history is arrested in the moment of the 'master's' perpetual triumph over the 'slave', a moment in which 'Humanity does not gradually progress fom combat to combat until it arrives at mutual reciprocity . . . [but] proceeds from domination to domination' (Foucault, 1984: 85).[2] Such is the apparent fate of the social subject.

Levinas: The Problem of the Same

If Sartre approaches recognition from the viewpoint of the subject who experiences objectification under the gaze of the other, then Levinas's disquisition proceeds from the opposite direction, namely from the ethically problematic nature of my endeavour to recognize, and so know, the other. The basic contention of Levinas's philosophical corpus can be expressed thus: Western philosophy has consistently suppressed the Other (*Autre*) by reducing it to the Same (*la même*). 'Western philosophy' writes Levinas 'is afflicted, from its childhood, with an insurmountable allergy: a horror of the Other which remains Other' (Davis, 1996: 32). Levinas sees the reduction of the Other to the Same as reaching its violent apotheosis in Hegelianism. The dialectical movement of the intersubjective encounter, following the path of *Verneinung*, *Aufhebung* and *Versöhnung* is the *sine qua non* of the reduction of Other to Same, the Many to the One, alterity to identity, transcendence to immanence, infinity to totality. Thus he writes that 'Hegelian phenomenology, where self-consciousness is the distinguishing of what is not distinct, expresses the universality of the same identifying itself in the alterity of objects thought and despite the opposition of self to self' (Levinas, 1969: 36). To 'recognize' the other, to render her known, understood, interpretable, is to rob her of her alterity or difference, to appropriate and assimilate her into a sameness with my own subjectivity. As such, this represents the abrogation of a primordial ethical responsibility, the respect for others in their alterity.

Levinas's own theory of ethical intersubjectivity consequently refuses the recognition-relation, and entails a stringent critique of the Hegelian position. This becomes clear if we consider two of the basic sets of distinction developed in *Totality and Infinity* (1969), namely that between the 'other' (*l'autre*) and 'Other' (*Autrui*), and that between 'need' and 'desire'. Here the other (*l'autre*) refers to that (ontological) otherness which can be assimilated by the subject into the Same. It is that which might confront the empirical self in its environment as alien, but which can be assimilated or appropriated so as to satisfy the self's 'need', and give it enjoyment (*jouissance*) as it feels exhilaration in taking possession of the world. This recuperation of the other (*l'autre*) within the Same, and the satisfaction of need thereby, reassures the self in its mastery of the world, affirms its self-sufficiency and so confirms the totality of Same (Levinas, 1969: 110–17,127–39,143–51). This is clearly taken to correspond to the movement of 'determinate negation' whereby the Hegelian subject overcomes the non-identity of the extant via its appropriative transformation. The Other (*Autrui*), in contrast, is that which is absolute (metaphysical) alterity, and which is in principle unassimilable, unapprehendable. The self's relation to the absolute Other is not that of appropriative 'need', but that of 'desire'. Since the Other is absolute exteriority, the desire for the Other is the desire for transcendence; whereas need reduces the other to the Same, desire does not, for precisely what desire desires is the *otherness* of the Other (Levinas, 1969: 33–40). The Other is desired because it offers an escape from Being and the Same, what Levinas calls an *excendance*, the desire of the self to escape beyond the existence to which it is bound (Davis, 1996: 18). The movement of desire does not effect a 'return to the Same', a movement of return which would reaffirm the closed circuit of the self in its solitude, self-mastery and potency. To put this another way, while 'need' corresponds to a *lack* which must be made good via the labour of assimilation and transformation, 'desire' responds to the *plenitude* or *fullness* of Being (*il y a*), the subject's confinement within an existence which it seeks to transcend or escape via its encounter with the other person as the 'trace' of an absolute alterity or exteriority.

In 'Violence and Metaphysics', his lengthy and influential discussion of *Totality and Infinity*, Derrida claims that 'This concept of desire is as anti-Hegelian as it can possibly be. It does not designate a movement of nega-tion and assimilation, the negation of alterity first necessary in order to become "self-consciousness" "certain of itself" . . .'. He goes on to claim that 'Hegelian desire would only be need, in Levinas' sense'; and whereas Levinas distinguishes 'desire' from such 'need', Hegel does not, thereby making 'need' the whole of his (Hegel's) conception of 'desire' (Derrida, 1978: 92–3). In other words, from the Levinasian perspective, Hegelian intersubjectivity *qua* recognition corresponds only to the experience of 'need' wherein the subject's ontological lack is made good by 'appropriating' the other for-itself. In compelling the other to recognize me in the terms defined by my own need, I turn the other into a mirror of myself, my 'spec-ular double' in whom I see only myself reflected back. As such, the other in his *otherness*, his fundamental difference from myself, is lost, discarded, vio-lated, consumed. The encounter of recognition is thus one of specular, cog-nitive and representational anthropophagy, voracious and cannibalistic, an imperialism whereby I colonize the other person as part of the circuit of my own self-conscious identification. Hence, for Levinas and the advocates of 'postmodern ethics' who follow his cue, the only morally viable mode of intersubjective relation is a relation of non-recognition which does not seek to identify the self in and through the other; one which does not reduce the other person to one's own definitional terms; which ultimately preserves the Other as absolute alterity, a mystery, in a 'relationless relation' (*rapport sans rapport*) which is without knowing, naming or understanding (Levinas, 1969: 38, 73; 1991: 45–51; Derrida, 1978: 147).[3]

Kojève's Hegel: Reclaiming Recognition

From the preceding exposition it is clear that the relation of recognition stands indicted for presupposing the reductive assimilation of the Other into the identity of the Same (Levinas) or as resulting in an interminable *agon* in which my freedom can only be purchased at the expense of the other's (Sartre). Consequently, our ethical-political options are either: (a) to reconcile ourselves to the impossibility of a mutually satisfactory settlement in which both my desire and that of the other can be satisfied, and so accept that the subject's 'self-certainty' inevitably requires the subordination of some other who mediates recognition; or (b) decide that any desire for mutual recognition must be eschewed all together, in favour of an ethics of surrender ('hostage') to a sublime, opaque and incomprehensible Other. Neither of these options holds out the possibility of thinking a political solidarity based on mutual affirmation and shared understanding. However, I believe that the dialectic of recognition can be defended against its representation as a 'pathological' relation of domination and identarian reduction. By reconsidering Kojève's reconstruction of Hegel's original formulation, I claim that we can establish the compatibility of recognition with both the *shared* realization of subjective freedom *and* the preservation of the other's alterity. Through such a theorization, recognition *and* difference can be brought together.

Perhaps the most efficacious way to proceed is to reconstruct Kojève's 'reading' of the 'master–slave' dialectic (at the risk of a little repetition), so as to show how a response to both Sartrean and Levinasian renditions emerges internally from the logic of the Kojèvian position. I have already adduced Kojève's starting point, namely his identification of desire, *qua* negativity or lack, as the fundamental constitutive condition and driving force behind the emergence of human self-consciousness. In Kojève's words:

> Desire is what transforms Being . . . into an 'object' revealed to a 'subject' by a subject different from the object and 'opposed' to it. It is in and by – or better still, as – 'his' Desire that man is formed and is revealed – to himself and to others – as an I, as the I that is essentially different from, and radically opposed to, the non-I. The (human) I is the I of a Desire or of Desire. (Kojève, 1969: 2–3)

This is the basis of the subject's 'negating' activity by which it transforms an 'alien reality' into its own through 'assimilation' and 'internalization' (as, for example, when one experiences a lack as hunger and internalizes the external objectivity of food so as to satisfy this desire) (Kojève, 1969: 3). However, this satisfaction of the subject's desire via the appropriation of the object is in itself insufficient to constitute the subject as a fully self-conscious human being. By relating to the world via the striving for the satisfaction of 'animal desire', the subject remains limited to 'Sentiment of self', an awareness of itself which is limited to the immediacy of its given desires. In Kojève's rendition:

> . . . the positive content of the I, constituted by negation, is a function of the positive content of the negated non-I. If, then, the Desire is directed toward a 'natural' non-I, the I, too, will be 'natural'. The I created by the active satisfaction of such a Desire will have the same nature as the things toward which that Desire is directed: it will be a 'thingish' I, a merely living I, an animal I. And this natural I, a function of a natural object, can be revealed to itself and

to others only as Sentiment of self, It will never attain self-consciousness.
(Kojève, 1969: 4–5)

In other words, the object (not-I) is only capable of satisfying a desire of a
certain kind (appetite, instinct) and so can only constitute or affirm the
subject in its subjectivity up to this point, as a 'desiring thing', an 'animal'.
Full human subjectivity, however, entails, beyond this, *self-consciousness*,
i.e. a certain awareness, perception and *understanding* of itself. Human subjectivity is defined not simply in terms of the specificity of its somatic
inclinations, but in terms of its reflexive self-relation, the meanings it attributes to itself. A human, self-conscious subject has a view of what kind of
subject it is or wishes to be: it *desires to realize itself according to a particular perception, understanding or image of itself as a human being* (e.g. as
'free', or 'autonomous', as possessed of 'value' and 'dignity', as deserving of
'respect', 'care', 'love' and so on). This desire to be affirmed in its self-
perception, to have its desire for its humanity answered, and thereby attain
its humanity as a fully constituted subject, cannot *in principle* be met by an
object. An object can satisfy an immediate desire (for example, for food,
warmth, shelter, sensuous gratification), but is incapable of giving *recognition* and thus affirmation that a subject is, in fact, the kind of subject which
it desires itself to be. On the contrary, this recognition or satisfaction, and
thus constitution of the subject as a subject proper, *can only be provided by
another subject*. The affirmation-constitution of ourselves as the kinds of
subjects we desire to be requires another *consciousness* (i.e. a subject) who
will be aware of us and thus capable of conferring recognition upon us in the
terms we wish to be 'taken'. Thus it is only via a *mediation* through the consciousness of another that the subject is able to identify itself, and so come
into itself as a self-conscious human subject. What this specifically 'human
desire' amounts to is a *desire to be desired, a desire for the desire of another*.
In other words,

> anthropogenetic Desire is different from animal Desire ... in that it is
> directed not toward a real, 'positive,' given object, but toward another Desire.
> Thus, in the relationship between man and woman, for example, Desire is
> human only if the one desires, not the body, but the Desire of the other; if he
> wants 'to possess' or 'to assimilate' the Desire taken as Desire – that is to say,
> if he wants to be 'desired' or 'loved,' or, rather, 'recognized' in his human
> value, in his reality as a human individual. (Kojève, 1969: 6)

And further that:

> ... to desire the Desire of another is in the final analysis to desire that the
> value that I am or that I 'represent' be the value desired by the other: I want
> him to 'recognize' my value as his value. I want him to 'recognize' me as an
> autonomous value. In other words, all human, anthropogenetic Desire – the
> Desire that generates Self-Consciousness, the human reality – is, finally, a
> function of the desire for 'recognition'. (Kojève, 1969: 7)

Thus the desire to become oneself as one wishes and wills oneself to be ('the act of transcending the given that is given to it') can only be satisfied via a recognition conferred by a subject other than the subject in question (Kojève, 1969: 5). The 'private idea that he has of himself' must be found 'in the external, objective reality' of others' affirmation (Kojève, 1969: 11). The subject's 'own subjective-certainty of himself' (i.e. 'the idea he has of himself, of the value that he attributes to himself') only becomes 'truth' (a reality that is objectively existing and valid) when it is intersubjectively affirmed (Kojève, 1969: 10–11).

Here we have reached the point of departure for Sartre's theorization of recognition, namely that this intersubjectively situated process has, in its origin, the character of a confrontation or struggle (*Kampf*) between a subject and its other(s). That is, in the first instance, the subject struggles to induce another subject or subjects to recognize and thus affirm it in the terms it has defined for itself (its idea of itself). In other words, it seeks to impose its subjective self-conception on others, thereby transforming it into an objectively (publicly) affirmed and valid reality which will be constitutive of others' conception of the subject, and correspondingly orient those others in their dispositions, evaluations and actions toward the subject. This is the heart of the 'master–slave' conflict as theorized by Hegel – subjects confront each other and vie with each other so as to successfully impel their other(s) to recognize them in their own terms, i.e. as they desire themselves to be objectively seen, treated and affirmed. Consequently, it seems that that struggle for recognition must lead to a contest of strength, in which compulsion becomes the means to force the other into accepting oneself on one's own terms. The resolution to such a struggle would be a situation in which the 'victor' (the one who succeeds in imposing his self-conception and self-evaluation on the other) comes to totally dominate the 'vanquished' other (who is reduced to accepting the victor's viewpoint, evaluations, etc.). Such would be a relation of 'master' and 'slave' – the latter submits to the former and places himself at the service of his vanquisher, giving himself over to realizing the desires and ends of the 'master'; he comes to live only for the other, the 'master', his own desire for his humanity having being eclipsed in favour of servitude to the desires of the other, which he has been compelled to accept as objectively valid and legitimate (Kojève: 1969: 15–16; Hegel, 1977: 115–16). As Hegel puts it: 'they exist as two opposed shapes of consciousness; one is the independent consciousness whose essential nature is to be for itself, the other is the dependent consciousness whose essential nature is simply to live or to be for another. The former is lord, the other is bondsman' (Hegel, 1977: 115). As such, the social formation that would emerge from the struggle for recognition is not a community of autonomous subjects mutually realizing their freedom, but a social structure of heteronomy in which the viewpoints, desires and ends of some (the 'masters') would be imposed upon defeated others (the 'slaves' or 'bondsmen') whose own self-conceptions (their idea of their own humanity) would be denied any social realization.

However, upon further reflection it becomes clear that such a relation of forced recognition, that of recognition via subordination and compulsion (as in Sartre's reading), cannot properly satisfy even the master's desire to achieve his self-conception as a recognized being (*anerkanntes Sein*). It will be recalled that an object is incapable of affirming the subject in its idea of itself because it is incapable of granting recognition – the satisfaction accomplished by mediation via an object will consequently be limited to a satisfaction of 'animal desire' and fall short of affirming the subject's desire for its humanity. Equally, however, recognition accomplished under conditions of subordination and compulsion (i.e. recognition of the subject's idea of itself emanating from the other who is a 'slave' or 'bondsman') will also fall short of an objective validation of the 'master's' 'subjective certainty of himself', and remain 'slavish' (Crossley, 1996: 18). The reason for this is as follows: for the other's recognition (positive perception and evaluation) of the subject to become valid as an objective truth, the other *has to be deemed capable and worthy of granting recognition*; in other words, the subject must trust and esteem the other's capacity for judgement, he must value the other's estimations as meaningful, significant and noteworthy, if the other's recognition of the subject is to 'count' and have any affirmatory power. In short, *the subject must recognize the other* as an autonomous, rational, valuable, fully conscious human being, before he himself can be similarly recognized by that other. In the 'master–slave' situation, these conditions cannot be met – precisely because the 'master' refuses to recognize the 'slave' (denies him the affirmation of his humanity), denies him his autonomy and freedom (including the freedom and autonomy of judgement and evaluation), and refuses to acknowledge the 'slave's' perceptions by forcing his own view of the world on the other, so the recognition 'won' by dint of force and compulsion fails to have any convincing validity (Hegel, 1977: 116–17). As Kojève puts it:

> The relation between Master and Slave ... *is not recognition properly so-called*. ... The Master is not the only one to consider himself Master. The Slave, also, considers him as such. Hence, he is recognized in his human reality and dignity. But this recognition is one-sided, for he does not recognize in turn the Slave's human reality and dignity. Hence, he is recognized by someone whom he does not recognize. And this is what is insufficient – what is tragic – in his situation. ... For he can be satisfied only by recognition *from one whom he recognizes as worthy of recognizing him*. (emphasis added; Kojève, 1969: 19)

This dilemma is *the absolute and singular source* of the emergence of relations of mutuality, of collective self-reassurance and self-realization, from the struggle for recognition. For a subject can only succeed in satisfying its 'human desire', its desire to have its 'idea of itself' objectively affirmed, if the other(s) who offer that recognition are themselves equally recognized in their own desire for their humanity and value. If the other is not recognized, then his recognition counts for nothing. I can only satisfy my own desire by simultaneously satisfying your desire – any attempt to win such satisfaction by force, compulsion or subordination is doomed to failure, as it undermines the very possibility of meaningful recognition from a subject who is deemed worthy and capable of granting it. Consequently, subjects' striving for the satisfaction of their own desire leads to the necessity of a relation of mutual affirmation with respect to other subjects' independence from oneself. I cannot affirm and accomplish my own desires without simultaneously recognizing others in their own terms.

After this lengthy exposition we can return to Levinas and Sartre, and draw out the implication that Kojève's account has for their 'pathologization' of recognition. First, with respect to Levinas, his equation of Hegelian recognition with 'need' is only partly true, for, as we have already seen, Hegelian desire is differentiated (in Kojève's terminology) between 'animal' and 'human'. Whereas 'animal desire' corresponds to Levinasian 'need', 'human desire' does not. Granted, Hegelian 'human desire' is a desire to constitute oneself according to idea-of-self, rather than to transcend oneself as Being. However, as the dialectic of recognition shows, 'human desire' (the desire to have one's idea of self objectively affirmed) cannot succeed by the assimilative logic of 'animal desire'. If desire assimilates the other, this destroys the other's independence, and with it the other's capacity to meaningfully grant recognition. Because the other must be seen as free and independent of oneself for his conferral of recognition to count, human desire necessarily must preserve the other *as other* for its own satisfaction. Hence Hegelian desire, as human desire for recognition, is not synonymous with the assimilating movement of Levinasian 'need', as Derrida supposes. On the contrary, if recognition properly speaking is to be achieved (i.e. if one is to pass beyond the failed recognition of the 'master–slave' scenario) then the difference of the other from myself, her independence as another who must be approached on her own self-established terms, becomes absolutely integral. Hence the mutuality of recognition is not coextensive with establishing an identity between myself and the other, i.e. recognizing in her only the very same characteristics I seek to have recognized in myself. To introduce such an isomorphism would be to 'take' the other on terms of my own definition, rather than on hers, and so abrogate her status as a free human being, thereby collapsing the necessary precondition for my own recognition. Indeed, it is worth recalling that Hegel's starting point is not a universal, identical subjectivity, but the singular subject of modernity (*das Einzelne*) whose right of self-satisfaction must be preserved in any intersubjective settlement (Lash, 1999: 138–9). It is on such a basis that Kojève insists that the egalitarianism envisaged by a recognition-theoretic perspective 'would imply the complete recognition of individual values', 'the formation of a society . . . in which the strictly particular, personal, individual value of each is recognized as such' (Kojève, 1969: 58; Butler, 1999: 77). In sum, far from appropriating, assimilating or 'saming' the other, this conception of recognition requires that I let the other remain an other if my mediated self-affirmation is to succeed.

With respect to Sartre, we again see that what he takes to be a relation of recognition is in fact not recognition proper at all. In Sartre's account, I as a free consciousness (*pour soi*) reduce the other to an object via the gaze (*en soi*) in order to assert my freedom and escape my own objectification by the other. Yet the moment I do this, I am no longer in a relation of recognition proper, since the other as object is exactly incapable of granting any meaningful recognition which would count for achieving the 'Being-for-myself of my consciousness'. In other words, my expropriation of the other's freedom (my denial of her status as also *pour soi*) robs me of the constitutive condition of affirming my own being-for-self as a 'reflective' (i.e. self-conscious) being. Thus from the standpoint of recognition proper, the inter-subjective affirmation of freedom, the affirmation of others as subjects rather than objects, is the necessary condition of the full and proper realization of my own desired possibilities.[4]

There are a number of other significant consequences which follow from a Kojèvian response to theorizations of recognition in the Sartrean vein. First, there is undoubtedly an ineliminable moment of contestation in the intersubjective encounter, as we each attempt to win the recognition of others on our self-established terms. However, this does not necessarily mean an encounter of seduction or compulsion (both of which efface the other's freedom), but one of *persuasion*. Indeed, we must question the peculiar torsion or warping that is introduced by a fixation on the *specular* conception of recognition, a conception which lends itself to seeing the encounter as reifying, objectifying and so on. If, in contrast, we make a move from specularity to *language*, we begin to appreciate the possibility of a *dialogic* conception of the intersubjective encounter (Kojève, 1969: 9; Barnett, 1998: 18–19). In such a situation recognition might be established through the process of mutual understanding, where I come to understand the other better in her uniqueness, and so become better positioned both to respond to her need for recognition in terms of her self-conceptions, and to better make myself understood as to what kind of recognition I myself desire.

This dialogic rendition of recognition can be approached along the lines mapped out by the hermeneutic tradition. Hermeneutic engagement entails a projection into a world of meanings outside one's own private, subjective sphere. The very notion of *understanding* presupposes an other, an outside, which must be met as something or someone unknowable from the vantage point of subjective interiority (Bleicher, 1990: 9, 57). The origin and impetus of *interpretation*, of *understanding*, (as opposed to reductive *explanation*) arises precisely out of the experience of the failure to simply fit the other's reality, existence and communications into our subjective framework – it is the *non-identity* between myself and my standpoint or truth, and that of someone else, 'that leads us to try and "understand" the text – historically, or psychologically – as the meaning of an Other' (Gadamer, in Bleicher, 1990: 80). Hermeneutic engagement requires a disposition of

attentiveness to alterity – as Gadamer puts it, 'Coming to an understanding
. . . presupposes that the partners are ready for it *and that they try to allow
for the validity of what is alien and contrary to themselves*' (emphasis added;
Gadamer, 1975: 348). To suppose that understanding the other is tantamount
to reducing the other to an identity with oneself is to miss the fundamentals
of the hermeneutic viewpoint – from Schleiermacher to Gadamer, hermeneutics depends precisely upon the fact that *the other is an other*, is not
simply the same as myself, and so must be met through an interpretive
engagement if she is to be understood in anything like her own terms.[5] If the
other were merely my mirror image, the *Doppelgänger* of my own subjectivity, a pure isomorphism, then the hermeneutic encounter would be entirely
unnecessary, redundant. The presumption of identity between subjects supports a *monological* stance in which I can know and anticipate everything
about the other by extrapolation from myself; conversely, it is the recognition
of the other *as* other which necessitates a *dialogical* engagement (Schleiermacher, 1998: 69–70, 113–14). From the specularist rendition of recognition
in much contemporary thought, such a hermeneutic possibility becomes lost.

Indeed, even from within a specularist formulation, the very specific
rendering of the 'look' as a kind of 'Medusan' reification and fixing simplifies the complex and polyvalent character of the visual dimensions of intersubjective encounters.[6] As Axel Honneth insightfully illustrates, quite apart
from the reifying look which 'robs' us of our possibilities, we can experience
looks as 'encouraging and disapproving, questioning or consenting, inviting
or sceptical', and as such 'they must not inevitably fix us simply to one particular goal of action'. On the contrary, they can affirm or question us in a
number of different ways, and we correspondingly answer to them either
negatively or positively dependent upon their specific valency, their relation
to the complexity of social contexts, structures of meaning and practices in
which they take place (Honneth, 1995a: 162–3). To illustrate this, Honneth
refers to Sartre's own famous example about the experience of shame (mentioned earlier). He points out that the negative experience of the other's look
in this instance isn't simply about the foreclosure of the spontaneity of my
pre-reflective, internal freedom, but is a moral reaction (*moralische
Gefühlsreaktion*) connected to the already existing normative infrastructure
of social interactions. In other words, I experience shame because the gaze
of the other reminds me that my actions are transgressive of a moral understanding about right or decent behaviour that the other and I already share
as part of a common structure of meanings (Honneth, 1995a: 163). What this
crucially illustrates is that the experience of recognition that is portrayed as
inherently negative by Sartre and others is in fact almost wholly dependent
for its valency upon certain normative self-understandings I have of myself.
If the look of the other confirms me with respect to self-understandings and
aspirations which are central to my idea-of-self or life narrative, then I will
welcome it as a moment contributing to the realization of my own aspirations
for selfhood. Sartre, in conceiving the freedom of the *en soi* as inhering only
in a permanent openness of existential possibility, misses the crucial fact

that freedom also and crucially consists in establishing for ourselves enduring personal identities which are consistently affirmed in our encounters
with others (Honneth, 1995a: 163–5). The same criticism may be levelled
at the Levinasian perspective, wherein the integrity of the Other depends
upon a suspension of judgement on my part – what this misses is precisely
what the Other might require of me, namely the looks, gestures, words or
acts of recognition which publicly affirm him in his aspirations for coherent
selfhood.[7] *Thus I am the* condition *for the realization of the other's possibilities, rather than their death, and he is the condition of mine.*

A final issue which needs to be tackled here is how the theory of recognition, with its emphasis on 'mutuality' and 'reciprocity', might retain the
element of 'spontaneity' or 'gratuitousness' in its understanding of the intersubjective encounter. In other words, it must be demonstrated that recognition does not reduce social relations to mere calculation, a disenchanted
vision of equilibristic exchange. The need for a moment of gratuity or asym-
metry in the ethical relation, of 'care' for the other without an anticipation
or requirement of remuneration, has been explored by Derrida in his excursus on 'the gift' (Derrida, 1987: 198–201).[8] From the recognition-theoretic
perspective presented above, there is a two-fold response as to why recognition entails an orientation of concern for the other. First, for Kojève as
much as for Levinas, the subject is 'tied' to the other as its condition of possibility. For Levinas, it is the primordial 'exposure' to alterity which enables
the separation in which the self knows itself as a self, as a self in its distinction from what it fundamentally *is not*. This is why, for Levinas, the
relation of self and Other is a metaphysical fundament, and why one's being
is always a being-for the Other (*pour l'autre*); to escape or efface this Other
is impossible, for to do so would destroy the condition of possibility of one's
own existence (Levinas, 1969: 210–11; 1991: 86–9, 109–18). Equally, we
can see that the establishment of the human subject as self-consciousness,
the Hegelian *für sich*, is tied to the other, to exteriority, as its constitutive
condition; the human is a being whose being is always 'outside of himself'
(Kojève, 1969: 13). This unavoidable condition of mutual dependence
means that the other's existence is something inextricably bound up with my
own, and the other's need is something which obtrudes upon my consciousness at the most fundamental level.[9] A second, and crucial element of 'care'
emerges within the recognition-led perspective from its dependence upon
an orientation of openness and understanding. As already argued, the
willingness to apprehend the experiential standpoint of the particular other
is an intrinsic moment in the successful effectuation of recognition. The
achievement of understanding can be said to subvene on the exercise of the
capacity for imaginative projection, what Hannah Arendt calls the development and deployment of 'an enlarged mentality' which liberates us from
subjective private conditions and introduces us to the experiential reality of
an other (Benhabib, 1992: 52–3; Yar, 2000: 16–17). Through such understanding we imaginatively reconstruct or anticipate what the world and its
experience *feel like* from the standpoint of the other, and it is this sharing

which furnishes a source of moral motivation oriented to the other's need; hence 'an affective openness to the particularity of the other', and a sense of 'asymmetrical obligation' to that particular other's need (Honneth, 1995b: 307–9), can be seen to emerge from the hermeneutic engagement within which the recognition-relation is played out.

The Political Future of Recognition

It is my hope that the preceding discussion has furnished an initial rationale and response for theoretically reclaiming the positive potentialities of recognition from its implicit or explicit pathologization in much recent work. My aim has been to show how a 'politics of recognition', properly understood, can support structures of intersubjective reciprocity, while incorporating a sensitivity to 'difference'. There are, however, a number of important dimensions along which the vision of a politically useful conception of recognition must be developed. The constraints of space have prevented their discussion in this contribution. However, in concluding, I would like to mention some of these axes briefly, so as to further establish the relevance of a recognition-led perspective for understanding the present and future of progressive politics. First, we can see that the process of intersubjective agreement entailed in recognition is generative of mediating structures, shared cultural and institutional forms which reconcile subjects in common normative and practical orientations of a *sittlich* kind. As such, the theory of recognition offers an invaluable resource for rethinking the vexed problem of 'community', namely the challenge of establishing substantive forms of solidarity in the context of late-modern, highly differentiated and pluralistic societies. Second, we see that the recognition perspective provides a normative ideal for self-realization, what Honneth calls a model of 'decentred autonomy', which can function as a critical yardstick in challenging existing structures of social and political relations. The experience of the refusal of recognition, or 'pseudo-recognition' in the form of a coercive identification embedded in unequal relations of power, can be seen as the incitement for social and emancipatory struggles (Honneth, 1996). As such, this rendition allies itself with a critical and transformative conception of political praxis, rather than seeing recognition as something which can simply be comfortably accommodated within the existing frameworks and structures of liberalism, a scenario in which the state and other key institutions retain their 'neutrality' with respect to fundamental conceptions of the 'good' (see, for example, attempts to incorporate a concept of recognition, as 'respect' for cultural minorities, into a model of 'liberal multiculturalism' – Kymlicka, 1995). Finally, the concept of recognition can rescue left-radical theorizations of politics from the 'false opposition' between the new 'cultural politics' of lifestyle and identity, and the older agenda of social justice *qua* politics of redistribution (Fraser, 1997). The concept of recognition enables us to see the distribution of material and other social goods (the division of the 'social surplus') as an intrinsic and critical component of any successful self-realization, i.e. of a person's securing for herself the public affirmation and social conditions needed to establish a positive self-relation. As such, the unhelpful divide between what Nancy Fraser has respectively termed the politics of 'insult' and 'injury', can be overcome. In sum, the ability of a recognition-theoretic perspective simultaneously to entertain the need for solidarity, the exercise of individual autonomy, a sensitivity to difference, the critique of power and the struggle for social justice, establishes its indisputable relevance for mapping the future of progressive politics.

Notes

I wish to express my thanks to the following: Jan Selby, for his careful reading and incisive comments on an earlier draft of this article; and the anonymous reviewer who provided detailed and insightful comments which were invaluable in strengthening the argument developed here.

1. Thus Jean Hyppolite claims that for Hegel desire is nothing other than 'the power of the negative in human life', and consequently the 'essence' of human life must be seen as that of a 'negating negativity' (Hyppolite, 1969: 27).

2. This is not to claim that Foucault is a Hegelian *avant la lettre*, but rather that he, like many 'anti-Hegelians', at crucial points plays out the Hegelian relation of constitutive specularity in an 'inverted' form. The extent to which the critics of Hegelianism remain within the ambit of Hegel's thought is something of which Foucault himself was well aware:

> But to truly escape Hegel involves an exact appreciation of the price we have to pay to detach ourselves from him. It assumes that we are aware of the extent to which Hegel, insidiously perhaps, is close to us; it implies a knowledge, in that which permits us to think against Hegel, of that which remains Hegelian. We have to determine the extent to which our anti-Hegelianism is possibly one of his tricks directed against us, at the end of which he stands, motionless, waiting for us. (Foucault, 1972: 235)

3. This becomes apparent in Levinas's elaboration of a theory of communication based on the distinction between 'Saying' (*le Dir*) and 'the Said' (*le Dit*). The former denotes the 'pre-original' exposure to alterity in language, the primordial action of signifying ('signifyingness'); the latter denotes the propositional content of language, the identifying, classifying, naming, clarifying, illuminating transmission which produces knowing and understanding. To relate to the Other in terms of the Said means to bring the Other into the realm of one's subjective comprehension, and thus into the totality of Same and identity. Hence, in order to preserve the radical alterity of the Other, Levinas must strive for a 'Saying without the Said', 'an incessant unsaying of the Said', such that communication without comprehension will preserve the Other as exteriority and mystery (Levinas, 1991: 5–7, 45–51).

4. Sartre's objection to the possibility of a 'successful' resolution to the 'master–slave' dialectic (i.e. the subject's achieving identity between its desire, its subjective idea-of-self, and the objective recognition furnished by the other) orients to the inability of the subject to know the other *as a subject* from the outside, i.e. to intuitively apprehend the other's immediate, interior, subjective experience, rather than seeing him only and always from the external standpoint as object. If I cannot apprehend the other's internal experience as *en soi*, and so I cannot know him as a

subject, his capacity for recognizing me fails. For Sartre, Hegel's postulation of a resolution depends on his untenable 'optimism' from the 'totalitarian standpoint'. By this he means the postulation of an objective standpoint, that of 'the vantage point of truth i.e., of Whole' from which Hegel can show how my consciousness reaches the other (Sartre, 1969: 242–3). This, however, depends on a misapprehension by Sartre, namely that my knowing the other as subject requires an *immediate* apprehension of the other in *intuition*; rather, from the Hegelian standpoint, self-recognition and self-consciousness proceed precisely via the sublation of immediate, intuitive apprehension into mediated awareness. Hence my 'reaching' the consciousness of the other is not dependent on our both being moments within a greater metaphysical whole, but rather upon the establishment of a mediating awareness between real pluralities (Hartmann, 1966: 118–19; Barnett, 1998: 20–1).

5. On the centrality of otherness in the development of the hermeneutic tradition see, for example, Andrew Bowie's illuminating introductory essay in Schleiermacher (1998).

6. Martin Jay sees this equation of visuality with objectification as an unwarranted simplification which takes the multiple and often contested 'scopic regimes' of modernity and reduces them to Cartesian perspectivalism (see Jay, 1992).

7. The normative dimension of self-realization as public affirmation, inherent in the concept of recognition, is readily apparent in our everyday usage – that is to say, we mean by this term not only a cognitive relation of correspondence ('I recognize this, I've seen it before . . .'), but also a normative acknowledgement of the moral and practical status of others ('I recognize your right to do this or that . . .', or 'She doesn't get the recognition she deserves . . .'). The reduction of recognition to a variant of epistemological objectivization misses this crucial dimension altogether.

8. For an attempt to develop a fully fledged theory of political practice from Derrida's notion of the gift, see Corlett (1989).

9. Levinas's citation of Paul Célan's verse – *ich bin du, wenn ich ich bin* – would thus apply equally to the Kojèvian position, insofar as it gestures to the inextricable relation of mutual dependence in which self and other are bound (Levinas, 1991: 99). The crucial difference here, I would argue, is the character of this relation: for the Levinasian, it must remain a 'relationless relation' (*rapport sans rapport*) of mutual incomprehension, lest the other's alterity be traduced; from the recognition-theoretic perspective developed here, this relation is socially accomplished through the dialogic establishment of understanding.

References

Althusser, Louis (1994) 'Ideology and Ideological State Apparatuses (Notes towards an Investigation)', pp. 100–40 in Slavoj Žižek (ed.) *Mapping Ideology*. London: Verso.

Barnett, Stuart (1998) 'Introduction: Hegel Before Derrida', pp. 1–37 in S. Barnett (ed.) *Hegel After Derrida*. London: Routledge.

Bauman, Zygmunt (1993) *Postmodern Ethics*. Oxford: Blackwell.

Benhabib, Seyla (1992) *Situating the Self: Gender, Community and Postmodernism in Contemporary Ethics*. Cambridge: Polity Press.

Bleicher, Josef (1990) *Contemporary Hermeneutics*. London: Routledge.

Butler, Judith (1997) *The Psychic Life of Power: Theories in Subjection*. Stanford, CA: Stanford University Press.

Butler, Judith (1999) *Subjects of Desire: Hegelian Reflections in Twentieth-century France*. New York: Columbia University Press.

Corlett, William (1989) *Community without Unity: A Politics of Derridean Extravagance*. Durham, NC and London: Duke University Press.

Crossley, Nick (1996) *Intersubjectivity: The Fabric of Social Becoming*. London: Sage.

Davis, Colin (1996) *Levinas: An Introduction*. Cambridge: Polity Press.

Derrida, Jacques (1978) 'Violence and Metaphysics', pp. 79–153 in *Writing and Difference*, trans. and intro. Alan Bass. London/Henley: Routledge and Kegan Paul.

Derrida, Jacques (1987) 'Women in the Beehive: A Seminar with Jacques Derrida', pp. 189–203 in A. Jardine and P. Smith (eds) *Men in Feminism*. Methuen: New York.

Derrida, Jacques (1997) *Politics of Friendship*, trans. George Collins. London: Verso.

Foucault, Michel (1972) *The Archaeology of Knowledge*. New York: Pantheon.

Foucault, Michel (1984) 'Nietzsche, Genealogy, History', pp. 76–100 in Paul Rabinow (ed.) *The Foucault Reader*. New York: Pantheon.

Fraser, Nancy (1997) *Justice Interruptus*. London: Routledge.

Gadamer, Hans-Georg (1975) *Truth and Method*. New York: Seabury Press.

Gilroy, Paul (1993) *The Black Atlantic: Modernity and Double Consciousness*. London: Verso.

Hartmann, Klaus (1966) *Sartre's Ontology: A Study of* Being and Nothingness *in the Light of Hegel's Logic*. Evanston, IL: Northwestern University Press.

Hegel, G.W.F. (1977) *Phenomenology of Spirit*, trans. A.V. Miller. Oxford: Oxford University Press.

Honneth, Axel (1995a) 'The Struggle for Recognition: On Sartre's Theory of Intersubjectivity', pp. 158–67 in *The Fragmented World of the Social*. Albany: SUNY Press.

Honneth, Axel (1995b) 'The Other of Justice: Habermas and the Ethical Challenge of Postmodernism', pp. 289–323 in Stephen K. White (ed.) *The Cambridge Companion to Habermas*. Cambridge: Cambridge University Press.

Honneth, Axel (1996) *The Struggle for Recognition: The Moral Grammar of Social Conflicts*, trans. Joel Anderson. Cambridge: Polity Press.

Howells, Christina (1992) 'Sartre and the Deconstruction of the Subject', pp. 318–52 in C. Howells (ed.) *The Cambridge Companion to Sartre*. Cambridge: Cambridge University Press.

Hyppolite, Jean (1969) 'The Concept of Existence in the Hegelian Phenomenology', in *Studies on Hegel and Marx*, trans. John O'Neill. New York: Basic Books.

Jay, Martin (1992) 'Scopic Regimes of Modernity', pp. 178–95 in Scott Lash and Jonathan Friedman (eds) *Modernity and Identity*. Oxford: Blackwell.

Jay, Martin (1994) *Downcast Eyes: The Denigration of Vision in Twentieth-century French Thought*. Berkeley/Los Angeles: University of California Press.

Kojève, Alexandre (1969) *Introduction to the Reading of Hegel*, trans. James H. Nichols. New York: Basic Books.

Kymlicka, Will (1995) *Multicultural Citizenship*. Oxford: Oxford University Press.

Lacan, Jacques (1977) *Écrits: A Selection*. London: Penguin.

Lash, Scott (1999) *Another Modernity, A Different Rationality*. Oxford: Blackwell.

Levinas, Emmanuel (1969) *Totality and Infinity: An Essay on Exteriority*, trans. Alphonso Lingis. Pittsburgh, PA: Duquesne University Press.

Levinas, Emmanuel (1991) *Otherwise Than Being or Beyond Essence.* trans. Alphonso Lingis. Dordrecht: Kluwer Academic Press.

Lingis, Alphonso (1994) *The Community of Those Who Have Nothing in Common.* Bloomington/Indianapolis: Indiana University Press.

Merleau-Ponty, Marcel (1968) *The Primacy of Perception and Other Essays.* Evanston, IL: Northwestern University Press.

Mulvey, Laura (1989) *Visual and Other Pleasures.* Bloomington: Indiana University Press.

Said, Edward W. (1991) *Orientalism: Western Concepts of the Orient.* London: Penguin.

Sartre, Jean-Paul (1969) *Being and Nothingness: An Essay on Phenomenological Ontology*, trans. Hazel E. Barnes. London: Routledge.

Sartre, Jean-Paul (1970) 'Intentionality: A Fundamental Idea in Husserl's Phenomenology', *Journal of the British Society for Phenomenology* 1(2): 4–5.

Sarup, Madan (1992) *Jacques Lacan.* Hemel Hempstead: Harvester Wheatsheaf.

Schleiermacher, Friedrich (1998) *Hermeneutics and Criticism and Other Writings.* Cambridge: Cambridge University Press.

Yar, Majid (2000) 'From Actor to Spectator: Hannah Arendt's "Two Theories" of Political Judgment', *Philosophy & Social Criticism* 26(2): 1–27.

Majid Yar is a Research Associate in the Institute for Environment, Philosophy and Public Policy (IEPPP), Lancaster University, UK. He has recently completed a PhD exploring the relation between ethical intersubjectivity, Hegel's concept of 'recognition' and the theorization of community. His primary research interests relate to the ethical dimensions of both European social thought and contemporary processes of social change, and he has authored a number of articles exploring these themes.

Oh, My Others, There is No Other!

Civic Recognition and Hegelian Other-Wiseness

John O'Neill

HERE ARE signs that our current political discourse has settled into a stalemate between what Lash nicely calls the two idioms of *community* and *difference*. Identity politics (race, sexuality, multiculturalism) now represents the main thrust in the politics of recognition. Yet I will argue there is a danger that cultural politics so strains towards the idiom of absolute otherness and non-identity as to lose what I call the *civic idiom of inter-subjectivity and community*. If this happens, the baby thrown out with the bathwater will be the unfinished project of a civic welfare state (O'Neill, 1994). Because I am concerned with the question of whether capital society has any civic limit or moral commons (O'Neill, 1994), I think it necessary to restate the case for a Hegelian politics of recognition. I am not unaware of the French case against Hegel (O'Neill, 1992, 1995), yet I think it can be questioned by showing what is at stake in the politics of welfare which I think must be defended against the current remoralization of a-civic autonomy. I shall argue, therefore, that a civic politics of recognition must be grounded in a proper grasp of the Hegelian fourfold structure of the intra-inter-subjective doubling of self/other relations (O'Neill, 1996). This structure of recognition or *other-wiseness* delimits both the absolute otherness of the other and the absolute selfness of the self. From an Hegelian standpoint the two idioms of otherness and selfness belong to the (im)possibility of the state of nature, i.e. they are subcultures of a regressive politics of arbitrariness and unknowability from which 'we' have already exited. Despite Derrida and Levinas, there is neither an absolute subject nor an absolute

■ *Theory, Culture & Society* 2001 (SAGE, London, Thousand Oaks and New Delhi),
   Vol. 18(2–3): 77–90
   [0263-2764(200104/06)18:2–3;77–90;017484]

otherness of the other except as filial phantasies of post-Hegelian decon-struction. Since I have argued this at length elsewhere (O'Neill, 1989, 1996, 1998, 1999) I will now restate the Hegelian position that is central to a *poli-tics of civic recognition*.

Identity politics tempts us to turn away from the more historically grounded project of revising capitalism's civic self-correction in the welfare state (O'Neill, 1997). The result will be to reduce further the welfare state both by *neo-right* arguments that employ the very multicultural relativism of identity politics to dissipate the project of social justice and by *left–liberal* (Derrida, 1992) arguments against the immorality of the subject/other gift which aggravates left/right discontent with the welfare state (O'Neill, 1999). The challenge to contemporary society is to sustain its secular gifting, which includes all forms of conventional charity and public transfers of income, education, health and civic infrastructures. The secular rationale for these gift practices need not pit independence against dependence or locate rationality in the market instead of the state. All society is post-individual (Durkheim, 1933: 277–80). Difference is a civilizational process. In archaic society (Mauss, 1990) alliances ruled the economy of difference whose excess could be destroyed in a festival of gifts beyond the everyday effort to bind exchange to solidarity. The challenge today is to raise the minimalist liberal political contract to a civic level of recognition under a rule of political tolerance extended to universal strangers as civic others (Rawls, 1971, 1993; O'Neill, 1994; Habermas, 1996, 1998). That is the ideal of the welfare state (Marshall, 1964; Titmuss, 1970). We are currently engaged in revising our political vision of one another. We do not need to ask who deserves citizenship because this perversely moralizes scarcity. But we should ask what is a socially just distribution of the goods (health, education, housing, employment) that underwrite civic cohesion. This is an exercise that presupposes we share some common institutions and that we understand and feel things in much the same way. A civic democracy is hardly imagin-able without such assumptions. We should not shed the long history of moral and political struggles through which we have created institutions that have softened the inequality of income, health and education that mark all of our lives. Rather, we share a common political will to alter our institutions in the direction of social justice and with a civic regard for the inclusion of the most disadvantaged and vulnerable members of society (Walzer, 1983). These arrangements constitute a social covenant that, despite their political differences, parties on the right and on the left have honoured without monopoly by either one and without any belief that this covenant should be broken.

As I see it, liberal democracies are risking a return to a 'state of nature' whose cruelty was considerably if not willingly counteracted in the civic practices of 19th-century capitalism. Even in the context of class struggle, or precisely because of the will-to-class struggle, the welfare state was the civilized peak of liberal capitalism, an achievement that we owe as much to the right as to the left (Wiener, 1981). What is abhorrent about the New Right is its ignorant will-to-destroy the civic covenant, thereby aggravating the fundamentalism and neo-ethnicism it so fears. If we do abandon the will-to-civic covenant, we shall lose what I call its *other-wiseness*. We shall lose our civic understanding that rich and poor, male and female, young and old, past and present, present and future are not entirely alien to one another but overlap and modify each other's claim upon our civic potential.

Capital Culture

The modern state owes its distinctive form to the ways in which it answers to the articulation of an industrial society. In short, the polity, economy and sociocultural institutions of modern society have assumed particular con-stellations at given stages of mercantile, industrial and post-industrial capi-talism. Whenever these constellations of capitalism begin to shift, we are driven to examine their history or genealogy in order to estimate their prob-able path. To delimit the contesting political discourses that emerge in a period of paradigm global shift, we are obliged to take a stand on the base grammar of capitalism. The globalized imperatives of the current stage of capitalism code the celebrated features of postmodernism (subjectivity, de-centring, pluralism, deconstructed racism and genderism) more for its symbolic elites than its production and service workers. What must be asked is whether these cultural dispensations are rather the ideological effects through which individuals misrecognize the evacuation of capital power from sites the techno-political centre once thought it needed to hold. Where nothing is contested by capitalist interests, nothing is gained by identifi-cation with the fallout from the erasure and realignment of institutional relations demanded periodically by capitalist elites. Every shift in the insti-tutional forces of capitalism offers us an opportunity to deepen our ignor-ance of those forces. Indeed, our contemporary ignorance is guaranteed if we proliferate difference and drift, despite the overwhelming global practice of mergers that narrow the rest of our civic practices. In fact, by allowing its loyal opposition to attack its presumed notions of authority, art, sexuality and politics, late capitalism achieves a benign solidity and tolerance. Neither mastery nor victimage can be espoused in a cultural system that can recycle all of its class, sexual, artistic and political symbols to re-embody a-temporal and a-spatial identities whose social contexts no longer delimit the space-time of late capitalism.

The global division of labour and the exodus of transnational corpor-ations that employ the state apparatus to offset the nation-state, have pro-duced a new configuration of the forces of integration and fragmentation within and between regional economies. Yet global capitalism is still cor-porate capitalism whose global consistency generates ubiquitous contra-dictions, foreclosures and marginalization. Meanwhile, the new division of globalized wealth and poverty is now declaring its own hard line on the ethics of survival and obsolescence. Today, we are told by the New Right that our civic covenant is an immoral and profligate exercise that can only be indulged by the nation-state through the blindness of its politicians to the morality of the new world order. In an explosion of Darwinistic fervour, we are called to believe that a sudden shift in our economic environment has left every one of our social institutions obsolete – except for the market. Only by downsizing our moral and political baggage can we enjoy the proper release of that lean and mean individual energy that is demanded and rewarded by the market (Gordon, 1996). In short, global capitalism proposes to remoralize us by returning us to a *state of nature* from which it would then draw us in accordance with the absolute law that our industry be ruled by a capital information elite. To understand what institutional re-orientation is involved here, we need to remind ourselves of the social compact that is now under reconstruction if not dismantlement. The primary social fact is that production relations generate class relations and state/economy relations. Production is primary in the material sense but not necessarily politically. In modern times this is because the liberal state is operative in the dominance of industrial over mercantile and agrarian capitalism. The liberal state may also operate as an imperial nation-state on behalf of the mass production phase of capitalism, with domestic class relations harmonized through a national pact between business, labour and government:

> A certain kind of political culture is, indeed, a condition for tripartism, one in which the state is regarded both as the instrument of civil society and at the same time as the agency for harmonizing civil society's divergent interests. Government is thought of both as the channel for procuring satisfaction for separate interests and as a force constraining these interests toward reconciliation. (Cox, 1987: 77–8)

Tripartism has, of course, never achieved perfect political balance; any partner to the pact may be seen to dominate it. With the globalization of production relations, we are experiencing the collapse of tripartism – the erosion of unionism, the hegemony of the global market and the subordination of the redistributive welfare state(s) that we have known for the last 50 years. We can now see that the neoliberal state was committed to growth as much as redistribution and to inflation as the price of tripartism. Inflation, however, when combined with the stagnation of the mid-1970s, began to erode the national income policies of tripartism. At the same time, the informal cooperation between the central agencies of government and the globalizing corporations was strengthened. Finally, the conflict between the interests of international capital accumulation and the national welfare of vulnerable groups has come to a head. National governments are now subordinate to international finance and trade institutions that enforce the new world order of production:

> The state disengages from civil society – it reverses the trend toward inter-penetration and blurring of the edges between state and society that corporatism promoted – in order to force more radically the adjustment of national economies to the world economy. (Cox, 1987: 289)

The result is that the civic capital expenditures of nation states have been severely discounted, resulting in lower credit ratings, i.e. higher interest rates that further aggravated the national deficit. Yet, it is the welfare component of the deficit that is blamed for the overall drag upon national economies.

Currently, there is a considerable withdrawal of the legitimacy accorded to the neoliberal welfare state, expressed in anti-state movements, tax revolts and new elite ideologies of self-interest and zero-altruism. These events, coupled with the severe polarization of incomes since the 1980s, have put considerable strain upon civic society, which is caught between the anomic violence of marginalized groups and a generalized fear of new scarcities and insecurities. Global capitalism imperils our political potential for civic 'other-wiseness', grounded in the welfare state. By rejecting the corporatist contract between business, government and labour that has softened class differences in the last half century, global capitalism now subjects everyone to the dominion of monetarism and the market, downsizing organizations and breaking unions. All this weakens the welfare state as a brake upon capitalism. Worse still, the fragmentation of social citizenship is now accelerated by the New Right's curious adoption of left cultural relativism, especially in media coverage of such events as the demonstrations against the World Trade Organization (WTO) in Seattle, Quebec City and Genoa, to claim that there are no objective moral principles to guide the pursuit of social justice:

> Ideas of social justice and of basic needs, which form the threadbare clothing of contemporary social democratic movements, are of minimal help here. Criteria of desert and merit, such as enter into popular conceptions of social justice, are not objective or publicly corrigible, but rather express private judgments grounded in varying moral traditions. Conceptions of merit are not shared as a common moral inheritance, neutrally available to the inner city Moslem population of Birmingham and the secularized professional classes of Hampstead, but instead reflect radically different cultural traditions and styles of life . . . The objectivity of basic needs is equally delusive. Needs can be given no plausible cross cultural content, but instead are seen to vary across different moral traditions. (Gray, 1983: 181–2)

The ideology of the New Right rejects any notion of the political manipulation of the allocative efficiency of the market that might redistribute income within or between nations. Just as the New Right rejects neo-Keynesian policies on the state level, so it rejects the last 50 years of state-driven development in the Third World. We are all asked to believe that there is no dual economy of labour, no comparative disadvantage or non-market mentality. Economics is a general science of human behaviour unless prohibited or violated by politics and morals. The only accountability is what is imposed by the market, namely, a rule against inefficiency but not any rule against inequality. Rather, markets encode inequalities as competitive differences that optimize social efficiency. According to the New Right, there can be no equation between inequality and injustice. The blindness of the market rather than the blindness of justice is the ultimate guarantee of merit and reward. Social inequality is natural and moral whereas the policies of equality are unnatural and immoral.

Capital Class

It is too early to abandon the welfare society. The abstractive power of capitalism lies in its power to absorb labour, race and gender subject to the maintenance of its own persistence as a system of class inequality invariant across all industrialized societies (Shavit and Blossfeld, 1993; Marshall, 1997). Poverty, racism and genderism are structural effects of a class society not of its sub-cultures. What cultural and value relativists overlook is that the differences that flourish *within* classes do not challenge but even confirm the difference *between* classes. Poverty is colourless and genderless however much it marks women and racial minorities. Likewise, although it has discriminated against women and ethnic groups (Williams, 1995), the welfare state remains a strategic resource for the reduction of inequality and the expansion of civic citizenship. I am therefore coming down on the side of the *class idiom* in the gender/race/class paradigm rather than on the side of the identity idiom in the paradigm (Brenkman, 1999). This is not because I think equality overrides identity but because I propose that the figure of *civic citizenship* draws together its constituent figures of *person* and *public* in our political tradition. The politics of race and gender must attach to this civic tradition, or else win cultural battles but lose the class war.

The structural agency of class cuts across race and gender and is analytically prior to them precisely because its referent is the abstract(ive) system of power that reproduces capitalist society. Class does not reside *in* a class but *between* social classes, i.e. in their relative wealth/poverty which hardly varies in the industrial world. This system has no borderlines or hybrids that can make any difference to it that is not a difference enjoyed by some group or other within the class system. Class is everywhere and nowhere – a feature described but not analysed in postmodern deconstructions of essence and appearance, race and gender, space and time:

> A culturalist politics, though it glances worriedly at the phenomenon of class, has in practice never devised a politics that would arise from a class 'identity.' For while it is easy enough to conceive of a self-affirmative racial or sexual identity, it makes very little sense to posit an affirmative lower-class identity, as such an identity would have to be grounded in the experience of deprivation per se. Acknowledging the existence of admirable and even heroic elements of working-class culture, the affirmation of lower-class identity is hardly compatible with a program for the abolition of want. The incommensurability of the category of class with that of race or gender (class cannot be constructed as a social identity in the *same way* as race or gender because it is not, in the current affirmative sense, a 'social identity' at all) does not, on the other hand, disenable a description of the relation between these social modalities. This was after all the problem sociology once addressed by means

of the distinction between class and *status*. The current equation of gender, race, and class as commensurable minority identities effaces just this structural distinction. (Guillory, 1993: 13)

It is therefore debatable whether multiculturalism constitutes an adequate basis for 'the politics of recognition' (Taylor, 1992) to eliminate racism and sexism. One could easily dismiss this move on the ground that it is a belated response to the hidden (ethnic) injuries of class (Sennett and Cobb, 1972) and civic deprivation (Hamacher, 1997). Once late capitalism has hollowed out all other identities than market position, one can expect a return of the cultural repressed (family, roots, ethnicity), played out in multicultural curricula, films, art, dress and food and furniture. In short, *capitalism has no Other* once it reaches its full development in global capitalism.

Because global capitalism is now its own Other – due to the transnational displacement of its major corporations – its domestic politics soon display a paranoid combination of elite distance and populist presence that undermines citizenship and civic politics. This is fertile ground for the return to a new liberal state of nature and its nasty narrative of fear, hunger and brute power. It is now clear that the New Right intends to remoralize political life by starving it to a bare minimum. The New Right wants class politics out of the state, out of business, out of work, out of the family. It wants to abandon the civic covenant like an old factory. The New Right proclamation of the end of class politics is only the beginning of its new politics of the market-place, of the dominion of international finance and the self-reporting corporate media endlessly discovering its own dictates in the quasi-natural movements of the global economy.

Hegelian Otherwise-ness not Post-political Alienation

As I see it, the postmodern dismissal of the Hegelian-Marxist grand narrative of the complementarity of reason and freedom (O'Neill, 1996) could not have been more ill-timed, let alone ill-advised. It is Hegel who explores the illusory idiom of the sovereign subject commanding nature and alien others in the name of its independent desire and purpose. Hence Hegel's experiment with the minimal conditions of the state of nature to show that, even at the level of animality, life presupposes certain general categories, e.g. edible/inedible, if it is to achieve its barest aims. The heart of the matter is reached when the predatory self realizes that, by projecting every other thing as its thing, it is condemned to a fate that is always potentially its own death or enslavement. Strictly speaking, this moment of reflection is not available in the state of nature. It involves a complex inter- and intra-subjective splitting and recognition of the desire for society. Human independence lies not in its origins but in its ends which we come to realize in society and history. Human nature, therefore, is second nature (*Bildung*). Any question about human origins or ends presupposes a cultural narrative that, in our case, is populated with the figures of Stoicism, Scepticism, the Covenant and the

Social Contract. This is the narrative through which we understand ourselves on the way to the romance of individualism (O'Neill, 1998).

Hegel mercilessly deconstructs the anthropological assumptions of foundationalist epistemology while simultaneously reconstructing it in terms of the historical transformation of the community of belief that it figurates (*Gestalt der Bildung*). There is neither justice nor injustice in the state of nature, no rights, no contracts and no law (Peperzak, 1995). In fact, there is no identity. This is because everybody is a *nobody*, i.e. merely the object of another's fear, appetite or desire. Bodies cannot exercise natural rights by recognizing common bodily states of desire, hunger and fear. To the contrary, so far from underwriting political society, natural rights derive from a moral community whose members recognize in one another those rights that become second nature to them in a given historical period. Hegel certainly understood how the subjective shape of modernity is reinforced by its political economy. What he opposed was the pathological individualism in modernity's appropriation of desire, knowledge and labour (Žižek, 1989). The reified self-concept of individuals systematically misrecognizes the collective reality (*die Sache selbst*) of their 'we-like' (*wirhaftige*) relations (Marcuse, 1987: 254). Lacking mutuality, the physical and sexual conquests of the natural self neither relieve loneliness nor shorten the shadow of death that it drags along with it. The critical task of the *Phenomenology*, therefore, lies in the restoration of the middle principle of the intersubjectivity of subjectivity (O'Neill, 1989). Short of this, the idealist and empiricist philosophies of individualism are tied to a state of nature and animality where desire is endlessly mortified for want of an encounter with an 'other' by whom its 'self' is neither aggrandized nor enslaved.

In the *Phenomenology*, Hegel historicizes consciousness as a structure *within* difference, as a living entity with subject (Ego) and object (Other) polarities that continually cancels any exclusivity in either object-awareness or self-awareness. In Figure 1, the desiring Ego (1) can never be satisfied on the level of appetite because the living body is a complex structure of differentiation and integration, involving higher levels of endo-/exo-structuring. Hence, in stages (2) and (3) Ego's senses are subject to fading and exhaustion in the wake of the embodied subject even before the Ego encounters the higher level of intersubjectivity. The projection of subject- and object-consciousness appears to break down in the experience of desire since, in cancelling its object, the desiring consciousness merely reproduces its object as the essence of desire. Consciousness is therefore obliged to treat the object of its desire as something living, as an Other endowed with an opposing consciousness. Having achieved primacy over the object, self-consciousness has still to press on with the articulation of its own self-determination. To achieve this, in stage (4) self-consciousness must both split and integrate its awareness of its self qua 'self' and its awareness of objects as other than its self. Thereafter, consciousness exists in a *double entente* of mutual recognition, i.e. as an intra-subjectivity that is an intersubjectivity. Each consciousness achieves a social identity

Dialectic of Desire and Recognition

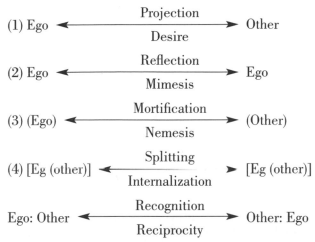

Figure 1

accorded to one another rather than the project of a possessive self excluding all others except as objects of appropriation and domination. Self-
consciousness must seek reason and freedom as higher goods than its own
independence since in the worst possible scenario only one self might
survive the struggle for life and death. But this negative freedom would
return us to the very impossibility of self-possession that the *Phenomenology* recounts.

We should not abandon the Hegelian-Marxist narrative unless we wish
to trash the narrative of the civic transformation of society, mind and personality that figurates Western history of philosophy, political economy
and sociology. The antagonism between the idioms of conformity and indi-
viduation, between lordship and bondage, between subjectivity and intersubjectivity demands their sublimation (*Aufhebung*) but not the suppression
of one or the other side. Sublimation is not repression. The desire to overcome repression without 'working through' (*durcharbeiten*) the necessity of
sublimation results in the oppression of opposites in an 'I' that merely
declares itself a 'We' or a 'We' that is nothing but an 'I', says Hegel (1910:
227). Individual and cultural maturity (*Mundigkeit*) is achieved through
compromise and reconciliation (*Versöhnung*), i.e. through dialectical
communication.

In Hegel the nature/culture relation does not involve an idealist
repetition of the material aspect of life. The subjective cohesiveness and
individuality achieved on the level of the economy is not identical with the
ethic-political achievement of community and reciprocity (Dickey, 1987).
A civic state exceeds the formal universalization of bourgeois private life
and property – but it does so without any metaphysical leap. Put another
way, Hegel's critique of political economy locates it at the first level of a

collective servitude to the quasi-natural laws of the market. The economy operates to atomize individuals and the effect is to divide political and economic life, excluding the propertyless, women and children. But there is a second level of the dialectic of recognition where the project of citizenship can only be achieved by responding to a political vocation on behalf of civic life (*Sittlichkeit*). Hegel is nevertheless determined not to speak of civic life in purely idealist terms. Civic life is impossible apart from the historical acquisition of the technical and socio-practical intelligence operative in the economy. Actually, Hegel locates the major shift in our cultural intelligence in the political articulation of the difference between economic morality (*subjective Sittlichkeit*) and civic intelligence (*objective Sittlichkeit*). The ethic of the market remains limited in its concept of human need even on its own level due to property restriction. But on the civic level, defined by the need for mutual recognition, the material ethic of political economy involves an even more restricted economy and is not at all the general economy it proclaims to be. Bourgeois prestige chokes upon itself like a lord whose honour prevents him from according any recognition to his slave. The lord's contempt for his slave starves himself as well as the slave, just as the sadist is bound to the empty fetish that enslaves the masochist. In each there is no recognition and no jouissance becase neither party can internalize a relationship that is constituted entirely through abjection and projection.

Post-script: Hegel in a Bottle

Let us reconsider the postmodern politics of identity and minority values. Can there be public discourse, evidence and argument on the nature of personal and social identity that rejects civic authority in the name of the contingency of values? What can be the appeal of an idiom of the subject that is limited by the contingency of every other subjectivity with whom it can presume no commonality of knowledge and values? Such a theory would require an epistemic loan while simultaneously renouncing the trust which underwrites it (Cole, 1994). Since even anti-social behaviour can only achieve its purpose through the social recognition it disclaims, what can be the objection to the advances of a civic idiom of social cohesion? We cannot achieve the aims of any personal behaviour, opinion or values without bringing them to a public forum for validation (O'Neill, 1994). We need a civic forum for the expression and evaluation of individual opinion precisely so that *one's* opinion can be given some common weight rather than remain on the level of personal taste. For here, too, one's public and private interests are not wholly different kinds of interests, as though a citizen differs entirely from a worker or consumer. To imagine that we have no way of translating and revising our interests as citizens and our interests insofar as class, race and gender weigh upon us, is to surrender politics to cultural fragmentation.

Today, we experience great difficulty in reconciling the idioms of civic community and ethical identity. Indeed, the rejection of 'we' formulations as authoritarian, essentialist and colonizing practices is taken for granted in enabling or empowering political identity. Yet, even on the level of ethical identity, we need translations between desire and value if we are to avoid the current endorsement of the idiom's impulse and anger as moral insight. The need for such translation or mediation in the constitution of ethical identity returns 'us' to the very civic reflexivity we reject but need if we are to avoid the reduction of intersubjective recognition to minoritarianism. In short, the welcome pluralization of ethical identity cannot be fulfilled without recognition of an implicit mediation process on the level of civic citizenship. The practice of minoritarian politics presupposes the civic recognition of ethical identity claims. Unless this is cancelled, one's life, reasons and desires only achieve currency in a public world and a public discourse that they presuppose for their identification, evaluation and acknowledgement. The self, in other words, is a communicative self, endlessly invoking another similarly communicative self to sustain its projects (O'Neill, 1989). This is a message that is lost once we put Hegel in a bottle and toss it out to sea – or into the Seine! The 'missing subject' at the heart of modernity is that the self-identity we have come to cherish involves misrecognition of the historical, social structures of mind, self and society:

> A certain mental breathing space seems indispensable to modern man, one in which his independence not only of any master but also of any god is affirmed, a space for his irreducible autonomy as individual, as individual existence. Here there is indeed something that merits a point-by-point comparison with a delusional discourse. It's one itself. It plays a part in the modern individual's presence in the world and in his relations with his counterparts. Surely, if I asked you to put this autonomy into words, to calculate the exact indefeasible freedom in the current state of affairs, and even should you answer, the *rights of man*, or *the right to happiness*, or a thousand things, we wouldn't get very far before realizing that for each of us this is an intimate, personal discourse which is a long way from coinciding with the discourse of one's neighbour whatsoever. (Lacan, 1993: 133)

Once again we are seducing ourselves with a delusional idiom of individualism. To accommodate global capital we are drawn to capital bodies, intelligence, sexuality and possessions. Once again, we are tempted to reject the unemployed, the welfare poor, immigrants and refugees as moral aliens whose fates lay no claim upon our own. We fancy that we can set up new walls between the rich and the poor, between personal and civic life, between today's enjoyment and tomorrow's misery that will fall upon children and youth who are not our own. In the name of an absent capital god we are being asked to break the civic covenant, to fragment our communities, to exit from the city in order to reconnect in an abstractive, vertical union with our global other in the world's finance, film and fashion houses. Meanwhile, the sweatshops, the refugee camps and the prisons do not close; exploitation and violation do not cease; hunger does not abate. We are asked to close our minds, to harden our hearts and not to cry out.

References

Brenkman, John (1999) 'Extreme Criticism', *Critical Inquiry* 26 (Autumn): 109–27.

Cole, Stephen E. (1994) 'Evading the Subject: The Poverty of Contingency Theory', pp. 38–45 in Herbert W. Simons and Michael Billig (eds) *After Postmodernism: Reconstructing Ideology, Critique*. London: Sage.

Cox, Robert (1987) *Production, Power and World Order: Social Forces in the Making of History*. New York: Columbia University Press.

Derrida, Jacques (1992) *Given Time: 1. Counterfeit Money*, trans. Peggy Kamuf. Chicago, IL: University of Chicago Press.

Dickey, Lawrence (1987) *Hegel: Religion, Economics and the Politics of Spirit 1770–1807*. Cambridge: Cambridge University Press.

Durkheim, Emile (1933) *The Division of Labor In Society*. London: Macmillan.

Gordon, David M. (1996) *Fat and Mean: The Corporate Squeeze of Working America and the Myth of Managerial 'Downsizing'*. New York: Free Press.

Gray, John (1983) 'Classical Liberalisms, Positional Goods, and the Politicization of Poverty', pp. 174–185 in Adrian Ellis and Kristian Kumar (eds) *Dilemmas of Liberal Democracies: Studies in Fred Hirsch's Social Limits to Growth*. London: Tavistock.

Guillory, John (1993) *Cultural Capital: The Problem of Literary Canon Formation*. Chicago, IL: University of Chicago Press.

Habermas, Jürgen (1996) *Between Facts and Norms: Contributions to a Discourse Theory of Law and Democracy*, trans. William Rehg. Cambridge, MA: MIT Press.

Habermas, Jürgen (1998) *The Inclusion of the Other: Studies in Political Theory*, ed. C. Cronin and P. de Grieff. Cambridge: Polity Press.

Hamacher, Werner (1997) 'One 2 Many Multiculturalisms', pp. 284–325 in Hent de Vries and Samuel Weber (eds) *Violence, Identity, and Self-Determination*. Stanford, CA: Stanford University Press.

Hegel, G.W.F. (1910) *The Phenomenology of Mind*, trans. J.B. Baillie. London: George Allen and Unwin. (Orig. pub. 1807.)

Lacan, Jacques (1993) *The Seminar of Jacques Lacan, Book III: The Psychoses 1955–1956*, ed. Jacques-Alain Miller, trans. with notes by Russel Grigg. New York: Norton.

Marcuse, Herbert (1987) *Hegel's Ontology and the Theory of Historicity*, trans. Seyla Benhabib. Cambridge, MA: MIT Press.

Marshall, Gordon (1997) *Repositioning Class: Social Inequality in Industrial Societies*. London: Sage.

Marshall, T.H. (1964) *Class, Citizenship and Social Development*. New York: Doubleday.

Mauss, M. (1990) *The Gift: The Form and Reason for Exchange in Archaic Societies*, trans. W.D. Hall, Foreword by M. Douglas. London: Routledge.

O'Neill, John (1989) *The Communicative Body: Studies in Communicative Philosophy, Psychology and Politics*. Evanston, IL: Northwestern University Press.

O'Neill, John (1992) *Critical Conventions: Interpretation in the Literary Arts and Sciences*. Norman: University of Oklahoma Press.

O'Neill, John (1994) *The Missing Child in Liberal Theory: Towards A Covenant Theory of Family, Community, Welfare and the Civic State*. Toronto: University of Toronto Press.

O'Neill, John (1995) *The Poverty of Postmodernism*. London: Routledge.

O'Neill, John (ed.) (1996) *Hegel's Dialectic of Desire and Recognition: Texts and Commentary*. Albany: State University of New York Press.

O'Neill, John (1997) 'The Civic Recovery of Nationhood', *Citizenship Studies* 1(1): 19–32.

O'Neill, John (1998) 'Lost in the Post: (Post) Modernity Explained to Children', pp. 128–38 in *The Politics of Jean-François Lyotard: Justice and Political Theory*, ed. Chris Rojeck and Bryan S. Turner. London: Sage.

O'Neill, John (1999) 'What Gives (with Derrida)?', *European Journal of Social Theory* 2(2): 131–46.

Peperzak, Adriaan (1995) 'Hegel and Hobbes Revised', pp. 199–218 in Ardis B. Collins (ed.) *Hegel on the Modern World*. Albany: State University of New York Press.

Rawls, John (1971) *A Theory of Justice*. Cambridge, MA: Harvard University Press.

Rawls, John (1993) *Political Liberalism*. New York: Columbia University Press.

Sennett, Richard and Jonathan Cobb (1972) *The Hidden Injuries of Clan*. New York: Knopf.

Shavit, Yoshi and Hans-Peter Blossfeld (1993) *Persistent Inequality: Changing Education Attainment in Thirteen Countries*. Boulder, CO: Westview Press.

Taylor, Charles (1992) *Multiculturalism and the Politics of Recognition*. Princeton, NJ: Princeton University Press.

Titmuss, Richard M. (1970) *The Gift Relationship: From Human Blood to Social Policy*. London: Allen and Unwin.

Walzer, Michael (1983) *Spheres of Justice: A Defense of Pluralism and Equality*. New York: Basic Books.

Wiener, Martin J. (1981) *English Culture and the Decline of the Industrial Spirit, 1850–1980*. Cambridge: Cambridge University Press.

Williams, Fiona (1995) 'Race/Ethnicity, Gender and Laws in Welfare States: a Framework for Comparative Analysis', *Social Politics: International Studies on Gender, State and Society* 2(2): 127–59.

Žižek, Slavoj (1989) *The Sublime Object of Ideology*. London: Verso.

John O'Neill is Distinguished Research Professor of Sociology at York University, Toronto, a Member of the Centre for Comparative Literature at the University of Toronto, and a Fellow of the Royal Society of Canada. He was Senior Scholar at the Laidlaw Foundation 1993–4, working on the Children at Risk Programme. He is the author of *Sociology as a Skin Trade* (1972), *Making Sense Together* (1974), *Essaying Montaigne* (1982) and *Five Bodies: The Human Shape of Modern Society* (1985). His more recent books are *The Communicative Body: Studies in Communicative Philosophy, Politics and Psychology* (1989), *Plato's Cave: Desire, Power and the Specular Functions* *of the Media* (1991), *Critical Conventions: Interpretation in the Literary Arts and Sciences* (1992), *The Missing Child in Liberal Theory* (1994) and *The Poverty of Postmodernism* (1995). He is Co-Editor of the *International Quarterly*, *Philosophy of the Social Sciences* and of the *Journal of Classical Sociology*. Currently, he is working on the political economy of child suffering, welfare state theory and civic practice.

Towards a Citizens' Welfare State
The 3 + 2 'R's of Welfare Reform

Ruth Lister

T HE LANGUAGE of 'recognition' and 'difference' is not, by and large, that in which mainstream debates about 'welfare' (aka social security) reform are couched, despite its relevance to welfare reform. Instead, in many Western societies the welfare agenda has become dominated by a false dichotomy between 'active' and 'passive' forms of welfare. Active (read positive) welfare is geared towards enhancing the employability of the workless and moving them from 'welfare to work'. Passive (read negative) welfare is about consigning the workless to a life of 'welfare dependency' in the name of better benefits.

The UK Welfare Reform Green Paper, published during the new Labour government's first year in office, epitomizes this thinking. It proposes as 'a third way' in welfare reform 'a modern form of welfare that believes in empowerment not dependency'. It conjures up an alluring vision of a modern welfare system, which extends 'the exits from welfare dependency, moving from a mass-production service, which merely pays benefit, to one offering a professional, tailor-made service for each individual' (DSS, 1998a: 19–20). In contrast, those who argue for better benefits are presented as antediluvians:

> . . . who believe that any changes to the Beveridge system are a betrayal of his vision, even though the world has changed so dramatically. They believe that cash is the answer to most of the problems, that poverty is alleviated by more money rather than more opportunity. They defend the *status quo*, but want benefits for all to be more generous. They believe that poverty is relieved exclusively by cash hand outs. (DSS, 1998a: 19)

A discourse of active modernization is used to promote the new welfare agenda. It is set against a negative discourse of a passive 'welfare dependency

■ *Theory, Culture & Society* 2001 (SAGE, London, Thousand Oaks and New Delhi),
   Vol. 18(2–3): 91–111
   [0263-2764(200104/06)18:2–3;91–111;017489]

culture', imported from the USA, which serves to stigmatize welfare benefits and those reliant upon them. In doing so, it constructs benefit recipients
as the 'other', thereby weakening any relations of solidarity based on recognition of common membership of society. The notion of a 'dependency
culture' does not derive from research-based evidence. As a careful initial
assessment of the UK 'welfare to work' programme observed:

> It is important to distinguish between long-term benefit receipt and 'benefit
> dependency'. Very few people appear to choose a life on benefits in prefer-
> ence to paid work. Indeed, the commitment to seek work is strong – usually
> only weakening when it conflicts with other responsibilities, such as caring
> for others. (Bennett and Walker, 1998: 2)

To challenge the active/passive welfare reform dichotomy is not to
question the importance of policies which promote paid work as the main
route out of poverty. Research in the UK and elsewhere has demonstrated
the relationship between changing labour market positions and poverty, the
importance to individual well-being and self-esteem of employment, and the
adverse and isolating effects of worklessness (Dean and Taylor-Gooby, 1992;
Jackson, 1994; Bryson et al., 1997; Clasen et al., 1998; McKendrick, 1998).
An analysis of longitudinal data confirms the crucial role which paid
employment can play in lifting people out of poverty (Jarvis and Jenkins,
1997, cited in Bennett and Walker, 1998). However, paid work does not
guarantee an exit from poverty; nor is it appropriate for all those who rely on
benefits for their main income.

The purpose of this article is not therefore to make a case against the
'active' side of the welfare dichotomy. It is, rather, to challenge the
dichotomy itself. It does so in two main ways, within the context of welfare
reform in the UK. First, it argues for a welfare reform agenda, which treats
improvements to social security benefits not as promoting 'passive' welfare
but as complementary to labour market activation policies. Second, it broad-
ens the notion of active welfare to incorporate notions of active citizenship,
which construct welfare subjects as actors in the political process of welfare
policy-making and delivery (see also Williams, 1999). The framework for
these arguments is what I have dubbed the three 'R's of welfare reform: risk
protection, redistribution and recognition. Running through these three 'R's
are the further two 'R's of rights and responsibilities, the latter being a dominant theme in the official welfare reform agenda.

Risk Protection

Social security is commonly understood as an institutional device for trans-
ferring money to certain groups of the population in order to protect them
against risk and to prevent or at least alleviate poverty; which benefits are
covered by the term varies between countries. However, social security is
not simply a means; it is also an end, i.e. a state of financial security in the
face of risk (Sinfield, 1989).

It is well known that the nature of these risks has changed. The post-war welfare state was built on the assumption that 'a Fordist economy guarantees decent pay and secure employment. The post-industrial economy is less likely to provide such guarantees; indeed, the average worker's life-cycle risks will increase substantially' (Esping-Andersen, 1994: 183). The theme was taken up by the Commission on Social Justice (CSJ),[1] which located these 'life-cycle risks' in both the workplace and the changing patterns of family life, warning that such risks are both 'less predictable and more probable than were those of the 1950s' (CSJ, 1994: 222). It argued that:

> . . . far from making the welfare state redundant, social and economic change creates a new and even more vital need for the security which the welfare state was designed to provide. Frightened people cannot welcome change; they can only resist it or be defeated by it. It takes secure people – secure in their abilities, their finances and their communities – to cope with change at the workplace or in the home. (CSJ, 1994: 222)

More recently, the then Secretary of State for Education and Employment, David Blunkett (2000), has spoken of the welfare state as 'an enabling force', 'helping [men and women] to overcome fear of change, minimize risk and seize the opportunities of the new economy'. However, in the same speech, he hinted at a further reduction in the overall welfare responsibilities of the state. The impact of 'the risk society' bears most heavily on those least able to negotiate its contingencies, reflecting class and other social divisions (Taylor-Gooby, 2000; Holzmann and Jørgensen, 2000). The continued importance of public social security provision in this context has been underlined by a Joseph Rowntree Foundation study.[2] This concluded that 'collectively financed social security may offer a better deal than is commonly supposed, not just for those with low incomes and at high risk, but also for those with average incomes and at more typical risk' (Burchardt and Hills, 1997:4). While the Commission did not see social security as the sole mechanism for helping people to deal with contemporary risks, it did, nevertheless, acknowledge its role as 'a crucial source of financial security for most people' within the context of a mixed economy of welfare (CSJ, 1994: 224). 'A modern system of social insurance tailored to changing employment risks and family needs' was a central plank in its welfare reform strategy (CSJ, 1994: 229).

The specific reforms it proposed were designed to address one of the key weaknesses of the national insurance system that stood at the heart of the Beveridge post-war model: its anachronistic template modelled on male employment patterns. This serves to exclude many women, including nearly 2 million in paid employment but with earnings below the national insurance lower earnings limit, below which contributions are not paid. According to a study carried out for the (government-appointed) Equal Opportunities Commission, this kind of low-paid employment is much more likely to be long-term for women than for men (who are much less likely to earn below the earnings limit anyway). The researchers called for reform of the national insurance system so as to include 'the vast majority of part-time and low paid workers' (McKnight et al., 1998).

There have been some minor policy initiatives in this direction, but overall the direction of policy is towards greater reliance on both means-tested and private forms of provision. The various Green Papers on welfare reform have not explicitly addressed the future of social insurance (apart from the occasional opaque reference). Adopting an incremental benefit-by-benefit approach to reform, the government is disinclined to debate the shape of the social security system's underlying architecture. The Social Security Secretary, Alistair Darling, has described such debates as 'dogmatic' (Darling, 1999). He is more interested in what is 'cost-effective'. Likewise, Prime Minister Tony Blair used his 1999 Beveridge lecture to stress that in the mix of 'universal and targeted help', 'the one is not "superior" or "more principled" than the other' (Blair, 1999). Many would disagree. While acknowledging that it is unrealistic to envisage a social security system with no means-testing, it is widely believed that means-testing is divisive, inefficient and a less effective form of protection against risks.

The danger is that the shift under the Conservatives, away from a social insurance-based social security system towards a means-tested-based one, is being continued by default without any public debate about the appropriate balance between the different kinds of benefits – contributory, means-tested and contingency. According to Nicholas Timmins, Public Policy Editor of the *Financial Times*, 'national insurance is dead. . . . Government ministers know they are accelerating its destruction, but do not want to talk about it much' (*Financial Times*, 22 November 1999).[3] The direction in which they are taking policy has been signposted by *The Economist*: 'Tony Blair's Government has crossed the Rubicon from . . . the left bank of welfare-for-all to the right bank of means testing' (6 March 1999). Even if possibly something of an overstatement (given, for example, counter-indications such as increases in the real value of child benefit, the universal benefit for children in the UK), these observations act as a hazard warning that we may be moving further down the road towards a residual poverty relief model of social security typical of liberal regimes such as the USA. This takes us further away from more institutionalized Continental European models, which, even if they are themselves also under pressure, have been more effective in guaranteeing genuine social security (Hirsch, 1997). According to a study of social insurance in Europe, 'Britain is unique with respect to the way in which its social insurance system has "withered"' (Clasen and Erskine, 1998: 4; Clasen, 1997).

One aspect of risk which has become of increasing significance is that faced by those who attempt to move to a new country as migrants or asylum seekers. The latter, moreover, are fleeing the risk of persecution and often violence. Western welfare states, for the most part, have become increasingly exclusionary in their response to those seeking entry and residence. An example is the decision of the UK Government, first Conservative and now

Labour, initially to restrict and now to remove the right to social security for asylum seekers. Instead, asylum seekers are to be given vouchers and a small amount of pocket money. Apart from the negative implications for the material security of this group of particularly vulnerable people, there is a danger that their use of vouchers, which act as a visible indicator of their status, could, in some instances, jeopardize their physical security in the face of racist and xenophobic opposition to their presence. At the very least, the use of vouchers is stigmatizing and potentially humiliating (Refugee Council, 1999).

Social security's function in relation to risk is not confined to that of protection. It also has a role to play in helping people to take risks. For instance, the provision of decent benefits for lone parents can be crucial in enabling women with children to leave violent or abusive relationships. Likewise, as Tony Giddens (1998: 116) has observed, 'deciding to go to work and give up benefits, or taking a job in a particular industry are risk-infused activities'. As part of a 'third way' approach to welfare reform, he calls for benefit systems to encourage a 'more active risk-taking attitude . . . wherever possible through incentives, but where necessary by legal obligations' (Giddens, 1998: 122).

Underlying this and similar justifications for 'activation' measures to encourage or oblige benefit claimants to take the risk of giving up the relative security of benefit payments for the insecurity of the modern labour market is an assumption that benefits for those out of work have to be kept as low as possible so as not to discourage such risk-taking. There is, though, another perspective on this which points to the very opposite policy conclusion. There is evidence to suggest that, without the protection of a reasonable safety net and the buffer of some savings, or if in debt, benefit claimants are less likely to be willing to take the risk of a job in a labour market, which offers most of the workless only temporary, part-time, self-employed or low-skill jobs (White and Forth, 1998). Some of this evidence has been collected together by Eithne McLaughlin who draws attention to a number of studies which:

> . . . show how the low level of out-of-work income available constrains the ability of unemployed people, especially parents, notwithstanding the availability of in-work means-tested benefits, to manipulate potential economic opportunities where those opportunities do not carry with them an immediate, weekly wage large enough to meet most of the individual's or household's basic needs. With no 'margin of error' in their incomes, and hence tight budgeting practices, the practicalities of moving out of unemployment into low-paid full-time, part-time, temporary (or otherwise uncertain) jobs, or economic opportunities which require some initial outlay . . . or of drawing on in-work benefit sources of income (family credit and housing benefit), all become considerably more difficult than policy-makers and other commentators appear to understand . . . it is important to note that current low levels of social security provision may act against unemployed people taking a chance on such opportunities as there are. (McLaughlin, 1994: 24)

Other research suggests that the greater the hardship experienced by lone mothers, the less likely they are to move into employment. The researchers speculate that 'hardship may influence employment rates by exhausting mothers and leaving them no time or money for job search' (Bryson et al., 1997: 29). It is through such evidence that the false dichotomy between 'active' and 'passive' welfare is revealed most sharply.

Redistribution

The issue of benefit levels is also an important one in its own right and represents one item on the wider agenda of redistribution. There is a considerable body of evidence, of various kinds, which testifies to the inadequacy of current benefit levels, particularly in the case of families with children reliant on benefit for more than a short period. Even with welcome significant increases in social assistance rates for young children, introduced by the Labour government, the independent Family Budget Unit estimates that they are still insufficient to secure 'a low cost but acceptable' standard of living (Parker, 1999). Without an adequate income, it is difficult for people living on benefit to be full participants in the wider society, enjoying full rights of citizenship and exercising their responsibilities as citizens.

There has been no official public review of benefit levels since they were set after the Second World War. The case has been made for a minimum income standard (MIS) that would function as a benchmark against which benefit levels can be assessed. An MIS stands regardless of and separate from other factors which shape benefit levels, such as public spending constraints and concerns about work incentives. It means, though, that need becomes an explicit element in the determination of benefit levels. Moreover, it opens up to public debate the whole issue of what it is appropriate to expect our fellow citizens to survive on. The European Commission has recommended that member states should set an MIS at a level 'considered sufficient to cover essential needs with regard to respect for human dignity' (Commission of the European Communities, 1992). As John Veit Wilson (1994, 1998) has pointed out, a number of other industrialized countries operate an MIS.

Despite some ad hoc improvements in benefits, targeted on those not expected to undertake paid work, the government has hitherto resisted a more comprehensive review of benefit levels.[4] This partly reflects the antipathy discussed above. It also signals the Labour government's rejection of what is regarded as an outdated model of 'tax and spend' in which the better off are taxed more in order to spend more on the worse off. Any redistribution which is effected (and recent Budgets have been reasonably redistributive) has to be 'quiet' or 'by stealth'. The retreat from noisy redistribution is, at one level, a political tactic designed to appease the *Daily Mail*-reading voters of Middle England whom the party continued to woo in order to win a second term.[5]

It is also a response to economic globalization, which is perceived as rendering unsustainable traditional 'tax and spend' policies, thereby exemplifying the 'post-Fordist' model of welfare described by Jessop (1994). This is typical of New Labour's reification and embrace of economic globalization as an uncontrollable fact of life to which governments and individuals have to adapt. Cloaked in a discourse of modernization, there is an implicit denial of the possibility of political choice in governmental responses to economic global forces (Finlayson, 1998; Hay, 1998; Andrews, 1999; Rose, 1999). Likewise, public opinion, which is read (not necessarily accurately, see Hills and Lelkes, 1999) as favouring tax cuts over public spending, is treated as something to be followed not led. The 1999 Anglo-German document, *Europe: The New Way*, repeatedly rejects the traditional 'tax and spend' approach of centre-left governments, going so far as to claim that 'public expenditure as a proportion of national income has more or less reached the limits of acceptability' (Blair and Schröder, 1999: 29).

These political stances are underpinned by a philosophical shift in official Labour Party thinking. The goal of (greater) equality (of outcome) has been replaced with that of equality of opportunity, to be achieved by the 'redistribution of possibilities' (Giddens, 1998: 101) rather than of resources. This was summed up by Gordon Brown, the Chancellor of the Exchequer, as a rejection by New Labour of 'equality of outcome as neither desirable nor feasible, imposing uniformity and stifling human potential; instead it espouses a view of equality of opportunity that is recurrent, life-long and comprehensive' (*Guardian*, 2 August 1997). Likewise, in his speech to the 1999 Labour Party conference, Blair called for 'true equality – equal worth, an equal chance of fulfilment, equal access to knowledge and opportunity', 'not equal incomes. Not uniform lifestyles or taste and culture'. In both cases, echoing the classic anti-egalitarian caricature, greater equality of outcome is being conflated with sameness and uniformity.

At the same time, according to Giddens, 'the new politics defines equality as inclusion and inequality as exclusion' (1998: 102). It does so using what Ruth Levitas (1998) has dubbed a social integrationist discourse of exclusion (SID), focused primarily on paid work, rather than an earlier redistributive, egalitarian discourse (RED) that embraces notions of citizenship and social rights. Arguably it is the latter that is better attuned to diversity, whereas the former promotes a uniform paid-work ethic, which obscures the variety of relationships to and positions in the labour market of different social groups.

The rejection of an explicit redistributionist egalitarian stance is occurring against the backdrop of a massive redistribution of resources towards the better off during the previous two decades. As the Treasury itself points out, in a report which documents the scale of inequality, 'income inequality has increased sharply over the last twenty years' and this 'is not representative of a world wide trend' (HM Treasury, 1999: 11). Between 1979 and 1996/7, the real incomes of the bottom tenth of the population fell by 9 percent compared with an increase of 70 percent for the top tenth and 44 percent overall (DSS, 1998b). The level of inequality in the 1990s was higher than at any time since the late 1940s (Hills, 1998).

In this context, any vision of equality of opportunity and social inclusion is a mirage. Massively unequal starting points cannot but affect the ability to grasp educational and other opportunities, and it is questionable how far genuine social inclusion can be achieved without addressing the inequalities which are the motor of social exclusion. As David Marquand (1998: 24) has commented, given the growing fault line 'between the winners and losers in the global marketplace . . . no project for social inclusion will work unless it captures some of the winners' gains and redirects them to the losers'.

Nor is it good enough in the long run to redirect some of those gains 'by stealth'. While any project of redistribution to the poor and powerless inevitably faces political and economic constraints, the political constraints are likely to be greater if there is no attempt to make the positive case for redistribution. Without such an attempt, it will be impossible to build the constituency of support for redistributive policies which is necessary if they are to take root. The rehabilitation of taxation as an expression of citizenship responsibility would help to counter the criticism, voiced by the leading political economist Will Hutton among others, that 'most of the obligations that accompany rights in a New Labour order are shouldered by the bottom of society rather than those at the top, which is let off largely scot-free' (*Observer*, 5 July 1998; see also Fitzpatrick, 1998; Chen, 1999).

A redistributive conceptualization of citizenship responsibilities can also be inscribed at the global level, as reflected in the Charter for Global Democracy launched in 1999 as a 'call for international accountability, equality, justice, sustainable development and democracy' (*Observer*, 24 October 1999). Relevant here are notions of global citizenship, which reflect, at the international level, some of the rights and responsibilities associated with national citizenship, as acknowledged to some extent in the June 2000 Berlin Communiqué on Progressive Governance for the 21st Century (see also Lister, 1997). The concept of global citizenship encourages a focus on the responsibilities of the more affluent nation-states towards poorer nations. It is accepted by a number of citizenship theorists that principles of distributive justice, combined with ecological imperatives, demand an internationalist interpretation of citizenship obligations (Weale, 1991; Oliver and Heater, 1994; Twine, 1994; Newby, 1996). Social policy analysts, such as Peter Townsend (1996), are likewise arguing that poverty and injustice have to be understood and tackled at the international as well as at the national level (see also Deacon et al., 1997). In the words of J.K. Galbraith, 'the responsibility for economic and social well being is general, transnational' (1996: 2). The impact of economic globalization has made the case all the more urgent. As the 1997 UN Human Development Report argues:

> International efforts must share the responsibility for providing the much-needed public good of equity and social cohesion through co-operation in its widest sense. Globalisation increases both the benefits from providing this international public good and the penalties from neglecting it. (UNDP, 1997: 91)

This message was reinforced in the 1999 Human Development Report whose main author, Richard Jolly, argues that 'the world is rushing headlong into greater integration, driven mostly by a philosophy of market profitability and economic efficiency. We must bring human development and social protection into the equation' (*Guardian*, 12 July 1999; see also UNDP, 2000).

The case for such an approach, and for an internationalist construction of citizenship responsibilities, is being actively promulgated by what has been termed an embryonic global civil society. Richard Falk, for instance, has painted the image of 'a citizen pilgrim . . . on a pilgrimage that loosens spatial connections' in the non-violent struggle for a better world for future generations. He suggests that 'traditional citizenship is being challenged and remoulded' by the emergence of a transnational activism, born of the new social movements, the political orientation of which is international rather than national (Falk, 1996: 24; 1994: 138).

Recent examples include the defeat (at least temporarily) by a global coalition, communicating mainly by Internet, of the Multilateral Agreement on Investment, which would have given significant rights to multinational corporations against national governments, without any corresponding responsibilities (Hall, 1998). This was one example of the resistance of a new 'global alliance of peoples' movements' to economic globalization and the World Trade Organization (Madeley, 1999). In 1999, an Intercontinental Caravan of over 400 activists and farmers from Latin America and the Indian subcontinent toured Europe to protest against economic globalization (*Guardian*, 26 and 27 May 1999) and a diverse coalition from across the globe came together in Seattle to disrupt the meeting of the World Trade Organization. This coalition has been described as 'a watershed towards the creation of a global citizen-based and citizen-driven democratic order' (Shiva, 1999). What we are seeing is the development of 'the globalisation of opposition' (Vidal, 2000) or what Boaventura de Sousa Santos has termed 'counter-hegemonic' forms of globalization.[6] Through these counter-hegemonic forms, excluded and oppressed groups around the world are joining to make their voices heard in an attempt to challenge hegemonic forms of economic and cultural globalization.

Recognition

This challenge is framed not only in a discourse of 'redistribution' but also in that of 'recognition', dubbed by Nancy Fraser as the 'paradigmatic form of political conflict' in the contemporary world (Fraser, 1995: 68; 1997: 11). Recognition can be understood as a 'vital human need' (Taylor, 1992: 26), which 'all too often goes unmet. Regularly, members of marginalized and subaltern groups have been systematically denied recognition for the worth of their culture or way of life, the dignity of their status as persons, and the inviolability of their physical integrity' (Anderson, 1995: x).

Recognition claims can be understood in a number of ways that are important for the reconstruction of welfare. One, raised by Nancy Fraser, is the recognition given by welfare systems to different kinds of activities, such as wage-earning and child-rearing.[7] To a greater or lesser degree, welfare systems tend to privilege wage-earning over child-rearing and other caring work in the allocation of social rights. In both Europe and North America, governments increasingly are elevating paid work to the supreme expression of citizenship responsibility. Thus, for instance, the Blair government is 'reforming welfare around the work ethic' and in the Netherlands 'work, work, and again work' has been the rallying cry of the Kok administration. In both cases, for work, read 'paid work'; other forms of work such as voluntary and community work, as well as care work, do not really count, even if lip service is paid to their value. A key issue in debates about social citizenship is how these different expressions of citizenship responsibilities can best be recognized and genuinely valued (Leisink and Coenen, 1993; Knijn and Kremer, 1997; Lister, 1997, 1999; Hirsch, 1999).

Another aspect of the recognition debate raises wider issues of equality and difference and of universal and particular claims (Lister, 1997). Here two different, but related, meanings of recognition can be discerned. One is the demands by marginalized groups for recognition of their *particular* perspectives and needs, couched in a discourse of difference. Thus, for example, racialized groups have resisted assimilation as the price of racial and ethnic equality and equal citizenship. For many gays and lesbians, equal citizenship is not about incorporation into heterosexist norms, but recognition of 'a plurality of relationships without a hierarchical ordering of them' (Donovan et al., 1999: 692; Richardson, 1998). Jan Pakulski has interpreted such positions through the lens of the notion of cultural citizenship rights: 'a new set of citizenship claims that involve the right to unhindered and legitimate representation, and propagation of identities and lifestyles through the information systems and in public fora'. He distinguishes three elements: 'the right to symbolic presence and visibility (vs. marginalization); the right to dignifying representation (vs. stigmatization); and the right to propagation of identity and maintenance of lifestyles (vs. assimilation)' (Pakulski, 1997: 80).

Although cultural citizenship rights are about the recognition of difference, Pakulski interprets them as also contributing to the further universalizing of citizenship. As such they provide a bridge to the other dimension of recognition demands, that is for recognition of the *common* humanity of different groups and the equal worth of each citizen, which flows from that. This is an argument sometimes used in support of the *universal* provision of welfare benefits and services. Common usage of the same health, education and social services and social security benefits strengthens the ties of equal citizenship. This aspect of the recognition argument also reinforces the case for a redistributive welfare state and more egalitarian society. In the words of Anne Phillips:

> A society that condones excesses of poverty in the midst of wealth, or arbitrarily rewards one skill with one hundred times the wages of another, is not recognizing its citizens as of equal human worth. . . . When the gap

between rich and poor opens up too widely, it becomes meaningless to pretend that we have recognized all adults as equals. (Phillips, 1999: 131)

The point here concerns not just the exclusion from the bonds of common citizenship of those at the bottom, but also the ways in which those at the top can exclude themselves from these bonds and thereby fail to recognize the equal worth of their fellow citizens.

A progressive welfare politics has to be able to embrace the two sides of the demand for recognition, difficult as this may sometimes be: 'particularities can only flourish in the context of shared, broad-based universalist-democratic and socialist-economic equality' (Werbner and Yuval-Davis, 1999: 9). Two examples illustrate how hitherto marginalized groups have been able to promote just such a dual recognition politics. The first is the success of the Northern Ireland Women's Coalition in writing into the Northern Ireland Peace Agreement a statement which could be taken as a paradigm of such an approach, even if only at the level of aspiration.[8] The Agreement declares that power:

> . . . shall be exercised with rigorous impartiality on behalf of all the people in the diversity of their identities and traditions and shall be founded on the principles of full respect for, and equality of, civil, political, social and cultural rights, of freedom from discrimination for all citizens, and of parity of esteem and of just and equal treatment for the identity, ethos and aspirations of both communities. (Governments of UK and Ireland, 1998: 2)

The second example is the disabled people's movement, which has had a considerable impact on welfare provision. The disabled people's movement has fought for welfare provisions to reflect the social model of disability, which it has developed, rather than the individualistic medical model deployed by welfare professionals. It has struggled for welfare provisions that reflect disabled people's own interpretations of their needs, and for adequate income maintenance provisions. In doing so, it has used a universalistic discourse of *equal* citizenship rights and social justice, while at the same time asserting disability as a *different* social and political category, not to be denied in the name of equality (Barton, 1996).

The disabled people's movement also provides a good example of the third dimension of recognition politics, on which I will focus in rather more detail. This is what we might call 'the politics of voice'. One of the achievements of the disabled people's movement has been to win recognition of disabled people as subjects or agents in welfare policy-making and implementation, as opposed to their more traditional construction as simply the objects of policy.

The demand for voice and recognition is becoming more vocal in the politics of poverty also. In her original article on the politics of redistribution and of recognition, Fraser (1995, 1997) roots the former in the struggle against socio-economic injustice and the latter in the struggle against cultural or symbolic injustice. Poverty is quintessentially the product of socio-economic injustice and anti-poverty campaigns are central to any politics of redistribution. At the same time, though, these campaigns increasingly deploy a discourse of recognition as well as of redistribution. Among the examples of cultural or symbolic injustice cited by Fraser are:

> ... nonrecognition (being rendered invisible via the authoritative representational, communicative, and interpretative practices of one's culture); and disrespect (being routinely maligned or disparaged in stereotypic public cultural representations and/or in everyday life interactions). (Fraser, 1995: 71; 1997: 14)

Nonrecognition and disrespect are the typical experience of those in poverty, especially when labelled pejoratively as an 'underclass' or as inhabiting a 'dependency culture' (for a critique, see Lister, 1996). At a National Poverty Hearing in London, organized by Church Action on Poverty (an ecumenical anti-poverty group), one of the most common refrains among those with experience of poverty was the desire to be treated with greater respect. 'I just wish people would give us a chance and treat us with some respect' and 'I just feel very angry sometimes that people are ignorant to the fact that we are humans as well and we do need to be respected' were typical of the comments made (Russell, 1996: 7, 10).

As Fraser acknowledges, economic and cultural forms of injustice tend 'to reinforce each other dialectically' so that 'economic disadvantage impedes equal participation in the making of culture, in public spheres, and in everyday life' (Fraser, 1995: 72–3; 1997: 15). In her critique of Fraser, Iris Marion Young places greater emphasis on the interrelationship between the two forms of injustice and politics. She maintains that 'we should show how recognition is a means to, or an element in, economic and political equality' and that 'so long as the cultural denigration of groups produces or reinforces structural economic oppressions, the two struggles are continuous' (Young, 1997: 156, 159). Drawing on Fraser's own work on a 'politics of needs interpretation', she argues for a 'materialist culturalist approach [which] understands that needs are contextualized in political struggle over who gets to define whose needs for what purpose' (Young, 1997: 155).

Such an approach is highly relevant to the politics of poverty. Here a politics of recognition is not about the assertion of group difference, as in the case of women, racialized groups, lesbians and gays, and disabled people (remembering that we are not, of course, talking about discrete groups). Indeed, a successful politics of redistribution could remove the category altogether, as 'the poor' are a group that are the product of the distribution of resources. A politics of recognition in this context is, instead, about the assertion of recognition in the sense of equality of status and respect. Equality of status and respect is critical to recognition of the full citizenship of those in poverty. At the same time, if citizenship is understood as a practice as well as a status (Oldfield, 1990; Lister, 1997), then the traditional exclusion of people in poverty from debates about poverty and from decision-making which affects their lives can be seen to reinforce the exclusion of those in poverty from full citizenship (Lister, 1990).

What is also at issue is the value accorded to poor people's own interpretation of their rights and needs and recognition of the expertise born of experience.[9] Moraene Roberts, another participant in the National Poverty Hearing, argued:

> No-one asks our views. . . . We are the real experts of our own hopes and aspirations. Service providers should ask the users before deciding on policies, before setting targets that will affect our lives. We can contribute if you are prepared to give up a little power to allow us to participate as partners in our own future, and in the future of our country. (Russell, 1996: 4)

Her statement links in with wider debates about user involvement and citizenship participation in the institutions of the welfare state. User involvement represents a different take on the notion of 'active' welfare. Here 'active' refers to the construction of welfare state users as active and creative participants in the process of welfare policy-making and delivery, again reflecting an understanding of citizenship as a practice as well as a status bestowing rights. Welfare user movements are 'creating a new vision of social policy' in which participation is prioritized as 'both the means and ends of social policy' (Beresford, 1999: 12). Research into user involvement suggests that the first-hand knowledge and experience of service users provide an invaluable basis for developing policy and practice better attuned to service users' concerns and needs (Beresford and Croft, 1993). Likewise, evaluation of the work of citizens' juries demonstrates that ' "ordinary citizens" can not only respond to issues raised with them by policy makers but can also come up with their own solutions and ideas unprompted by official proposals' (Barnes, 1999: 70; see also Coote and Lenaghan, 1997).[10]

Ultimately, this is not only a question of recognition of expertise and of equality of status and respect, but also a question of power. In the words of the 1997 United Nations Human Development Report:

> Poor people should be politically empowered to organize for themselves for collective action and to influence the circumstances and decisions affecting their lives. For their interests to be advanced, they must be visible on the political map. (UNDP, 1997: 10)

Earlier, the Declaration of the UN World Summit for Social Development committed governments to implementation of national poverty plans, underlining that 'the full participation of people living in poverty is a fundamental and equally obligatory part of the process' (cited in ATD Fourth World, 1999: 6).[11]

Despite New Labour's commitment to a more inclusive politics and to 'listening to the people', little attempt has been made hitherto to involve those in poverty in the development of policies to tackle poverty and social exclusion. There is recognition of the case for inclusion at neighbourhood level, notably through the work of the Social Exclusion Unit (SEU).[12] For instance, the SEU acknowledges, in its consultation report on neighbourhood renewal, that policies to tackle social exclusion are unlikely to work if the communities affected are not involved in their development (Social Exclusion Unit, 2000). Indeed, Tony Blair echoes this in his Foreword. However, the speed with which the SEU has had to work has made it difficult for it always to engage in genuine consultation with those affected by the problems it is tackling.

There is also, with one or two exceptions, a resistance in government to a more participatory approach in relation to national anti-poverty and social exclusion policies. Yet, in the context of international development, it has argued the point itself: 'a human rights perspective on participation means moving beyond and above local-level processes of consultation through to ensuring poor people's participation in broader formal and informal systems of decision-making'. This is part of the wider case made by the Department for International Development for 'empowering all people to make decisions about their own lives, rather than being the passive objects of choices made on their behalf' (DfID, 2000: paras 5.3, 1.2).

Applying this philosophy on the domestic front, the SEU would be well placed to develop, in partnership with the voluntary and community sectors, what we might call a 'participatory infrastructure'. This would provide channels through which those excluded from the formal political system could make their views known and debate them. One of the lessons from the attempt to develop a more participatory anti-poverty strategy in the Republic of Ireland is that training of those involved is an important component of any such infrastructure: 'participation from citizens is not viewed as a spontaneous, inherent capacity but rather a capacity that requires forming, building and investment' (Ralaheen Ltd and Community Technical Aid, 1998: 42).

The importance of adequate training for all those involved (providers as well as users) is also underlined in work on user involvement in welfare services (Beresford and Croft, 1993). User involvement tends to be recognized in the sphere of welfare services but not benefits. Thus, although the Welfare Reform Green Paper highlighted 'the rise of the demanding, sceptical, citizen-consumer' (DSS, 1998a: 16), it did not discuss how we might apply to social security the principles of user involvement developed elsewhere in the welfare system and establish systematic mechanisms for involving benefit recipients as users (see also Stafford and Bates, 1997; Walker, 1998). Its proposals for 'an active modern service' appealed to a consumer rather than a citizenship ethos, ignoring the 'citizen' in the 'citizen-consumer'. This perhaps reflects a higher value accorded to consumerism than to citizenship, as reflected in Blair's statement in the government's first Annual Report that 'in all walks of life people act as consumers not just citizens' (1998: 6).

Conclusion

The conception of 'active' welfare developed here is one rooted in a participatory reading of citizenship rather than in a false dichotomy, which devalues welfare as intrinsically inferior to paid work. It is not inconsistent with policies to promote paid work, which remain crucial. However, I have argued that such policies need to be part of a broader welfare strategy, which promotes the three 'R's of risk protection, redistribution and recognition.

Such a strategy also means addressing the growing tension in the relationship between the other two 'R's of rights and responsibilities. On the one hand, Western governments are placing increasing emphasis on individual responsibilities in the construction of welfare citizenship. Giddens has gone so far as to propose 'no rights without responsibilities' as 'a prime motto for the new politics' (1998: 65). Writing in the *Daily Mail* (10 February 1999), Blair summed up 'the new ethic of rights and responsibilities at the heart of our welfare state' as 'the end of the something-for-nothing welfare state'. The 'new welfare contract' elaborated in the Welfare Reform Green Paper is framed exclusively in the language of duties, referring to rights only in relation to matching responsibilities. The (partial) embrace of the agenda for strengthening civil and political rights by New Labour, for instance through the introduction of a Human Rights Act and constitutional reform, has not been matched by equal enthusiasm for developing social rights (Lister, 1998).

On the other hand, in the words of the European Anti-Poverty Network:

> ... poverty is increasingly seen to be a denial of fundamental rights. This is how those affected experience it themselves. . . . The worse-off individuals and families are, the more of all their civil, political, economic, social and cultural rights they lose. These situations clearly show how indivisible and interdependent rights are in daily life. (EAPN, 1999: 6)[13]

The Network proposes the promotion of 'the effective exercise of fundamental rights by all' as a central pillar of a European strategy to combat social exclusion. Its assertion of the indivisibility of rights receives support in a report from the European Commission's Expert Group on Fundamental Rights:

> Any attempt to explicitly recognise fundamental rights must include both civil and social rights. To ignore their interdependence questions the protection of both. It is in this sense that their indivisibility has over and over again been affirmed. (1999: 21)

In Axel Honneth's (1995) theorization of recognition politics, rights are crucial to self-respect, which is one element of the struggle for mutual recognition as autonomous human agents. What this discussion of rights points to, taken together with the three 'R's of risk protection, redistribution and recognition, is an egalitarian, inclusive and participatory welfare state in which the citizenship of all members of society is underpinned by a strong floor of social rights.

Notes

1. The Commission on Social Justice (1994), of which I was a member, was established by the late John Smith, Leader of the Labour Opposition, as an independent body 'to develop a practical vision of economic and social reform for the 21st century'. It reported after John Smith's death and although some of its ideas have been tacitly incorporated into the government's reform agenda, New Labour has distanced itself from a report which, although in many ways embracing a modernizing agenda, is now associated with the pre-New Labour era.

2. The Joseph Rowntree Foundation is one of the main funders of social policy research in the UK.

3. See also the recent report of the House of Commons Social Security Select Committee on *The Contributory Principle* (HC 56–1, 2000) and the 12th Report of the official Social Security Advisory Committee (1999).

4. These improvements have included a 72 percent real increase in the social assistance rates for young children over three years, although the government tends not to trumpet this significant concession.

5. The *Daily Mail* is seen by New Labour as a key tabloid newspaper on the political right.

6. The term was put forward during the Future of Political Culture seminar, 21–2 May 1999, Goldsmiths College, London.

7. Paper given at the Future of Political Culture seminar.

8. The cross-community Northern Ireland Women's Coalition was formed to contest the elections to the All-Party Talks to determine the future of Northern Ireland in 1996. Two women were elected in a country which has had only three women Members of Parliament since its founding in 1922.

9. See also Lister and Beresford (2000) for an exploration of the implications of this approach for research into poverty.

10. Citizens' juries, which originated in the USA and Germany (known there as planning cells) are increasingly being used by local and health authorities in the UK to promote citizen participation in discussions of public policy. They enable a random 'jury' of citizens to engage with 'experts' in policy deliberation (Barnes, 1999).

11. See also ATD Fourth World (2000) and the report of the independent Commission on Poverty, Participation and Power (2000), which is examining the barriers to the involvement of people in poverty in decisions which affect their lives and ways of overcoming these barriers.

12. The Social Exclusion Unit was established early in the new Labour government within months of coming to power. Its purpose is to 'co-ordinate and improve Government action to reduce social exclusion' (Social Exclusion Unit Home Page http://www.cabinet-office.gov.uk/seu/index.htm). Participation is to be written in as a condition of funding under the new strategy for neighbourhood renewal.

13. See also the *Human Development Report 2000* (UNDP, 2000).

References

Anderson, J. (1995) 'Translator's Introduction', in A. Honneth, *The Struggle for Recognition*. Cambridge: Polity Press.

Andrews, G. (1999) 'New Left and New Labour: Modernisation or a New Modernity?', *Soundings* 13: 14–24.

ATD Fourth World (1999) 'Towards Copenhagen + 5', *Fourth World Journal* Spring: 6.

ATD Fourth World (2000) *Participation Works. Involving People in Poverty in Policy-making*. London: ATD Fourth World.

Barnes, M. (1999) *Building a Deliberative Democracy: An Evaluation of Two Citizens' Juries*. London: Institute for Public Policy Research.

Barton, L. (1996) 'Citizenship and Disabled People: A Cause for Concern', in J. Demaine and H. Entwhistle (eds) *Beyond Communitarianism: Citizenship, Politics and Education*. Basingstoke: Macmillan.

Bennett, F. and R. Walker (1998) *Working with Work. An Initial Assessment of Welfare to Work*. York: Joseph Rowntree Foundation.

Beresford, P. (1999) 'Participation', *SPA News* October/November.

Beresford, P. and S. Croft (1993) *Citizen Involvement: A Practical Guide for Change*. Basingstoke: Macmillan.

Blair, T. (1998) 'The Government's Strategy', *The Government's Annual Report*. London: HMSO.

Blair, T. (1999) 'Beveridge Lecture', Toynbee Hall, London, 18 March.

Blair, T. and G. Schröder (1999) 'Europe: The Third Way/Die Neue Mitte', reproduced in *The Spokesman* 66: 27–37.

Blunkett, D. (2000) 'On Your Side: The New Welfare State as the Engine of Economic Prosperity', Speech given to the Institute for Public Policy Research, London, 7 June.

Bryson, A., R. Ford and M. White (1997) *Making Work Pay: Lone Mothers, Employment and Well-being*. York: Joseph Rowntree Foundation.

Burchardt, T. and J. Hills (1997) 'Private Welfare Insurance and Social Security', *Social Policy Research Findings* 111. York: Joseph Rowntree Foundation.

Chen, S. (1999) *Citizens and Taxes*. London: Fabian Society.

Clasen, J. (ed.) (1997) *Social Insurance in Europe*. Bristol: Policy Press.

Clasen, J. and A. Erskine (1998) 'Meltdown Inevitable? National Insurance in Britain', *Benefits* 23: 1–4.

Clasen, J., A. Gould and J. Vincent (1998) *Voices Within and Without: Responses to Long-term Unemployment in Germany, Sweden and Britain*. Bristol: Policy Press.

Commission of the European Communities (1992) 'Council Recommendation of 24 June 1992 on Common Criteria Concerning Sufficient Resources and Social Assistance in Social Protection Systems [92/441/EEC]', *Official Journal of the European Communities* 26 August.

Commission on Poverty, Participation and Power (2000) *Listen Hear: The Right to be Heard*. Bristol: Policy Press in association with the UK Coalition against Poverty.

Commission on Social Justice (CSJ) (1994) *Social Justice: Strategies for National Renewal*. London: Vintage.

Coote, A. and J. Lenaghan (1997) *Citizens' Juries: Theory into Practice*. London: Institute for Public Policy Research.

Darling, A. (1999) *House of Commons Hansard*, 19 December, col. 309.

Deacon, B. with M. Hulse and P. Stubbs (1997) *Global Social Policy*. London: Sage.

Dean, H. and P. Taylor-Gooby (1992) *Dependency Culture*. Hemel Hempstead: Harvester Wheatsheaf.

DfID (2000) *Human Rights for Poor People*. London: Department for International Development.

Donovan, C., B. Heaphy and J. Week (1999) 'Citizenship and Same Sex Relationships', *Journal of Social Policy* 28(4): 689–709.

DSS (1998a) *New Ambitions for Our Country: A New Contract for Welfare*. London: HMSO.

DSS (1998b) *Households Below Average Income 1979–1996/7*. Leeds: Corporate Document Services.

EAPN (European Anti-Poverty Network) (1999) *EAPN Network News* 67.

Esping-Andersen, G. (1994) 'Equality and Work in the Post-industrial Life-cycle', pp. 167–85 in D. Miliband (ed.) *Reinventing the Left*. Cambridge: Polity Press.

Expert Group on Fundamental Rights (1999) *Affirming Fundamental Rights in the European Union*. Luxembourg: Office for Official Publications of the European Communities.

Falk, R. (1994) 'The Making of Global Citizenship', pp. 127–40 in B. Van Steenbergen (ed.) *The Condition of Citizenship*. London: Sage.

Falk, R. (1996) 'An Inquiry into the Political Economy of the World Order', *New Political Economy* 1(1): 13–26.

Finlayson, A. (1998) 'Tony Blair and the Jargon of Modernisation', *Soundings* 10: 11–27.

Fitzpatrick, T. (1998) 'The Rise of Market Collectivism', in E. Brunsdon, H. Dean and R. Woods (eds) *Social Policy Review* 10. London: Social Policy Association.

Fraser, N. (1995) 'From Redistribution to Recognition? Dilemmas of Justice in a "Post-socialist" Age', *New Left Review* 212: 68–93.

Fraser, N. (1997) *Justice Interruptus*. New York and London: Routledge.

Galbraith, J.K. (1996) *The Good Society*. London: Sinclair-Stevenson.

Giddens, A. (1998) *The Third Way: The Renewal of Social Democracy*. Cambridge: Polity Press.

Governments of United Kingdom and Ireland (1998) *The Agreement*. Belfast: Governments of United Kingdom and Ireland.

Hall, R. (1998) 'The Deal's Off', *Red Pepper* December: 20.

Hay, C. (1998) 'Globalisation, Welfare Retrenchment and the "Logic of No Alternative"; Why Second-best Won't Do', *Journal of Social Policy* 27(4): 525–32.

Hills, J. (1998) *Income and Wealth: The Latest Evidence*. York: Joseph Rowntree Foundation.

Hills, J. and O. Lelkes (1999) 'Social Security, Selective Universalism and Patchwork Redistribution', in R. Jowell, J. Curtice, A. Park and K. Thomson (eds) *British Social Attitudes, the 16th Report: Who Shares New Labour Values?* Aldershot: Ashgate.

Hirsch, D. (1997) *Social Protection and Inclusion, European Challenges for the United Kingdom*. York: Joseph Rowntree Foundation.

Hirsch, D. (1999) *Welfare beyond Work: Active Participation in a New Welfare State*. York: Joseph Rowntree Foundation.

HM Treasury (1999) *Tackling Poverty and Extending Opportunity*. London: HM Treasury.

Holzmann, R. and S. Jørgensen (2000) *Social Risk Management: A New Conceptual Framework for Social Protection and Beyond*. Social Protection Discussion Paper No. 0006. Washington, DC: World Bank.

Honneth, A. (1995) *The Struggle for Recognition*. Cambridge: Polity Press.

Jackson, P.R. (1994) 'Influences on Commitment to Employment and Commitment to Work', in A. Bryson and S. McKay (eds) *Is it Worth Working? Factors Affecting Labour Supply*. London: Policy Studies Institute.

Jarvis, S. and S. Jenkins (1997) 'Low Income Dynamics in 1990s Britain', *Fiscal Studies* 18(2): 123–42.

Jessop, B. (1994) 'The Transition to Post-Fordism and the Schumpeterian Workfare State', in R. Burrows and B. Loader (eds) *Towards a Post-Fordist Welfare State?* London and New York: Routledge.

Knijn, T. and M. Kremer (1997) 'Gender and the Caring Dimension of Welfare States: Towards Inclusive Citizenship', *Social Politics* 4(3): 328–61.

Leisink, P. and H. Coenen (1993) 'Work and Citizenship in the New Europe', in H. Coenen and P. Leisink (eds) *Work and Citizenship in the New Europe*. Aldershot: Edward Elgar.

Levitas, R. (1998) *The Inclusive Society? Social Exclusion and New Labour*. Basingstoke: Macmillan.

Lister, R. (1990) *The Exclusive Society*. London: Child Poverty Action Group.

Lister, R. (1996) 'Introduction: In Search of the "Underclass"', in R. Lister (ed.) *Charles Murray and the Underclass: The Developing Debate*. London: Institute of Economic Affairs.

Lister, R. (1997) *Citizenship: Feminist Perspectives*. Basingstoke: Macmillan.

Lister, R. (1998) 'Vocabularies of Citizenship and Gender: The UK', *Critical Social Policy* 18(3): 309–31.

Lister, R. (1999) ' "Reforming Welfare around the Work Ethic": New Gendered and Ethical Perspectives on Work and Care', *Policy & Politics* 27(2): 233–46.

Lister, R. and P. Beresford, with D. Green and K. Woodard (2000) 'Where are "the Poor" in the Future of Poverty Research?', in J. Bradshaw and R. Sainsbury (eds) *Researching Poverty*. Aldershot: Ashgate.

McKendrick, J. (1998) 'The "Big" Picture: Quality in the Lives of Lone Parents', in R. Ford and J. Millar (eds) *Private Lives and Public Responses: Lone Parenthood and Future Policy*. London: Policy Studies Institute.

McKnight, A., P. Elias and R. Wilson (1998) *Low Pay and the National Insurance System: A Statistical Picture*. Manchester: Equal Opportunities Commission.

McLaughlin, E. (1994) *Flexibility in Work and Benefits*. London: Institute for Public Policy Research.

Madeley, J. (1999) 'Dodging the Paupers' Custard Pies', *New Statesman* 12 February: 27.

Marquand, D. (1998) 'The Blair Paradox', *Prospect* May.

Newby, H. (1996) 'Citizenship in a Green World: Global Commons and Human Stewardship', in M. Bulmer and A.M. Rees (eds) *Citizenship Today*. London: UCL Press.

Oldfield, A. (1990) *Citizenship and Community: Civic Republicanism and the Modern World*. London: Routledge.

Oliver, D. and D. Heater (1994) *The Foundations of Citizenship*. Hemel Hempstead: Harvester Wheatsheaf.

Pakulski, J. (1997) 'Cultural Citizenship', *Citizenship Studies* 1(1): 73–86.

Parker, H. (1999) 'Tackling Poverty – An Acceptable Living Standard', *Poverty* 103: 12–15.

Phillips, A. (1999) *Which Equalities Matter?* Cambridge: Polity Press.

Ralaheen Ltd and Community Technical Aid (1998) *Final Report on Models of Consultation and Ongoing Participation between the Statutory Sector and the Community and Voluntary Sector to Inform the Implementation of the National Anti-Poverty Strategy*. Dublin: Combat Poverty Agency.

Refugee Council (1999) 'Life without Cash', *Inexile* June: 14–15.

Richardson, D. (1998) 'Sexuality and Citizenship', *Sociology* 32(1): 83–100.

Rose, N. (1999) 'Inventiveness in Politics', *Economy and Society* 28(3): 467–93.

Russell, H. (1996) *Speaking from Experience: Voices at the National Poverty Hearing*. Manchester: Church Action on Poverty.

Shiva, V. (1999) 'This Round to the Citizens', *Guardian* 8 December.

Sinfield, A. (1989) *Social Security and its Social Division: A Challenge for Sociological Analysis*. Edinburgh: New Waverley Papers, University of Edinburgh.

Social Exclusion Unit (2000) *National Strategy for Neighbourhood Renewal: A Framework for Consultation*. London: Social Exclusion Unit.

Stafford, B. and C. Bates (1997) *Partnership in Social Security: Giving Benefit Recipients a Voice*. Loughborough: Social Security Unit/Centre for Research in Social Policy.

Taylor, C. (1992) 'The Politics of Recognition', in A. Gutmann (ed.) *Multiculturalism and 'The Politics of Recognition'*. Princeton, NJ: Princeton University Press.

Taylor-Gooby, P. (2000) 'Risk, Contingency and the Third Way: Evidence from BHPS and Qualitative Studies', paper presented at Social Policy Association Annual Conference, July, University of Surrey, Roehampton.

Townsend, P. (1996) *A Poor Future*. London: Lemos and Crane.

Twine, F. (1994) *Citizenship and Social Rights*. London: Sage.

UNDP (1997) *Human Development Report 1997*. New York and Oxford: Oxford University Press.

UNDP (2000) *Human Development Report 2000*. New York and Oxford: Oxford University Press.

Veit Wilson, J. (1994) *Dignity not Poverty*. London: Institute for Public Policy Research.

Veit Wilson, J. (1998) *Setting Adequacy Standards*. Bristol: Policy Press.

Vidal, J. (2000) 'The world@war', *Guardian* 19 January.

Walker, R. (1998) 'Promoting Positive Welfare', *New Economy* 5(2): 77–82.

Weale, A. (1991) 'Citizenship beyond Borders', in U. Vogel and M. Moran (eds) *The Frontiers of Citizenship*. Basingstoke: Macmillan.

Werbner, P. and N. Yuval-Davis (1999) 'Women and the New Discourse of Citizenship', in N. Yuval-Davis and P. Werbner (eds) *Women, Citizenship and Difference*. London and New York: Zed Books.

White, M. and J. Forth (1998) *Pathways through Employment*. York: Joseph Rowntree Foundation.

Williams, F. (1999) 'Good Enough Principles for Welfare', *Journal of Social Policy* 28(4): 667–87.

Young, I.M. (1997) 'Unruly Categories: A Critique of Nancy Fraser's Dual Systems Theory', *New Left Review* 222:147–60.

Ruth Lister is Professor of Social Policy at Loughborough University. She is a former Director of the Child Poverty Action Group and was a member of the Commission on Social Justice, the Opsahl Commission on the Future of Northern Ireland and, most recently, a Commission on Poverty, Participation and Power. Her publications include *Citizenship: Feminist Perspectives* (Macmillan/New York University Press, 1997). She is a founding academician of the Academy of Learned Societies in the Social Sciences.

From Community to Coalition
The Politics of Recognition as the
Handmaiden of the Politics of Equality in an
Era of Globalization

Sylvia Walby

L
ASH (1996B) HAS rightly argued in his debate with Bauman (1996)
that there is a need to go beyond the polarities of individualism and
communitarianism. There is a need to ground analysis in a presumption of social bonding, in the face of the relentless over-preoccupation of
much contemporary theory with difference, while rejecting the hierarchy
which is integral to communitarianism. In the introduction to this volume,
Featherstone and Lash (2001) argue that 'recognition' is a useful concept in
the analysis of political culture which opens up the space limited by the
assumptions involved in either 'community' or 'difference'. I am going to
argue here that, while the problems they identify are real, the concept of
'recognition' is not the solution. This is because 'recognition' is still too
rooted in the present order of things and speaks insufficiently to issues of
change. It is situated at a level of abstraction which makes it hard to analyse
the empirical realities of political cultures which are always riddled with
complexity, cross-cutting relations with other political cultures, coalitions
and alliances. Most particularly, the idiom and metaphor of 'community' on
which it draws so heavily is too limited a conceptualization of the 'social'.
Rather we need to draw more deeply upon the larger sociological vocabulary of concepts of the social.

The debate that Lash (2001) foregrounds has a long history in moral and
political philosophy. It is time to turn to Sociology for some answers (Calhoun,
1995). Rather than abstractly ponder the basis of ethical and political claims,
there is much to be learnt from analyses of how people actually do make

■ *Theory, Culture & Society* 2001 (SAGE, London, Thousand Oaks and New Delhi),
    Vol. 18(2–3): 113–135
    [0263-2764(200104/06)18:2–3;113–135;017492]

ethical and political claims. Sociological analysis of the practical reasoning that people make, the frames of reference they utilize when making judgements, their practical juggling of various and competing identity claims, the various ways that these political cultures are historically sedimented in surviving social institutions, and the competition and contestation between social institutions with rival claims has much to offer to ground and resolve or by-pass many of these philosophical debates. There are two key issues here, one is the use of the weak conceptualization of the social, especially the use of the concept of community as if it signified the social, but which is actually too narrow and specific an operationalization of the concept of the social. Second, and relatedly, there is an absence of discussion of how people actually do theorize their political cultures, just how and with what use of universal as opposed to contextual frames of reference.

The global is becoming the defining horizon for some political projects (Benhabib, 1999; Castells, 1996, 1997, 1998; Standing, 1999). Globalization today re-frames the notion of the universal. Yet the global is not the same as the abstract universal. Rather, the global is a practical, special and time-specific realm, even as it can be purported to encompass the totality of contemporary human life. The global and the universal have an uneasy and ambiguous relationship in many contemporary analyses. This is because many political projects today make claims to justice on the basis of an ambiguously defined conception of the global/universal. This is a different trend from the practice within some political projects towards a focus on ever more tightly and narrowly defined social groupings, which occurred especially in the projects at the intersection of gender/ethnic concerns (Felski, 1997; Mohanty, 1991; Spellman, 1988).

I shall situate my analysis within presumptions about modernity, reflexivity (Beck et al., 1994), complex globalization (Castells, 1996, 1997, 1998) and the challenge of difference (Calhoun, 1995). I start by engaging with some of the theoretical debates on recognition and redistribution. I use substantive examples of political coalitions in contemporary global politics. Throughout, I discuss the elements which need to be included in an analysis of political culture and which are insufficiently dealt with in accounts of recognition: complexity and sociological concepts of the social beyond community; the relationship between equality and recognition; the separation of ethos and polis; the relationship between the global and the universal.

The Community and the Universal

The central dilemmas articulated by philosophers and social theorists here centre on the nature of the grounding of the rules by which the justice of political and ethical claims may be judged. This alterity between community and individualism/universalism is a key theme in the social philosophy recently discussed in *Theory, Culture & Society* (Bauman, 1996; Gardiner, 1996; Hutchings, 1997; Lash, 1996a, 1996b). On the one hand, liberalism and universalism appear to offer a plea to a free-floating form of reason which is universal, drawing on a Kantian heritage. There is a claim to universally valid truth, which usually assumes a coherent individual as the seeker/knower. On the other hand, communitarianism appears to offer a grounding in the particular standards of a specific community (Sandel, 1998; Taylor et al., 1994). There is the notion that truth is always partial and situated, that we are limited by the communities in which we are located. Of course, in practice, most contemporary writers reject the polar extremes as untenable. Some simultaneously reject both poles and with them the search for certain foundations for contemporary ethics and political projects (Bauman, 1991, 1993, 1996, 1997). Bauman's rejection of both these choices follows his earlier rejection of the morality of modernity because of its association with the holocaust (Bauman, 1989). Others seek a resolution or compromise, either by refining the procedures for assessment of justice claims (Benhabib, 1992; Habermas, 1989, 1991), or by integrating the concerns of the individual and the community (Kymlicka, 1991, 1995).

There have been many attempts to find a resolution to this debate. Habermas (1989, 1991) seeks a resolution by attempting to establish universally valid procedures by which truth may be established, utilizing the dynamics within an assumed desire to communicate to drive the process, and locating it within an idealized situation of equality of contribution. However, by such a location, Habermas, despite his intentions, situates rather than universalizes the conditions for truth, since the conditions of free and equal contribution are actually socially specific, not least in their presumption of the implications of democratic involvement. Benhabib's (1992) attempt at overcoming the same dualism by demanding a focus on the other has similar strengths and weaknesses to that of Habermas despite her attempt to move beyond (Hutchings, 1997). Benhabib seeks to avoid commitment to the communitarian stance, by making an appeal to the ostensibly universally valid criteria of judgement of recognizing the standpoint of the other. But the process of recognizing the standpoint of the other is not natural and automatic, but depends upon socially variable conditions. Thus Benhabib merely displaces the problem of universalism on to these new procedures for judgement which are not sufficiently universal to be adequate to the task demanded of them. The act of 'recognition' requires a social process of assessment as to what constitutes the same or different from oneself. The abstractions of social philosophy constitute a serious limitation here, since they neglect the complex social dimensions of the processes involved.

Kymlicka (1991, 1995) attempts a way forward by softening the polarities of the debate through grounding them in a comparative analysis of practical attempts at their resolution. By including substantive analysis he is able to provide a more nuanced conceptualization of the groups involved and of the bases of the claims to justice that they make. Kymlicka's (1991) analysis focuses on minority groups in North America, especially those which pre-dated white settlement: the Indian, Inuit and Metis aboriginal peoples. He discusses in detail both the foundations and the working of the provisions which were introduced into the Canadian Constitution to give special rights to these aboriginal minorities in order to protect their cultural heritage, and how they might appear to cut across individual rights of Canadian citizenship. He notes the need to exclude non-Indians from rights of voting and property ownership if the cultural rights of the Indians are to be maintained, thus grounding his analysis in a sociological understanding of power. He also notes that in so compromising conventional liberal individual rights there is a potential to undermine the rights of other groups, such as women seeking protection from gender discrimination through the use of the liberal principles enshrined in law. His aim is to reconcile principles of justice so as to sustain both cultural communities such as aboriginal life-styles, while leaving intact liberal principles which protect other social groups from discrimination. He seeks to achieve this by a reconsideration of the theory of the self within liberal theory, effectively seeking a more social, more sociologically grounded, conception of the self than is customary within abstract philosophy. Kymlicka argues that core to liberalism is the right to choose one's way of life, and that in order to achieve this, there needs to be respect for collective cultural membership. Kymlicka argues that, in practice, liberalism has respected collective rights of minority communities and has understood this as part of a liberal respect for freedom to choose one's own way of life, which involves recognition of communities as a whole within a larger polity, and that this can be articulated theoretically within his modified account of liberal philosophy.

Kymlicka's work is strongest when he is engaging with communities which are defined in terms of ethnicity or nation, in which there is a fully rounded and cohesive culture. It is weakest in relation to cross-cutting forms of difference, such as gender. When forms of difference are not coincident with holistic communities, Kymlicka, while empirically noting the issues involved, does not have concepts adequate to incorporating this complexity within his theoretical schema. Thus, while empirically Kymlicka sensitively notes the significance of gender divisions within a community when he discusses the politics of pornography, he does not integrate this insight into his conclusions. This is because of his use of the notion of 'community' as his dominant conceptualization of the social. His analysis is strong when the forms of difference are articulated through cohesive communities. But he is unable to offer solutions to the reality of the complexity of modern social life where there are divisions and social fractures which cross-cut ethnic and national groups, such as gender. The reason for this lack of integration into his theory of the full range of differences that he notes empirically is due to his choice of the concept of 'community' as a metaphor for the social. The use of 'community' pulls him back into the simplicities which he has tried so hard to escape. In the end, Kymlicka's analysis can deal with one set of differences, but not with the diverse range of cross-cutting and multiple differences that actually exist in the world. Cohesive 'communities' devoid of internal divisions of gender, class and further minority ethnic and religious groups do not exist in the modern world. The concept of 'community' does not capture the nature of the social as it is actually riddled with diverse cross-cutting differences.

I seek to build on the strengths of Kymlicka's approach, in advancing philosophical debates on justice through grounded social analysis and developing his as yet incomplete project more adequately, capturing the diversity of social life.

Recognition Politics?

Fraser (1995) has produced one of the clearest statements on recognition politics and attempts both to engage with theory and to ground it in practice. She makes critical distinctions not only between the politics of recognition and the politics of redistribution but also introduces a third category of the politics of transformation. She suggests that the politics of redistribution is bound up with notions of equality and is focused substantively on economic issues while, in contrast, the politics of recognition is bound up with notions of difference and is focused substantively on cultural issues. While Fraser notes that both redistribution and recognition are needed, she suggests that there has been a shift from the politics of redistribution to the politics of recognition, by which she means a double shift involving a movement from socio-economic politics to cultural politics and from the goal of equality to that of recognition. 'Cultural recognition displaces socio-economic redistribution as the remedy for injustice and the goal of political struggle' (Fraser, 1997: 11). Further, in relation to the politics of gender, Fraser argues normatively for the politics of transformative redistribution by the liberal welfare state together with the cultural politics of deconstructive politics.

There are three main limitations to Fraser's analysis. First, I think she is empirically incorrect to suggest that the politics of economic redistribution have given way to the politics of cultural recognition. Second, she underestimates the rise of coalition building as a method of organizing which engages with difference within feminist and other politics, which is not dependent on the communities which are the basis of the politics of recognition. Third, she insufficiently addresses the relationship between redistribution and recognition and produces an abstract account which is at odds with the empirical evidence. Her abstract account of the role of a liberal welfare state and cultural feminism is that they affirm women's position, yet the gender regime is currently undergoing a radical transformation.

The first of these problems with Fraser's work is with her claim that the politics of recognition is replacing the politics of equality and that the recognition of ethnicities and genders is replacing class-based projects for equality. This is unfounded, notwithstanding the frequency with which this assertion is made (see also Featherstone and Lash, 2001; Maffesoli, 1996; Phillips, 1999). This is a sociological claim, not merely one of ethics or high theory. However, Fraser provides no evidence to support her assertions. While it is the case that feminist and anti-racist politics have become more vibrant and more deeply rooted than politics ostensibly based on class alone, it is a mistake to see this as a triumph of the politics of recognition over the politics of equality. The politics of equality is thriving in both feminist and anti-racist politics (Charles, 2000; Lovenduski and Randall, 1993; Rees, 1992). There has been a decline in the politics in which largely white men made claims which they legitimated by an appeal to class, but these were often claims which privileged their own ethnic and gender specific interests, not those of their class alone. There is a reconfiguration of the cross-cutting alliances around gender, ethnicity and class, but that is not the same as the demise of the politics of equality. Rather we have seen its re-birth within a new political project in which class, gender and race interests are differently balanced. This is a complex networked and coalition-based politics in which claims to recognition are made in order to have the capacity to make effective claims for equality more effectively (Ledwith and Colgan, 2000). In the UK and other Western countries there has been an increased involvement of women in the politics of economic redistribution, as they increasingly participated in the labour market and the institutions associated with it, such as trade unions and professional associations (Gagnon and Ledwith, 2000; Ledwith and Colgan, 1996). As women have entered the labour market in larger numbers over the last few decades, they have become increasingly involved in the politics of economic redistribution (Acker, 1989; Evans and Nelson, 1989; Shaw and Perrons, 1995).

While men's membership of trade unions has been falling significantly, data from the Labour Force Survey and the Certification Officer for 1999 show that there has been a near convergence with women's rates of unionization. Young educated women, in particular, are joining trade unions. Among people under 40 the rate of unionization of women and men is the same, though there is a gender gap among older people. Among those with degrees women are significantly more likely than men to be in trade unions, 45 percent as compared with 30 percent (Hicks, 2000). Trade unions are now more likely to engage with issues of concern to women workers than they used to, constructing an agenda of equality issues (Ellis and Ferns, 2000). The proportion of women in decision-making positions in unions, while not yet reflecting their membership proportions, has significantly increased. In UNISON, the largest union in the UK, the proportion of members who are women rose from 68 percent in 1994 to 72 percent in 1999/2000, while over the same time period the proportion of women who were members of the national executive rose from 42 percent to 62 percent, as a proportion of conference attendees from 46 percent to 58 percent, as a proportion of national full-time officers from 20 percent to 21 percent (Ledwith and Colgan, 2000). Women are increasingly, not decreasingly, engaged in the politics of economic distribution.

In both the US and the EU there has been pressure to introduce legislation to provide equal treatment for women at work, the implementation of which often depends on worker and other organizations (Acker, 1989; Evans and Nelson, 1989; Rees, 1998). The European Union has passed a plethora of legally binding Directives as well as advisory Recommendations which require the equal treatment of women and men in employment and in employment-related activities (European Commission, 1999; European Parliament, 1994; Hantrais, 1995; Pillinger, 1992). These Directives were passed not merely as a result of the interest of the European Commission, but as a result of political pressure from women activists (Hoskyns, 1996; Rees, 1998). The implementation of these is uneven across the EU, generating more activity in support of them in the UK (and Ireland) as compared with many other member states (European Commission, 1994). This was a result not only of women's willingness to take cases to national tribunals and courts, but also due to financial and moral support from the EOC and trade unions. Without trade union support, it is unlikely these cases would be fought. There is increased representation of women and their interests in trade union activities at both national and EU levels (Pascual and Behning, 2000). In the USA there has also been a series of attempts to use the law to improve the position of women in employment, from the pay equity movement (Acker, 1989) to the development of maternity leave policies (Kelly and Dobbin, 1999). Again, this is an arena of significant political activity by women in pursuit of their economic interests, the politics of redistribution. Women are demanding economic equality at work as never before, in new and complex alliances.

Further, there is an intensified struggle over the distribution of the world's resources between North and South, including contestation over the economic policies and priorities of the World Bank, World Trade Organization and the International Monetary Fund. These are quintessentially about the politics of power and distribution of resources between the First and Third Worlds, the rich North and the poor South (Moghadam, 1996b; UNDP, 1999).

A further area of politics which has developed over the last 30 years is that of campaigns to stop violence against women. Again this is about power, the unequal power between men and women. The feminist demand is to de-legitimize, to criminalize, to punish men's use of coercive force against women. They want the priorities of the criminal justice system re-ordered so that police resources are used to hunt down and arrest violent men. They demand financial resources from the state to support refuges and rape crisis centres to help women who have been abused by men (Dobash and Dobash, 1992; Hague and Malos, 1993). Insofar as these politics include a politics of recognition, it is as a handmaiden to the politics of equality. There is a demand for the recognition of the problem and the recognition of the voices speaking out on the topic. But the goal is the reduction and elimination of men's violence in order to curtail men's power over women – this is the politics of equality.

Second, Fraser neglects the actual development of coalition rather than recognition politics. She suggests that coalition-building might be a good idea, thus significantly underestimating the extent to which it is already a typical rather than exceptional practice within contemporary feminist politics. Rather, we have seen the development of the politics of coalition instead of the politics of community become the dominant mode of organizing within at least feminist politics in the West and global feminist coalitions.

The use of networks and coalitions has been an increasingly important mode of organizing, especially when this crosses national frontiers (Keck and Sikkink, 1998). Jakobsen (1998) argues that the analysis and practice of political cultures which focuses on recognizing difference underestimate complexity. In a world with many political cultures, there are overlaps which means that it is always impossible to identify a 'pure' instance of one of the political communities which are to be recognized. They are always already complex, with each individual subject to cross-cutting claims. Her empirical analysis is on the nature of politics among the US left, especially in anti-racist and feminist politics since the 1960s. She notes that there is never a pure 'African-American' group which can be recognized, because of cross-cutting political communities around at least 'class', 'feminism' and 'locality'. As a consequence of this complexity, there is never a pure political culture available to be recognized. Indeed, Jakobsen argues that awareness of this has in fact lain behind the practice of much political organizing since the 1960s. It is the theorists who have been slow to develop concepts to catch up with the world. She describes movement-based texts from the 1960s and 1970s which engaged with complex cross-cutting inequalities within their political practice. And how wave after wave of theorists kept discovering difference as if it was a theoretical discovery. The theorists, in their focus on difference, have tended to miss the way that practical politics in the modern world has always engaged with complexity. In practice, coalition rather than community is the key to understanding contemporary political movements. The awareness of this complexity has given rise to coalition rather than community-based politics.

Third, the relationship between the role of recognition and redistribution politics is not that of alternates, in which recognition is replacing redistribution, as Fraser argues, but is actually one in which the politics of recognition is the handmaiden of the politics of redistribution. Fraser suggests that the liberal welfare state and cultural feminism represent a politics of affirmation of existing gender identities. However, the empirical evidence suggests rather that the USA, with a liberal welfare state and cultural feminism, is currently undergoing a major transformation of the gender regime as women increasingly participate in employment (ILO, 1999), even when they are the mothers of young children, changing traditional family practices (South and Spitze, 1994) and cultural conceptions of femininity and masculinity as a consequence. The deep structures of gender relations are currently changing in the USA, not being affirmed, alongside a liberal welfare state (Bergmann, 1986). Additionally, her abstract account of cultural feminism as affirming femininity is also mistaken. Cultural feminism seeks to encourage women to experiment with a greater diversity of gender practices, especially sexual ones, not affirming old ones (Franklin et al., 1991). In short, Fraser's abstract philosophizing is not supported by the evidence.

Fraser has addressed an important issue in her account of the role of the welfare state in contemporary gender and class relations. However, the gender regime is in transition from a domestic to a public form in most industrialized countries, whatever the kind of welfare state. By 'gender regime' I mean the system of gender relations, which is constituted by several structures or domains, especially those of paid work, housework, the state, male violence against women, sexuality and culture, together with a set of associated practices. The domestic form of gender regime is one in which women are primarily located in the home and dominated and exploited by their husband or father and restricted from entry into the public sphere of employment and the state. In the transition to the public form of the gender regime, the restrictions on women's entry to the public sphere are eliminated and women enter employment and the state, though they still suffer from forms of disadvantage associated with segregation (Walby, 1990, 1997).

A key issue in welfare politics is that of the reference group to which voters relate. Women here are divided as much by age as any other social indicator, in both the US and the UK, in that younger women are more likely to support the policies which facilitate women's waged employment than are older women (Fawcett Society, 2000; Manza and Brooks, 1998). The gender gap in US voting intentions is significantly structured by women's employment status in that women in employment are significantly more likely to vote for the party which will provide social service spending (Manza and Brooks, 1998). This social division of age/gender is not captured by the concept of 'community', yet this divide is key to the explanation of women's interests and political preferences.

The Global and Castells

Contemporary politics cannot be understood without an analysis of the global framing of issues. The nature of this global framing is especially important given the ease with which an elision between the global and the universal can be made. The global is no more than a specific social construction situated in a specific time. In this way it is quite different from the universal which is usually seen as timeless as well as lacking spatial specificity. I am going to argue that the appeal to the global/universal is becoming an increasingly common feature of contemporary politics, especially radical politics.

However, many writers have seen globalization as a process against which people protest, rather than as endorsing a set of political claims. In particular, Castells (1996, 1997, 1998) provides accounts of political movements which mostly, though not always, object to globalization, which is perceived as undermining their community's conditions of existence. Castells sees three different kinds of political identity in relation to globalization: legitimizing, resistance and project. Castells uses 'identity' as his core concept to engage simultaneously with difference and community. Today 'meaning is organized around a primary identity, one identity which frames the others' (1997: 7). Legitimizing identity is bound up with an integrated society, but such legitimizing identities are disappearing along with civil society, democracy and nation-states as a result globalization. Castells is dismissive of this first set of political projects, those which engage in 'legitimizing', since he considers that globalization undermines the political units he considers necessary for such projects, that is, nation-states. Resistance identities, the second type, are defensive identities and are the main basis of the various forms of resistance to globalization. Examples include religious fundamentalism, Islamic and Christian among others, nationalism, for instance in the post-Soviet republics and Catalunya, and local territorial identity, for instance urban social movements. The third type of identity, project identity, is less well developed, even though it is crucial. This seeks transformation rather than retrenchment. However, it is only considered to be viable if a core set of values can be identified. Castells does not find many examples of this. He considers whether the European Union might be an example, but concludes that the project is doubtful. This is because, although there are some potential common values, such as those of universal human rights and of a notion of political culture as rooted in political democracy and participation, nevertheless, primary identity in this part of the world is still lodged in nation-states.

Castells is thus sceptical of the likelihood of success of existing instances of rights-based politics, as a result of his dismissal of both legitimizing and project-based identities. I think this is a mistake for two reasons. First, he underestimates the extent to which the 'global' level, in its guise as the 'universal', could be used to legitimate political projects, especially those utilizing a conception of rights couched within the discourse of universal human rights. Despite his path-breaking work on politics beyond the nation-state, he curiously underestimates the extent to which the global itself can act as a frame for positive political action. While rightly pointing to some of the ways in which the nation-state is undermined as a focus for democratically inspired politics by globalization, he underestimates the way in which alternative frames could be found for this type of politics. In particular, he underestimates the extent to which the global itself, when re-invented as the universal, could provide an alternative frame of reference for democratically inspired politics. Second, Castells is limited by his utilization of the concept of 'identity' as core to his notion of politics. He uses the concept of identity despite his powerful deployment of the concept of network to describe the transmission of power in a global age. It is a limitation of his work that he does not extend the use of this concept of network to his analysis of political projects. Instead his utilization of the concept of 'identity' to underpin political projects is a relatively weak part of his analysis, despite the rich empirical detail. This is because of his misleading assumption that a primary identity must underlie each political project if it is to be successful. But the world is not like this. Most people simultaneously hold several, if not many, identities. This concern with a primary identity is contradicted by the evidence. For instance, the European Union is a powerful and successful polity which has a very limited common ethos and is instead built on political coalitions. A common ethos is not necessary for polis, nor for a political project. The complexity of the many overlapping and cross-cutting 'communities' in the contemporary social world is not adequately grasped by a notion of 'identity' which rests on a presumption of coherence. Castells does not have a concept which adequately addresses the complexity and inter-connecting and overlapping forms of 'community' which exist. This is related to a tendency to conflate the concepts of 'politics' and 'culture' in a way which can be misleading in that it overly simplifies the social world. For instance, the European Union contains many cultures yet functions as a polity and as a political project. The easy equation of 'ethos' and 'polis' needs to be disrupted. There can be political coalitions between groups with quite different 'cultures' which can nonetheless be effective, as the EU demon-strates.

Nevertheless, despite these weaknesses, Castells has ensured that the significance of politics focused on the global level is taken seriously. He is right to argue that globalization has altered the political choices and prospects available. His concepts of networked forms of power have added to our conceptual vocabulary. My argument is that he did not push the innovations he made in parts of his analysis far enough. The concept of network which he used in relation to power should also be applied to politics, so that political networks rather than identities are the key concept. The utilization of the new framing of the global by progressive social movements should be considered, not merely when it is used by those resisting these changes. The example of the movement to stop violence against women analysed below is an instance of this.

From 'Community' to 'Social': Sociological Conceptions of the Self and 'Other'

Ironically, for all the invocation of 'the other' in the politics of recognition, there is a tendency to reduce the complexity of the social world too far. This is because insufficient attention is given to the variety of social institutions. There is more to social life than the individual, the universal and com-munities. The development of social philosophy, while illuminating in its own field, underestimates the complexity of the social, reducing it to 'com-munity', and could usefully integrate a wider range of concepts of the social from Sociology. There are more divisions within social life than can be expressed by the concept of community. There are cross-cutting divisions of gender, age, religion, language, sexual orientation and many more. Sociology has a rich conceptual vocabulary to grasp a wide range of types of social divisions, which is insufficiently utilized by philosophers and social theorists. Instead we have the reduction of the complexity of the social world to the simplicities of the very specific social form of 'community'.

We need a better developed set of concepts for the diversity of the social, which goes beyond the simplicities of 'community'. We need to analyse a range of social institutions and a range of levels of abstraction, from system and structure to practices. One starting point for this is the reconsideration of the sociology of reference groups, which was developed several decades ago to address the issue why social groups chose some standards rather than others as constitutive of their interests and chose others as the focus of their aspirations.

The selection of which 'other' is to be chosen to be recognized is treated in much of the social philosophy literature as obvious, whether it is presumed to be everyone else, or merely the person or 'community' one is engaging with. However, there are many options of which 'other' is to be the focus and many complex reasons why one is chosen and not another. There is a vast sociological literature on this topic, much, though not all, focused around the concept of reference group. This literature has sophisticated discussions of at least two key processes. First, the identification of the group with which one identifies or draws one's normative values from. This is not obviously a group which is the 'same' as oneself, since there is a question as to the selection of the issues on which likeness is to be ascertained. In complex societies there will be many possibilities. Second, there is the identification of the group with which one compares oneself. In complex modern societies there is likely to be a wide choice of groups from which a choice of comparator can be made. Reference group theory debated the conditions under which people chose one group or another as the one to which they referred for their own norms and those to which they aspired (Runciman, 1966; Urry, 1973).

The development of reference group theory depended upon the prior development of a sociological theory of the self. A key figure here was Mead (1934), who developed a theory of the self as composed of an internal relationship between the 'I' which acted and the 'me' which was the product of the complex and deeply sedimented memory of the experience of social life. This internal complexity went radically beyond the notion of the self as a fixed essential coherent unity, and posited it rather as always in a state of becoming in relationship to the social. Symbolic interactionist theorists, such as Blumer (1969) developed this further, considering three processes as key: interaction, negotiation and meaning. Such theoretical development underpinned the work of Goffman (1963, 1969) on the presentation of the self in everyday life, and his development of a series of theatrical metaphors, including that of performance, front stage and back stage. Such work was applied to substantive topics such as that of becoming homosexual by Plummer (1975). This is a more developed theory of the self and performance than we see in social philosophers such as Butler (1990), who, despite being widely credited with inventing the concept of performativity, uses a concept which is simpler and does not draw on the earlier sociological work of Mead, Blumer and Goffman.

In order to understand the reasoning behind the selection of one social group as the basis for one's own self-definition and another one as a point of comparison, it is necessary to have an understanding of the historical processes which have led these social groups to be positioned in this way. Yet political cultures are always changing. We are always out of date as to the characteristics of the political culture that we are intending to recognize. Likewise, the divisions within political cultures and the relations with other political cultures are always changing. We are always out of date in relation to this. For instance, groups in the diaspora will often 'freeze' their political culture, while that of those in their place of origin, which may be looked upon as their authentic reference point, is actually changing (Medaglia, 2001). Which is the 'real' political culture to be recognized – the practice of the diaspora population, the previous practice of those in the 'homeland' or the current practice of those in the 'homeland'? The analysis of the selection of the groups for identification and for comparison thus requires a historical sociological analysis, not merely a description of the present. Political cultures are usually the outcome of complex processes of development with historic compromises between different political forces which shape the pathways of development. Too great a concern for the present can lead to an unfortunate voluntarism and lack of depth of understanding of the nature of constraints resulting from prior historic events.

The process of selection of points of comparison brings into question some of the easy polarities which have been perceived between the politics of equality and the politics of recognition (Meehan and Sevenhuijsen, 1991). The different political cultures in which equality and difference are rooted have been seen as irreconcilable, based on different ethics and principles of justice. However, there have been attempts at a reconciliation, which are based on a deconstruction of the concept of equality (Holli, 1997; Scott, 1988). The core issue is that of which equalities matter (Phillips, 1999), and what we mean by equality (Holli, 1997; Lorber, 2000). As Holli shows, in a grounded empirical analysis of equality politics in Scandinavia (1997), the definition and substantive content of equality are open to considerable debate and contestation. There is not an a priori given of what aspects of social life we intend to refer to when we speak of equality. In some circumstances, the goal of 'equality' might be construed as 'equal pay', in others as 'equal treatment', in others as 'equal respect'. In order to be able to judge something to be equal or unequal we must agree on the standard against which we are judging. Equality politics presumes a prior agreement on the identification of the issue at stake.

The issue of which comparisons matter lies at the heart of debates on globalization. To what extent are frames of reference being shifted in a global direction? To what extent is the notion of the particular becoming simultaneously that of the global?

The Global and the Universal

The appeal to the global level is often presented as if it were an appeal to a timeless universal. This is an increasingly common feature of feminist (Peters and Wolper, 1995), environmental (Beck, 1992), development (UNDP, 1999) and labour movement politics (Valticos, 1969), as well as extending into the treatment of international war crimes and other issues. This appeal to a global level is especially occurring in the case of the appeal to 'universal' human rights. A successful elision between the global and the universal is an important move in contemporary politics. The ability to claim access to a universal standard of justice has been used by an increasing number of political projects as a powerful form of legitimation.

The appeal to the notion of universal human rights has been a continuing strand in political life for centuries (Held, 1995; Paine, 1984), although subject to criticism, not only by communitarians, as discussed above, but also by socialists and feminists seeking radical transformations (Young, 2000). My argument here is that the appeal to universal human rights is newly re-invigorated by the development of global institutions and perspectives. The appeal to universal human rights depends not only upon a philosophy and commonly accepted rhetoric, but also upon a set of institutional practices which give it practical expression. This set of institutional practices is increasing with globalization. There are at least three elements here. First, increased global communications which shrink the distance in time and space between events, so that live news footage of a conflict can be beamed to millions around the world. This increases awareness of quite general publics about incidents beyond their own country. Second, increased global communications which facilitate interconnections between political activists, especially cheaper air travel, faster trains and the development of cheaper and more reliable phone, fax and email. These facilitate the exchange of ideas and practices between people located in different countries and regions of the world. Third, the development of global institutions, events and conferences has increased the number of spaces where international interactions, dialogues and networking between activists can take place. These include international conferences and agencies, the increased salience of the World Bank and the International Monetary Fund. Fourth, the increased salience of the UN, as custodian of the Universal Declaration of Human Rights, through its global conferences (such as Rio on the environment, Beijing on women), and UN agencies.

The elision of the 'universal' with the 'global' lies at the heart of this development. It is implied that if all the world agrees to something through open debating in forums of persons selected in a representative manner from each country then the Habermas-type conditions of procedure have been met, which in turn means that truth is approached as closely as is humanly possible. Simultaneously, there is an appeal to the liberal principle of universal individual human rights, as if this is above time-bound and space-bound calculations of interest. In these developing global fora, political activists devise and change those principles of justice understood as human rights. They successfully treat the global as if it is the same as the universal, the better to claim authority for their actions.

An example of such a move from the global to the universal can be found in the work of Amartya Sen. This influential economist and philosopher has constantly scoured philosophical literature for justifications of distributive justice whilst also being an economist with impeccable credentials (Sen, 1984, 1987, 1992, 1999). Sen (1999) has re-described the project of development as one which increases freedom. This shifts the focus from a needs-based to a rights-based justification of this project and enables a claim to justice which is expressed in terms of universal human rights. By this move Sen has shifted the project from being 'merely' global, to one which is justified by 'universal' standards.

Sen's philosophy has underpinned the attempt by the United Nations Development Project (UNDP, 1999) to insert values of distributive justice into the indicators of global progress to be used by national governments, the UN and other global economic bodies. The UNDP has created performance indicators of human development (which include education, literacy and longevity as well as income). By setting global standards it was hoped to influence the nature of national development projects, which already address a global frame of reference, not least because of their partial dependence for credit and capital on global financial bodies. This was a deliberate attempt to construct an alternative global standard to the narrowly focused performance indicator of economic growth used by the World Bank, the International Monetary Fund and many national governments. It was a self-conscious move to change the goals of national and global financial bodies by making appeals to improve human capacities and capabilities understood in terms of the broader demands of justice and need, as well as economic efficiency. It was an attempt to set global standards, in a context of developing global governance, in which access to credit by developing countries is affected by their willingness to conform to global standards.

There are many examples of political projects newly using universal human rights as the basis of their politics. In a second example below I will examine feminist politics in relation to violence against women.

Women's Rights as Human Rights

Contemporary feminist politics is framed by the global, even as it is simultaneously deeply engaged with difference (Benhabib, 1999; Felski, 1997). Political activists constantly balance and re-balance priorities and practices in response to the changing tensions involved. Feminist political activists endeavour to reach beyond the particularism of any grouping with which they might appear to be identified. This occurs in two main ways. First, there is an increasing tendency to legitimate claims by reference to universal rights. This is articulated through the notion that women's rights are human rights which are universal human rights. Second, there is the use of coalitions rather than democratic centralist forms of organization in order to deal constructively with issues of difference.

The claim to universal human rights has a long history in feminism and is now undergoing a resurgence. It was a key, though not sole, legitimating principle during suffrage struggles over the last hundred years (Banks, 1981; Jayawardena, 1986; Ramirez et al., 1997). It was present in claims to equal worth, equal pay and equal treatment at work in the reconstruction of the European Union in the 1980s and 1990s (European Commission, 1999; European Parliament, 1994; Pillinger, 1992), in Japan (Yoko et al., 1994) and elsewhere around the world (Nelson and Chowdhury, 1994). This claim to universalism is often knowing, by which I mean that the protagonists know that the 'universal' is but a contingent social construct (Bunch, 1995). Indeed, much feminist activity is devoted to redefining and reconstructing what constitutes 'universal' human rights (Peters and Wolper, 1995; UNIFEM, 2000a, 2000c). This occurs in UN conferences, which attract a massive attendance of feminist activists from around the world, both North and South, who supplement and influence the official delegations (UNIFEM, 2000e).

In 1993 in a UN conference in Vienna, violence against women was constructed for the first time as a violation of women's human rights and thus of human rights (Bunch, 1995; UNIFEM, 2000d). This UN conference concluded with a statement that violence against women is a violation of human rights and thus that national governments must strengthen the response of their criminal justice systems in support of women. This is done as if this was an always already existing universal human right, even as many activists know that it was recently constructed through struggle. This involves a major reconceptualization of the issue of male violence against women. It involves a shift away from constructing men as the beneficiaries of this form of power, instead seeing such violence as a minority form of socially unacceptable conduct. Since this conduct is now held to violate women's human rights, which are newly considered human rights, it makes it an issue on which progressive men can stand as allies with women in a human rights struggle, rather than uncomfortably on the margins. This reconfiguration makes it harder to reject action against violence against women on the grounds that the analysis is extreme; rather, all humanity is considered to have an interest in the elimination of such violent conduct (Bunch, 1995; Davies, 1993; Heise, 1996; Peters and Wolper, 1995).

There is much exchange of information, ideas and practices about politics against violence against women around the world. This takes place not only at conferences, but through the Internet, letters, phone calls, books, journals, magazines and other publications (Counts et al., 1992; Heise, 1996; Keck and Sikkink, 1998). There is the use of modern technologies, as in the use of web sites and video-conferences (UNIFEM, 2000b, 2000d). There is effectively a global feminist civil society in existence. The discussion of difference is a constant feature of this politics. The policies and practices used in response are reflexively monitored and adapted to particular circumstances. The use of coalitions as a method of organizing across difference is now taken for granted. Such transnational feminist coalitions have worked hard to engage constructively with issues of difference within the overall project (Friedman, 1995; Mayer, 1995; Rao, 1995).

The movement against violence against women, in its aim to reduce and eliminate men's violent power over women, has always been a politics seeking equality rather than mere recognition. There has been a major shift in tactics involved in the adoption of a human rights discourse instead of the earlier more confrontational strategy which named men as the oppressive 'other'. Nevertheless, this is still a politics about power and inequality. While this has involved an attempt to get women's voices recognized as legitimate on the global political stage, this has only been as a handmaiden to the politics of equality. It is a politics which is more actively seeking coalitions and alliances, which is itself made easier by the creative and innovative re-working of the discourse of universal human rights using global institutions.

By this example, I want to suggest that some of the polarities in philosophy, while ostensibly having analytic purchase, are far behind existing social and political practice. There is a universalist framing, but it is known to be contingent and constructed. Differences are treated seriously, but not essentialized. They are addressed through coalitions, rather than being for ever obstacles to action. Identities are as much constituted through actions as they are the basis of actions.

Conclusions

The alterity between liberalism and communitarianism has provided not a dead end, but a creative tension, in political thought, once it is recognized that both polar positions are untenable. The route through this philosophical dilemma is via sociological analysis. The concept of community is a poor and overly narrow operationalization of the social which is unable to articulate sufficiently the complexities of cross-cutting differences. Rather, we should invoke a wider range of sociological concepts of social divisions, accepting that they cross-cut in complex ways.

Some modern political actors have already found a way through the dilemmas of difference and the desire for a less particularistic conception of justice. This has been through the utilization of networks and coalitions, and the overt abandonment of the assumption that political projects are to be based on culturally cohesive communities. In particular, we need to abandon any notion that ethos and polis do or should map onto each other. The purity demanded by such a project is unachievable in the modern world.

The reframing of contemporary politics by globalization has given rise, not only to politics opposed to this change, but also to the creative and innovative adaptation and expansion of the notion of universal human rights. This new framing elides the distinction between the global and the universal as part of its legitimation strategy. The attempted reference group for these politics is that of a common humanity. This opens up a new round of political struggles in the construction of such rights, even as they are held up as timeless and universal (Walby, 2002).

The politics of equality is still vibrant in the modern world, in both the North and the South. While emergent political voices will seek recognition in political institutions and fora, this is usually merely in order to achieve their goals of redistribution of resources. The politics of recognition is but the handmaiden of the politics of redistribution.

References

Acker, Joan (1989) *Doing Comparable Worth: Gender, Class and Pay Equity*. Philadelphia, PA: Temple University Press.

Banks, Olive (1981) *Faces of Feminism: A Study of Feminism as a Social Movement*. Oxford: Martin Robertson.

Bauman, Zymunt (1989) *Modernity and the Holocaust*. Cambridge: Polity Press.

Bauman, Zygmunt (1991) *Modernity and Ambivalence*. Cambridge: Polity Press.

Bauman, Zygmunt (1993) *Postmodern Ethics*. Oxford: Blackwell.

Bauman, Zymunt (1996) 'On Communitarians and Human Freedom: or, How to Square the Circle', *Theory, Culture & Society* 13(2): 79–90.

Bauman, Zygmunt (1997) *Postmodernity and its Discontents*. Cambridge: Polity Press.

Beck, Ulrich (1992) *Risk Society*. London: Sage.

Beck, Ulrich, Anthony Giddens and Scott Lash (1994) *Reflexive Modernization: Politics, Tradition and Aesthetics in the Modern Social Order*. Cambridge: Polity Press.

Benhabib, Seyla (1992) *Situating the Self: Gender, Community and Postmodernism in Contemporary Ethics*. Cambridge: Polity Press.

Benhabib, Seyla (1999) 'Sexual Difference and Collective Identities: The New Global Constellation', *Signs* 24(2): 335–61.

Bergmann, Barbara R. (1986) *The Economic Emergence of Women*. New York: Basic Books.

Blumer, H. (1969) *Symbolic Interactionism*. Englewood Cliffs, NJ: Prentice-Hall.

Bunch, Charlotte (1995) 'Transforming Human Rights from a Feminist Perspective', in Julie Peters and Andrea Wolper (eds) *Women's Rights, Human Rights: International Feminist Perspectives*. London: Routledge.

Butler, Judith (1990) *Gender Trouble: Feminism and the Subversion of Identity*. New York: Routledge.

Calhoun, Craig (1995) *Critical Social Theory*. Oxford: Blackwell.

Castells, Manuel (1996) *The Information Age: Economy, Society and Culture; Volume 1: The Rise of the Network Society*. Oxford: Blackwell.

Castells, Manuel (1997) *The Information Age: Economy, Society and Culture; Volume II: The Power of Identity*. Oxford: Blackwell.

Castells, Manuel (1998) *The Information Age: Economy, Society and Culture; Volume III: End of Millennium*. Oxford: Blackwell.

Charles, Nickie (2000) *Feminism, the State and Social Policy*. Basingstoke: Macmillan.

Counts, D.A., J.K. Brown and J.C. Campbell (eds) (1992) *Sanctions and Sanctuary – Cultural Perspectives on the Beating of Wives*. Boulder, CO: Westview Press.

Davies, M. (ed.) (1993) *Women and Violence: Realities and Responses Worldwide*. London: Zed.

Dobash, R. Emerson and Russell P. Dobash (1992) *Women, Violence and Social Change*. London: Routledge.

Ellis, Valerie and Sue Ferns (2000) 'Equality Bargaining', in Suzanne Gagnon and Sue Ledwith (eds) *Women, Diversity and Democracy in Trade Unions*. Oxford: Oxford Brookes University.

European Commission (1994) *Sex Equality Legislation in the Member States of the European Community* by Barry Fitzpatrick, Jeanne Gregory and Erika Szysczak. Brussels: DGV, European Commission.

European Commission (1999) 'Gender Mainstreaming in the European Employment Strategy', Doc. EQOP 61–99 DG EMPL/D/5 1 October 1999. Brussels: European Commission.

European Parliament, Directorate General for Research (1994) *Measures to Combat Sexual Harassment at the Workplace: Action taken in the Member States of the European Community*, Working Paper in the Women's Rights Series. Strasbourg: European Parliament.

Evans, Sara M. and Barbara J. Nelson (eds) (1989) *Wage Justice: Comparable Worth and the Paradox of Technocratic Reform*. Chicago, IL: University of Chicago Press.

Fawcett Society (2000) *The Gender/Generation Gap*. London: Fawcett Society.

Featherstone, Mike and Scott Lash (2001) 'Introduction', *Theory, Culture & Society* 18(2–3).

Felski, Rita (1997) 'The Doxa of Difference', *Signs* 23(1): 1–22.

Franklin, Sarah, Celia Lury and Jackie Stacey (eds) (1991) *Off-Centre: Feminism and Cultural Studies*. London: HarperCollins.

Fraser, Nancy (1995) 'From Redistribution to Recognition? Dilemmas of Justice in a "Postsocialist" Age', *New Left Review* 212: 68–93.

Fraser, Nancy (1997) *Justice Interruptus: Critical Reflections on the 'Postsocialist' Condition*. London: Routledge.

Friedman, Elisabeth (1995) 'Women's Human Rights: The Emergence of a Movement', in Julie Peters and Andrea Wolper (eds) *Women's Rights, Human Rights: International Feminist Perspectives*. London: Routledge.

Gagnon, Suzanne and Sue Ledwith (eds) (2000) *Women, Diversity and Democracy in Trade Unions*. Oxford: Oxford Brookes University.

Gardiner, Michael (1996) 'Alterity and Ethics: A Dialogical Perspective', *Theory, Culture & Society* 13(2): 121–43.

Goffman, Erving (1963) *Stigma: Notes on the Management of Spoiled Identity*. Englewood Cliffs, NJ: Prentice-Hall.

Goffman, Erving (1969) *The Presentation of Self in Everyday Life*. London: Allen Lane.

Habermas, Jürgen (1989) *The Theory of Communicative Action, Volume Two: The Critique of Functionalist Reason*. Cambridge: Polity Press.

Habermas, Jürgen (1991) *The Theory of Communicative Action, Volume One: Reason and the Rationalization of Society*. Cambridge: Polity Press.

Hague, Gill and Ellen Malos (1993) *Domestic Violence: Action for Change*. Cheltenham: New Clarion Press.

Hantrais, Linda (1995) *Social Policy in the European Union*. Basingstoke: Macmillan.

Heise, Lori L. (1996) 'Violence against Women: Global Organizing for Change', in Jeffrey L. Edleson and Zvi C. Eisikovits (eds) *Future Interventions with Battered Women and their Families*. London: Sage.

Held, David (1995) *Democracy and the Global Order: From the Modern State to Cosmopolitan Governance*. Cambridge: Polity Press.

Hicks, Stephen (2000) 'Trade Union Membership 1998–9: An Analysis of Data from the Certification Officer and Labour Force Survey', *Labour Market Trends* July: 329–40.

Holli, Anne Maria (1997) 'On Equality and Trojan Horses: The Challenges of the Finnish Experience to Feminist Theory', *European Journal of Women's Studies* 4(2): 133–64.

Hoskyns, Catherine (1996) *Integrating Gender: Women, Law and Politics in the European Union*. London: Verso.

Hutchings, Kimberly (1997) 'Moral Deliberation and Political Judgement: Reflections on Benhabib's Interactive Universalism', *Theory, Culture & Society* 14(1): 131–42.

ILO (1999) *Yearbook of Labour Statistics*. Geneva: International Labour Office.

Jakobsen, Janet R. (1998) *Working Alliances and the Politics of Difference: Diversity and Feminist Ethics*. Bloomington: Indiana University Press.

Jayawardena, Kumari (ed.) (1986) *Feminism and Nationalism in the Third World*. London: Zed.

Keck, Margaret E. and Kathryn Sikkink (1998) *Activists Beyond Borders: Advocacy Networks in International Politics*. Ithaca, NY: Cornell University Press.

Kelly, Erin and Frank Dobbin (1999) 'Civil Rights Law at Work: Sex Discrimination and the Rise of Maternity Leave Policies', *American Journal of Sociology* 105(2): 455–92.

Kymlicka, Will (1991) *Liberalism, Community and Culture*. Oxford: Clarendon Press.

Kymlicka, Will (1995) *Multicultural Citizenship: A Liberal Theory of Minority Rights*. Oxford: Clarendon Press.

Lash, Scott (1996a) 'Introduction to the Ethics and Difference Debate', *Theory, Culture & Society* 13(2): 75–7.

Lash, Scott (1996b) 'Postmodern Ethics: The Missing Ground', *Theory, Culture & Society* 13(2): 91–104.

Ledwith, Sue and Fiona Colgan (eds) (1996) *Women in Organisations: Challenging Gender Politics*. Basingstoke: Macmillan.

Ledwith, Sue and Fiona Colgan (2000) 'Women, Democracy and Diversity and the New Trade Unionism', in Suzanne Gagnon and Sue Ledwith (eds) *Women, Diversity and Democracy in Trade Unions*. Oxford: Oxford Brookes University.

Lorber, Judith (2000) 'Using Gender to Undo Gender: A Feminist Degendering Movement', *Feminist Theory* 1(1): 79–95.

Lovenduski, Joni and Vicky Randall (1993) *Contemporary Feminist Politics: Women and Power in Britain*. Oxford: Oxford University Press.

Maffesoli, Michel (1996) *The Time of Tribes: The Decline of Individualism in Mass Society*. London: Sage.

Manza, Jeff and Clem Brooks (1998) 'The Gender Gap in US Presidential Elections: When? Why? Implications?', *American Journal of Sociology* 103(5): 1235–66.

Mayer, Ann Elizabeth (1995) 'Cultural Particularism as a Bar to Women's Human Rights: Reflections on the Middle Eastern Experience', in Julie Peters and Andrea Wolper (eds) *Women's Rights, Human Rights: International Feminist Perspectives*. London: Routledge.

Mead, George Herbert (1934) *Mind, Self and Society*. Chicago, IL: University of Chicago Press.

Medaglia, Azadeh (2001) *Patriarchal Structures and Ethnicity in the Italian Community in Britain*. Avebury: Ashgate.

Meehan, Elizabeth and Selma Sevenhuijsen (eds) (1991) *Equality Politics and Gender*. London: Sage.

Moghadam, Valentine M. (1996a) 'The Fourth World Conference on Women: Dissension and Consensus', *Indian Journal of Gender Studies* 3(1): 93–102.

Moghadam, Valentine M. (ed.) (1996b) *Patriarchy and Development*. Oxford: Clarendon Press.

Mohanty, Chandra Talpade (1991) 'Under Western Eyes: Feminist Scholarship and Colonial Discourses', in Chandra Talpade Mohanty, Ann Russo and Lourdes Torres (eds) *Third World Women and the Politics of Feminism*. Bloomington: Indiana University Press.

Nelson, Barbara J. and Nalma Chowdhury (eds) (1994) *Women and Politics Worldwide*. New Haven, CT: Yale University Press.

Paine, T. (1984) *The Rights of Man*. Harmondsworth: Penguin.

Pascual, Amparo Serrano and Ute Behning (eds) (2000) *Gender Mainstreaming in the European Employment Strategy*. Brussels: European Trade Union Institute.

Peters, Julie and Andrea Wolper (eds) (1995) *Women's Rights, Human Rights: International Feminist Perspectives*. London: Routledge.

Phillips, Anne (1999) *Which Equalities Matter?* Cambridge: Polity Press.

Pillinger, Jane (1992) *Feminising the Market: Women's Pay and Employment in the European Community*. Basingstoke: Macmillan.

Plummer, Kenneth (1975) *Sexual Stigma: An Interactionist Account*. London: Routledge.

Ramirez, Francisco O., Yasemin Soysal and Suzanne Shanahan (1997) 'The Changing Logic of Political Citizenship: Cross-national Acquisition of Women's Suffrage Rights, 1890–1990', *American Sociological Review* 62: 735–45.

Rao, Arati (1995) 'The Politics of Gender and Culture in International Human Rights Discourse', in Julie Peters and Andrea Wolper (eds) *Women's Rights, Human Rights: International Feminist Perspectives*. London: Routledge.

Rees, Teresa (1992) *Women and the Labour Market*. London: Routledge.

Rees, Teresa (1998) *Mainstreaming Equality in the European Union: Education, Training and Labour Market Policies*. London: Routledge.

Runciman, W. Gary (1966) *Relative Deprivation and Social Justice: A Study of Attitudes to Social Inequality in Twentieth-century England*. London: Routledge.

Sandel, Michael J. (1998) *Liberalism and the Limits of Justice*, 2nd edn. Cambridge: Cambridge University Press.

Scott, Joan W. (1988) 'Deconstructing Equality-versus-Difference: or, The Uses of Poststructuralist Theory for Feminism', *Feminist Studies* 14(1): 33–49.

Sen, Amartya (1984) *Resources, Values and Development*. Oxford: Blackwell.

Sen, Amartya (1987) *On Ethics and Resources*. Oxford: Blackwell.

Sen, Amartya (1992) *Inequality Re-examined*. Oxford: Clarendon Press.

Sen, Amartya (1999) *Development as Freedom*. Oxford: Oxford University Press.

Shaw, Jenny and Diane Perrons (eds) (1995) *Making Gender Work: Managing Equal Opportunities*. Buckingham: Open University Press.

South, Scott J. and Glenna Spitze (1994) 'Housework in Marital and Non-marital Households', *American Sociological Review* 59: 327–47.

Spellman, Elizabeth V. (1988) *Inessential Woman: Problems of Exclusion in Feminist Thought*. Boston, MA: Beacon Press.

Standing, Guy (1999) *Global Labour Flexibility: Seeking Distributive Justice*. Basingstoke: Macmillan.

Taylor, Charles et al. (1994) *Multiculturalism: Examining the Politics of Recognition*. Princeton, NJ: Princeton University Press.

UNDP (1999) *Human Development Report 1999*. New York: Oxford University Press.

UNIFEM (2000a) *Progress of the World's Women*. (http://www.undp.org/unifem/progressww/).

UNIFEM (2000b) *A World Free of Violence Against Women: UN Inter-Agency Global Videoconference*. (http://www.undp.org/unifem/campaign/violence/videocon.htm).

UNIFEM (2000c) *Promoting Women's Human Rights*. (http://www.undp.org/unifem/hrights.htm).

UNIFEM (2000d) *Women @ Work to End Violence: Voices in Cyberspace*. (http://www.undp.org/unifem/w@work/w@work11.htm).

UNIFEM (2000e) *Bringing Equality Home: Implementing the Convention on the Elimination of All Forms of Discrimination Against Women, CEDAW*. (http://www.undp.org/unifem/cedaw/cedawen5.htm).

Urry, John (1973) *Reference Groups and the Theory of Revolution*. London: Routledge and Kegan Paul.

Valticos, Nicolas (1969) 'Fifty Years of Standard-setting Activities by the International Labour Organisation', *International Labour Review* 100(3).

Walby, Sylvia (1990) *Theorizing Patriarchy*. Oxford: Blackwell.

Walby, Sylvia (1997) *Gender Transformations*. London: Routledge.

Walby, Sylvia (2002) *Globalisation, Modernity and Difference*. London: Sage (forthcoming).

Yoko, Nuita, Yamaguchi Mitsuko and Kubo Kimiko (1994) 'The UN Convention on Eliminating Discrimination Against Women and the Status of Women in Japan', pp. 398–414 in Barbara J. Nelson and Nalma Chowdhury (eds) *Women and Politics Worldwide*. New Haven, CT: Yale University Press.

Young, Brigette (2000) 'Disciplinary Neoliberalism in the European Union and Gender Politics', *New Political Economy* 5(1): 77–98.

Sylvia Walby is Professor of Sociology at the University of Leeds. She was the founding Director of the Gender Institute at the LSE and of the Women's Studies Research Centre at Lancaster University. She was the first President of the European Sociological Association and Chair of the Women's Studies Network UK. She is author of *Gender Transformations* (Routledge, 1997), *Theorising Patriarchy* (Blackwell, 1990), *Patriarchy at Work* (Polity, 1986); joint author of *Sex Crime in the News* (Routledge, 1991), *Localities, Class and Gender* (Pion, 1985), *Contemporary British Society* (Polity, 1988, 1994,

2000), *Restructuring Place Class and Gender* (Sage, 1990) and *Medicine and Nursing: Professions in a Changing Health Service* (Sage, 1994); editor of *Gender Segregation at Work* (Open University Press, 1988) and *New Agendas for Women* (Macmillan, 1999); and co-editor of *Out of the Margins: Women's Studies in the Nineties* (Falmer, 1991)and *European Societies: Fusion or Fission* (Routledge, 1999).

The Great War of Recognition

Zygmunt Bauman

S AID BRUNO LATOUR: 'we might be leaving the time of time – suc-
cessions and revolutions – and entering a very different time/space:
that of coexistence'. The type of change that it is hoped will sweep clean
the lumber and mess from the social site for the eager land-developers to
start work on it from scratch is no longer on the cards in our time/space of
'liquid modernity'.[1] There is more change these days than ever before – but
(as Milan Kundera observed) change nowadays is as disorderly as the state
of affairs which it is meant to replace and which has prompted it in the first
place. Things today are moving sideways, aslant or across rather than
forward, often backward, but as a rule the movers are unsure of their direction and the nature of successive steps is hotly contested. Changes happen
all over the place and all the time – sometimes converging, some other times
diverging. One change starts before another has been completed and, most
importantly, the sediments and imprints of one change are not wiped clean
or erased before another change starts to scatter its own. In short – forms of
life do not *succeed* each other: they settle aside each other, clash and mix,
crowd together in the same time/space and are bound to do so for a long time
to come. 'There is still an arrow of time', says Latour, 'but it no longer goes
from slavery to freedom, it goes from entanglement to more entanglement.'
Like before (perhaps more than ever before), the 'great simplification', remaking the world to order, is a dream dreamt by many, but more than ever
before it looks like a pipe-dream. Variety of life-forms is here to stay. And
so is the imperative of their coexistence.

Coexistence comes in many shapes and colours. One of these shapes
– a basic one in fact (as Georg Simmel explained well before most sociolo-
gists noted that there was something to explain) – is *confrontation and strife*.
Conflict is the birth-act of coexistence (since coexistence is a state that
needs to be born daily anew, to speak of a birth-*process* rather than *act* would
be more to the point). Conflict means *engagement*, and it is in the course of

■ *Theory, Culture & Society* 2001 (SAGE, London, Thousand Oaks and New Delhi),
Vol. 18(2–3): 137–150
[0263-2764(200104/06)18:2–3;137–150;017481]

hostile confrontations and struggle that *Weltanschauungen*, values, ideals and preferences are first set against each other, compared, scrutinized, criticized, tested, valued or de-valued. Conflict lifts a mere 'entanglement' to the level of mutual engagement and so triggers the protracted, convoluted and contorted process of getting to know each other, coming to terms with each other, striking a bargain, seeking and finding a *modus vivendi* or rather *coexistendi*. Without conflict, no engagement. Without engagement, no hope for coexistence.

Conflict, I suggest, is in the 'liquid stage' of modernity the prevalent form of coexistence (this stage, together with the preceding 'solid' stage of modernity, I described more fully in Bauman, 2000). No longer can it be treated as a temporary irritant – a hiccup of an imperfectly modernized state of affairs and a hurdle to be leaped over or kicked out of the way by more modernization. It would not be proper to dismiss it as a symptom of back-wardness even if the meaning of 'backwardness' were not itself the focus of a most hectic and fiery of conflicts. The growing volume and intensity of local and segmental conflicts cannot be played down as the feature of 'the state of transition' that leads to something variously (but invariably wrongly) called 'global culture', 'global society', or even (wistfully and romantically) 'global community'. It should be seen instead as a permanent, perhaps constitutive, attribute of a fast globalizing 'liquid modern' world – its staple and massive product rather than a side-effect of a preliminary, yet unfinished but finite and transient stage of globalization. Just as continuous (obsessive and unstoppable) modernization is not a process leading to modernity, but the substance of modernity itself, so the incessant and permanently unfinished *globalization* is the essence of the new *globality* of human condition.

That 'globality', to deploy Norbert Elias's terms, means no more but no less either than the presence of a 'global figuration': the network of depen-dencies, in which human thought and action are entangled, has extended to encompass the whole of the planet and to reach every nook and cranny, however remote and sheltered. 'Global figuration' means the ubiquity of 'butterfly effects': the consequences of a thoroughly local event may well reverberate throughout the planet. Actions, as before, have local (and local-izable) origins, but now they have also global repercussions: it is only at their own peril that the actors fail to reckon with factors remote from the locality in which their own actions have been begotten and in which their designs are inscribed. What 'globality' does *not* mean, however (thus far at any rate), is the emergence or the imminence of a comparable global totality in other dimensions of human existence, notably political and cultural. On the con-trary, the 'incompleteness', the one-dimensionality of the global figuration, the absence of the overlapping/complementing/integrating political and cul-tural networks of a matching size and potency is the most prominent, and perhaps the most consequential, trait of 'globality'. In his widely debated article for *Die Zeit* of 16 April 1999, dedicated to the NATO decision to bomb Yugoslavia, Jürgen Habermas pointed out that, in the absence of any binding and authoritative code of 'global law', actors can only refer to their utterly subjective and so inherently questionable intuitions of what is a proper way to act and react to other actors' actions.

There may be something like a global trade-and-finance system in the making, but there are few if any signs of anything approximating a global political, legal, military or cultural system. It may be argued that this striking imbalance is a question of time-lag or 'relative retardation' of the global 'superstructure', but equally strong or stronger arguments can be advanced for the supposition that the imbalance or the absence of coordination in question is an integral and potentially permanent feature of globality – at least in its current economy-led, and thus far the only known and practised, form.

In the 'solid stage' of modernity the actions classified as 'economic' took place inside the political and cultural cocoon of the nation-state, simultaneously a greenhouse and an internment camp. All the factors of economic activity having been similarly confined, 'solid modernity' was an era of *mutual* dependency, mutual engagement, production and servicing of *mutually* binding and durable bonds. The defining trait of 'liquid modernity' is, on the contrary, *dis*-engagement. It is a time when economics, or rather its driving and propulsive forces, break free from the (obligingly dismantled from inside) carapace of politics and culture and accelerate beyond the slowing-down, let alone the catching-up capacity of state institutions (to use Manuel Castells's apt expression – new global powers flow away from politics which remains as grounded and territorially confined as before). Modernity started from the disengagement and separation of business from the household (and so, obliquely, the emancipation of business from ethical constraints). It has led to the disengagement and separation of business from the nation-state (and so, obliquely, to the emancipation of business from political constraints).

On politics, this latest development is making an impact the extent of which we are only beginning to assess, searching for a conceptual net in which new realities could be caught to be adequately examined. Most of the concepts inherited from the times of 'solid modernity' conceal more than they reveal of the new arrangement and delay noticing what is truly novel and fast-growing in importance. Particularly prominent among such concepts is that of power. Central to political science and the sociological study of politics, the concept of 'power' had been from the start of the modern era 'state-oriented', made to the measure of 'affairs of state'. Its uses in the modelling of areas of life other than those administered by the state had a metaphorical character: the birth-marks of the concepts were difficult, perhaps impossible to erase, whatever their uses. The umbilical cord which tied the idea of power to such inalienable attributes of the state as (territorial) sovereignty, domination, coercion and enforcement, the expectation of discipline and pattern promotion, protection and maintenance, was never cut. With whatever qualifier it has been supplemented and to whatever area of human cohabitation it was applied, the idea of power tacitly assumed a close and unbreakable *engagement* between the sides: between the dominant and dominated, the rulers and the ruled, the governing and the governed, administrators and the administered, managers and the managed – all tied fast together for better or worse in a durable and non-negotiable bond of mutual dependency (permanent in its intention, if not in fact).

It is precisely that assumption of lasting mutual dependency that can no longer be credibly upheld. The power flowing in the liquid-modernity global network has got rid of the ballast of durable bonds and commitments. Coercion need not be therefore its principal resource – nor does the drive towards monopoly of the means of coercion need to be its principal stratagem. Power is measured these days by the agent's ability to break the bond, to escape dependency unilaterally. As the engagements become fragmentary and episodic, the agents who are free to move away from the confrontation and shed the commitments of which their bond had been woven move to the dominant side of power-relationship; and the agents incapable of holding their partners-in-engagement in place, and arresting or at least slowing down their movements, drop and settle on the dominated pole.

Domination now has no need of coercion and would gladly do without it, since coercion, as much as the responsible and thus cumbersome cares of wardenship, calls for engagement – and engagement means *constraint on mobility*. It is the fragility of bonds, their in-built transience and 'until-further-noticeness', coupled with temporariness of commitment and revocability of obligations, that constitutes the new frame (if perpetual frame-breaking can be called a frame) of power-relationships. Once the mobility and evasiveness of some cast the rest into a position of acute and disabling uncertainty, the expectation of submission and obedience need not rest on surveillance, disciplining drill or ideological indoctrination. The new power hierarchy is built of speed and slowness, of freedom to move and immobility. At stake in the power struggles is the liberty of one's own movements, coupled with the constraints imposed on the movements of others. Among the most coveted spoils of victory is enhanced mobility, protected by 'slowing down' capacity.

The power hierarchy is steep and is a site of continuous and permanently inconclusive combat. The distinctive mark of liquid modernity is, so to speak, continuous 'disembedding' with little prospect of reliable 're-embedding'; extant frames go on being dismantled but are no longer replaced by 'new and improved ones', since fluid power relations are seldom durable enough to solidify into institutional frames and since a fluid *modus vivendi* hardly ever emerges from the tug-of-war stage for a time-span long enough to ossify into habitual routines.

In the absence of institutionalized frames and with powers-that-be lukewarm at best, but more often than not hostile to their re-assembly and instead bent on further de-regulation, the boundary between coercion (that is legitimate, read: habitualized, violence) and violence (to wit illegitimate, read: contingent, coercion) cannot but be hotly contested. The redrawing of this boundary is the object of ubiquitous 'reconnaissance skirmishes' whose aim is to find out how far one can move and how much ground one can capture with no fear of a potent counter-attack, or how much punishment the other side will take without responding in kind.

Boundaries are as fluid as the power-balances whose projections they are. No wonder that liquid-modern society is a vast theatre of boundary wars – the battleground of endless 'reconnaissance skirmishes'. As in the case of Wagner's endless melody or Derrida's infinite deconstruction, there is no plausible finishing line to this kind of 'bargaining through trial of strength': each successful challenge throws open new battlegrounds and prompts further challenges.

It was one of the more salient characteristics of modernity in its 'solid' stage to visualize an a priori limit to order-building endeavours – be it an ideal model of stable economy, a fully equilibrated system, a just society or a code of rational law and ethics. Liquid modernity, on the other hand, sets the forces of change free to 'find their own level' after the pattern of the stock exchange or financial markets, and then go on seeking better or more suitable levels, never accepting any of the (by definition interim) levels as final and irrevocable. True to the spirit of that fateful transformation, the model of 'social justice' as the ultimate horizon of trial-and-error sequence has been all but abandoned in favour of the 'human rights' rule/standard/ measure to guide the never-ending experimentation with satisfying and/or acceptable forms of cohabitation. If models of 'social justice' struggled to be substantive and comprehensive, the human rights principle cannot but stay formal and open-ended. The sole substance of that principle is a standing invitation to register claims and to bid for the claims' recognition. The question of which one of the rights, and of which of the many groups or categories of humans, has been (wrongly) overlooked, neglected, refused recognition or insufficiently catered for, is not and cannot be pre-empted or decided in advance. The set of possible answers to that question is in principle infinite, and the choice of answers is always open to renegotiation: in practice, to 'reconnaissance battles'. With all its universalistic ambitions, the practical consequence of the 'human rights' appeal for the claims of recognition is a perpetual differentiation and divisiveness.

As Jonathan Friedman (1999) suggested, we have been landed now with modernity without modernism: a passion for transgression without a clear vision of ultimate purpose and destination. More than that has changed, though: the new global power elite, exterritorial and uninterested in 'engagement on the ground' or downright resentful of it, particularly of a till-death-us-do-part sort of engagement, no longer entertains the ambition to design order nor has much taste for order-administration and day-to-day management. The projects of 'high civilization, high culture, high science', converging and unifying in their intention if not in practice, are no longer in fashion, and those cropping up occasionally are not treated differently from sci-fi products, are cherished mostly for their entertainment value and on the whole muster no more than fleeting interest. To quote Friedman once more: 'In the decline of modernism . . . what is left is simply difference itself and its accumulation.' '[O]ne of the things that is not happening is that boundaries are disappearing. Rather, they seem to be erected on every new street corner of every declining neighbourhood of our world' (1999: 239, 241).

It is in the nature of 'human rights' that although they are meant to be enjoyed *separately* (they mean, after all, the entitlement to have one's own difference recognized and so to remain different without fear of reprimand or punishment), they have to be fought for and won *collectively*, and only collectively can they be granted. Hence the zeal for 'boundary erecting': in order to become a 'right', a difference needs to be shared by a group or a category of individuals and so become a stake in collective vindications. The fight for and the apportionment of individual rights result in intense community-building – digging trenches and training and arming assault units. Being different becomes a value in its own right, a quality worth fighting for and preserving at all costs, and a clarion call to enlist, to close ranks and to march in step. First, however, the difference must be *recognized*: more exactly, a difference must be found or construed fit to be acknowledged as an entitlement to claims under the 'human rights' rubric. For all these reasons, the principle of 'human rights' is a catalyst triggering production and self-perpetuation of difference.

When human rights replace the project of a good society and social justice as the last-resort attempt to find a guiding principle of human co-existence, in a world that no longer holds the promise of domesticating contingency and taming spontaneity – an environment is created that is hospitable and fertile for the intense production of difference. As Eric Hobsbawm observed, 'never was the word "community" used more indiscriminately and emptily than in the decades when communities in the sociological sense became hard to find in real life' (1994: 428); 'Men and women look for groups to which they can belong, certainly and forever, in a world in which all else is moving and shifting, in which nothing else is certain' (Hobsbawm, 1996: 40). Jock Young supplies a succinct and poignant gloss: 'Just as community collapses, identity is invented' (1999: 164). Another gloss is called for, however: 'identity' is the community's posthumous life – the ghost of the deceased community; but it is also a potent tool in the hard labour of the 'invention of community' masquerading as community-resurrection.

Commenting on Søren Kierkegaard's proto-psychoanalytical call to 'destroy the self' for the sake of freedom to race up to the complex reality of existence, Ernest Becker compared 'identity' to a painstakingly built prison mistaken for a shelter. Kierkegaard, in Becker's opinion:

> . . . knew how comfortable people were inside the prison of their character defenses. Like many prisoners they are comfortable in their limited and protected routines, and the idea of a parole into the wide world of chance, accident and choice terrifies them. . . . In the prison of one's own character one can pretend and feel that he is *somebody*, that the world is manageable, that there is a reason for one's life, a ready justification for one's action. (1997: 86–7)

Writing from the depth of 'solid modernity', Kierkegaard rebelled against imprisonment, rather than objecting to his fellow-citizens pining after self-made prisons. The kind of prisons Kierkegaard saw around survive however today mostly in the form of myth and misdirected nostalgia. Today's prisons – the self-built prisons, the prisons which Becker calls on us to dismantle – are responses to the breakdown of those that used to appal Kierkegaard. Desperate and passionate these responses may be, but they are bound to be indecisive, inconclusive and in the end self-destructive.

The fragility of identities which – however painstakingly construed and valiantly defended, can never hold as fast as the 'preordained' essences which they earnestly try to emulate, simulate or dissimulate – is one reason for this state of affairs. But there is another reason, more potent than the first. We live, after all, in a time which de-legitimizes all sacrifice of freedom in the name of security, let alone for the sake of a prison-style comfort. The kind of freedom that has been lifted to the rank of the topmost value of liquid modernity means, to quote Christopher Lasch, 'keeping your options open'. Identities need to be fit to 'be adopted and discarded like a change of costume' (Lasch, 1983: 38). Which does not diminish the zeal with which the prisons of identities are coveted and patched together: it only tops up that zeal with seething passions, perpetual suspicion and fits of desperation. The inner incurable contradiction of the project results in an erratic, disjointed conduct which further adds to the confusion and anxiety from which it was meant to provide an escape.

Another escape is therefore needed: this time from the awesome truth that the project of the original escape (as Ulrich Beck put it: of finding biographical solutions to systemic contradictions) has been faulty from the start and will not work. Such an escape is sought, again in vain yet at enormous psychological and social cost, in Jock Young's 'essentialism': the tendency to 'cast difference in an essentialist mould' which is 'always liable to demonization and conflict'. The demonization of others who are blamed for the failure of 'identity project' is difficult to avoid: it is, after all, 'based on the ontological uncertainties of those who would site themselves at the centre stage' (Young, 1999: 148, 165) – and ontological uncertainties are endemic to the 'liquid modernity' condition and removable, if at all, only together with that condition. If solid modernity was an era of the wars of liberation, liquid modernity is the time of the wars of recognition.

Much as one can, after Isaiah Berlin, distinguish between 'negative' and 'positive' freedom, one can speak of *negative* and *positive* recognition of identity (one could have said 'different identity', if not for the fact that 'identity' and 'difference' connote the same concern and strategy and can be interpreted as synonymous notions).

More often than not, negative recognition is what the currently fashionable 'multiculturalist' stance of the new global business-and-information elite boils down to. In Mary Kaldor's words, there is:

> . . . growing cultural dissonance between those who see themselves as part of an international network, whose identity is shaped within a globally linked

and oriented community of people who communicate by e-mail, faxes, telephone, and air travel, and those who still cling to or who have found new types of territorially based identities . . . (1996: 43)

The latter are, first and foremost, the excluded, the disempowered, the 'tied to the ground' and hotly-resented-when-on-the-move populations, confined to their 'home territory' and criminalized when they rebel against their confinement. For such populations, the place they occupy acquires a brand-new significance since (as Joan Cocks explains) that place, unless their sovereign rights to it are recognized, 'cannot be counted on or remain intact' (2000: 46).[2] These are the kind of concerns, however, which the merely negative recognition willingly granted by the global elite would not address.

Negative recognition consists in a 'let it be' stance: you have the right to be what you are and are under no obligation to be someone else, as there will be no pressure to 'acculturate' or 'assimilate': in stark opposition to the era of nation-states building in the times of 'solid' modernity, there will be no cultural crusades, no proselytizing, no missionaries, no demand to convert. Negative recognition may well boil down to the tolerance of the otherness – a posture of indifference and detachment rather than the attitude of sympathetic benevolence or willingness to help: let them be, and bear the consequences of what they are. In such a case, insisting on difference and refusing to compromise may have to be paid for with distributive handicap; in the competitive game for resources and rewards, 'being different' may well prove a liability even if discrimination is formally outlawed.

If this is not a sufficient reason to render the prospect of negative recognition unappetizing and – when granted – unsatisfactory, there is another potent reason why the groups or categories demanding acknowledgement of their separate identity would not easily settle for merely negative recognition: just 'being tolerated' would not endow the identity they claim with the comforting and healing faculties for which it has been desired. The cognitive frame in which tolerance is granted is totally out of tune with the frame in which it is sought and received. Tolerance is granted in the spirit of a (joyfully embraced, or resignedly accepted, as the case may be) *relativism*. Those who grant tolerance consider a way of life different from their own to be a matter not important enough to wage a war for; or suspect that the war is lost before it has been started or too costly to undertake. For one reason or another, they 'agree to disagree' – yet their agreement more often than not is unilateral (a contradiction in terms, as agreements go) and so the truce is likely to be observed by one side only. The act of tolerance diminishes, instead of magnifying, the identity's importance which for the fighters for recognition was the most precious and avidly desired stake of the struggle – the prime cause of going to war. Since the tolerant are (as Nicholas Lobkowitz [1999: 173–7] convincingly argued), overtly or implicitly, relativists – the gift they offer to the seekers of recognition is tainted – unattractive and so unwanted.[3] Unlike the tolerance-givers, the seekers of recognition are, outspokenly or covertly, essentialists or fundamentalists:

whatever formula they may use to match the prevailing mood and so to serve better their cause (paying lip-service to the principle of equality in particular), the difference for which they seek recognition is not one of many, equal among equals – but a quality not just precious in its own right but endowed with a unique value which other forms of life lack: perhaps even superior to such forms of life as could be adopted without worry about their recognition and so would not raise the issue of recognition were the carriers of difference allowed, able and willing, to practise it matter-of-factly. Only a difference endowed with such a status would fit the bill issued to the postulated identity.

Only *positive* recognition is therefore on a par with the purpose of war: only positive recognition may insure the seekers of recognition against the unduly high costs of staying different, and only positive recognition can endorse the intrinsic value of the difference and thus sustain the dignity which it bestows on its bearers. Positive recognition, it is hoped, will fulfil both these ends (and so re-forge the liabilities into assets) through tying the postulate of recognition to *distributive* justice. 'Positive recognition', unlike negative recognition, augurs 'positive discrimination', 'affirmative action' and subsidizing the cultivation of identity; in short, an entitlement to preferential treatment and to the award of extra points on the ground of being different from the rest. Distributive justice is the natural sequel of the war of recognition; the second is incomplete until it finds fulfilment in the first.

Nancy Fraser was therefore right when she complained about 'widespread decoupling of the cultural politics of difference from the social politics of equality' and insisted that 'justice today requires *both* redistribution and recognition' (1999).

> It is unjust that some individuals and groups are denied the status of full partners in social interaction simply as a consequence of institutionalized patterns of cultural value in whose construction they have not equally participated and which disparage their distinctive characteristics or the distinctive characteristics assigned to them.

I have indicated before that the logic of the war of recognition presses the combatants to absolutize the difference: it is difficult to eradicate the 'fundamentalist' streak in any claim which makes recognition demands, in Fraser's terminology, 'sectarian'. Placing the issue of recognition in the frame of social justice, instead of the context of 'self-realization' (where, for instance, Charles Taylor or Axel Honneth prefers to put it) has a de-toxicating effect: it removes the poison of sectarianism (with all its unprepossessing consequences like social separation, communication break-down and self-perpetuating hostilities) from the sting of recognition claims. It also stops the recognition of difference just on the edge of the relativist precipice. If recognition is defined as the right to equal participation in social interaction, and if that right is conceived in its turn as a matter of social justice, then it does not follow (to quote Fraser once more) that 'everyone has an equal right to social esteem' (that, in other words, all values are equal and each difference is worthy just because of being different), but only that 'everybody has an equal right to pursue social esteem under fair conditions of equal opportunity'. Cast in the framework of self-assertion and 'self-realization' and allowed to stay there, recognition wars lay bare their agonistic (as the recent experience has confirmed, ultimately genocidal) potential; if returned to the problematics of social justice where they belong, recognition claims and the policy of recognition turn into a recipe for dialogue and democratic participation.

All this, I suggest, is not a question of philosophical hair-splitting, nor is it just philosophical elegance or theorizing convenience that are here at stake. The blend of distributive justice and the policy of recognition is, one may say, a natural sequel to the modern promise of social justice under conditions of 'liquid modernity' or, as Jonathan Friedman put it, 'modernity without modernism', which is, as Bruno Latour suggests, the era of reconciliation to the prospect of perpetual coexistence and so a condition which, more than anything else, needs the art of peaceful and humane cohabitation; an era which no longer can (or would wish to) entertain hope of a radical one-fell-swoop eradication of human misery followed by a conflict-free and suffering-free human condition. If the idea of 'good society' is to retain meaning in the liquid-modernity setting, it may only mean a society concerned with 'giving everyone a chance' and removing all impediments to taking that chance up one by one, as obstacles are revealed and brought to attention by successive recognition claims. Not every difference has the same value, and some ways of life and of living together have superiority over others – but there is no way to find out which is which unless each one is given equal opportunity to argue and prove its case.

Richard Rorty hails the passage from 'movement politics' to 'campaign politics'. The first (a characteristic mark, let me add, of 'solid modernity' bent on replacing melted solids with solids that would not melt) is needed to provide a large context within which politics is no longer just politics, but rather the matrix out of which will emerge something like Paul's 'new being in Christ' or Mao's 'new socialist man' . . . This kind of politics assumes that things will be changed utterly, that 'a terrible new beauty will be born'. .

In 'movement politics', not just its ultimate purpose but the sole criterion to measure the propriety of each current move lies far ahead and permanently beyond reach – in the unknown or rather unknowable future, that is Emmanuel Levinas's 'absolute Other'. For this reason, movement politics is immune to reality testing and so unable to self-correct, but is exquisitely capable instead of multiplying present miseries in the name of the happiness to come (closer to our point – to refuse, and in good conscience, to give voice to, let alone recognize the legitimacy of such claims as have no place in the perfect world yet to come). On the other hand, a 'campaign' is 'something finite, something that can be recognized to have succeeded or to have, so far, failed'. Thanks to being finite, campaign politics is conscious of the need to fight human misery here and now, and to measure its own success or failure by the effects of that fight.

> Campaigns for such goals as the unionization of migrant farm workers, or the overthrow (by votes or by force) of a corrupt government, or socialized medicine, or legal recognition of gay marriage can be conducted without much attention to literature, art, philosophy, or history. (Rorty, 1998a: 114–15)

Let me note that in all specimens of 'campaign politics' listed by Rorty the concerns of recognition politics and distributive justice merge. Through blending them into one no longer divisible whole, campaign politics reflects and brings into the open the shared fate of the battles waged on both fronts: recognition is deceitful or at any rate incomplete unless coupled with distributive corrections, and distributive justice has no chance without the recognition of the right to participate, on an equal footing, in negotiating the mode of existence.

We may conclude that melting together the tasks of distributive justice and the policy of recognition is the meaning of social justice in the present 'liquid-modernity' era, while campaign politics compounding the two is its prime, and perhaps its sole, available strategy.

And obversely: the separation of the politics of recognition from the question of distributive justice – a fashion already widespread and spreading wider yet in the current intellectual debates – delivers a 'double whammy' to the prospects of a humane and peaceful coexistence which is no longer a matter of choice, either in reality or in fantasy.

On one hand, this fashion endorses the present trend to counter *distributive* claims with the all-too-real threat of social reprobation, degradation and 'outcasting', using the allegedly demeaning effect of 'dependency' to justify withdrawal of esteem; on top of the pain inflicted on 'claimants', the censure and deprecation of 'dependency' stokes awesome dangers for the ethical standards of society, since the assumption of the Other's dependency is both the cornerstone and touchstone of all morality.

On the other hand, separating the politics of recognition from the issue of distributive justice, and enclosing it in the frame of self-realization, endorses the new policy consistently pursued by the fast globalizing powers of the 'liquid-modernity' era and carries potentially devastating consequences: the policy of (deliberate) precarization, as Pierre Bourdieu named it – domination attained through, founded on and reinforced by actual or threatened disengagement and the refusal to bear responsibility for its social costs. Cutting off the claims of recognition from their natural distributive consequences makes the granting of recognition as toothless and ineffective as it becomes easy.

The demand for recognition is a claim to humanity and the right to participate in shaping it and enjoying it. Potent forces released by the one-sided globalizing process and aided and abetted by many a current intellectual fashion (notably by much of the 'communitarian' philosophy), conspire to neutralize and defuse that claim by forcing it and encouraging it to be, or re-presenting it as a call 'to be left alone'. The wars of recognition are here to stay. It is the joint task and responsibility of politics and social theory to release their potential as a powerful instrument of justice and humanity, dialogue and cooperation.

The demand for recognition is a bid for full citizenship in a 'global community' not yet in existence, but which is likely to emerge only if that demand is met and honoured. Contrary to the communitarian ideology, the ultimate horizon of the on-going wars of recognition is the promotion of shared humanity, which may only take the form of autonomous individuals able to exercise their autonomy in order to promote and sustain their common property – the autonomous society.

We are still at an enormous distance from that horizon: much needs to be done to bring that horizon any closer. As Michael Lerner and Peter Gabel pointed out recently,

> . . . we were astounded to learn, and after three decades of knowing this still find it difficult to assimilate, that far more people are killed by the ordinary workings of a worldwide system of inequality than were killed by Hitler or Stalin. The reality we don't face is this: every year, over 30 million people starve to death or die of diseases that could have been prevented by providing access to adequate nutrition – while we throw away enough food to feed millions of them. These deaths are the result of what we call 'structural murder', because no one in particular pulls the trigger, but the dead are just as dead. (1999: 10)

I am not sure whether Lerner and Gabel are right when they say that the truth they portray is 'difficult to assimilate'. As a matter of fact, the secret of our triumphant and self-congratulating society celebrating the dawn of the New Millennium as the 'end of history', is the finding of ways to assimilate it without much damage to its balance of mind and without much more than ritual soul-searching and occasional carnivals of charity. If the on-going, year in year out murder which Lerner and Gabel write about can be truly called 'structural', it is because of the accomplishment of the structural feat of separating the question of human rights from the right of humans to participate in joint humanity, and the question of distributive justice from the recognition of difference, and so the choice of forms of life from life's ethical meaning.

As to the conclusion which needs to be drawn, Richard Rorty put it better than I'd be able to express:

> We should raise our children to find it intolerable that we who sit behind desks and punch keyboards are paid ten times as much as people who get their hands dirty cleaning our toilets, and a hundred times as much as those who fabricate our keyboards in the Third World. We should ensure that they worry about the fact that the countries which industrialized first have a hundred times the wealth of those which have not yet industrialized. Our children need

to learn, early on, to see the inequalities between their own fortunes and those of other children as neither the Will of God nor the necessary price of economic efficiency, but as an evitable tragedy. They should start thinking, as early as possible, about how the world might be changed so as to ensure that no one goes hungry while others have a surfeit. (1998b: 203–4)

Which words in the quoted sentences refer to distributive justice, and which to the need for recognition? The power of Rorty's statement, its ethical as well as political potential, stems precisely from the fact that such distinction cannot be easily made.

Notes

1. The concept of 'liquid modernity' has been discussed in my book of the same title (Bauman, 2000).

2. Cocks points out that 'travelling for the pleasure of relaxing while consuming a variety of geographical and cultural contexts, world-tourists prompt the reshaping of places to meet their material expectations, helping to corrode, in the long run, the differentiated landscapes and cultures they supposedly wish to enjoy' (2000). The same applies, in much greater measure yet, to the corrosive impact of the global and exterritorial capitalist market.

3. According to Lobkowitz (1999), the question 'how to be tolerant without succumbing to relativism' is nowadays the most daunting issue democracy has to confront.

References

Bauman, Zygmunt (2000) *Liquid Modernity*. Cambridge: Polity Press.

Becker, Ernest (1997) *The Denial of Death*. New York: Free Press.

Cocks, Joan (2000) 'A New Cosmopolitanism? V.S. Naipaul and Edward Said', *Constellations* 1: 46–61.

Fraser, Nancy (1999) 'Social Justice in the Age of Identity Politics: Redistribution, Recognition, and Participation', in Detlev Claussen and Michael Werz (eds) *Kritische Theorie der Gegenwart*. Hanover: Institut für Soziologie an der Universität Hannover.

Friedman, Jonathan (1999) 'The Hybridization of Roots and the Abhorrence of the Bush', in Mike Featherstone and Scott Lash (eds) *Spaces of Culture: City–Nation–World*. London: Sage.

Hobsbawm, Eric (1994) *The Age of Extremes*. London: Michael Joseph.

Hobsbawm, Eric (1996) 'The Cult of Identity Politics', *New Left Review* 217: 40.

Kaldor, Mary (1996) 'Cosmopolitanism vs. Nationalism: The New Divide?', in Richard Caplan and John Feffer (eds) *Europe's New Nationalism*. Oxford: Oxford University Press.

Lasch, Christopher (1983) *The Minimal Self: Psychic Survival in Troubled Times*. London: Pan Books.

Latour, Bruno (1998) 'Ein Ding ist ein Thing', *Concepts and Transformations* 1–2: 97–111.

Lerner, Michael and Peter Gabel (1999) 'Why we're Hopeful about the New Millennium', *Tikkun* November/December: 10.

Lobkowitz, Nicholas (1999) 'Remarks on Tolerance', in Jiři Fukač, Zdeněk, Chlup, Alena Mizerova and Alena Schauerova (eds) *Crossroads of European Culture 1999: Responsibilities and Hopes*. Brno: Vitium Press.

Rorty, Richard (1998a) 'Movements and Campaigns', in *Achieving Our Country: Leftist Thought in Twentieth-Century America*. Cambridge, MA: Harvard University Press.

Rorty, Richard (1998b) 'Failed Prophets, Glorious Hopes', in *Philosophy and Social Hope*. Harmondsworth: Penguin.

Young, Jock (1999) *The Exclusive Society*. London: Sage.

Zygmunt Bauman is Professor Emeritus of Universities of Leeds and Warsaw. Latest publications: *Individualised Society and Community: Seeking Safety in an Uncertain World* (2001).

Joined-up Politics and Postcolonial Melancholia

Paul Gilroy

WRITING AT the dawn of the Cold War, George Orwell likened the predicament of socialists to the position of a doctor struggling against the odds to keep a 'hopeless case' alive. More than 20 years beyond the finest flowering of this country's anti-racist youth movements, its residual anti-racists have grown accustomed to similar feelings of obligation, determination, constraint and misplaced hope. This consideration of the diversification and transformation of our country must begin by honouring those who, like the Lawrence family[1] and their core support, have struggled for so long to make Britain a freer, more just and more humane place. I would like to communicate respect and appreciation for those brave and diligent people who have worked in climates of hatred, ridicule and indifference to try and make what we used to call 'anti-racism' part of the process of calculation engaged in by governments, markets and other social institutions. I feel that we value them and their half-hidden and often disreputable traditions of political action most effectively at this point, by moving firmly against the recent but nonetheless mythical notion that Britain has sorted out the discrete issues of 'race' and ethnicity in an exemplary manner and is now a wholly successful multicultural society to which the rest of Europe can turn for inspiration and guidance. That view is tempting. It has a certain superficial plausibility, but we must be cautious about buying into it. It is attractive above all because it suggests that there is nothing else to be done. The hard work is in the past. From this angle, the belated official response to the murder of Stephen Lawrence and the institutional failures that compounded that tragedy provide solid proof of an irreversible commitment to taking racism out of our civic culture. This convenient view fits easily into the idea that widespread shame at the failures of our police and courts has made some degree of opposition to racism an essential component in the

■ *Theory, Culture & Society* 2001 (SAGE, London, Thousand Oaks and New Delhi),
Vol. 18(2–3): 151–167
[0263-2764(200104/06)18:2–3;151–167;017482]

cathartic redefinition of British decency we have just witnessed – a historic triumph which may in due course be claimed for the tattered regimental honours of New Labour.

In contrast to that mistaken approach, I want to suggest that a great deal more hard work lies ahead. This apprehension also obliges me to say unambiguously that, especially when seen through the blood-stained frame of racialized politics, New Labour's postcolonial Britain is in a precarious, divided and volatile condition. Everything is not all right. Social inequalities may be decreasing but economic inequality is growing. The politics of 'race' is inescapably intertwined with them both. Better tests of Britain's cultural diversity will materialize when economic conditions are worse than they are now.

The great tide of sympathy for the Lawrence family suggests that some denizens of Middle England have turned away from the sly, self-effacing but always statesmanlike, populist race-talk of Enoch Powell[2] and his many followers, but that historic opportunity has not been seized upon by New Labour and identified as a powerful means to communicate their 'modernizing' break with that unsavoury past. We need to consider exactly why it is William and Ffion[3] rather than Tony and Cherie[4] who felt they had something to gain by demonstrating their command of the postcolonial art of jumping up in the Grove. The role of Paul Dacre's *Daily Mail*[5] in the Lawrence case confirms that the Tories know something about the political calculus of 'race' and gender that Millbank[6] is still waiting to learn. Our rulers appear to be caught between one world, where the idea that Britain has nurtured relatively peaceful encounters with difference is a minor political asset, and another more important one where being tough on immigrants of all types affords them real political advantages. The media narration of the Lawrences' tragedy demonstrated a reversal of the comforting Powellite scenario in which feral black youth preyed on frail, vulnerable and aged inner-city whites. But where the vestiges of Powell's construction persist, contact with aliens, blacks and any other outsiders can represent only the decline of the United Kingdom and the debasement of time-worn British identity. As you know, that noble history is already being sullied and undone by the corrosive influence of immigrants and the malign activities of stealthy foreigners hell-bent on seizing that critical element of Britain's deepest identities: its currency.

Whatever the spin doctors and public relations people currently suggest, 'diversity' is one area in which Tonyism is loathe to take risks and follow the race-shedding cues offered by the globalizing corporate world to which it usually defers. The problems articulated around 'race', culture and plurality are not amenable to being solved on a once-and-for-all basis. They cannot be divorced from widespread anxieties over nationality and the integrity of national culture under pressure from globalization and transnationalism. They cannot be placed in cold storage by a grand governmental gesture, nor can they be left quietly to sort themselves out under the benevolent eye of a beefed up CRE,[7] until the next shocking revelation comes along to trigger some new spiralling plunge into the depths of amnesia. This very indeterminacy suggests that nothing much can be done. There will always be a more urgent reason to avoid any risk to Labour's electoral apple-cart. Tony may walk on water but even he and Clare Short[8] cannot bring Joy Gardner[9] and the rest back from the dead.

In pointing out these difficulties I am not making the romantic argument that racial identification enjoys an ontic, primordial or spiritual character that resists political initiatives. I want to emphasize that consistent, wholehearted and serious governmental solutions have not been attempted. If things are to improve, if the body-count is to decline, and the legacy of compounded injustice diminish, then the conflicts and hurt that racism creates have to be articulated as political problems and brought fully into the formal language and rationality of political and judicial processes. There are obvious difficulties in securing that outcome, particularly where racialized inequalities are exceptionally recognized as matters of minority concern but are not thought to be sufficiently important to merit sustained attention. The power of race-thinking to divide, destroy and distort constitutes one dense layer of conflicts, the characteristic patterns of refusal and denial that surround it in British political life present substantial problems of a rather different order. Recognizing this double task suggests that making 'race' political *enough* is a far larger task than it may initially appear to be. It is certainly more difficult than many well-intentioned people would like. Just appreciating the scale of that democratic commitment is an important first step. The refusal to concede its dimensions can be interpreted as a recurrent effect of an underlying malaise that resides in the distinctive combination of two closely aligned responses: the inability to take racism seriously and an iron-jawed disinclination to recognize the equal human worth and dignity of people who are not 'white'.

That precious 'whiteness' should not be reified either and may yet have important implications for the future of Europe. So far there is no consensus about its ethnic or cultural contents. The idea of purity, with which it has been associated, requires and creates a void – a blank, bleached space. No actually existing culture can possibly measure up to the impossible standards of perfection that this racializing discourse demands. The same void makes anxious folk vulnerable to the appeal of a casual, normative, white supremacism that conceals and negotiates its own disappointments and discomforts by endlessly holding off the moment in which it has to confront its own strange reflection. To keep that critical, edgy encounter between perfect, abstract whiteness and empirical 'white trash' at bay, white supremacism promotes the colour-coded concepts of national belonging that can cancel all premature celebrations of the cool multiculturalism that is yet to come. Today, the notable sporting achievements of Linford, Lennox, Incey and Denise Lewis[10] notwithstanding, to be recognized as belonging means being just like those decaying chalk cliffs which we are told met the anxious gaze of the invader in this country's finest hours. It is to be immobile, silent, apparently unchanging and blankly, blindness-inducingly, white. Whatever,

the actual ecology of that great symbolic fortification – reported recently to be
slowly turning yellow much to the disgust of more metaphysically patriotic
locals – its frontier refers us to stories of our nation at war. Heroic tales of
danger, fraternity and enhanced self-understanding are everywhere as
comedy, tragedy, sport, news and politics. They are repeatedly invoked not
only because they still construct immigration as another invasive military
campaign but because of an enduring capacity to isolate and exclude aliens
and, in doing so, to produce the pleasures of an impossibly unanimous nation
in all its imaginary simplicity. These militaristic operations tap into the
murkiest layers of the English vernacular. The masculinist 'two world wars
and one world cup' mentality they celebrate is, of course, also absolutely
incompatible with all notions of cultural diversity, however meek, mild and
piously Christian they might aspire to be. In a sense, then, when it comes to
'race' and nation, we have grown used to living under martial rules. Until
that cultural and psychological complex begins to shift, nothing else will be
able to change.

The choice posed by Enoch Powell's death was a pivotal moment: an
early chance to examine New Labour's determination to practise what they
call joined-up politics. They passed that test at no discernible cost.[11] Perry
Worsthorne's[12] apology for the way that he had been led astray by the great
man was the first lonely swallow in another British summer that never came.
Still, after those brown faces had been spotted in the crowds weeping over
Diana, few respectable commentators wanted to be seen to be racists, and
that was well before the iconic presence of Stephen Lawrence blazed through
the media heavens and the righteous tenacity of his parents had underlined
Britain's present difficulties. But even after that episode, many voices, inside
and outside the bounds of political institutions, were alert to the conspicuous payoff that can follow from manipulating the tacit, race-friendly and
race-producing codes of Brit nationalism. Those cynical operations can still
conjure racialized sentiments into logic-defying life and they nurture several
distinctly unwholesome desires. They feed an old bipartisan yearning to
keep the idea of 'race' away from the centre of political calculation and are
equally determined to see those rare moments when the damage done by
race-thinking to British law, morality and politics becomes apparent, not just
as embarrassing, but as useless, unproductive and unhealthy. Rather than
being actively claimed and then used to build up and enhance our flagging
democracy, these unsought opportunities must be closed down as quickly as
possible lest they distract proper political sentiment and divert precious
political resources towards ignoble and unworthy goals.

This is the influential current in which the eloquent immigrant voice
of Michael Ignatieff has been raised. He says that there are important
political and ethical points at stake in his obstinate refusal to acknowledge
the power of racism to distort and corrode democratic social and civic interaction. These days, Ignatieff speaks in the name of 'liberal realism' seemingly from somewhere inside the trouser turn-ups of the late Isaiah Berlin.
The blank refusal distilled in Ignatieff's recent warning: 'If racism is in the

eye of the beholder, we will never be finished with it', is itself a revealing gesture, and was not born from the author's impatience at the wretched speed at which a race-less world is emerging. It was designed, apparently, to relay stern instructions to the mouthy, justice-seeking minorities who, Ignatieff believes, 'often inhabit unfathomably different universes': stop whinging, he tells them, straighten up and fly right, or it's back to your unfathomably different universes you must go.

In his response to the Macpherson report, Ignatieff (1999) presented police incompetence and police racism as mutually exclusive alternative explanations of the wrongs suffered by the Lawrence family. There was no sense that racism had to be addressed specifically as an aspect of the injustice he claims to abhor, no understanding that after all the deaths in custody, all the choke holds, the sticky tape, the forced deportations and the contemptuous, dismissive official silences, it might be worth taking the patterned indifference that would deny blacks full humanity, seriously at all. For him, the guilty and wrong-headed developments associated with anti-racist training are unwelcome because they tune citizens in to the wrong channels of their civic identities. They make the easily influenced over-sensitive to the spurious claims of differentiation. Britain's ageing institutions may need to be reformed in this area but the truly modern answer to any race-based discrimination is to *train* state servants to treat those they interact with as sovereign interchangeable individuals rather than representatives of any larger collective groups. Why this has not happened already does not need to be considered. Rejoice, we have the technology. Politics can either be safely renounced because it doesn't apply in this zone or re-directed towards other more profitable areas of intervention. Ultimately, the grey poetry management-speak takes over.

The path identified by Ignatieff in his role as Witchfinder General to Britain's B52 liberals has been followed to the snowy peaks of Uncle Enoch's Shangri-La by a number of others. The dust in Old Compton Street[13] had barely settled before Ros Coward entered the lists as a would-be champion of the 'ordinary' British people who react against minorities with violence because they, like her, are inclined to see Britain's ethnic populations as being privileged rather than discriminated against. For these two rather desperate but usefully typical refugees from the debris of the Left, all politically correct remedies against discriminatory attitudes and behaviour are worse than the unavoidable ailments at which they have been aimed. Misguided reforming initiatives prompted by the purveyors of 'identity politics' supply conclusive proof that the world has been turned upside down, not so much by the racists and homophobes but by the alien interlopers whose impossible demands to be recognized if not more actively tolerated, have triggered the reasonable and comprehensible antipathy of their hosts.

Coward's blame-the-victim utopia was an especially strange place in which Britain's minorities were required, in fact, not to be minorities at all and where, if we are to avoid the all-too-understandable violence directed at us by ordinary British folk, we must learn to be confident in the power of the phantom presence she blithely labels 'the shared values of the majority'. Minimal exposure to one of Ali G's[14] great ethnographic expeditions into darkest England is sufficient to detonate the anachronistic assumptions there. It is not only that any shared values are no longer binding but that the absence of cultural mortar from the national necropolis is a significant source of amusement and pleasure for as many people as it alarms. The sharp divisions exposed not only by responses to the Lawrence case but by a whole sequence of other profound political conflicts over hunting, say, the monarchy or recreational drug use, should surely have undermined the resort to such simplistic formulae, but no, Coward went on to blame the fallout from Macpherson's enquiry for producing the bad responses involved in her unsatisfactory experiences at the local swimming pool. My perspective, the precise inversion of hers, would argue that it is only episodes like the Lawrence family's tragedy that make this nation's dwindling fund of common values momentarily apparent.

Though the news evidently couldn't reach Coward in her suburban eyrie, under the exceptional conditions that followed the publication of Macpherson's strategically overpriced report, most liberals and some conservatives could agree with the hitherto contentious proposition that 'race' is an unhelpful fiction best set aside and kept out of respectable politics. However, their minimal sense of what that extensive task involves often undermined their good intentions. They make the Herculean labours involved in purging race-thinking from Britain's body-politic appear too easy, quick and straightforward. There is a real danger that this critical insight could be abused. The argument runs like this: if we agree that 'race' doesn't exist, then why do we still need special arrangements to address its consequences? In the practical terms now favoured by government, this stance would mean that police anti-racism, and any other forms of special intervention designed to de-legitimize prejudice, make temporary restitution or promote equality of opportunity, can quite reasonably be done away with. This is something that figures like Ignatieff and Coward seem prepared to flirt with when they endorse the idea that 'special pleading for minorities actually confers advantages that "ordinary" people don't have'. That chorus is set to grow and it must be answered with a tactical emphasis not on 'race' but on the lore and relations of inequality that bring it to life.

These depressing arguments have not as yet won the ear of government but it's easy to see how they will eventually provide an obvious get-out from the conceits of misplaced governmental efforts at social engineering. Their complacency has been rather unsystematically denounced by the voices of a second, broadly differentiated constituency. Affiliates of this group may not agree over what to do about it, but they share a sense that racialized difference and the violence that flows from it have to be recognized as something substantive. This group encompasses those who bravely argue that encounters with difference can be enriching and see diversity as constitutive of society. It also includes some voices from defensively minded community-based organizations which, in their efforts to take the destructive impact of race-thinking seriously, have sometimes become too comfortable with the cheap and automatic solidarity offered by ethnic absolutism. When their ultra-nationalist, fraternalist and occult antics get out of hand, it's worth remembering that Britain's black communities have repeatedly turned away from all attempts to articulate their miseries as part of a separatist political agenda. For a whole host of demographic and historical reasons, their battles over identity, religion and ethnic tradition have been more intensely conducted in the hidden spheres of home, family and interpersonal relations. At the moment, their fledgling fundamentalisms are essentially private matters. As far as public and political conduct goes, for decades now, they have usually been inclined to engage the 'host' society with the greatest possible patience and politeness, seeking colour-blind justice in more than their own immediate interests at a time when most people in this country give little thought to its enhancement. Remember too that monolingualism is not their norm. Specific grievances have been patiently translated into local and regional idioms. There have been no riotous protests in the name of Stephen Lawrence. Britain's struggles for civil liberties and judicial and constitutional reform are both heavily indebted to long-standing minority efforts, which have been built through a moral economy and with a political rhetoric that project community as more than a spatial concentration of strange or different people. Ignatieff boasts provocatively and dismissively that Britain's black community is an entirely fictional entity, however this second group sees that fragile counterpower springing to life intermittently, not necessarily as some essential collective but as a transitional but nonetheless effective, political and moral response to repeated wrongs. It is understood by many of them as a practical example of the responsible democratic activity proper to a citizenship more authentic than anything they knew in the officially forgotten days of the colour bar, the paki-bashers, the skinheads and those 'virginity tests' in Heathrow airport. Like all that shocking black grief over Diana, the conspicuous dignity of the Lawrences is only really a surprise if you are used to imagining black people as hyper-emotional, child/savages. The vivid associational life of the community in which they stand has been constituted from its contemporary mobilizations as much as any ethnic inheritance. That black community emerges in seeking justice as an interpretative community and a community that, in recognition of its internal differentiation and its transient status as an effect of prejudice and discrimination, sometimes even looks forward to its own abolition. The language of community should be welcomed rather than disparaged; historians will eventually note that the conflicts in which it has circulated have functioned to integrate immigrant people and their descendants almost exactly as the political theory of procedural liberalism would anticipate that it should.

This second group can be both liberal and not so liberal. Where it becomes explicitly anti-racist, its members have been drawn into a loose coalition because they can discover no significant compromise of civic or democratic principles arising from the suggestion that the workings of racism, past and present, might be acknowledged as an important public issue by government and its agencies. For many on this side of Ignatieff's Alamo-style line in the dust, the abstract universality so beloved of liberals who will not concede the destructive transnational power of race-thinking, has had to be set aside because it has proved to be an insufficient cloak against bullets, bombs and blades. On this side of the street, individuals are more likely to be seen as culturally specific though not always as culture-bound. Here, it is easier to appreciate that though people can mould their 'ethnicity' more than they sometimes like to admit, there are no good reasons why it should be driven from the public realm to seek its only legitimate expressions in private.

I want to speak now as an anti-racist and as anti-anti-racist simultaneously. I confess that I share a lot of hospitable liberalism's hankering after a race-free world. Unlike them, I favour a planetary rather than a market universalism but I agree that we'd all be better off without reified racial and ethnic categories mystifying the world at a time when our relationship with our own species life is assuming a new and potentially wonderful complexity. It has been good that liberals have queried the easy resort to particularity and interrupted the cheap invocations of incommensurability that have trivialized both political solidarity and the hard work involved in learning once again to translate, listen and evaluate, contrast and compare across the leaky but not insignificant boundaries of discrepant cultures. The anti-racists are right where they have challenged the mistaken view that an undiscriminating, 'universal love of mankind and the world' necessarily involves diminishing the value of love. On the other hand, they have been wrong where their view of pluralism as a motionless mosaic capitulates weakly to the narcissism of minor differences. The difference-mongers have sometimes placed the image of the victim at the heart of political hopes that have been articulated in rather too anthropological terms, but they have made other good points where they have advocated not only an indivisible but an explicitly non-racial justice; where they have drawn attention to the stubborn links between inequality and racialized hierarchy; and where they have defended the presence of other cultures in an expanded and invigorated, cosmopolitan public sphere endowed with new strength as a result of its ability to experience exposure to otherness as more than the danger, stress and loss we're always told it must entail.

It's important to appreciate that just understanding these contrasting responses to the trials of multiculture necessitates a journey to the limits of our available political language. Liberals, civic and ethnic, old, new and neo- are still, after all, liberals, and they can be present on both sides of Ignatieff's fence. Similarly, racial conservatism knows no colour line and, now that socialists are silent on these matters and feminists have been diverted by their own paralysing encounters with the idea of absolute difference, this argument over the status of 'race', nationality and ethnicity can be recognized as a dispute about what liberalism is to be in future. Is it compatible with the recognition of particularity? What forms of tolerance can it endorse? Considering the wrongs involved in race-thinking creates a test of social pluralism as well as a compass with which to locate liberal responses in a rapidly changing political topography.

It should be obvious that the real divisions here are more than simply ideological. They are moral and philosophical. They ask us honestly to address not real or even reified racial differences, coded on or in the body, but the systems of thought that produced and still produce difference as gross inequality and catastrophic violence. The deepest divisions are thus between those who are committed to a lengthy and serious detour through the history of race-thinking's corrosive impact upon the very democratic political traditions that liberals prize without ever taking their compromised character into account, and those who dismiss that terrifying task as trivial, loony or politically correct. Against them I would say that if Britain's fragile democratic resources are to be renewed and extended, their long, complex and deeply ambivalent relation to the idea of 'race' must be brought to light. Only then might the precious idea of universal humanity be plausibly offered back to those who have been excluded from its inner circle on raciological grounds.

The national convulsion which followed the publication of Macpherson's report was not the healing moment that it could have been. The apologies were mostly too easy or grudging, and sometimes they were patently insincere. Frequently, they were offered by the wrong people, exceptional individuals who had themselves been fighting long battles for non-racial justice inside the organizations they were required, on this special occasion, to represent as their in-house proprietors of the race problem. The language employed was often emotional but it was not charged with any moral significance and, for the celebrity apostles of the Third Way, compromised by the traditional habits of an emphatically anti-modern police service, the post-Macpherson spasm amounted to a spot of bad weather that could soon be made to blow over. This rare moment offered plenty of additional proof as to how much Britain's chronic political crisis became and remains intelligible principally as a crisis of national identity, but its patterns of media representation and information were only briefly outside those of the governmental machine. Once the looming figures of predatory White Wolves were replaced by the far less menacing image of a dangerous but isolated eccentric, the work involved in tracing and unravelling the web of associations that linked Tyndal to Tebbitt, Baldwin to Blair, Enoch to the Acourts and Straw to Howard, Hurd and Clarke[15] could be closed down. Any remaining political ground was swiftly ceded to the lawyers who could be left to dispute Macpherson's more contentious recommendations over freedom of information, inquests and the accountability of the Metropolitan Police, many of which were replete with echoes of more radical work done towards the same ends by the GLC Police Committee during the 1980s.[16] Once again, the government's taste for practical solutions turned out to be less than consistent.

A fully independent system for managing complaints against the police is as far away as ever, but there were new departures. In one decisive step beyond the analysis offered by Lord Scarman,[17] getting rid of racism emerged from this episode as a matter of administrative and managerial technique. The idea that 'institutional racism' could have significant implications for how political processes were conducted or understood did not appear to dawn on anybody. Here, again, the populist legacy of Conservative rule was the main intimidating factor. Paul Boateng, his youthful GLC days long forgotten and now eagerly playing a fawning Smithers to the whims of Jack Straw's Monty Burns, was first dispatched to defend Commissioner Condon[18] against the un-joined-up demand that he resign, and then to warn the nation's black muggers and marginals that they would not be able to 'use the Macpherson Report as a cloak for their criminal activities'. He continued: 'Stop and search is there to be used as part of the police's armoury. We expect the police to use it. There's no softly, softly policy there's no hands-off policy. We believe in stop and search . . .'. In this lost world of politics without conflict, division or even debate, the spin doctors are always right. You can have business as usual in the street-level operations of police power but you can also 'use' stop and search 'in a way that attracts the support of the whole community black and white'. The compromised imperatives of sensible, joined-up politics dictate that no one is to be estranged, offended or perturbed, everyone can board this privatized bus to post-political utopia. You can please all of the people all of the time. So much for hard choices.

Power is there to be administered and Middle England will never be inner London. Politics, joined-up or otherwise, eventually yields meekly to the different rules of statecraft. In the key constituencies where control of government will be lost or retained, the British love of playing fair does not currently include recognizing the possibility that blacks can belong. Far better, then, to manage the problem of diversity and inclusivity, theatrically and aesthetically by, for example, putting up Trevor Phillips[19] to be a celebrity mayor, or by gilding the withering boughs of the House of Lords with the delicate blooms represented by a few carefully selected ethnic peerages. Minority business people, mentored and marshalled by Keith Vaz and then cheered on by Lord Taylor of Warwick[20] will supply the incontrovertible proof that this country is, after all modern! Their knee-bending legions are to be the final evidence that Britain really has changed for the better. Under the arc lights, colour turns out to be a critical index after all, and, surprise surprise, the American corporate model is once more decisive. To quote Vaz: 'Bill Clinton showed an acute appreciation of the fact that in the modern world good race relations and good business practice are synonymous'. It's hard to see how this deluded profundity might have helped Stephen Lawrence, but then he seems to have passed outside the present. That wrong resolved, to all intents and purposes, into a financial transaction that provides an uncomfortable alternative to more substantive forms of judicial restitution.

By now we have no excuse not to know that our political culture is being transformed by management technique, celebrity and a host of bad habits drawn from unchecked commerce and rampant corporate life. But how does that big shift impact upon the politics of diversity? Is the best we can hope for the idea that, driven onward by the rhythms of a planetary economy, racial division will wither away and become an ephemeral, insubstantial moment in the operations of regionalized consumer preference? The situation is dominated by the anti-historical fantasies of the advertising people whose creative input sculpted Labour's brand identity and fed their corporate populism. Meanwhile, mass electoral abstention and routine image manipulation tell a different story about the health of British democracy.

According to media legend, Macpherson's biggest achievement was his unanticipated redefinition of institutional racism to include the 'unintentional' in addition to the unwitting and unconscious behaviours previously identified. This, taken together with his timely consumerist emphasis on collective organizational failure, compounded our present difficulties by breathing new life into an anachronistic definition drawn from the wilder backwoods of early-1970s ethnic sociology. His report yields a view of racism as either everywhere equally, mysteriously coating the institutional landscape like an unexpected fall of snow, or as far too closely specified: exclusively concentrated in the bleak environment favoured by Kentish London's criminal shock troops.[21] This utterly false and paralysing choice cannot produce anything helpful. The best response to it relies heavily on the slow and unglamorous labour that can reveal racism to be a persistent factor in political and economic relations, by demonstrating, for example, where the injustice of the judicial system and the incompetence of the police in the Lawrence investigations operated with and through the language and concepts of racial and ethnic division. Sadly, outside the theatres where it has done a roaring trade, this worthwhile alternative is still being dismissed as unthinkable. To follow that path away from Eltham and to carry the same type of analysis into the corridors of Whitehall, the Inner Temple or White City is dismissed defensively as manifestly stupid or, in quieter tones, as a disproportionate reaction. Nobody seems inclined to acknowledge the ways that race-thinking has shaped the wider common assumptions of the political culture – its premium identities, its shifting sense of nationality, its ideas of belonging, of progress, of democracy and, indeed, of history. All of this while the time-reversing, anti-cosmopolitan nail bombs were going off and Hitler was getting reincarnated in the form of 'Slobba'.

The widespread re-appearance and imitation of fascist political styles in various parts of Europe ought to warn us that race-thinking is in transition too. It is being updated to offer certainty and consolation to its anxious adherents and stabilizes their uncomfortable experiences of an accelerating world. It gives them meaning, hope and even love. Where national and ethnic identity are represented raciologically and projected as pure, exposure to difference threatens them with dilution and compromises their prized purities with the ever-present possibility of contamination. Crossing, as mixture and movement, must be guarded against. New hatreds and violence arise not, as they did in the past, from supposedly reliable anthropological knowledge of the identity and difference of the Other, but from the novel problem of not being able to locate the Other's difference in the common-sense lexicon of alterity. Different people are certainly hated and feared, but the timely antipathy against them is nothing compared to the hatreds turned towards the greater menace of the half-different and the partially familiar. To have mixed is to have been party to a great betrayal. Any unsettling traces of hybridity must be excised from the tidy, bleached-out zones of impossibly pure culture.

Our transitional predicament obliges us to try and understand these local preoccupations in their larger historical setting. The disappointing responses to the Lawrence tragedy raise urgent and immediate matters for Britain, but they also represent only one instance of an equally pressing and more general set of difficulties: the wider political and moral crisis being identified in overdeveloped nation-states under the sign of multiculturalism. All the key terms in these debates are blurry and yet the divisions between their protagonists produce unexpectedly strong feelings. In Britain, these currents are so strong and so bitter that there are good grounds to wonder what else is at stake. Whatever the immediate institutional setting – poverty, criminal justice, work and education – the familiar abstractions about multiculture, diversity and plurality become intensely animated. Across Europe these debates are haunted by other histories, usually but not only those that involve colonial guilt and postcolonial shame. The residues of imperial and colonial culture live on wherever 'race' is invoked. Locally, they promote a nostalgia and sanction a violence which ensure that Britain stays paralysed by the inability to really work through the loss of global prestige and the economic and political benefits that once attended it. 'Race', or rather the presence of supposedly alien peoples for which it supplies the cipher, constitutes the visible link to a cultural pathology that is hard to analyse but which reaches nonetheless into the innermost ways in which British society operates. We might tentatively name this ugly formation postcolonial melancholia. It bears repetition that it is not some-thing precipitated by the intrusive presence and unsettling, noisome habits of migrants, their children, their grandchildren or any other permanently strange folk. They have been caught up in it but it preceded their settlement and it is not their problem. It is, at root, the morbid core of England and Englishess in remorseless decline, the same strain that feeds interminable and increasingly desperate speculations about the content and character of the shrinking culture that makes England distinctive.

That observation provides an opportunity to turn towards the idea of culture and the distinctive accents it acquires when brought into the field of national and racialized identity. Taking elementary defensive action against openly belligerent crusaders for ethno-unanimity and essential or absolute difference – whatever 'colour' they may be – should not mean that we overlook the different perils surrounding the insubstantial pluralism which has largely failed to answer their calls to arms. Though that pluralistic mentality may provide assistance in the storms ahead, it is a flimsy formation that suffers in particular from the limited ways in which it conceptualizes culture. During the last 30 years of British political history it has been engaged not so much with the project of assimilation but on the different tasks involved in giving minorities their difference and then expecting them to celebrate it interminably, usually under the beneficent eye of governmental institutions fed by their gratitude. Perhaps that form of official recognition is something we can now do without? The agenda it promotes is problematic, first, because it leaves the position of the majority intact. The hard, moral and political work involved in negotiating the fears of the majority and accommodating their expectations need not even be identified. From this angle, as well, politics is clearly not an issue. Culture, conceived reductively and mechanistically provides an alternative form of solidarity as well as a principle for recognizing, rationalizing and manipulating difference and the various identities it supports. Each warring element of the fixed mosaic totality is projected as separate, entire of itself and sealed off – no civic cement in this model – from the influence of other similar formations which can only be mutually destructive and compromising. Just as they were in the 19th century, the dangers are greatest for those at the top of the heap, for the culture that has the most to lose in its tumble from the top rung of the developmental ladder.

In the postcolonial twilight, to encounter difference produces only jeopardy. In response to that threat, the historic obligation to conserve culture produces a different conservatism: readily racialized, nationalized and now gene biologized under the brittle shells of protective, know-nothing ethnicity. It has acquired many compelling variants. Englishness, Scottishness, Irishness even Welshness can construct the same little parcels of ossified culture equivalent to the steel pans and samosas that were once the synecdochical meltdown of torrid, colonial histories. Culture is now analysed as property rather than process.

That powerful fantasy of how culture operates has some reputable sociological hallmarks. It is nonetheless locked in an inescapable confrontation with the easy, informal and downbeat urban culture that contributed heavily to the climate in which 'Cool Britannia' looked plausible, and which still draws young people from right across Europe towards London. Its postcolonial character means that difference is routine. This otherness is magnetic but need not be exotic. There are still conflicts, but there is also a savvy, agonistic humanism around. It has become vital to the sustenance of metropolitan life and to the confidence of the fragmentary but really cosmopolitan public culture that has established itself in unbleached parts of this city. This precious life-form has crepuscular habits. It rarely emerges into full daylight. It has certainly not been planned or orchestrated from above by visionary municipal thinkers or a modernizing political leadership. It is not amenable to being disciplined, ventriloquized or iconized. If we desire to develop and protect it as a civic asset, we have to be aware that it exists in spite of governmental interventions and is all the more precious because of its profound antipathy towards many of them. We must remember, too, that this surreptitious multiculture is not *always* a prestige object in the economy of governmental signs. It is too disreputable, too spontaneously democratic, too closely associated with youth culture, too hostile both to class hierarchy and to the shiny corporate authority that strives to replace it, for that.

Though I am inclined to be utopian, I am not naive. I know that the joys of shuttling between little Englandism and generic xenophobia have found some of their most enthusiastic practitioners among Britain's young people for whom those endlessly stylish Nazis are German first and Fascist only secondarily, if at all. Nothing here can be taken for granted, but the dissident forms of youth's surreptitious multiculture require that we re-think the habits of the redundant culturalist analysis produced to account for racial and ethnic divisions in the era of Jenkins and Hattersley and scarcely touched since then. Think, for example, of the crude generational and cultural models that govern political and institutional analysis. Their time horizons will hardly stretch beyond two generations. The first, the immigrants, has been succeeded by the second. It is composed of their offspring: younger people caught effectively between the ethno-cultural monolith that shaped their parents and the altogether different body of culture that constitutes the life of the host community into which they are thrown: ill prepared, reviled and disadvantaged both by their own migrant burdens and the explosive antipathy of their English not-quite-peers. Cross-cultural contact is contaminating, tragic and dangerous. The decisive moment in the larger scheme of identity crisis emerges from the lives of the second generation. Right and left, radical and conservative, all endorse variants of this stale script held together only by a disavowed subscription to hidden racial codes. It will make life more difficult in the short term, but we will have to learn not to judge the behaviours of different groups against a spurious characteristic sense of how we think they should be living out their ethnic differences. The politics of diversity, tolerance and recognition is being played out differently at various generational stages. Even when draped in archaic ethnic symbols, modern, protectionist demands for the coherence and integrity of minority groups conflict sharply with the unstoppable postmodern desire to make and play with mutable individuality. That desire to be free and to be free from 'race' and ethnicity can be both destructive and liberating. Understanding this complex context provides a better grasp of its cultural dynamics and its political possibilities. For me, it enhances the value of the libertarian and cosmopolitan forms that have been the finest gifts of Britain's most recent black settlers to their fellow citizens and to the world.

The global selling of black bodies as a prestigious element in the economy of health, sports and fitness industries means that blackness is now largely uncoupled from the theme of immigration which overdetermined it for so long, but the pattern set by bipartisan policies oriented to the twin benefits of restriction and integration endures today in the brutal and unjust regime that keeps asylum seekers and refugees at bay and is, as we have seen, also fortuitously the best means to keep Middle England content. Against the expectations of the rigid two-and-then-three-cultures model,

Britain's black populations are increasingly differentiated culturally, economically, ideologically and politically. If the automatic links between blackness and poverty have been partially broken, most postcolonial settlers do remain both socially excluded and economically marginal. For every hypervisible corporate or entrepreneurial success, there are plenty of other grimmer tales to tell. Racial division is still integral to the workings of schools, courts and markets, and the political goals that follow from imagining a world without racial hierarchies are still being trivialized. Our prisons – until very recently being run by Richard Tilt, someone who thought that his black charges had different necks from the rest of the prison population, and who has now been rewarded with a Knighthood for his pains – are brimming over. Young black and Asian people are shut out from education, harassed in the streets and criminalized with the connivance of the media, eager to initiate celebrations when British multiculture becomes a matter of occasional national festivity, but more or less routinely nostalgic for simpler, easier times, when it was possible to pretend that this was an exclusively white country. That yearning is yet to find a respectable political vehicle, but even in its mute state it still gives real cause for alarm. I hope it is not melodramatic to suggest that a storm is on the way, and that both peace and democracy will be at stake when it breaks.

It is here that we should be prepared to become immersed in the historians' task of periodizing changes to the economic and political institutions of the overdeveloped countries under the impact of the great communicative, technological and scientific revolution that may be bringing the time of nation-states to an end. Brazilianization is not quite the right concept with which to begin the work of enumerating these processes, but it points towards the poorer parts of our planet as places in which significant clues to our own fate may lie. We need to know where the divisive, race-entrenching tendencies, far better described as the South Africanization of our social and economic life, cut into our cities and polities. That investigative, forensic work has so far proved difficult to combine with more abstract considerations of diversity, recognition and difference promoted by the speculative, philosophical writings of Charles Taylor, James Tully, Michael Walzer and company (see for example Walzer, 1997). The more open-ended discussions cannot be abandoned, particularly where they have raised the question of whether non-specific theories of political recognition are an adequate vehicle for the elaboration of what might be termed a principled multiculturalism. Rather than find a conclusion in that direction, I prefer to suggest that, for Britain at least, the turn towards those epochal questions, diversity, recognition and difference, might itself be interpreted as a hopeful sign – something promising that communicates more than the exhaustion of political culture as it has been practised in the past, and the redundancy of many of the theories that purport to explain its postmodern workings. Consolidating that promising shift presupposes not so much the inexorable decay of our immediate political culture, but a longer and more detailed history of 20th-century cultural politics. This was something quite different from both typically ancient and modern definitions of political practice and assumed coherent shape only recently. A disenchanted Walter Benjamin offered a notable early diagnosis of it, based on glimpses of its novel techno-logical bases as well as its links to war, ultra-nationalism and Fascism. His contemporary, Edward Bernays, began to try and systematize it into what he saw as a properly scientific and usable technique for managing the inter-relation of information and power. With their prescient analyses of the aestheticization and theatricalization of politics and commerce in mind, we can perhaps accept that this discussion of the challenge posed by multi-culture must approach it as more than one small but telling manifestation of Britain's chronic post-imperial decline. The justification for that change of perspective lies in the ways that Britain's crisis is still routinely being registered as 'race', lived as 'race', most vividly projected and powerfully symbolized in racialized terms. We cannot then hide from 'race', but to understand how that continuing crisis has been articulated as a matter of 'race' and nation, culture and identity is not for a moment to suggest that it can be resolved at those levels, in that decaying hall of mirrors.

Notes

1. Stephen Lawrence was brutally and tragically murdered in Eltham, south-east London on 22 April 1993, initiating a process of political struggle that changed the way that Britain understood itself. See Macpherson (1999) and Cathcart (1999).

2. Enoch Powell, an esteemed Conservative politician from the Midlands, articu-lated a populist and ultra-nationalist politics around the catastrophic intrusion of blacks and other aliens into the heartlands of Britain. He is remembered now for his mentoring of Margaret Thatcher and for his April 1968 speech which used the idea of 'rivers of blood' to prophesy race war in England. See Gilroy (1999).

3. This refers to the leader of Britain's Conservative opposition party and his spouse.

4. Tony Blair and Cherie Booth, his consort.

5. Britain's leading conservative daily newspaper, read predominantly by women.

6. This is the address of the Labour Party's strategic office. It has come to refer to the work of their 'spin' doctors.

7. The Commision for Racial Equality is the paragovernmental body charged with the task of implementing Britain's race-equality legislation.

8. Minister of Overseas Development who, before her elevation, took a strong inter-est in race politics.

9. A Jamaican woman living in north London who died in front of her small son as a result of being forcibly manhandled by immigration authorities intent on deport-ing her from the country.

10. These are England's most prominent black athletes.

11. The Labour Party greeted news of Powell's passing with an appreciative com-mentary on his parliamentary competence and statesmanship. There was no mention of his aggressive and obscene racist commentaries on Britain's undesired black set-tlers.

12. Sir Peregrine Worsthorne was one of the journalists who had taken the political

imperatives of Powellism over into the pages of respectable print media. After Powell died he acknowledged that he had been wrong in endorsing the prophecy of race war.

13. This refers to a bomb placed in the Admiral Duncan pub in the centre of Soho's gay district on 30 April 1999. Three people were killed by the blast, Andrea Dykes, John Light and Nicholas Moore.

14. Ali G is the creation of comedian Sacha Baron-Cohen. He is a rude boy who specialized in interviewing pompous and right-wing members of Britain's political establishment using terminology drawn from the black vernacular that they could not possibly have been expected to understand. A video of his material was Britain's best-selling comedy item towards the end of 1999.

15. The Acourts were two brothers implicated in the murder of Stephen Lawrence; Straw is Jack Straw the Labour Home Secretary. Hurd, Howard and Clarke were his Conservative predecessors.

16. This refers to initiatives undertaken by the Greater London Council towards the goal of police accountability during the early 1980s following the riots in Brixton and elsewhere. A number of New Labour figures were associated with this development though the figurehead for it was Ken Livingstone, MP.

17. Lord Scarman produced a judicial inquiry into the riots that had erupted all over Britain during the summer of 1981 (Scarman, 1981).

18. Sir Paul Condon was Commissioner of the Metropolitan (London) Police during the years when the Lawrence tragedy was at its most intense.

19. Mr Phillips is a long-standing member of the Labour Party who has also made several careers as broadcaster, television presenter and businessman.

20. Lord Taylor is Britain's most prominent black Tory.

21. This is a reference to the killers of Stephen Lawrence who came from the south-east area of the city, i.e. the area closest to the county of Kent.

References

Cathcart, Brian (1999) *The Case of Stephen Lawrence*. London: Viking.

Gilroy, Paul (1999) 'A Lundun sumting "dis"', *Critical Quarterly* 41(3): 57–69.

Macpherson, Sir William (1999) *The Stephen Lawrence Inquiry*, CM-4261-I. London: HMSO.

Scarman, Lord (1981) *The Brixton Disorders 10–12 April 1981*, Cmnd. 8427. London: HMSO.

Walzer, Michael (1997) *On Toleration*. New Haven, CT: Yale University Press.

Vertigo and Emancipation, Creole Cosmopolitanism and Cultural Politics

Françoise Vergès

I
N THIS article, I wish to explore the meanings and politics of Creole cosmopolitanism. The term 'Creole', which takes different meanings with regard to its geographical, linguistic and historical location,[1] refers here to the identities created in the Creole societies of the French colonial empire – Martinique, Guadeloupe, Réunion Island – slave societies, colonies of France and, since 1946, French overseas departments. Cosmo-politanism, a term which has reappeared in recent years to describe an alternative way of being-in-the world that challenges national identity,[2] is taken here to describe the politics of Creole intellectuals who, whether during colonial times or in our current postcolonial times, projected them-selves onto the world from their particular position. Originally a central concept of European philosophy, cosmopolitanism designated a universal humanism transcending regional particularism. In the colonized world of the late 20th century, Creoles adopted that notion but creolized it: their uni-versal humanism was informed by their opposition to racism and colonial exploitation.[3] Their cosmopolitanism embodied a translocal experience that was a particular aspiring to the universal. Postcolonial Creoles criticized certain aspects of that universalism, arguing that nationalism was an emancipatory and potent force against colonialism. The particular could not be reduced to tradition and reaction. Creole cosmopolitanism is close to Paul Gilroy's analytical description of the translocal identities of the *Black Atlantic*, an analysis which he has pursued further in *Between Camps*. It is a cosmopolitanism grounded in the rejection of ethnic or nationalist abso-lutism from a (post)colonial position. This article is *situated*, it does not

■ *Theory, Culture & Society* 2001 (SAGE, London, Thousand Oaks and New Delhi),
Vol. 18(2–3): 169–183
[0263-2764(200104/06)18:2–3;169–183;017486]

pretend to possess the key to cosmopolitanism. I have wished to present a *cosmopolitics*, that emerged in a contact-zone. The article is part of a continuous reflection on the culture and politics of (post)colonial emancipation, the diasporic structures of the Creole world of the Indian Ocean and the importance of hatred, love, desire, mimicry and interdependency in the constitution of subjects.

Creole cultures are cultures of survival. They were invented and elaborated upon an experience of destruction and erasure: destruction of social, cultural and political ties, erasure of native languages and cultures. Hence, on Réunion Island, slaves from Madagascar, Africa, Malaysia and India were thrown together by the yoke of history, forced to invent and forge new languages, new social and family relations. This situation was, of course, not specific to the French slave societies. What was specific was a series of political and cultural conditions that led, on the one hand, to a strong feeling of disjunction (present to this day) between cultural and political identity and, on the other, to the desire to project oneself onto the world in order to escape the local disjunction, the lack of political horizon and the betrayal of the revolutionary promise.[4] The different waves of forced immigration were thoroughly creolized. The late date of the abolition of slavery (1848) meant that emancipation in the colonies occurred in a context of political modernization and internal colonization of the colonial power (expansion of civil rights, public education, new strategies of discipline and colonization). Techniques of discipline and discursive strategies were either first experienced in the colony and transferred to the metropole, or translated from the metropole to the colony. Political emancipation in the colonies was expressed in terms of assimilation, of following, of imitating the republican ideals of the colonial power. Scholars have shown how that approach has continued to frame the political demands of recognition and difference in Creole societies (Confiant, 1994; Toumson and Henry-Valmore, 1994; Vergès, 1999). Yet, I argue that what has been seen as mere mimicry and lack of creativity may be seen as a more widely existing form of political expression than we might wish to think. The ideal of authentic individual auto-creation, of a radical difference, still informs most postcolonial studies. In the effort of bringing back to life the diversity of political and cultural expressions in the non-West, most of us in the postcolonial world, as Anthony K. Appiah (1992) has shown, have fallen into the trap of celebrating one as the Other. The analysis of mimicking, imitating and borrowing as sources of creativity deserves to be pursued further in Creole societies. *Métissage* and *marooning* framed their experience from the beginning of their existence (on *métissage* and recognition see Gruzinski, 1999; Laplantine and Nouss, 1997; Subrahmanyam, 1999; Vergès, 1999). Creole cultures thus emerged as profoundly diverse and mobile. This led to a difficulty, an impossibility: there was no cultural particularism upon which to build a collective strategy. The foundations of the recognition of the Creole difference have remained a vexed question: if variety, change, fluidity, constant re-adaptation described the Creole difference, how can we demand recognition? Does not recognition of difference *demand* some form of stability? The political translation of the Creole difference has focused locally around the recognition of the Creole language as a *language*.[5] I argue that, confronted with the difficulty of translating the Creole difference into a collective strategy locally or nationally, Creoles turned to cosmopolitanism. They saw themselves as able to play a cosmopolitan role because of their difficulty in devising a Creole politics. Cosmopolitanism was a way of being in the world as Creoles.

Jacky Dahomay (2000) has argued that the goal of Creole culture is to bring back into the world (*remondanéiser*) the group marked by slavery. This explains, Dahomay suggests, the polemical character of Creole culture: it sets itself against the colonial project of exclusion from the world (*démondanéisation*). Creole cultures offer an affiliation to three communities of recognition. One community is local. It experiences a culture of reaction, whose reactive principle leads to a constant adaptation of its forms and expressions. It is a fluid, changing, anthropophagous culture. This character has led observers either to celebrate the amorphous nature of Creolization (as a postmodern rather than a postcolonial expression)[6] or to dismiss it (it cannot be clearly defined, or generalized). Another community is the political community of the French Republic: the community seeks political assimilation as the sign of recognition within the nation. A third community elaborates itself around a discourse of cosmopolitanism. Creole cosmopolitanism answers to the desire of being connected with the world, with humanity. Creole identity cannot be tied to a national territory, or to a political identity. It is a here-and-now way of living in the world. Creole cosmopolitanism represents a projection onto the world, beyond the ties of the reactive community (which protects the Creole difference) and the republican community (which does not recognize the Creole difference). Creole cosmopolitanism gives access to the universal, which localized Creole identities have seemed unable to provide.

I will examine two discourses of Creole cosmopolitanism. One, which I call 'universalist cosmopolitanism', emerged in the first half of the 20th century; the other, which I call 'revolutionary internationalism', was contemporary with the movement for decolonization in the second half of the 20th century. In my conclusion, I will reflect on the actuality and relevance of Creole cosmopolitanism in a period of intense globalization.

Creole Universalist Cosmopolitanism

In the last years of the 19th and the early years of the 20th century, the colonized educated elite and the organized working class of the 'Old Colonies' (Martinique, Guadeloupe, Réunion), identified themselves with the principles of European liberal democracy and the cultural politics of anti-colonialism. The abolition of slavery in 1848 had given citizenship to the slaves and the right to vote and be elected to men, yet had maintained the colonial status of the territories. The transformation of feudal colonialism into republican colonialism opened up the colonial public space. A small educated elite of colour emerged, which adopted the vocabulary of

French republicanism, creolized it and developed its own claims for rights and justice. Starting in the 1900s, the French colonial administration sent Creoles to its African and Asian colonies. It hoped that the difference created between assimilated colonized (with access to citizenship) and the other colonized (without access to rights) would work in their interest, i.e. that Creoles would prove to be the perfect representatives of republican colonialism, which they were, in their majority. However, this led to unforeseen consequences. Creoles took seriously the principles of democracy and therefore challenged their violation in the empire. For instance, in 'Cochin-China', the Réunionnais Georges Garros published in 1920 a scathing indictment of French colonial racism; in Madagascar, the Réunionnais Paul Dussac formed, with Malagasy friends, an anti-colonial movement; the Martinican René Maran, a former colonial administrator in West Africa, denounced the violation by European powers of the principles associated with the respect of humanity. He wrote in 1921:

> Civilization, civilization, pride of Europe. Charnel house of innocents, one day, in Tokyo, the Hindu poet, Rabindranâth Tagore, described what you were! You built your kingdom on corpses. Despite your claims, you lie. One sees you and cries tears of grief and shouts with fear. To you, might is right. You are not a torch but a blaze. Everything you touch is destroyed . . . (Maran, 1921, cited in Dewitte, 1985: 68–9)

Travelling across the French empire transformed the Creoles and led them to develop a cosmopolitanism grounded in the understanding of a shared humanity, against racial ideology.

The imperial discourse of cultural authenticity and pure identities was constantly exposed as a fantasy. To be sure, it was a fantasy whose practitioners enjoyed extraordinary resources: science, literature, media, joined their forces to transform a desire (to be 'the best, the first') into a truth. Yet, despite its continuous effort, imperialism could not fulfil its appetite for omnipotence. On the margins, as well as in the heart of the empire, in the interstices of colonial society and the imperial metropole, processes of hybridity and creolization occurred, as they had occurred during colonial slavery, the first emergence of a global economy. Creole cosmopolitanism emerged then as a response to colonial racism and as an expression of a translocal sensibility. Creoles were the products of colonization and slavery. Their ancestors came from Africa (East and West), from Madagascar, from Asia (East and South), from the Levant, from Europe. There was no native land to return to, no fantasy of origins. Upon that legacy, Creoles constituted themselves as an 'open' community, one that sought to build translocal connections. Solidarity with non-European peoples provided a training for emergent anti-colonial sensibilities. Creoles discovered bridges between the African, Asian, Caribbean and Indian Ocean worlds. With Creole cosmopolitanism, intellectuals of the French post-slavery colonies escaped the narrow world of local politics and the closed world of republican politics.

With Creole cosmopolitanism, they could identify with a larger community. It constituted an expansion of their world. They could defend the principles of shared humanity rights from *their* position: their past did not define their present. Ancestry and blood could not play an important role, rather it was dispersion and adaptation.

The First World War accelerated the movement of translocal anti-colonial politics. More than 100,000 soldiers came from the French colonial empire to fight in Europe. After the war, tens of thousands of them stayed in France. They constituted the first important non-European diasporic community in France, important not only because of their numbers – close to 30,000 individuals – but also because their encounter with the imperial metropole radically changed them and the metropole. Reviews, journals, books, pamphlets were published, in which a transcontinental, cultural and political, consciousness was debated and reinforced. The sheer existence of journals and reviews, the diversity of the themes they tackled, the polemics that took place, testified to the emergence on the cultural and political scene of a new group, which saw its role as that of a relentless critic of racism and colonialism and as creator of a new culture. The themes discussed were assimilation, *métissage*, black identity, rejection of Europe, Negritude, African civilization, racism, the unity of the anti-colonial diaspora, the 'two Frances' – the 'legitimate' France of liberty, equality, fraternity, of the Declaration of the Rights of Man and the Citizen, and the 'illegitimate' France, colonial France where these principles were violated. Creoles moved from the colony to the empire, from the empire to the metropole, and back to the colony. They imagined themselves belonging a greater community than the native one: the community of the colonized.

Cosmopolitan Creoles asserted their emerging autonomy through a process of 'deterritorialization' – the process whereby there is a subversion of discourse conventions that wrench the hegemonic language from the possession of its cultural overlords. Their movement announced postmodern and postcolonial practices of creolization. Innovative works of historical, cultural, political and aesthetic significance emerged in which practitioners sought to question the legacy of the dominant paradigms. There were the Nardal sisters, Jane, Paulette and Andrée Nardal, daughters of a black Martinican bourgeois family, who had been sent to French universities. They opened a *salon*, after the intellectual and cultural salon of the 18th century, which they wished to be the centre of the intellectual life of *Paris Noir*. The end of the 1920s were a very active period for translocal politics and culture: in 1928, André Maurois published an article on African-American poetry in the mainstream review *Candide*; Léopold Sédar Senghor arrived in Paris; the Haitian Jean Price-Mars published his novel *Ainsi parla l'oncle*, a revolution in literature; the review *La Dépêche africaine* was created, with among its editors René Maran, Paul Guillaume, the famous advocate and critic of *Art Nègre*, and the Nardal sisters; the monthly *L'Action coloniale* (1918–28) in which René Maran, Nguyen Ai Quoc, best known as Ho Chi Minh, and the Réunionnais poet Barquissau wrote. In 1929, the African-American writer and poet, Claude McKay, published *Banjo* which became a 'Bible of inspiration' to Léopold Sédar Senghor, Aimé Césaire (who arrived in Paris in 1932) and the Guyanese poet Léon Damas. The notions of a new humanism, the desire to go beyond traditional assimilation, and the elaboration of cultural miscegenation were evoked in *La Revue du Monde Noir*, Paulette Nardal's review.

By the early 1930s, new themes emerged. The threat of fascism and Nazism with their racist ideologies brought some urgency to the debate about non-European cultures and identities. There was an emphasis on the fundamental contribution of non-European cultures to the world. 'African collectivism has nothing to envy in European Marxism. No member of another race has received, since its infancy, an education as collectivist as the Negro', the Dahomean Vincent Durand wrote (Durand, 1928). In 1939, Césaire published *Cahier d'un retour au pays natal* in which he spoke of 'Those who have invented neither gunpowder nor compass/ those who tamed neither steam nor electricity/ those who explored neither the sea nor the sky/ but those without whom the earth would not be the earth'. Slaves who had built the wealth of Europe and who now inhabit the West Indies, 'the hungry West Indies, pitted with smallpox, dynamited with alcohol, stranded in the mud of this bay, in the dirt of this city sinisterly stranded' (Césaire, 1971). The Martinican poet Gilbert Gratiant spoke for the first time of 'Creole civilization' and sought to define a mulatto identity (Gratiant, 1935). Miscegenetion, *métissage* as a process of identification, inspired colonial poets and writers. They reacted against a legal, medical and psychological discourse which argued that *métissage* would inevitably lead to 'vulgarity, degeneration, perversion, morbidity' (Vergès, 1999). To *La Revue du Monde Nègre*, *métissage* was a 'vital necessity'. *Métissage,* Creole intellectuals affirmed, offered the possibility to go beyond an 'either–or' position, either the culture of the colonizers, or an idealized native world. Advocating *métissage* and creolization was also a response to racist discourses about blood purity. In his novels *Karim* (1935) and *Mirages de Paris* (1937), the Senegalese writer Ousmane Socé advocated cultural and biological *métissage*. Fara, his hero in *Mirages de Paris*, answers his friend Sidia for whom 'men of pure race are superior to the *métis*': 'I would say that if the mixing of the races continue, the *métis* will be the man of the future (Socé, 1937; see also Lüsebrink, 1992). But to Senghor, the function of *métissage* was the erasure of differences.

At the 1937 International Congress for the Cultural Progress of Colonial Peoples, the writer from Mali, Fily Dabo Sissoko, declared: 'The black man must remain black, in his life and in his education.' The Senegalese writer Abdoulaye Sadji violently attacked *métissage* in his novel *Nini, mulâtresse du Sénégal*. It was a denunciation of the mixed-blood community of Senegal which wanted to pass, and Sadji mocked the mixed-blood women whose only dream was to marry a white man. Socé declared in 1942: 'One day, cultural hybridity would be global (*interplanétaire*)' (Socé, 1942).

The Second World War brought back the question of allegiance. To whom did colonial peoples owe allegiance? To the international brotherhood of the oppressed? To their fatherland? To Communism? To France? Upon learning that the Senegalese veterans had reaffirmed their indestructible attachment to France under German threat, Léon Damas, the Guyanese poet, questioned the Senegalese's apish loyalty in his 1937 poem *Pigments*:

> To the Senegalese veterans
> To the future Senegalese soldiers
> I
> I say to them
> Merde and
> Other things as well
> I
> I ask them to renounce the need they may have
> to loot
> to steal, to rape
> to defile the banks
> of the Rhine
> I ask them
> to start by invading
> Senegal. (cited in Kesteloot, 1978: 68; my translation)

Creole universalist cosmopolitans followed the debates around similar themes that were happening in London and New York (on the relations between these movements see Jules-Rosette, 2000; Mudimbe, 1992; Stovall, 1996). Though they shared with the Pan-African Congress or the Harlem Renaissance the desire to explore the specificity of African civilizations and their contribution to humanity, as well as a common indictment of racism and colonial violence, Creole universalist cosmopolitans favored the notions of hybridity and creolization over the notion of race. The emphasis on *métissage*, hybridity and creolization operated a division between francophone and anglophone colonial intellectuals (a division that continues to operate).

After the war, the movement of decolonization transformed the terms of the debate. The advocacy of violence, the research for a *national* identity and culture radically altered Creole cosmopolitanism. Creole universalist cosmopolitanism emerged at a specific moment. It saw itself as the heir of the Creole world built by the slaves; it advocated a humanism in which the idiom of creolization and *métissage* countered the obsession with blood purity and national absolutism; it sought to organize an Afro-Asian movement. To be sure, cosmopolitan Creoles had underestimated the intimate relationship that existed between liberal democracy and the violation of its principles in the empire. They had framed their demands in the language of justice and rights, unable to foresee the emergence of nationalism in the empire. Yet their belief in the strength of hybridity and creolization to counter the discourse and practices of racial hierarchy weakened their political impact. To be sure, racism was their enemy, but they thought that peoples could be enlightened through a programme of education that would stress the universality of processes of creolization, presenting them not only as inevitable processes but, above all, as the desirable future. As such, their discourse offered a horizon of opened identities rather than closed, reified, blood-based identities. Yet, as they had underestimated the power of passion, anger and hatred in politics and the role of emotions in the processes of recognition and difference, their discourse appeared, to the following generation, as a discourse abstracted from the realities of politics and the formation of communities. The demonstration by Europe of its capacity for destruction and the violence of decolonization raised new questions for Creole cosmopolitanism: could it still offer a politics of resistance, of belonging, of emancipation? Was not its universalism a mask for its inability to think conflict and political struggle?

Creole Cosmopolitanism as Revolutionary Internationalism

Frantz Fanon sought to answer these questions in the context of colonial war. As a Creole of Martinique, Fanon had preferred to distance himself from local politics. The political assimilation defended by Aimé Césaire appeared meek and weak. Creole culture seemed to be a mere mimicking of the French. It looked as if Creoles were unable to project themselves onto the world. Yet, the politics of revolutionary solidarity emerging throughout the world offered a new space to elaborate new identities, new strategies of resistance and belonging. A French Creole could still play a role as a cosmopolitan intellectual. He (the Fanonian cosmopolitan was a 'he') knew the enemy because his people had for so long tried to imitate them, because the enemy had been the 'master' of his enslaved ancestors. They were intimate enemies. He knew about race, about exclusion, about the politics of visual representation, about the psychology of identifications, because his world had been entirely modelled by these processes. Yet, his territory was not his island, because he refused a burden imposed upon him by the colonial power. His battlefield was the world of the wretched of the earth. Revolutionary internationalism revived Creole cosmopolitanism by giving it a new vocabulary (the vocabulary of Third World's revolution), a new face (the angry young man), a new discourse (the redemptive role of violence).

In the last chapter of *The Wretched of the Earth*, Frantz Fanon evoked the mental disorders brought by the 'total war' waged by the French army against the Algerian people. War affected both sides, colonized and colonizers were psychically disturbed or destroyed by conflicting loyalties, violence and fear. On both sides, people were haunted by the perception that the 'other side' wished one's own destruction. At the end of the Algerian war, the *Organisation de l'Armée Secrète* (OAS), a French terrorist and racist armed group, exploited that perception among the *pied-noirs*. Sharing a territory became impossible, the majority of *pied-noirs* refused to accept what 'sharing' would mean: the loss of privileges and access to a different yet still unknown future. The logic of war required that borders between communities were clear-cut, that differences were clarified. France had stubbornly refused equal rights to Algerians. Further, its presence in Algeria could not, at any rate, be justified.

The idiom of war helped the Algerians in their identification with the forthcoming nation (the French state and army were obviously the enemy), but it also forced them to accelerate the processes of identification with a future identity whose contours were defined according to the idiom of nationalism and modernization that dominated the movements of decoloniz-ation. War imposed an idealized self, both to counter the destructive images of Algerians that French colonialism had constructed and to contain the diversity of identities in a multicultural Algeria. In its last years, the war imposed tight borders between worlds, yet there were moments when these borders were disrupted, when actions against the 'other side' and the demands of loyalty within one's group deeply affected a subject's psyche.

The war was waged not only on bodies but on psyches as well, and both sides manipulated neuroses, feelings of paranoia, the death drive and sui-cidal impulses. It is known that both sides used marginalized individuals or people suffering from mental disorders to conduct attacks. The French army used psychiatric asylums as jails, nationalists as refuges.

The collective anxiety, which had been partly contained during the war, exploded after 1962. It was neither mediated nor re-oriented (Poinson-Quinton, 1964). Algerian women and men, expressing their anguish after seven years of war, deportation and the violent breaking of traditional ties and customs, found no space to express their grief and fears. The Algerian government adopted the idiom of modernization and saw every manifestation of psychic resistance as an expression of backwardness. Community and difference were reconstructed along lines that agreed with the ideology of a nascent class whose goal was to transform a multicultural country into an 'Arabic-Algerian' nation. Expressions of individual and collective anxiety belied the discourse of national oneness. The new community was haunted by the war and its aftermath. The war had brought vertigo and anguish, peace could not easily assuage these feelings.

The Algerian government shared, with the majority of movements of decolonization, the belief that an Ideal (that was said to be common to all citizens) would provide a common culture, a common identity and a common social geography of history. The Ideal (the Algerian nation) demanded unconditional adoption of an Ideal Ego but denied its incorporation into a signifying system. In other words, in 1962, the name 'Algerian' was not a name incorporated into a line of signifiers, of names that recognized a diver-sity of names (Muslim, Christian, Jew, animist, Man, Woman, Berber, Arab). The demands of the Ideal Ego clashed with the demands of the subject to be re-inscribed in a symbolic order. The clash produced a feeling, which Frantz Fanon had already observed during the war: vertigo.

Vertigo was provoked by the gap between group identification and identification with a shared humanity. Political struggle demands loyalty to a group, that the other group be considered an enemy to be destroyed, while political discourse demanded identification with the community of human beings. The division had always existed, but in the colonial situation, in which colonizer and colonized had been intimate enemies, the gap produced anxiety.[7]

Discussing the case of an African who suffered from insomnia, suicidal obsessions and vertigo after he had placed a bomb in a café, Fanon wondered if it was ever possible to avoid the feeling of 'vertigo'. Though there was no reason to repudiate the action, the café was a 'meeting place for notorious racists', the African activist suffered psychologically.

> Some months after his country's independence was declared, he had made the acquaintance of certain nationals of the former colonial power, and he had found them very likeable. . . . He wondered with a feeling of anguish whether among the victims of the bomb there had been people like his new acquaintances. (Fanon, 1990: 203)

Fanon observed that though the demands of revolutionary politics clashed with the soldier's psyche, it was a fact he had to live with. 'We are forever pursued by our actions', Fanon remarked. The feeling of 'vertigo haunts the whole of existence' (1990: 203). In politics, there is no escape, no possibility of peaceful harmony. We must act and live with the consequences. Vertigo is inseparable from a politics of emancipation.

Fanon foresaw that a victory would not erase the sources of collective anxiety. He puzzled over complex and troubling political narratives in the chaos of war, wishing that independence would bring some sense of homecoming and yet knowing that 'home' as a sign of stability was not easily sustainable. Yet, the construction of 'home' produced vertigo, regrets and anxiety. These feelings were inevitable and, to avoid the morbid melancholia associated with regrets, Fanon chose the 'home' of revolutionary camaraderie, the translocal imagined community of anti-colonial men. Identification with home meant being recognized as 'one of us' by revolutionary brothers. Being-at-home-in-a-community meant constructing a community whose contours were fluid but which obeyed the principles of revolutionary politics: against injustice and racism, against exploitation and for a new humanism. The idiom of revolutionary internationalism gave a more grounded politics to Creole universalist cosmopolitanism. The former re-territorialized Creole cosmopolitanism through a rejection of the interdependence inherent in human relations (cosmopolitan revolutionary internationalism in its Fanonian expression accepted the existence of psychological interdependence but rejected political interdependence).[8] In other words, where Creole universalist cosmopolitanism had sought to construct a theory of shared humanity regardless of race and class, cosmopolitan revolutionary internationalism reintroduced race and class. Both performed exclusionary practices, that have been described elsewhere, such as in the feminist critique of nationalism and socialism, in the queer critique of sexual politics, or in the critique by ethnic minorities of the national narrative.

Creole Cosmopolitanism in the Context of Globalization

Creole universalist cosmopolitanism did not prove to be strong enough against nativism, ethnic and national absolutism. Yet, it opened the way to more radical demands, and their humanism prefigured current debates about identity and difference. Its debates foreshadowed current debates about the function of hybridization and creolization. Cosmopolitanism as revolutionary internationalism introduced new theoretical approaches. Its debates announced current debates about belonging and resistance. Yet, what is really the actuality of Creole cosmopolitanism in the context of globalization?

Creolization is now widely used to describe processes of deterritorialization, hybridity, mixing. Rather than debating the pertinence of the polysemic nature of the term, I will, for the moment, keep it grounded in the experience of Creole societies that I have described. Edouard Glissant has been the foremost theorist of creolization in these societies. He has been, since Edward Kamau Braithwaite (see Braithwaite, 1971), the postcolonial scholar who has repeatedly sought to define the notion of creolization, and Creole as the identity produced by creolization. Glissant (1997: 36) has argued that 'Creole' refers to a mode of cultural construction that is *absolutely* original. Creolization emerges from the contact of different cultures in a defined place. The result is a new emergence, but one which cannot be determined, planned or guessed at. It is entirely unpredictable. This is an important aspect of Glissant's theory: whereas the result of *métissage* can be foreseen, it is fundamental to understand that the result of creolization will remain unforeseen. Creolization is *not* multiculturalism, or simply an expression of the paradoxes of postmodern subjectivities. Creolization produces identities that are not rooted but grow as rhizomes (Glissant borrows Deleuze and Guattari's notion) and which do not seek to delimit a territory on which to express themselves. With creolization, one can envision a future in which humanity will be diverse, multiple and whose identities will be based on *relation* rather than on filiation, blood, ancestry, land. The cosmopolitanism that Glissant's creolization provides is an Ideal, and as an Ideal may open our mental space, expand our imagined community: the world is my territory, I am not like a tree but like a plant with multiple roots (mangrove, banyan), I conceive my encounter to the Other as a relation, not as a confrontation. The poetics of relation constitutes a crucial aspect of Glissant's creolization, and, as such, can be compared to the theories elaborated by Homi Bhabha on vernacular cosmopolitanism and hybridity, Stuart Hall on diasporic identities or Paul Gilroy on cosmopolitan humanism.[9] In which ways is 'Creole' different from diasporic, from hybrid? It is a vexed question, which can be answered only through a careful study of current processes of creolization, in their localization and specificity. Whether such studies will, or can, yield a model that can be generalized cannot be answered at this point. Furthermore, though Glissant's description of creolization is very attractive (as well as the derivative discourse of Créolité), it fails to provide an explanation for the continuing paradox in the Creole societies which have been our site of reference.

The question remains: can there be a revivification of Creole cosmopolitanism in the context of globalization? Or might we be forced to conclude that Creole cosmopolitanism was a response grounded in a specific time and space and that the current context of globalization has radically transformed the problematic? I wish to propose two conclusions. One is that Creole cosmopolitanism can be revivified in the French Creole societies as an alternative to an assimilation in the French discourse on human rights based on the 'right to interfere' and as an alternative to new forms of local nativism, which I describe below. The other conclusion is that Creole cosmopolitanism cannot pretend to constitute a model for analogous problems that have emerged in the current context of globalization. I find myself absolutely unable to make such generalizations.

As examples of solidarity and affinity that have worked in the 1930s and 1960s, Creole cosmopolitanism might provide ideas for new translocal circuits of political culture. Creoles of the French post-colonies might find that the reactive, imitative, mimicking character of their culture is a strength. What is seen as a lack − lack of strong roots, of stable identities, of a national culture − might constitute the grounds upon which to build a process of identifications based on adaptation and fluidity. At that point, observers would say: what about the paranoid character of social relations? What about the social violence? What about the suffering produced by the disjunction that you are proposing as foundation for community and difference (on social violence and paranoia, see André, 1987; Reverzy and Marimoutou, 1990)? What you describe dismisses the economic and political reality of dependence. It is a nice but stupid dream. Though I would consider these questions carefully, I would also propose that Creole cosmopolitanism will not be a healing process, or a response to social and political problems. It is a framework for imagining oneself in the world, it can provide a localized answer to the assimilative project of the former colonial centre (France), a regionalized answer to the discourses of regional powers (India, China which are reorganizing the periphery into new centres and new peripheries), and, finally, it can contribute to the larger debate on difference and recognition.

The postcolonial world is still trapped in colonial history. The subject seeks relief for its multiple splits through identification with strong signifiers (belonging to a strong nation-state, to an imperial history). We witness the emergence in the French Creole post-colonies of forms of nativism and of 'civilizationalism', i.e. of tradition and its reinterpretation.[10] For instance, one can hear, in Martinique, Guadeloupe and Réunion, demands for independence that do not question *privileges* inherited from colonialism such as the status of civil servants (their salary is higher than in France, but they pay less taxes). One can also witness new ethnicisms that use civilizationalism to ground their claims. Hence, in Réunion Island, the *Malbars*, the descendants of low-caste indentured workers from India are reconstructing themselves as descendants of high castes, turning their back on the syncretic religion of their forebears with its sacrifice of living animals and other rituals, and turning to a more 'civilized' form of ritual: vegetarianism, meditation and Eastern philosophy. It is no small irony that, in their attempt to construct a new ethnicity, Malbars adopt rituals that are more closely associated with 'Eastern mysticism' in the West, a mysticism which has become highly fashionable. Yet, one can also observe new strategies of resistance through the affirmation of cultural and religious differences (African; Muslim; Asian). Groups are reaffirming their difference, expressions of their capacity for 'giving meaning' to their exclusion from the French republic.[11] It remains to be seen whether creolization and Creole cosmopolitanism will disappear under the emergence of these new differences.

Notes

1. For instance, in Haiti, 'Creole' (the light-skinnned, wealthy, educated group) is opposed to 'Bossale' (dark-skinned, poor, uneducated); in Mauritius, 'Creole' is claimed by the descendants of African and Malagasy slaves to counter the hegemonic narrative of Mauritius as 'Asian'; in the English-speaking Caribbean islands, the term 'Creole' is barely used to claim an identity.

2. Cosmopolitanism has been discussed by people with different interpretations of the terms. See Archibugi and Held (1995); Heater (1996); Held (1995); Gilroy (2000).

3. One might observe that forms of Creole cosmopolitanism existed in the 19th century (see the poet Leconte de Lisle's project of universal fraternity). More research is needed to explore the different forms of Creoles' relation with the world.

4. In the French colonies, the class of landowners never elaborated a real autonomous political programme, they never claimed a specific political identity. They wanted minimal participation in the political life of the nation, their only demand being that France would maintain slavery and the economic rights associated with that system.

5. The recent recognition by the French Socialist government of Creole as a 'regional language', with respect to the European Charter on Regional Languages, has led again to furious debates in Creole societies. When the Minister of Education announced in November 2000 that there will be a CAPES exam for Creole (school-teachers must pass the CAPES to be allowed to teach in high schools), there was also an uproar. Advocates and opponents traded insults.

6. I follow Anthony K. Appiah's argument on African identities: they are not 'post-colonial' or 'postmodern' but belong to a 'postmodernization' moment, i.e. they question the colonial discourse (but not from a 'pre-colonial' position) *and* the post-colonial discourse of modernization.

7. See Mannoni, 1990; Memmi, 1965; Tillon, 1960. A comparison can be made with civil wars.

8. I have explored that apparent contradiction elsewhere. See Vergès (1996, 1997, 1998).

9. A comparison with the theories proposed by philosophers, such as Jean-Luc Nancy and Giorgo Agamben, who discussed a 'community into being', a 'forthcoming community' could also be fruitful. There seem to be more similarities

between these discourses than a territorialized glance ('European philosophy' vs 'Caribbean discourse') might allow.

10. Civilizationism is a term proposed by Kuan-Hsing (1998: 1–56).

11. See Farhad Khosrokhavar (2000) for a comparative analysis of the Beurs's Islam.

References

André, Jacques (1987) *L'Inceste focal dans la famille noire antillaise*. Paris: PUF.

Appiah, Anthony K. (1992) *In My Father's House*. Oxford: Oxford University Press.

Archibugi, Danielle and David Held (1995) *Cosmopolitan Democracy. An Agenda for a New World Order*. Cambridge: Polity Press.

Braithwaite, Edward Kamau (1971) *The Development of Creole Society in Jamaica, 1770–1820*. Oxford: Clarendon Press.

Césaire, Aimé (1971) *Cahier d'un retour au pays natal* (Return to my Native Land), trans. Emile Snyder. Paris: Présence Africaine.

Confiant, Raphaël (1994) *Aimé Césaire: une traversée paradoxale du siècle*. Paris: Stock.

Dahomay, Jacky (2000) 'Identité culturelle et identité politique: le cas antillais', pp. 99–118 in Will Kymlicka and Sylvie Mesure (eds) *Comprendre les identités culturelles*. Paris: PUF.

Dewitte, Philippe (1985) *Les Mouvements nègres en France, 1919–1939*. Paris: L'Harmattan.

Durand, Vincent (1928) 'Le Collectivisme africain', *La Dépêche Africaine* 6.

Fanon, Frantz (1990) *The Wretched of the Earth*, trans. Constance Farrington. London: Penguin Books.

Gilroy, Paul (2000) *Against Race*. Cambridge, MA: Harvard University Press.

Glissant, Edouard (1997) *Traité du tout-monde*. Paris: Gallimard.

Gratiant, Gilbert (1935) 'Mulâtres: pour le bien et pour le mal', *L'Étudiant Noir* 1.

Gruzinski, Serge (1999) *La Pensée métisse*. Paris: Fayard.

Heater, David (1996) *World Citizenship and Government: Cosmopolitanism Ideas in the History of Western Political Thought*. New York: St Martin's Press.

Held, David (1995) *Democracy and the Global Order: From the Modern State to Cosmopolitan Governance*. Cambridge: Polity Press.

Jules-Rosette, Benetta (2000) *Black Paris*. Chicago: University of Illinois Press.

Kesteloot, Lylian (1978) *Anthologie négro-africaine*. Paris: Verviers.

Khosrokhavar, Farhad (2000) 'L'Islam des jeunes musulmans', pp. 81–97 in Will Kymlicka and Sylvie Mesure (eds) *Comprendre les identités culturelles*. Paris: PUF.

Kuan-Hsing Chen (1998) 'The Decolonization Question', pp. 1–56 in Kuan-Hsing Chen (ed.) *Trajectories. Inter-Asia Cultural Studies*. London: Routledge.

Laplantine, François and Alexis Nouss (1997) *Le Métissage*. Paris: Flammarion.

Lüsebrink, Hans-Jürgen (1992) 'Métissage culturel et société coloniale: émergence et enjeux d'un débat de la presse coloniale aux premiers écrivains africains (1935–1947)', *Métissages* 1 (La Réunion).

Mannoni, Octave (1990) *Prospero and Caliban: The Psychology of Colonization*, trans. Pamela Powesland. Ann Arbor: University of Michigan Press.

Maran, René (1921) *Batouala, véritable roman nègre*. Paris: Albin Michel.

Memmi, Albert (1965) *The Colonizer and the Colonized*. New York: Orion Press.

Mudimbe, Valentin (1992) *The Surreptitious Speech*. Chicago, IL: University of Chicago Press.

Parry, Benita (1991) 'The Contradictions of Cultural Studies', *Transition* 53.

Pheng Cheah and Bruce Robbins (eds) (1998) *Cosmopolitics: Thinking and Feeling beyond the Nation*. Minneapolis: University of Minnesota Press.

Poinson-Quinton, Jean-Louis (1964) unpublished thesis.

Reverzy, Jean-François and Carpanin Marimoutou (eds) (1990) *Cultures, exils et folies dans l'Océan Indien*. Paris: INSERM, L'Harmattan.

Socé, Ousmane (1937) *Mirages de Paris*. Paris.

Socé, Ousmane (1942) 'L'Évolution culturelle de l'A.O.F.', *Dakar-Jeunes* 4 (29 janvier).

Stovall, Tyler (1996) *Paris Noir: African-Americans in the City of Light*. New York: Houghton Mifflin.

Subrahmanyam, Sanjay (1999) *L'Empire portuguais d'Asie, 1500–1700*. Paris: Maisonneuve et Larose.

Tillon, Germaine (1960) *Les ennemis complementaires*. Paris: Éditions de Minuit.

Toumson, Roger and Simonne Henry-Valmore (1994) *Aimé Césaire, le nègre inconsolé*. Paris: Syros (2nd edn 1996).

Vergès, Françoise (1996) 'Chains of Madness, Chains of Freedom', pp. 46–75 in Alan Read (ed.) *The Fact of Blackness: Frantz Fanon and Visual Representation*. London: ICA.

Vergès, Françoise (1997) 'To Cure and to Free: The Fanonian Project of Decolonized Psychiatry', pp. 85–99 in Lewis R. Gordon, T. Denean Sharpley-Whiting and Renée T. White (eds) *Fanon: A Critical Reader*. Oxford: Blackwell.

Vergès, Françoise (1998) 'Creole Skin, Black Mask: Fanon and Disavowal', *Critical Inquiry* 23(3): 578–95.

Vergès, Françoise (1999) *Monsters and Revolutionaries*. Durham, NC: Duke University Press.

Françoise Vergès is MA Convenor and Lecturer at the Centre for Cultural Studies, Goldsmiths College, University of London. She has written extensively on postcolonial politics and culture, slavery and memory, psychiatry and psychoanalysis.

Nuestra America

Reinventing a Subaltern Paradigm of Recognition and Redistribution

Boaventura de Sousa Santos

The European American Century

ACCORDING TO Hegel, we recall, universal history goes from the East to the West. Asia is the beginning, while Europe is the ultimate end of universal history, the place where the civilizational trajectory of humankind is fulfilled. The biblical and medieval idea of the succession of empires (*translatio imperii*) becomes in Hegel the triumphal way of the Universal Idea. In each era a people takes on the responsibility of conducting the Universal Idea, thereby becoming the historical universal people, a privilege which has in turn passed from the Asian to the Greek, then to the Roman, and, finally, to the German peoples. America, or rather, North America, carries, for Hegel, an ambiguous future, in that it does not collide with the utmost fulfilling of the universal history in Europe. The future of (North) America is still a European future, made up of Europe's left-over population.

This Hegelian idea underlies the dominant conception of the 20th century as the American century: the European American century. Herein implied is the notion that the Americanization of the world, starting with the Americanization of Europe itself, is but an effect of the European universal cunning of reason, which, having reached the Far West and unreconciled with the exile to which Hegel had condemned it, was forced to turn back, walk back upon its own track and once again trace the path of its hegemony over the East. Americanization, as a hegemonic form of globalization, is thus the third act of the millennial drama of Western supremacy. The first act, to a large extent a failed act, was the Crusades, which started the second millennium of the Christian era; the second act, beginning halfway through

■ *Theory, Culture & Society* 2001 (SAGE, London, Thousand Oaks and New Delhi),
   Vol. 18(2–3): 185–217
   [0263-2764(200104/06)18:2–3;185–217;017485]

the millennium, was the discoveries and subsequent European expansion. In this millennial conception, the European American century carries little novelty; it is nothing more than one more European century, the last one of the millennium. Europe, after all, has always contained many Europes, some of them dominant, others dominated. The United States of America is the last dominant Europe; like the previous ones, it exerts its uncontested power over the dominated Europes. The feudal lords of 11th-century Europe had and desired as little autonomy vis-a-vis Pope Urban II, who recruited them for the Crusades, as the European Union countries today vis-a-vis the USA of President Clinton, who recruits them to the Balkan wars.[1] From one episode to the other, only the dominant conception of the dominant West has been restricted. The more restrictive the conception of the West, the closer the East. Jerusalem is now Kosovo.

In these conditions it is hard to think of any alternative to the current regime of international relations which has become a core element of what I call hegemonic globalization. However, such an alternative is not only necessary but urgent, since the current regime, as it loses coherence, becomes more violent and unpredictable, thus enhancing the vulnerability of subordinate social groups, regions and nations. The real danger, both as regards intranational and international relations, is the emergence of what I call societal fascism. Fleeing from Germany a few months before his death, Walter Benjamin wrote his *Theses on the Theory of History* (1980) prompted by the idea that European society lived at the time in a moment of danger. I think that today we live in a moment of danger as well. In Benjamin's time the danger was the rise of fascism as a political regime. In our time, the danger is the rise of fascism as a societal regime. Unlike political fascism, societal fascism is pluralistic, coexists easily with the democratic state, and its privileged time-space, rather than being national, is both local and global.

Societal fascism is a set of social processes by which large bodies of populations are irreversibly kept outside or thrown out of any kind of social contract (Santos, 1998a). They are rejected, excluded and thrown into a kind of Hobbesian state of nature, either because they have never been part of any social contract and probably never will (I mean the pre-contractual underclasses everywhere in the world, the best example of which are probably the youth of urban ghettos); or because they have been excluded or thrown out of whatever social contract they had been part of before (I mean the post-contractual underclasses, millions of workers of post-Fordism, peasants after the collapse of land-reform projects or other development projects).

As a societal regime, fascism manifests itself as the collapse of the most trivial expectations of the people living under it. What we call society is a bundle of stabilized expectations from the subway schedule to the salary at the end of the month or employment at the end of college education. Expectations are stabilized by a set of shared scales and equivalences: for a given work a given pay, for a given crime a given punishment, for a given risk a given insurance. The people who live under societal fascism are deprived of shared scales and equivalences and therefore of stabilized expectations. They live in a constant chaos of expectations in which the most trivial acts may be met with the most dramatic consequences. They run many risks and none of them is insured. Gualdino Jesus, a Pataxó Indian from Northeast Brazil, symbolizes the nature of such risks. He had come to Brasilia to take part in the march of the landless. The night was warm and he decided to sleep on a bench at the bus stop. In the early morning hours he was killed by three middle-class youths, one the son of a judge, another the son of an army officer. As the youngsters confessed later on to the police, they killed the Indian for the fun of it. They 'didn't even know he was an Indian, they thought he was a homeless vagrant'. This event is mentioned here as a parable of what I call societal fascism.

One possible future is therefore the spread of societal fascism. There are many signs that this is a real possibility. If the logic of the market is allowed to spill over from the economy to all fields of social life and to become the sole criterion for successful social and political interaction, society will become ungovernable and ethically repugnant and whatever order is achieved will be of a fascistic kind, as indeed Schumpeter (1962) and Polanyi (1957) predicted decades ago.

It is important, however, to bear in mind that, as my example shows, it is not just the state that may become fascistic; social relations – local, national and international relations – may also become so. The disjuncture in social relations between inclusion and exclusion has already gone so deep that it becomes increasingly a spatial disjuncture: included people live in civilized areas, excluded people in savage areas. Fences are raised between them (closed condominiums, gated communities). In the savage zones, because they are potentially ungovernable, the democratic state is democratically legitimated to act fascistically. This is more likely to occur the more the dominant consensus about the weak state is left unchecked. It is today becoming clear that only a strong democratic state can produce effectively its own weakness, and that only a strong democratic state can promote the emergence of a strong civil society. Otherwise, once the structural adjustment is accomplished, rather than with a weak state we will be confronted with strong mafias, as is today the case of Russia.

In this article I argue that the alternative to the spread of societal fascism is the construction of a new pattern of local, national and transnational relations, based both on the principle of redistribution (equality) and the principle of recognition (difference). In a globalized world, such relations must emerge as counter-hegemonic globalizations. The pattern sustaining them must be much more than a set of institutions. Such a pattern entails a new transnational political culture embedded in new forms of sociability and subjectivity. Ultimately it implies a new revolutionary 'natural' law, as revolutionary as the 17th-century conceptions of natural law were. For reasons that will soon become clear, I will call this new 'natural' law a baroque cosmopolitan law.

At the margins of the European American century, as I argue, another century, a truly new and American century, emerged. I call it the *Nuestra America* American century. While the former carries the hegemonic global-ization, the latter contains in itself the potential for counter-hegemonic globalizations. Since this potential lies in the future, the *Nuestra America* American century may well be the name of the century we are now entering. In the first section of my article I explain what I mean by globalization, and particularly counter-hegemonic globalization. Then I specify in some detail the most outstanding features of the idea of *Nuestra America* as it conceived of itself in the mirror of the European American century. In the following section I analyze the baroque ethos, conceived of as the cultural archetype of *Nuestra America* subjectivity and sociability. My analysis highlights some of the emancipatory potential of a new baroque 'natural' law, conceived of as cosmopolitan law, a law based neither on God nor on abstract nature, but rather on the social and political culture of social groups whose everyday life is energized by the need to transform survival strategies into sources of innovation, creativity, transgression and subversion. In the last sections of the article, I will try to show how this emancipatory counter-hegemonic potential of *Nuestra America* has so far not been realized, and how it may be realized in the 21st century. Finally, I identify five areas, all of them deeply embedded in the secular experience of *Nuestra America*, which in my view will be the main contested terrains of the struggle between hegemonic and counter-hegemonic globalizations, and thus the playing field for a new transnational political culture and the baroque 'natural' law that legitimates it. In each one of these contested terrains, the emancipatory potential of the struggles is premised upon the idea that a politics of redistribution cannot be successfully conducted without a politics of recognition, and vice versa.

On Counter-hegemonic Globalizations

Before I proceed, let me clarify what I mean by hegemonic and counter-hegemonic globalization. Most authors conceive of one form of globalization only, and reject the distinction between hegemonic and counter-hegemonic globalization.[2] Once globalization is conceived of as being one alone, resist-ance to it on the part of its victims – granted that it may be possible to resist it at all – can only take the form of localization. Jerry Mander, for example, speaks of 'ideas about the viability of smaller-scale, localized diversified economies, hooked into but not dominated by outside forces' (1996: 18). Similarly Douthwaite affirms that:

> [S]ince a local unsustainability cannot cancel local sustainability elsewhere, a sustainable world would consist of a number of territories, each of which would be sustainable independently of the others. In other words, rather than a single global economy which would damage everyone if it crashed, a sus-tainable world would contain a plethora of regional (sub-national) economies producing all the essentials of life from the resources of their territories and therefore largely independent of each other. (1999: 171)

According to this view, the shift toward the local is mandatory. It is the only way of guaranteeing sustainability.

I start from the assumption that what we usually call globalization consists of sets of social relations; as these sets of social relations change, so does globalization. There is strictly no single entity called globalization; there are, rather, globalizations, and we should use the term only in the plural. On the other hand, if globalizations are bundles of social relations, the latter are bound to involve conflicts, hence, both winners and losers. More often than not, the discourse on globalization is the story of the winners as told by the winners. Actually, the victory is apparently so absolute that the defeated end up vanishing from the picture altogether.

Here is my definition of globalization: it is the process by which a given local condition or entity succeeds in extending its reach over the globe and, by doing so, develops the capacity to designate a rival social condition or entity as local.

The most important implications of this definition are the following. First, in the conditions of the Western capitalist world system there is no genuine globalization. What we call globalization is always the successful globalization of a given localism. In other words, there is no global condition for which we cannot find a local root, a specific cultural embeddedness. The second implication is that globalization entails localization, that is, localization is the globalization of the losers. In fact, we live in a world of localization, as much as we live in a world of globalization. Therefore, it would be equally correct in analytical terms if we were to define the current situation and our research topics in terms of localization, rather than globalization. The reason why we prefer the latter term is basically because hegemonic scientific discourse tends to prefer the story of the world as told by the winners. In order to account for the asymmetrical power relations within what we call globalization, I have suggested elsewhere that we distinguish four modes of production of globalization: globalized localisms, localized globalisms, cosmopolitanism, and common heritage of humankind (Santos, 1995: 252–377). According to this conception, the two first modes comprise what we call hegemonic globalization. They are driven by the forces of global capitalism and characterized by the radical nature of the global integration they make possible, either through exclusion or through inclusion. The excluded, whether people or countries, or even continents like Africa, are integrated in the global economy by the specific ways in which they are excluded from it. This explains why, among the millions of people who live on the streets, in urban ghettos, in reservations, in the killing fields of Urabá or Burundi, the Andean Mountains or the Amazonic frontier, in refugee camps, in occupied territories, in sweatshops using millions of bonded child labourers, there is much more in common than we are ready to admit.

The two others forms of globalization – cosmopolitanism and common heritage of humankind – are what I call counter-hegemonic globalizations. All over the world the hegemonic processes of exclusion are being met with different forms of resistance – grassroots initiatives, local organizations, popular movements, transnational advocacy networks, new forms of labor internationalism – that try to counteract social exclusion, opening up spaces for democratic participation, community building, alternatives to dominant forms of development and knowledge, in sum, for social inclusion. These local–global linkages and cross-border activisms constitute a new transnational democratic movement. After the demonstrations in Seattle (November 1999) against the World Trade Organization and those in Prague (September 2000) against the World Bank and the International Monetary Fund, this movement is becoming a new component of international politics and, more generally, part of a new progressive political culture. The new local–global advocacy networks focus on a wide variety of issues: human rights, environment, ethnic and sexual discrimination, biodiversity, labor standards, alternative protection systems, indigenous rights, etc. (Casanova, 1998; Keck and Sikkink, 1998; Tarrow, 1999; Brysk, 2000; Evans, 2000).

This new 'activism beyond borders' constitutes an emergent paradigm which, following Ulrich Beck, we could call a transnational, emancipatory sub-politics, the political *Geist* of counter-hegemonic globalizations. The credibility of the transnational sub-politics is still to be established, and its sustainability is an open question. If we measure its influence and success in light of the following four levels – issue creation and agenda setting; changes in the rhetoric of the decision-makers; institutional changes; effective impact on concrete policies – there is enough evidence to say that it has been successful in confronting hegemonic globalization at the two first levels of influence. It remains to be seen how successful it will be, and within what span of time, at the two last and more demanding levels of influence.

For the purposes of my argument in this article, two characteristics of transnational sub-politics must be highlighted at this point. The first one, a positive one, is that, contrary to the Western modern paradigms of progressive social transformation (revolution, socialism, social-democracy), the transnational sub-politics is as much involved in a politics of equality (redistribution) as in a politics of difference (recognition). This does not mean that these two kinds of politics are equally present in the different kinds of struggles, campaigns, and movements. Some struggles may privilege a politics of equality. This is the case of campaigns against sweatshops or of new movements of labor internationalism. Other struggles, on the contrary, may privilege a politics of difference, as is the case of some campaigns against racism and xenophobia in Europe or of some indigenous, aboriginal, and tribal rights movements in Latin America, Australia, New Zealand and India. Still other struggles may explicitly combine the politics of equality with the politics of difference. Such is the case of some other campaigns against racism and xenophobia in Europe, women's movements throughout the world, and campaigns against the plundering of biodiversity (or biopiracy), most of it located in indigenous territories, as well as of most indigenous movements. The articulation between redistribution and recognition becomes far more visible once we look at these movements, initiatives, and campaigns as a new constellation of political and cultural emancipatory meanings in an unevenly globalized world. So far, such meanings have not yet conquered their self-reflexivity. One of the purposes of this article is to point to one possible path toward this end.

The other characteristic of transnational sub-politics, a negative one, is that, so far, theories of separation have prevailed over theories of union among the great variety of existing movements, campaigns and initiatives. Indeed, truly global is only the logic of hegemonic globalization, poised to keep them separate and mutually unintelligible. For this reason, the notion of a counter-hegemonic globalization has a strong utopian component, and its full meaning can only be grasped through indirect procedures. I distinguish three main procedures: the sociology of absences, the theory of translation and *Manifesto* practices.

The *sociology of absences* is the procedure through which what does not exist, or whose existence is socially ungraspable or inexpressible, is conceived of as the active result of a given social process. The sociology of absences invents or unveils whatever social and political conditions, experiments, initiatives, conceptions have been successfully suppressed by hegemonic forms of globalization; or, rather than suppressed, have not been allowed to exist, to become pronounceable as a need or an aspiration. In the specific case of counter-hegemonic globalization, the sociology of absences is the procedure through which the incompleteness of particular anti-hegemonic struggles, as well as the inadequacy of local resistance in a globalized world, is constructed. Such incompleteness and inadequacy derive from the absent (suppressed, unimagined, discredited) links that might connect such struggles with other struggles elsewhere in the world, thus strengthening their potential to build credible counter-hegemonic alternatives. The more expertly the sociology of absences is performed, the greater the perception of incompleteness and inadequacy. At any rate, the universal and the global constructed by the sociology of absences, far from denying or eliminating the particular and the local, rather encourage them to envision what is beyond them as a condition of their successful resistance and possible alternatives.

Central to the sociology of absences is the notion that social experience is made up of social inexperience. This is taboo for the dominant classes that promote hegemonic capitalist globalization and its legitimizing cultural paradigm: on the one hand, Eurocentric modernity or what Scott Lash calls high modernity (1999), on the other, what I myself call celebratory postmodernity (1999b). The dominant classes have always taken as a given their particular experience of having to suffer the consequences of the ignorance, baseness or dangerousness of the dominated classes. Absent from their minds has always been their own inexperience of the suffering, death, pillage, imposed as experience upon the oppressed classes, groups or peoples.[3] For the latter, however, it is crucial to incorporate in their experience the inexperience of the oppressors concerning the suffering, humiliation and exploitation imposed upon the oppressed. The practice of the sociology of absences is what endows counter-hegemonic struggles with cosmopolitanism, that is, openness towards the other and increased knowledge. This is the kind of knowledge Retamar has in mind when he asserts: 'There is only one type of person who really knows in its entirety the literature of Europe: the colonial' (1989: 28).

To bring about such openness, it is necessary to resort to a second procedure: the *theory of translation*. A given particular or local struggle (for instance, an indigenous or feminist struggle) only recognizes another (for instance, an environment or labor struggle) to the extent that both lose some of their particularism and localism. This occurs as mutual intelligibility between struggles is created. Mutual intelligibility is a prerequisite of what I would call the internal, self-reflexive mix of the politics of equality and the politics of difference among movements, initiatives, campaigns, networks. It is the lack of internal self-reflexivity that has allowed theories of separation to prevail over theories of union. Some movements, initiatives and campaigns rally around the principle of equality, others around the principle of difference. The theory of translation is the procedure that allows for mutual intelligibility. Unlike a general theory of transformative action, the theory of translation keeps intact the autonomy of the struggles in question as a condition for the translation, since only what is different can be translated. To render mutually intelligible means to identify what unites and is common to entities that are separate by their reciprocal differences. The theory of translation permits common ground to be identified in an indigenous struggle, a feminist struggle, an ecological struggle, etc., etc., without canceling out in any of them the autonomy and difference that sustain them.

Once it is identified, what unites and is common to different anti-hegemonic struggles becomes a principle of action only to the extent that it is identified as the solution for the incompleteness and inadequacy of the struggles that remain confined to their particularism and localism. This step occurs by means of *Manifesto practices*. I mean clear and unequivocal blueprints of alliances that are possible because based on common denominators, and mobilizing because yielding a positive sum, that is to say, because they grant specific advantages to all those participating in them and according to their degree of participation.

Thus conceived, transnational emancipatory sub-politics or counter-hegemonic globalization has demanding conditions. What one expects from it is a tense and dynamic equilibrium between difference and equality, between identity and solidarity, between autonomy and cooperation, between recognition and redistribution. The success of the above-mentioned procedures depends, therefore, on cultural, political and economic factors. In the 1980s, the 'cultural turn' contributed decisively to highlight the poles of difference, identity, autonomy and recognition, but it often did so in a culturalist way, that is to say, by playing down economic and political factors. Thus were the poles of equality, solidarity, cooperation and redistribution neglected. At the beginning of the new century, after almost 20 years of fierce neoliberal globalization, the balance between the two poles must be retrieved. From the perspective of an oppositional postmodernity, the idea that there is no recognition without redistribution is central (Santos, 1998b: 121–39). Perhaps the best way to formulate this idea today is to resort to a modernist device, the notion of a fundamental meta-right: the right to have rights. We have the right to be equal whenever difference diminishes us; we have the right to be different whenever equality decharacterizes us. We have here a normative hybrid: it is modernist because based on an abstract universalism, but it is formulated in such a way as to sanction a postmodern opposition based on both redistribution and recognition.

As I have already said, the new constellations of meaning at work in transnational emancipatory sub-politics have not yet reached their self-reflexive moment. That this moment must occur, however, is crucial to the reinvention of political culture in the new century and millennium. The only way to encourage its emergence is by excavating the ruins of the marginalized, suppressed or silenced traditions upon which Eurocentric modernity built its own supremacy. They are another 'another modernity' (Lash, 1999).

To my mind, the *Nuestra America* American century has best formulated the idea of social emancipation based on the meta-right to have rights and on the dynamic equilibrium between recognition and redistribution presupposed by it. It has also most dramatically shown the difficulty of constructing successful emancipatory practices on that basis.

The *Nuestra America* American Century

'*Nuestra America*' is the title of a short essay by José Martí, published in the Mexican paper *El Partido Liberal* (30 January 1891). In this article, which is an excellent summary of Martian thinking to be found in several Latin American papers at the time, Martí expresses the set of ideas which I believe were to preside over the *Nuestra America* American century, a set of ideas later pursued by, among many others, Marietegui and Oswald de Andrade, Fernando Ortiz and Darcy Ribeiro.

The main ideas in this agenda are as follows. First, *Nuestra America* is at the antipodes of European America. It is the America *mestiza* founded at the often violent crossing of much European, Indian and African blood. It is the America that is capable of delving deeply into its own roots and from there to produce a knowledge and a government that are not imported, but rather adequate to its reality. Its deepest roots are the struggle of the Amerindian peoples against their invaders, where we find the true precursors of the Latin American *independentistas* (Retamar, 1989: 20). Asks Martí: 'Is it not evident that America itself was paralysed by the same blow that paralysed the Indian?' And he answers: 'Until the Indian is caused to walk, America itself will not begin to walk well' (1963, VIII: 336–7). Although in '*Nuestra America*' Martí deals mainly with anti-Indian racism, elsewhere he refers also to black people: 'A human being is more than white, more than mulatto, more than black. Cuban is more than white, more than mulatto, more than black. . . . Two kinds of racist would be equally guilty: the white racist and the black racist' (1963, II: 299).

The second idea about *Nuestra America* is that its mixed roots gave rise to infinite complexity, a new form of universalism that made the world richer. Says Martí: 'There is no race hatred because there are no races' (1963, VI: 22). In this sentence reverberates the same radical liberalism that had encouraged Simon Bolívar to proclaim that Latin America was 'a small humankind', a 'miniature humankind'. This kind of situated and contextualized universalism was to become one of the most enduring leitmotifs of *Nuestra America*.

In 1928, the Brazilian poet Oswald de Andrade published his *Anthropophagous Manifesto*. By anthropophagy he understood the American's capacity to devour all that was alien to him and to incorporate all so as to create a complex identity, a new, constantly changing identity:

> Only what is not mine interests me. The law of men. The law of the anthropophagous. . . . Against all importers of canned consciousness. The palpable existence of life. Pre-logical mentality for Mr. Levy-Bruhl to study. . . . I asked a man what is law. He said it is the guarantee of the exercise of possibility. This man's name was Galli Mathias. I swallowed him. Anthropophagy. Absorption of the sacred enemy. To turn him to totem. The human adventure. Earthly finality. However, only the pure elites managed to accomplish carnal anthropophagy, the one which carries with itself the highest meaning of life and avoids the evils identified by Freud, the catechetical evils. (Andrade, 1990: 47–51)

This concept of anthropophagy, ironic in itself in relation to the European representation of the 'Carib instinct', is quite close to the concept of transculturation developed by Fernando Ortiz in Cuba somewhat later (1940) (Ortiz, 1973). For a more recent example, I quote the Brazilian anthropologist Darcy Ribeiro in a burst of brilliant humour:

> It is quite easy to make an Australia: take a few French, English, Irish, and Italian people, throw them in a deserted island, they kill the Indians and make a second-rate England, damn it, or third-rate, that shit. Brazil has to realize that that is shit, Canada is shit, because it just repeats Europe. Just to show that ours is the adventure of making the new humankind, *mestizaje* in flesh and spirit. Mestizo is what is good. (1996: 104)

The third founding idea of *Nuestra America* is that for *Nuestra America* to be built upon its most genuine foundations, it has to endow itself with genuine knowledge. Martí again: 'The trenches of ideas are worth more than the trenches of stone' (1963, VI: 16). But, to accomplish this, ideas must be rooted in the aspirations of the oppressed peoples. Just as 'the authentic mestizo has conquered the exotic Creole . . . , the imported book has been conquered in America by the natural man' (1963, VI: 17). Hence Martí's appeal:

> The European university must yield to the American university. The history of America, from the Incas to the present, must be taught letter perfect, even if that of the Argonauts of Greece is not taught. Our own Greece is preferable

to that Greece that is not ours. We have greater need of it. National politicians must replace foreign and exotic politicians. Graft the world into our republics, but the trunk must be that of our republics. And let the conquered pedant be silent: there is no homeland of which the individual can be more proud than our unhappy American republics. (1963, VI: 18)

This situated knowledge, which demands a continuous attention to identity, behavior and involvement in public life, is truly what distinguishes a country, not the imperial attribution of levels of civilization. Martí distinguishes the intellectual from the man whom lived life's experience has made wise. He says: 'There is no fight between civilization and barbarism, rather between false erudition and nature' (Martí, 1963, VI: 17).

Nuestra America thus carries a strong epistemological component. Rather than importing foreign ideas, one must find out about the specific realities of the continent from a Latin American perspective. Ignoring or disdaining them has helped tyrants to accede to power, as well as grounded the arrogance of the USA vis-a-vis the rest of the Continent.

The contempt of the formidable neighbor who does not know her is the major threat to *Nuestra America*; and he must know her urgently to stop disdaining her. Being ignorant, he might perhaps covet her. Once he knew her, he would, out of respect, take his hand off her. (Martí, 1963, VI: 22)

A situated knowledge is, therefore, the condition for a situated government. As Martí says elsewhere, one cannot:

. . . rule new peoples with a singular and violent composition, with laws inherited from four centuries of free practice in the United States, and nineteen centuries of monarchy in France. One does not stop the blow in the chest of the plainsman's horse with one of Hamilton's decrees. One does not clear the congealed blood of the Indian race with a sentence of Sieyès.

And Martí adds: 'In the republic of Indians, governors learn Indian' (Martí, 1963, VI: 16–17).

One fourth founding idea of *Nuestra America* is that it is Caliban's American, not Prospero's. Prospero's America lies to the North, but it abides also in the South with those intellectual and political elites who reject Indian and black roots and look upon Europe and the USA as models to be imitated and upon their own countries with the ethnocentric blinders that distinguish civilization and barbaric wilderness. Martí has particularly in mind one of the earliest Southern formulations of Prospero's America, the work of an Argentinian, Domingo Sarmiento, entitled *Civilization and Barbarism* published in 1845 (Sarmiento, 1966). It is against this world of Prospero that Andrade pushes with his 'Carib instinct':

However, it was not the Crusaders who came, but rather the runaways from a civilization we are now eating up, for we are strong and vengeful like the

> Jabuti . . . We did not have speculation. But we did have divination. We had
> politics, which is the science of distribution. It is a social-planetary
> system. . . . Before the Portuguese discovered Brazil, Brazil had discovered
> happiness. (Andrade, 1990: 47–51)

The fifth basic idea of *Nuestra America* is that its political thinking, far
from being nationalistic, is rather internationalistic, and is strengthened by
an anti-colonialist and anti-imperialist stance, aimed at Europe in the past
and now at the USA. Those who think that neoliberal globalization from
NAFTA to the Initiative for the Americas and the World Trade Organization
is something new should read Martí's reports on the Pan-American Congress
of 1889–90 and the American International Monetary Commission of 1891.
Mere are Martí's remarks on the Pan-American Congress:

> Never in America, since independence, was there subject matter demanding
> more wisdom, requiring more vigilance or calling for clearer and closer atten-
> tion than the invitation that the powerful United States, filled with unsaleable
> products and determined to expand domination over America, addresses to
> the American nations with less power, linked by free, Europe-friendly trade,
> to form an alliance against Europe and cut off their contacts with the rest of
> the world. America managed to get rid of Spain's tyranny; now, having looked
> with judicious eyes upon the antecedents causes and factors of such an
> invitation, it is imperative to state, because it is true, that the time has come
> for Spanish America to declare her second independence. (1963, VI: 4–6)

According to Martí, the dominant conceptions in the USA concerning
Latin America must incite the latter to distrust all proposals coming from
the North. Outraged, Martí accuses:

> They believe in necessity, the barbaric right, as the only right, that 'this will
> be ours because we need it'. They believe in incomparable superiority of the
> 'Anglo-Saxon race as opposed to the Latin race'. They believe in the baseness
> of the negro race which they enslaved in the past and nowadays humiliate,
> and of the Indian race, which they exterminate. They believe that the peoples
> of Spanish America are mainly constituted of Indians and negros. (Martí,
> 1963, VI: 160)

The fact that *Nuestra America* and European America are geographi-
cally so close, as well as the former's awareness of the dangers issuing from
the power imbalance between both, soon forced *Nuestra America* to claim
her autonomy in the form of a thought and a practice from the South: 'The
North must be left behind' (Martí, 1963, II: 368). Martí's insight derives from
his many years of exile in New York, during which he became well
acquainted with 'the monster's entrails':

> In the North there is no support nor root. In the North the problems increase
> and there is no charity and patriotism to solve them. Here, men don't learn
> how to love one another, nor do they love the soil where they are born by

chance. Here was set up a machine that deprives, more than it can gratify, the universal craving for products. Here are piled up the rich on one side and the desperate on the other. The North clams up and is full of hatred. The North must be left behind. (Martí, 1963, II: 368)

It would be difficult to find a more clairvoyant preview of the European American century, and the need to create an alternative to it.

According to Martí, such an alternative resides in a united *Nuestra America* and the assertion of her autonomy vis-a-vis the USA. In a text dated 1894, Martí writes: 'Little is known about our sociology and about such precise laws as the following one: the farther away they keep from the USA, the freer and more prosperous will the peoples of America be' (1963, VI: 26–7). More ambitious and utopian is Oswald de Andrade's alternative: 'We want the Caribbean Revolution greater than the French Revolution. One unification of all efficacious revolts on behalf of man. Without us, Europe would not even have its poor declaration of the rights of man' (Andrade, 1990: 48).

In sum, for Martí the claim of equality grounds the struggle against unequal difference as much as the claim of difference grounds the struggle against the unequal equality. The only legitimate cannibalization of difference (Andrade's anthropophagy) is the one of the subaltern because only through it can Caliban recognize his own difference vis-a-vis the unequal differences imposed upon him. In other words, Andrade's anthropophagus digests according to his own guts.

The Baroque Ethos: Prolegomena for a New Cosmopolitan Law

Nuestra America is no mere intellectual construct for discussion in the salons that gave so much life to Latin American culture in the first decades of the 20th century. It is a political project, or rather, a set of political projects and a commitment to the objectives contained therein. That was the commitment that dragged Martí to exile and later to death fighting for Cuba's independence. As Oswald de Andrade was to say epigrammatically: 'Against the vegetal elites. In contact with the soil' (Andrade, 1990: 49). But before it becomes a political project, *Nuestra America* is a form of subjectivity and sociability. It is a way of being and living permanently in transit and transitoriness, crossing borders, creating borderland spaces, used to risk – with which it has lived for many years, long before the invention of the 'risk society' (Beck, 1992) – used to enduring a very low level of stability of expectations in the name of a visceral optimism before collective potentiality. Such optimism led Martí to assert in a period of *fin-de-siècle* Vienna cultural pessimism: 'A governor in a new nation means a creator' (1963, VI: 17). The same kind of optimism made Andrade exclaim: 'Joy is counter proof' (1990: 51).

The subjectivity and sociability of *Nuestra America* are uncomfortable with institutionalized, legalistic thought and comfortable with utopian thinking. By utopia I mean the exploration by imagination of new modes of human possibility and styles of will, and the confrontation by imagination of the necessity of whatever exists – just because it exists – on behalf of something radically better that is worth fighting for, and to which humanity is fully entitled (Santos, 1995: 479). This style of subjectivity and sociability is what I call, following Echeverria (1994), the baroque ethos.[4]

Whether as an artistic style or as an historical epoch, the baroque is most specifically a Latin and Mediterranean phenomenon, an eccentric form of modernity, the South of the North, so to speak. Its eccentricity derives, to a large extent, from the fact that it occurred in countries and at historical moments in which the center of power was weak and tried to hide its weakness by dramatizing conformist sociability. The relative lack of central power endows the baroque with an open-ended and unfinished character that allows for the autonomy and creativity of the margins and peripheries. Because of its eccentricity and exaggeration, the center reproduces itself as if it were a margin. I mean a centrifugal imagination which becomes stronger as we go from the internal peripheries of the European power to its external peripheries in Latin America. The whole of Latin America was colonized by weak centers, Portugal and Spain. Portugal was a hegemonic center during a brief period of time, between the 15th and the 16th centuries, and Spain started to decline but a century later. From the 17th century onwards, the colonies were more or less left alone, a marginalization that made possible a specific cultural and social creativity, now highly codified, now chaotic, now erudite, now vernacular, now official, now illegal. Such *mestizaje* is so deeply rooted in the social practices of these countries that it came to be considered as grounding a cultural ethos that is typically Latin American and has prevailed from the 17th century to the present. This form of baroque, inasmuch as it is the manifestation of an extreme instance of the center's weakness, constitutes a privileged field for the development of a centrifugal, subversive and blasphemous imagination.

As an epoch in European history, the baroque is a time of crisis and transition. I mean the economic, social and political crisis that is particularly obvious in the case of the powers that fostered the first phase of European expansion. In Portugal's case, the crisis implies even loss of independence. For reasons to do with the monarchic succession, Portugal was annexed to Spain in 1580, and only regained its independence in 1640. The Spanish monarchy, particularly under Felipe IV (1621–65), underwent a serious financial crisis that was actually also a political and cultural crisis. As Maravall has pointed out, it begins as a certain awareness of uneasiness and restlessness, which 'gets worse as the social fabric is seriously affected' (1990: 57). For instance, values and behaviors are questioned, the structure of classes undergoes some changes, banditism and deviant behavior in general increase, revolt and sedition are constant threats. It is indeed a time of crisis, but a time also of transition towards new modes of sociability made possible by the emergent capitalism and the new scientific paradigm, as well as towards new modes of political domination based not only on coercion, but also on cultural and ideological integration. To a large extent, baroque culture is one such instrument of consolidation and legitimation of power. What nonetheless seems to me inspiring in baroque culture is its grain of subversion and eccentricity, the weakness of the centers of power that look for legitimation in it, the space of creativity and imagination it opens up, the turbulent sociability that it fosters. The configuration of baroque subjectivity that I wish to advance here is a *collage* of diverse historical and cultural materials, some of which in fact cannot be considered technically as belonging to the baroque period.

Baroque subjectivity lives comfortably with the temporary suspension of order and canons. As a subjectivity of transition, it depends both on the exhaustion and the aspiration of canons; its privileged temporality is perennial transitoriness. It lacks the obvious certainties of universal laws – in the same way that baroque style lacked the classical universalism of the Renaissance. Because it is unable to plan its own repetition *ad infinitum*, baroque subjectivity invests in the local, the particular, the momentary, the ephemeral and the transitory. But the local is not lived in a localist fashion, that is, it is not experienced as an orthotopia; the local aspires, rather, to invent another place, a heterotopia, or even a utopia. Since it derives from a deep feeling of emptiness and disorientation caused by the exhaustion of the dominant canons, the comfort provided by the local is not the comfort of rest, but a sense of direction. Again, we can observe here a contrast with the Renaissance, as Wölfflin has taught us: 'In contrast to the Renaissance, which sought permanence and repose in everything, the baroque had from the first moment a definite *sense of direction*' (Wölfflin, 1979: 67).

Baroque subjectivity is contemporaneous with all the elements that it integrates, and hence contemptuous of modernist evolutionism. Thus, we might say, baroque temporality is the temporality of interruption. Interruption is important on two accounts: it allows for reflexivity and surprise. Reflexivity is the self-reflexivity required by the lack of maps (without maps to guide our steps, we must tread with double care). Without self-reflexivity, in a desert of canons, the desert itself becomes canonical. Surprise, in turn, is really suspense; it derives from the suspension accomplished by interruption. By momentarily suspending itself, baroque subjectivity intensifies the will and arouses passion. The 'baroque technique', argues Maravall, consists in 'suspending resolution so as to encourage it, after that provisional and transitory moment of arrest, to push further more efficiently with the help of those retained and concentrated forces' (Maravall, 1990: 445).

Interruption provokes wonder and novelty, and impedes closure and completion. Hence the unfinished and open-ended character of baroque sociability. The capacity for wonder, surprise and novelty is the energy that facilitates the struggle for an aspiration all the more convincing because it can never be completely fulfilled. The aim of baroque style, says Wölfflin, 'is not to represent a perfect state, but to suggest an incomplete process and a moment towards its completion' (Wölfflin, 1979: 67).

Baroque subjectivity has a very special relationship with forms. The geometry of baroque subjectivity is not Euclidean; it is fractal. Suspension of forms results from the extreme uses to which they are put: Maravall's *extremosidad* (Maravall, 1990: 421). As regards baroque subjectivity, forms are the exercise of freedom *par excellence*. The great importance of the exercise of freedom justifies that forms be treated with extreme seriousness, though the extremism may result in the destruction of the forms themselves. The reason why Michelangelo is rightly considered one of baroque's fore-fathers is, according to Wölfflin, 'because he treated forms with a violence, a terrible seriousness which could only find expression in formlessness' (Wölfflin, 1979: 82). This is what Michelangelo's contemporaries called *terribilità*. The extremism in the use of forms is grounded on a will to grandiosity that is also the will to astound so well formulated by Bernini: 'Let no one speak to me of what is small' (Tapié, 1988, II: 188). Extremism may be exercised in many different ways, to highlight simplicity, or even asceticism, as well as exuberance and extravagance, as Maravall has pointed out. Baroque extremism allows for ruptures emerging out of apparent conti-nuities and keeps the forms in a permanently unstable state of bifurcation, in Prigogine's terms (1996). One of the most eloquent examples is Bernini's *The Mystical Ecstasy of Santa Teresa*. In this sculpture, St Teresa's expres-sion is dramatized in such a way that the most intensely religious represen-tation of the saint is one with the profane representation of a woman enjoying a deep orgasm. The representation of the scared glides surreptitiously into the representation of the sacrilegious. Extremism of forms alone allows baroque subjectivity to entertain the turbulence and excitement necessary to continue the struggle for emancipatory causes, in a world in which emancipation has been collapsed into or absorbed by hegemonic regulation. To speak of extremism is to speak of archeological excavation into the regu-latory magma in order to retrieve emancipatory fires, no matter how dim.

The same extremism that produces forms, also devours them. This voracity takes on two forms: *sfumato* and *mestizaje*. In baroque painting, *sfumato* is the blurring of outlines and colors amongst objects, as clouds and mountains, or the sea and the sky. *Sfumato* allows baroque subjectivity to create the near and the familiar among different intelligibilities, thus making cross-cultural dialogues possible and desirable. For instance, only resorting to *sfumato* is it possible to give form to configurations that combine Western human rights with other conceptions of human dignity existing in other cul-tures (Santos, 1999a). The coherence of monolithic constructions disinte-grates, its free-floating fragments remain open to new coherences and inventions of new multicultural forms. *Sfumato* is like a magnet that attracts the fragmentary forms into new constellations and directions, appealing to their most vulnerable, unfinished, open-ended contours. *Sfumato* is, in sum, an antifortress militancy.

Mestizaje, in its turn, is a way of pushing *sfumato* to its utmost, or extreme. While *sfumato* operates through disintegration of forms and retrieval of fragments, *mestizaje* operates through the creation of new forms of constellations of meaning, which are truly unrecognizable or blasphemous in light of their constitutive fragments. *Mestizaje* resides in the destruction of the logic that presides over the formation of each of its fragments, and in the construction of a new logic. This productive-destructive process tends to reflect the power relations among the original cultural forms (that is, among their supporting social groups) and this is why baroque subjectivity favors the *mestizajes* in which power relations are replaced by shared authority (*mestiza* authority). Latin America has provided a particularly fertile soil for *mestizaje*, and so the region is one of the most important excavation sites for the construction of baroque subjectivity.[5]

Sfumato and *mestizaje* are the two constitutive elements of what I call, following Fernando Ortiz, transculturation. In his justly famous book, *Contrapunteo Cubano*, originally published in 1940, Ortiz proposes the concept of transculturation to define the synthesis of the utterly intricate cultural processes of deculturation and neoculturation that have always characterized Cuban society. In his thinking, the reciprocal cultural shocks and discoveries, which in Europe occurred slowly throughout more than four millennia, occurred in Cuba in sudden jumps over less than four centuries (1973: 131). The pre-Colombian transculturations between paleolithic and neolithic Indians were followed by many others after the European 'hurricane', amongst various European cultures and between those and various African and Asian cultures. According to Ortiz, what distinguishes Cuba, from the 16th century on, is the fact that its cultures and peoples were all equally invaders, exogenous, all of them torn away from their original cradle, haunted by separation and transplantation to the new culture that was being created (1973: 132). This permanent maladjustment and transitoriness allowed for new cultural constellations which cannot be reduced to the sum of the different fragments that contributed to them. The positive character of this constant process of transition between cultures is what Ortiz designates as transculturation. To reinforce this positive, new character, I prefer to speak of *sfumato* instead of deculturation and *mestizaje* instead of neoculturation. Transculturation designates, therefore, the voraciousness and extremism with which cultural forms are processed by baroque sociability. This self-same voraciousness and self-same extremism are also quite present in Oswald de Andrade's concept of anthropophagy.

The extremism with which forms are lived by baroque subjectivity stresses the rhetorical artifactuality of practices, discourses and modes of intelligibility. Artifice (*artificium*) is the foundation of a subjectivity suspended among fragments. Artifice allows baroque subjectivity to reinvent itself whenever the sociabilities it leads to tend to transform themselves into micro-orthodoxies. Through artifice, baroque subjectivity is lucid and subversive at the same time, as the baroque feast so well illustrates. The importance of the feast in baroque culture, both in Europe and in Latin America, is well documented.[6] The feast turned baroque culture into the first instance of mass culture of modernity. Its ostentatious and celebratory character was used by political and ecclesiastical powers to dramatize their greatness and reinforce their control over the masses. However, through its three basic components – *disproportion, laughter* and *subversion* – the baroque feast is invested with an emancipatory potential.

The baroque feast is out of proportion: it requires an extremely large investment which, however, is consumed in an extremely fleeting moment and an extremely limited space. As Maravall says, 'abundant and expensive means are used, a considerable effort is exerted, ample preparations are made, a complicated apparatus is set up, all that only to obtain some extremely short-lived effects, whether in the form of pleasure or surprise' (Maravall, 1990: 488). Nevertheless, disproportion generates a special intensification that, in turn, gives rise to the will to motion, the tolerance for chaos and the taste for turbulence, without which the struggle for the paradigmatic transition cannot take place.

Disproportion makes wonder, surprise, artifice and novelty possible. But above all, it makes playful distance and laughter possible. Because laughter is not easily codifiable, capitalist modernity declared war on mirth, and so laughter was considered frivolous, improper, eccentric, if not blasphemous. Laughter was to be admitted only in highly codified contexts of the entertainment industry. This phenomenon can also be observed among modern anti-capitalist social movements (labor parties, unions and even the new social movements) that banned laughter and play, lest they subvert the seriousness of resistance. Particularly interesting is the case of unions, whose activities at the beginning had a strong ludic and festive element (workers' feasts) which, however, was gradually suffocated, until at last union activity became deadly serious and deeply anti-erotic. The banishment of laughter and play is part of what Max Weber calls the *Entzäuberung* of the modern world.

The reinvention of social emancipation, which I suggest can be achieved by delving into baroque sociability, aims at the re-enchantment of common sense, which in itself presupposes the carnivalization of emancipatory social practices and the eroticism of laughter and play. As Oswald de Andrade said: 'Joy is counter proof' (1990: 51). The carnivalization of emancipatory social practice has an important self-reflexive dimension: it makes the decanonization and subversion of such practices possible. A decanonizing practice which does not know how to decanonize itself, falls easily into orthodoxy. Likewise, a subversive activity which does not know how to subvert itself, falls easily into regulatory routine.

And now, finally, the third emancipatory feature of the baroque feast: subversion. By carnivalizing social practices, the baroque feast displays a subversive potential that increases as the feast distances itself from the centers of power, but that is always there, even when the centers of power themselves are the promoters of the feast. Little wonder, then, that this subversive feature was much more noticeable in the colonies. Writing about carnival in the 1920s, the great Peruvian intellectual Marietegui asserted that, even though it had been appropriated by the bourgeoisie, carnival was indeed revolutionary, because, by turning the bourgeois into a wardrobe, it was a merciless parody of power and the past (Marietegui, 1974: 127).

Garcia de Leon also describes the subversive dimension of baroque feasts and religious processions in the Mexican port of Vera Cruz in the 17th century. Up front marched the highest dignitaries of the viceroyalty in their full regalia – politicians, clergymen and military men; at the end of the procession followed the populace, mimicking their betters in gesture and attire, and thus provoking laughter and merriment among the spectators (Leon, 1993). This symmetrical inversion of the beginning and end of the procession is a cultural metaphor for the upside-down world – *el mundo al revés* – which was typical of Vera Cruz sociability at the time: 'mulattas' dressed up as queens, slaves in silk garments, whores pretending to be honest women and honest women pretending to be whores; Africanized Portuguese and Indianized Spaniards.[7] The same *mundo al revés* is celebrated by Oswald de Andrade in his *Anthropophagous Manifesto*: 'But we have never admitted to the birth of logic among us. . . . Only where there is mystery is there no determinism. But what have we to do with this? We have never been catechized. We live in a sleepwalking law. We made Christ be born in Bahia. Or in Belém-Pará' (Andrade, 1990: 48).

In the feast, subversion is codified, in that it transgresses order while knowing the place of order and not questioning it, but the code itself is subverted by the *sfumatos* between feast and daily sociability. In the peripheries, transgression is almost a necessity. It is transgressive because it does not know how to be order, even as it knows that order exists. That is why baroque subjectivity privileges margins and peripheries as fields for the reconstruction of emancipatory energies.

All these characteristics turn the sociability generated by baroque subjectivity into a subcodified sociability: somewhat chaotic, inspired by a centrifugal imagination, positioned between despair and vertigo, this is a kind of sociability that celebrates revolt and revolutionizes celebration. Such sociability cannot but be emotional and passionate, the feature that most distinguishes baroque subjectivity from high modernity, or first modernity in Lash's terms (1999). High modern rationality, particularly after Descartes, condemns the emotions and the passions as obstacles to the progress of knowledge and truth. Cartesian rationality, says Toulmin, claims to be 'intellectually perfectionist, morally rigorous and humanly unrelenting' (Toulmin, 1990: 198). Not much of human life and social practice fits into such a conception of rationality, but it is nonetheless quite attractive to those who cherish the stability and hierarchy of universal rules. Hirschman, in his turn, has clearly shown the elective affinities between this form of rationality and emergent capitalism. Inasmuch as the interests of people and groups began centering around economic advantage, the interests that before had been considered passions became the opposite of passions and even the tamers of passion. From then on, says Hirschman, 'in the pursuit of their interests men were expected or assumed to be steadfast, single-minded and methodical, in total contrast to the stereotyped behavior of men who are buffeted and blinded by their passions' (Hirschman, 1977: 54). The objective was, of course, to create a 'one-dimensional' human personality. And Hirschman concludes: '[I]n sum, capitalism was supposed to accomplish exactly what was soon to be denounced as its worst feature' (1977: 132).

Cartesian and capitalist recipes are of little use for the reconstruction of a human personality with the capacity and desire for social emancipation. The meaning of the emancipatory struggles at the beginning of the 21st century can neither be deduced from demonstrative knowledge nor from an estimate of interests. Thus, the excavation undertaken by baroque subjectivity in this domain, more than in any other, must concentrate on suppressed or eccentric traditions of modernity, representations that occurred in the physical or symbolic peripheries where the control of hegemonic representations was weaker – the Vera Cruzes of modernity – or earlier, more chaotic representations of modernity that occurred before the Cartesian closure. For example, baroque subjectivity looks for inspiration in Montaigne and the concrete and erotic intelligibility of his life. In his essay 'On Experience', after saying that he hates remedies that are more troublesome than the disease, Montaigne writes:

> To be a victim of the colic and to subject oneself to abstinence from the pleasure of eating oysters, are two evils instead of one. The disease stabs us on one side, the diet on the other. Since there is the risk of mistake let us take it, for preference, in the pursuit of pleasure. The world does the opposite, and considers nothing to be useful that is not painful; facility rouses suspicions. (Montaigne, 1958: 370)

As Cassirer (1960, 1963) and Toulmin (1990) have shown for the Renaissance and the Enlightenment respectively, each era creates a subjectivity that is congruent with the new intellectual, social, political and cultural challenges. The baroque ethos is the building block of a form of subjectivity and sociability interested in and capable of confronting the hegemonic forms of globalization, thereby opening the space for counterhegemonic possibilities. Such possibilities are not fully developed and cannot by themselves promise a new era. But they are consistent enough to provide the grounding for the idea that we are entering a period of paradigmatic transition, an in-between era and therefore an era that is eager to follow the impulse of *mestizaje*, *sfumato*, hybridization and all the other features that I have attributed to the baroque ethos, and hence to *Nuestra America*. The progressive credibility conquered by the forms of subjectivity and sociability nurtured by such ethos will gradually translate into new interstitial normativities. Both Martí and Andrade have in mind a new kind of law and a new kind of rights. For them the right to be equal involves the right to be different, as the right to be different involves the right to be equal. Andrade's metaphor of anthropophagy is a call for such a complex interlegality. It is formulated from the perspective of subaltern difference, the only 'other' recognized by Eurocentric high modernity. The interstitial normative fragments we collect in *Nuestra America* will provide the seeds for a new 'natural' law, a cosmopolitan law, a law from below, to be found in the streets where survival and creative transgression fuse in an everyday-life pattern.

In the following I will elaborate on this new normativity in which redistribution and recognition come together to build the new emancipatory blueprints which I have called *New Manifestos*. But before that I want to dwell for a moment on the difficulties confronted by the *Nuestra America* project throughout the 20th century. They will help to illuminate the emancipatory tasks ahead.

Counter-Hegemony in the 20th Century

The *Nuestra America* American century was a century of counter-hegemonic possibilities, many of them following the tradition of others in the 19th century after the independence of Haiti in 1804. Amongst such possibilities, we might count the Mexican Revolution of 1910; the Indigenous movement headed by Quintin Lame in Colombia, 1914; the Sandinista movement in Nicaragua in the 1920s and 1930s, and its triumph in the 1980s; the radical democratization of Guatemala in 1944; the rise of Peronism in 1946; the triumph of the Cuban Revolution in 1959; Allende's rise to power in 1970; the Landless Movement in Brazil since the 1980s; the Zapatista Movement in Mexico since 1994.

The overwhelming majority of these emancipatory experiences were aimed against the European American century or, at least, had for their background the latter's political ambitions and hegemonic ideas. Indeed, the training ground for American, neoliberal, hegemonic globalization, which nowadays spreads throughout the entire globe, was in *Nuestra America* from the beginning of the 20th century. Not allowed to be the New World on the same footing with European America, *Nuestra America* was forced to be the Newest World of the European America. This poisoned privilege turned *Nuestra America* into a fertile field of cosmopolitan, emancipatory, counter-hegemonic experiences, as exhilarating as painful, as radiant in their promises as frustrating in their fulfillments.

What failed and why in the *Nuestra America* American century? It would be silly to propose an inventory before such an open future as ours. Nonetheless, I'll risk a few thoughts, which actually claim to account more for the future than the past. In the first place, to live in the 'monster's entrails' is no easy matter. It does allow a deep knowledge of the beast, as Martí so well demonstrates, but, on the other hand, it makes it very difficult to come out alive, even when one heeds Martí's admonishment: 'The North must be left behind' (Martí, 1963, II: 368). In my way of thinking, *Nuestra America* has been doubly living in the monster's entrails: because it shares with European America the continent that the latter had always conceived of as its vital space and zone of privileged influence; because, as Martí says in '*Nuestra America*', '*nuestra America* is the working America' (1963, VI: 23) and, thus, in its relations with European America, it shares the same tensions and sorrows that plague the relations between workers and capitalists. In this latter sense, *Nuestra America* has failed no more, no less than the workers of all the world in their struggle against capital.

My second thought is that *Nuestra America* did not have to fight only against the imperial incursions of its northern neighbor. The latter took over and became at home in the South, not just socializing with the natives but becoming a very native in the form of local elites and their transnational alliances with US interests. The Southern Prospero was present in Sarmiento's political-cultural project, in the interests of agrarian and industrial bourgeoisie, specially after the Second World War, in the military dictatorships of the 1960s and 1970s, in the fight against the communist threat and in the drastic neoliberal structural adjustment. In this sense, *Nuestra America* had to live trapped in and dependent on European America, just like Caliban vis-a-vis Prospero. That is why Latin American violence has taken the form of civil war much more often than the form of the Bay of Pigs.

The third thought concerns the absence of hegemony in the counter-hegemonic field. While it is a crucial instrument of class domination in complex societies, the concept of hegemony is equally crucial inside the struggles against such domination. Among the oppressed or dominated groups one must emerge, capable of converting its specific interests in liberation into the common interests of all the oppressed, and thus become hegemonic. Gramsci, we recall, was convinced that the workers constituted the group in question. We do know that things did not happen like that in the capitalist world, less so today than in Gramsci's own time, and far less so in *Nuestra America* than in Europe or European America. Indigenous, peasants, workers, *petit bourgeois*, black movements and struggles always occurred in isolation, antagonizing one another, ever without a theory of translation and devoid of the *Manifesto* practices referred to above. One of the weaknesses of *Nuestra America*, actually quite obvious in Martí's work, was to overestimate the communality of interests and the possibilities of uniting around them. Rather than uniting, *Nuestra America* underwent a process of Balkanization. Before this fragmentation, the union of European America became more efficacious. European America united around the idea of national identity and manifest destiny: a promised land destined to fulfill its promises at any cost for the outsiders.

My final thought concerns the cultural project of *Nuestra America* itself. To my mind, contrary to Martí's wishes, the European and North American university never gave entirely way to the American university. As witness the

> . . . pathetic bovarism of writers and scholars . . . which leads some Latin Americans . . . to imagine themselves as exiled metropolitans. For them, a work produced in their immediate orbit . . . merits their interest only when it has received the metropolis' approval, an approval that gives them the eyes with which to see it. (Retamar, 1989: 82)

Contrary to Ortiz's claim, transculturation was never total, and in fact it was undermined by power differences among the different components that contributed to it. For a very long time, and perhaps more so today at a time of vertiginous deterritorialized transculturation in the guise of hybridization, the questions about the inequality of power remained unanswered: who hybridizes whom and what? With what results? And for whose benefit? What, in the process of transculturation, did not go beyond deculturation or *sfumato* and why? If indeed it is true that most cultures were invaders, it is no less true that some invaded as masters, some as slaves. It is perhaps not risky today, 60 years later, to think that Oswald de Andrade's anthropophagous optimism was exaggerated: 'But no Crusaders came. Only runaways from a civilization which we are eating up, because we are strong and vengeful like the Jabuti' (Andrade, 1990: 50).

The European American century ended triumphantly, the protagonist of the last incarnation of the capitalist world system – hegemonic globalization. On the contrary, the *Nuestra America* American century ended sorrowfully. Latin America has imported many of the evils that Martí had seen in the monster's entrails, and the enormous emancipatory creativity it has demonstrated – as witness the Zapata and Sandino movements, the indigenous and peasant movements, Allende in 1970 and Fidel in 1959, the social movements, the ABC trade unions movement, the participatory budgeting in many Brazilian cities, the landless movement, the Zapatist movement – either ended in frustration or face an uncertain future. This uncertainty is all the greater since it is foreseeable that extreme polarization in the distribution of world wealth during the last decades, should it go on, will require an even more despotic system of repression worldwide than currently exists. With remarkable forethought, Darcy Ribeiro wrote in 1979: 'The means of repression required to maintain this system threaten to impose upon all the peoples such rigid and despotically efficient regimes as are without parallel in the history of iniquity' (1979: 40). It comes as no surprise that the intellectual and social climate of Latin America has been invaded in the past decades by a wave of cynical reason, a cultural pessimism utterly unrecognizable from the point of view of *Nuestra America*.

Counter-Hegemonic Possibilities for the 21st Century: Towards New *Manifestos*

In the light of the preceding, the question must be asked whether *Nuestra America* can in fact continue to symbolize a utopian will to emancipation and counter-hegemonic globalization, based on the mutual implication of equality and difference. My answer is positive but depending on the following condition: *Nuestra America* must be deterritorialized and turned into the metaphor for the struggle of the victims of hegemonic globalization wherever they may be, North or South, East or West. If we revisit the founding ideas of *Nuestra America*, we observe that the transformations of the last decades have created the conditions for them to occur and flourish today in other parts of the world. Let us examine some of them. First, the exponential increase of transborder interactions – of emigrants, students, refugees, as well as executives, tourists – is giving rise to new forms of *mestizaje*, anthropophagy and transculturation all over the world. The world becomes increasingly a world of invaders cut off from an origin they never had or, if they did, where they suffered the original experience of being invaded. Against celebratory postmodernism, more attention must be paid than was paid in the first century of *Nuestra America* to the power of the different participants in the processes of *mestizaje*. Such inequalities accounted for the perversion both of the politics of difference (recognition became a form of miscognition) and the politics of equality (redistribution ended up as the new forms of poor relief advocated by the World Bank and IMF).

Second, the recent ugly revival of racism in the North points to an aggressive defense against the unstoppable construction of the multiple little humankinds Bolivar talked about, where races cross and interpenetrate in the margins of repression and discrimination. As the Cuban, in Martí's voice, could proclaim to be more than black, mulatto or white, so the South African, the Mozambican, the New Yorker, the Parisian, the Londoner can proclaim today to be more than black, white, mulatto, Indian, Kurd, Arab, etc., etc. Third, the demand to produce or sustain situated and contextualized knowledge is today a global claim against the ignorance and silencing effect produced by modern science as it is used by hegemonic globalization. This epistemological issue gained enormous relevance in recent times with the newest developments of biotechnology and genetic engineering and the consequent struggle to defend biodiversity from biopiracy. In this domain, Latin America, one of the great stores of biodiversity, continues to be the home of *Nuestra America* but many other countries are in this position, in Africa or Asia. Fourth, as hegemonic globalization deepened, the 'entrails of the monster' have drawn closer to many other peoples in other continents. The closeness effect is today produced by information and communication capitalism and by consumer society. Hereby are multiplied both the grounds for the cynical reason and the postcolonial impulse. No other counter-hegemonic internationalism seems to loom on the horizon, but chaotic and fragmentary internationalisms have become part of our quotidian life. In a word, the new *Nuestra America* is today in a condition to globalize itself and thereby propose new emancipatory alliances to the old *Nuestra America*, since localized.

The counter-hegemonic nature of *Nuestra America* lies in its potential to develop a progressive transnational political culture. Such a political culture will concentrate on (1) identifying the multiple local/global linkages among struggles, movements and initiatives; (2) promoting the clashes between hegemonic globalization trends and pressures, on one side, and the transnational coalitions to resist against them, on the other, thus opening up possibilities for counter-hegemonic globalizations; (3) promoting internal and external self-reflexivity so that the forms of redistribution and recognition that are established among the movements mirror the forms of redistribution and recognition that transnational emancipatory sub-politics wishes to see implemented in the world.

Towards New Manifestos

In 1998 the *Communist Manifesto* celebrated its 150th anniversary. The *Manifesto* is one of the landmark texts of Western modernity. In a few pages and with unsurpassed clarity, Marx and Engels offer there a global view of society in their own time, a general theory of historical development, and a short- and long-term political program. The *Manifesto* is a Eurocentric document that conveys an unswerving faith in progress, acclaims the bourgeoisie as the revolutionary class that made it possible, and by the same token prophesies the defeat of the bourgeoisie vis-a-vis the proletariat as the emergent class capable of guaranteeing the continuity of progress beyond bourgeois limits.

Some of the themes, analyses and appeals included in the *Manifesto* are still up to date. However, Marx's prophecies were never fulfilled. Capitalism did not succumb at the hands of the enemies it created itself and the communist alternative failed utterly. Capitalism globalized itself far more effectively than the proletarian movement, while the latter's successes, namely in the more developed countries, consisted in humanizing, rather than overcoming, capitalism.

Nonetheless, the social evils denounced by the *Manifesto* are today as grievous as then. The progress achieved in the mean time has gone hand in hand with wars that killed and go on killing millions of people, and the gap between the rich and the poor has never before been so wide as today. As I mentioned above, in the face of such a reality, I believe that it is necessary to create the conditions for not one but several new *Manifestos* to emerge, with the potential to mobilize all the progressive forces of the world. By progressive forces are meant all those unreconciled with the spread of societal fascism, which they do not see as inevitable, and who therefore go on fighting for alternatives. The complexity of the contemporary world and the increasing visibility of its great diversity and inequality render impossible the translation of principles of action into one single manifesto. I have therefore in mind several manifestos, each one of them opening up possible paths toward an alternative society vis-a-vis societal fascism.

Moreover, unlike the *Communist Manifesto*, the new manifestos will not be the achievement of individual scientists observing the world from one privileged perspective alone. Rather, they will be far more multicultural and indebted to different paradigms of knowledge, and will emerge, by virtue of translation, networking and *mestizaje*, in 'conversations of humankind' (John Dewey) involving social scientists and activists engaged in social struggles all over the world.

The new *Manifestos* must focus on those themes and alternatives that carry more potential to build counter-hegemonic globalizations in the next decades. In my view, the five following themes are the most important ones in this respect. In regard to each one of them, *Nuestra America* provides a vast field of historical experience. *Nuestra America* thus emerges as the most privileged site where the challenges posed by the emergent transnational political culture can be confronted. I here enumerate the five themes in no order of precedence.

1. Participatory Democracy. Along with the hegemonic model of democracy (liberal, representative democracy), other, subaltern models of democracy have always coexisted, no matter how marginalized or discredited. We live in paradoxical times: at the very moment of its most convincing triumphs across the globe, liberal democracy becomes less and less credible and convincing, not only in the 'new frontier' countries but also in the countries where it has its deepest roots. The twin crises of representation and participation are the most visible symptoms of such deficit of credibility and, in the last instance, of legitimacy. On the other hand, local, regional and national communities in different parts of the world are undertaking democratic experiments and initiatives, based on alternative models of democracy, in which the tensions between capitalism and democracy and between redistribution and recognition become alive and turn into positive energy behind new, more comprehensive and more just social contracts, no matter how locally circumscribed they may be.[8] In some countries in Africa, Latin America and Asia, traditional forms of authority and self-government are being revisited to explore the possibility of their internal transformation and articulation with other forms of democratic rule.

2. Alternative Production Systems. A market economy is of course possible and, within limits, even desirable. On the contrary, a market society is impossible and, if possible, would be morally repugnant, and indeed ungovernable. Nothing short of societal fascism. One possible response to societal fascism is alternative production systems. Discussions about counter-hegemonic globalization tend to focus on social, political and cultural initiatives, only rarely focusing on the economic ones, that is, on local/global initiatives consisting of non-capitalist production and distribution of goods and services, whether in rural or urban settings: cooperatives, mutualities, credit systems, farming of invaded land by landless peasants, sustainable water systems and fishing communities, ecological logging, etc. These initiatives are those in which local/global linkages are most difficult to establish, if for no other reason than because they confront more directly the logic of global capitalism that lies behind hegemonic globalization, not only at the level of production but also at the level of distribution. Another important facet of alternative production systems is that they are never exclusively economic in nature. They mobilize social and cultural resources in such a way as to prevent the reduction of social value to market price.

3. Emancipatory Multicultural Justices and Citizenships. The crisis of Western modernity has shown that the failure of progressive projects concerning the improvement of life chances and life conditions of subordinate groups both inside and outside the Western world was in part due to lack of cultural legitimacy. This applies even to human rights movements since the universality of human rights cannot be taken for granted (Santos, 1999a). The idea of human dignity can be formulated in different 'languages'. Rather than being suppressed in the name of postulated universalisms, such differences must be mutually intelligible through translation and what I call diatopical hermeneutics. By diatopical hermeneutics I understand an interpretation of isomorphic concerns of different cultures conducted by partners who are able and willing to argue with one foot in one culture and the other foot in another (Santos, 1995: 340–2).

Since modern nation-building was accomplished more often than not by smashing the cultural and national identity of minorities (and sometimes even majorities), the recognition of multiculturalism and of multinationhood carries with it the aspiration to self-determination, that is to say, the aspiration to equal recognition and differentiated equalities. The case of the indigenous peoples is paramount in this regard. Even though all cultures are relative, relativism is wrong as a philosophical stance. It is therefore imperative to develop (transcultural?) criteria to distinguish emancipatory from retrogressive forms of multiculturalism or self-determination.

The aspiration to multiculturalism and self-determination often takes the social form of a struggle for justice and citizenship. It involves the claims for alternative forms of law and justice and for new regimes of citizenship. The plurality of legal orders, which has become more visible with the crisis of the nation-state, carries with it, either implicitly or explicitly, the idea of multiple citizenships coexisting in the same geopolitical field and, hence, the idea of the existence of first-, second- and third-class citizens. However, non-state legal orders may also be the embryo of non-state public spheres and the institutional base for self-determination, as in the case of indigenous justice: forms of community, informal, local, popular justice that are part and parcel of struggles or initiatives pertaining to any of the three above-mentioned themes. For instance, community or popular justice as an integral component of participatory democracy initiatives; indigenous justice as an integral component of self-determination or conservation of biodiversity. The concept of 'multicultural citizenship' (Kymlicka, 1995) is the privileged site upon which to ground the kind of mutual implication of redistribution and recognition I am advocating in this article.

4. Biodiversity, Rival Knowledges and Intellectual Property Rights. Due to the advancement of the last decades in the life sciences, biotechnology and microelectronics, biodiversity has become one of the most precious and sought after 'natural resources'. For biotechnology and pharmaceutical firms, biodiversity appears increasingly at the core of the most spectacular and thus profitable product developments in the years ahead. By and large, biodiversity occurs mainly in the so-called Third World and predominantly in territories historically owned or long occupied by indigenous peoples. While technologically advanced countries seek to extend intellectual property rights and patent law to biodiversity, some peripheral countries, indigenous peoples' groups and transnational advocacy networks on their behalf are seeking to guarantee the conservation and reproduction of biodiversity by granting special protected status to the territories, ways of life and traditional knowledges of indigenous and peasant communities. It is increasingly evident that the new cleavages between the North and the South will be centered around the question of access to biodiversity on a global scale.

Though all the above-mentioned themes raise an epistemological issue, to the extent that they claim the validity of knowledges that have been discarded by hegemonic scientific knowledge, biodiversity is probably the topic in which the clash between rival knowledges is more evident and eventually more unequal and violent. Here equality and difference are the building blocks on new *mestiza* epistemological claims.

5. New Labor Internationalism. As is well known labor internationalism was one of the most blatantly unfulfilled predictions of the *Communist Manifesto*. Capital globalized itself, not the labor movement. The labor movement organized itself at the national level and, at least in the core countries, became increasingly dependent upon the welfare state. It is true that in our century international links and organizations have kept alive the idea of labor internationalism, but they became prey to the Cold War and their fate followed the fate of the Cold War.

In the post-Cold War period, and as a response to the more aggressive bouts of hegemonic globalization, new and as yet very precarious forms of labor internationalism have emerged: the debate on labor standards; exchanges, agreements or even institutional congregation among labor unions of different countries integrated in the same economic regional bloc (NAFTA, European Union, Mercosul); articulation among struggles, claims and demands of the different labor unions representing the workers working for the same multinational corporation in different countries, etc.

Even more directly than alternative-production systems, the new labor internationalism confronts the logic of global capitalism on its own privileged ground: the economy. Its success is dependent upon the 'extra-economic' linkages it will be able to build with the struggles clustered around all the other four themes. Such linkages will be crucial to transform the politics of equality that dominated the old labor internationalism into a new political and cultural mix of equality and difference.

None of these themes or thematic initiatives taken separately will succeed in bringing about transnational emancipatory sub-politics or counter-hegemonic globalization. To be successful their emancipatory concerns must undergo translation and networking, expanding in ever more socially hybrid but politically focused movements. In a nutshell, what is at stake in political terms at the beginning of the century is the reinvention of the state and of civil society in such a way that societal fascism will vanish as a possible future. This is to be accomplished through the proliferation of local/global public spheres in which nation-states are important partners but not exclusive dispensers of either legitimacy or hegemony.

Conclusion: Which Side are You On, Ariel?

Starting from an analysis of *Nuestra America* as the subaltern view of the American continent throughout the 20th century, I identified *Nuestra America*'s counter-hegemonic potential and indicated some of the reasons why it failed to fulfill itself. Revisiting the historical trajectory of *Nuestra America* and its cultural conscience, the baroque ethos, and proceeding on that basis, I then reconstructed the forms of sociability and subjectivity that might be interested in and capable of confronting the challenges posed by counter-hegemonic globalizations. The symbolic expansion made possible by a metaphorical interpretation of *Nuestra America* permits us to view the latter as the blueprint of the new transnational political culture called for in the new century and millennium. The normative claims of this political culture are embedded in the lived experiences of the people for whom *Nuestra America* speaks. Such claims, however embryonic and interstitial, point to a new kind of 'natural law' – a situated, contextualized, postcolonial, multicultural, bottom-up, cosmopolitan law.

The fact that the five themes selected as testing grounds and playing fields of the new political culture have deep roots in Latin America justifies, from an historical and political point of view, the symbolic expansion of the idea of *Nuestra America* proposed in this article. However, in order not to repeat the frustrations of the last century, this symbolic expansion must go one step further and include the most neglected trope in the *Nuestra America* mythos: Ariel, the spirit of air in Shakespeare's *The Tempest*. Like Caliban, Ariel is Prospero's slave. However, besides not being deformed like Caliban, he gets much better treatment from Prospero, who promises him freedom if he serves Prospero faithfully. As we have seen, *Nuestra America* has looked upon itself predominantly as Caliban in constant and unequal struggle against Prospero. This is how Andrade, Aimé Césaire, Edward Braithwaite, George Lamming, Retamar and many others see it (Retamar, 1989: 13). While this is the dominant vision, it is not the only one. For instance, in 1898 the Franco-Argentinian writer Paul Groussac spoke of the need to defend the old European and Latin American civilization against the 'Calibanesque Yankee' (Retamar, 1989: 10). On the other hand, the ambiguous figure of Ariel inspired several interpretations In 1900, the writer José Enrique Rodó published his own *Ariel*, in which he identifies Latin America with Ariel, while implicitly North America gets identified with Caliban. In 1935, the Argentine Anibal Ponce saw in Ariel the intellectual, tied to Prospero in a less brutal way than Caliban, but nonetheless at his service, much according to the model that Renaissance humanism conceived for the intellectuals: a mixture of slave and mercenary, indifferent to action and conformist vis-a-vis the established order (Retamar, 1989: 12). This is the intellectual Ariel reinvented by Aimé Césaire in his play of the late 1960s: *Une tempête: adaptation de 'La Tempête' de Shakespeare pour un théâtre nègre*. Now turned into a mulatto, Ariel is the intellectual permanently in crisis.

This said, I suggest it is high time we give a new symbolic identification to Ariel and ascertain of what use he can be for the promotion of the emancipatory ideal of *Nuestra America*. I shall conclude, therefore, by presenting Ariel as a baroque angel undergoing three transfigurations.

His first transfiguration is Césaire's mulatto Ariel. Against racism and xenophobia, Ariel represents transculturation and multiculturalism, *mestizaje* of flesh and spirit, as Darcy Ribeiro would say. In this *mestizaje* the possibility of interracial tolerance and intercultural dialogue is inscribed. The mulatto Ariel is the metaphor of a possible synthesis between recognition and equality.

Ariel's second transfiguration is Gramsci's intellectual, who exercises self-reflexivity in order to know on whose side he is and what use he can be. This Ariel is unequivocally on the side of Caliban, on the side of all the oppressed peoples and groups of the world, and keeps a constant epistemological and political vigilance on himself lest his help becomes useless or even counterproductive. This Ariel is an intellectual trained in Martí's university.

The third and last transfiguration is more complex. As a mulatto and an organic intellectual, Arial is a figure of intermediation. In spite of the most recent transformations of the world economy, I still think that there are countries (or regions, sectors) of intermediary development which perform the function of intermediation between the core and the periphery of the world system. Particularly important in this regard are countries like Brazil, Mexico and India. The first two countries only came to recognize their multicultural and pluri-ethnic characters at the end of the 20th century. Such recognition came at the end of a painful historical process in the course of which the suppression of difference (for example, in Brazil 'racial democracy' and in Mexico 'assimilationism' and the *mestizo* as the '*raza cosmica*'), rather than opening up the space for republican equality, led to the most abject forms of inequality. Just like the Ariel of Shakespeare's play, rather than uniting amongst themselves and with many others coming from Caliban-countries, these intermediation countries have been using their economic and populational weight to try to gain privileged treatment from Prospero. They act in isolation hoping to maximize their possibilities of success alone.

As I have argued in this article, the potential of their populations for engaging in transnational emancipatory sub-politics and thus in counter-hegemonic globalizations depends upon their capacity to transfigure themselves into an Ariel unequivocally solidary with Caliban. In this symbolic transfiguration resides the most important political task of the next decades. On them depends the possibility of a second century of *Nuestra America* with greater success than the first one.

Notes

I would like to thank Diane Soles, Paula Meneses and Luis Carlos Arenas, my research assistants, for their help.

My thanks also to Maria Irene Ramalho for her comments and editorial revisions.

1. On the relations between the Pope and the feudal lords concerning the Crusades, see Gibbon (1928, vol. 6: 31).

2. From very different perspectives Robertson (1992); Escobar (1995); Castells (1996); Hopkins and Wallerstein (1996); Mander and Goldsmith (1996); Ritzer (1996); Chossudovsky (1997); Bauman (1998); Arrighi and Silver (1999); Jameson and Miyoshi (1999) converge on this.

3. A brilliant exception is Montaigne's essay on 'The Cannibals' (1958), written at the very beginning of Eurocentric modernity.

4. The baroque ethos I propound here is very different from Lash's 'Baroque melancholy' (1999: 330). Our differences are due in part to the different loci of the baroque we base our analysis on, Europe in the case of Lash, Latin America in my case.

5. Among others see Alberro (1992); Pastor et al. (1993). With reference to Brazilian baroque Coutinho (1990: 16) speaks of 'a complex baroque *mestiçajem*'. Cf. also the concept of the 'Black Atlantic' (Gilroy, 1993) to express the *mestizaje* that characterizes black cultural experience, an experience that is not specifically African, American, Caribbean or British, but all of them at one and the same time. In the Portuguese-speaking world, the *Anthropophagous Manifesto* of Oswald de Andrade remains the most striking exemplar of *mestizaje*.

6. On the baroque feast in Mexico see Leon (1993), and in Brazil (Minas Gerais) see Ávila (1994). The relationship between the feast, particularly the baroque feast, and utopian thinking remains to be explored. On the relationship between *fouriérisme* and *la société festive*, see Desroche (1975).

7. Ávila concurs, stressing the mixture of religious and heathen motifs: 'Amongst hordes of negroes playing bagpipes, drums, fifes and trumpets, there would be, for example, an excellent German "impersonator" tearing apart the silence of the air with the loud sound of a clarinet, while the believers devoutly carried religious banners or images' (1994: 56).

8. I studied participatory budgeting in the city of Porto Alegre (Santos, 1998c).

References

Alberro, Solange (1992) *Del Gachupin al Criollo*. Mexico City: El Colégio de Mexico.

Andrade, Oswald de (1990) *A utopia antropofágica*. São Paulo: Globo.

Arrighi, Giovanni and Beverly Silver (eds) (1999) *Chaos and Governance in the Modern World System*. Minneapolis: University of Minnesota Press.

Ávila, Affonso (1994) *O lúdico e as projecções do mundo barroco – II*. São Paulo: Editora Perspectiva.

Bauman, Zygmunt (1998) *Globalization: The Human Consequences*. New York: Columbia University Press.

Beck, Ulrich (1992) *The Risk Society: Towards a New Modernity*. London: Sage.

Beck, Ulrich (1995) 'The Reinvention of Politics: Towards a Theory of Reflexive Modernization', pp. 1–55 in Ulrich Beck, Anthony Giddens and Scott Lash (eds) *Reflexive Modernization: Politics, Tradition and Aesthetics*. Cambridge: Polity Press.

Benjamin, Walter (1980) 'Uber den Begriff der Geschichter', in *Gesammelte Schriften, Werkausgabe*, vol. 2. Frankfurt am Main: Suhrkamp.

Brysk, Alison (2000) *From Tribal Village to Global Village: Indian Rights and International Relations in Latin America*. Stanford, CA: Stanford University Press.

Casanova, Pablo Gonzalez (1998) 'The Theory of the Rain Forest against Neo-liberalism and for Humanity', *Thesis Eleven* 53: 79–92.

Cassirer, Ernst (1960) *The Philosophy of the Enlightenment*. Boston, MA: Beacon Press.

Cassirer, Ernst (1963) *The Individual and the Cosmos in Renaissance Philosophy*. Oxford: Blackwell.

Castells, Manuel (1996) *The Rise of the Network Society*. Cambridge, MA: Blackwell.

Chossudovsky, Michel (1997) *The Globalization of Poverty: The Impacts of IMF and World Bank Reforms*. London: Zed Books.

Coutinho, Afrânio (1990) 'O barroco e o maneirismo', *Claro Escuro* 4–5: 15–16.

Desroche, Henri (1975) *La Société festive: du fouriérisme aux fouriérismes pratiqués*. Paris: Seuil.

Douthwaite, Richard (1999) 'Is It Impossible to Build a Sustainable World?', in Ronaldo Munck and Dennis O'Hearn (eds) *Critical Development Theory: Contributions to a New Paradigm*. London: Zed Books.

Echeverria, Bolívar (1994) *Modernidad, mestizaje, cultura, ethos barroco*. Mexico: UNAM, El Equilibrista.

Escobar, Arturo (1995) *Encountering Development: The Making and Unmaking of the Third World*. Princeton, NJ: Princeton University Press.

Evans, Peter (2000) 'Fighting Marginalization with Transnation Networks. Counter-hegemonic Globalization', *Contemporary Sociology* 29(1): 231–41.

Falk, Richard (1995) *On Human Governance: Toward a New Global Politics*. University Park, PA: Pennsylvania State University Press.

Featherstone, Mike and Scott Lash (eds) (1999) *Spaces of Culture: City, Nation, World*. London: Sage.

Gibbon, Edward (1928) *The Decline and Fall of the Roman Empire*, vol. 6. London: J.M. Dent and Sons.

Gilroy, Paul (1993) *The Black Atlantic: Modernity and Double Consciousness*. Cambridge, MA: Harvard University Press.

Hirschman, Albert (1977) *The Passions and the Interests*. Princeton, NJ: Princeton University Press.

Hopkins, Terence and Immanuel Wallerstein (1996) *The Age of Transition: Trajectory of the World-System 1945–2025*. London: Zed Books.

Jameson, Fredric and Masao Miyoshi (eds) (1999) *The Cultures of Globalization*. Durham, NC: Duke University Press.

Keck, Margaret and Kathryn Sikkink (1998) *Activists beyond Borders: Advocacy Networks in International Politics*. Ithaca, NY: Cornell University Press.

Kymlicka, Will (1995) *Multicultural Citizenship*. Oxford: Oxford University Press.

Lash, Scott (1999) *Another Modernity, a Different Rationality*. Oxford: Blackwell.

Leon, Antonio Garcia (1993) 'Contrapunto entre lo barroco y lo popular en el Vera Cruz colonial', paper presented at International Colloquium Modernidad Europea, Mestizaje Cultural y Ethos Barroco, Universidad Nacional Autónoma de Méjico, 17–20 May.

Mander, Jerry (1996) 'Facing the Rising Tide', pp. 3–19 in J. Mander and E. Goldsmith (eds) *The Case against the Global Economy: And for Turn toward the Local*. San Francisco, CA: Sierra Club Books.

Mander, Jerry and Edward Goldsmith (1996) *The Case against the Global Economy: And for Turn toward the Local*. San Francisco, CA: Sierra Club Books.

Maravall, José Antonio (1990) *La cultura del barroco*, 5th edn. Barcelona: Ariel.

Marietegui, José Carlos (1974) *La novela y la vida*. Lima: Biblioteca Amanta.

Martí, José (1963) *Obras completas*. La Habana: Editorial Nacional de Cuba.

Marx, Karl (1973) 'The Communist Manifesto', *The Revolution of 1848. Political Writings*, Vol. I. London: Penguin Books.

Montaigne, Michel de (1958) *Essays*. Harmondsworth: Penguin.

Ortiz, Fernando (1973) *Contrapunteo cubano del tabaco y el azucar*. Barcelona: Ariel.

Pastor, Alba et al. (1993) *Aproximaciones al mundo barroco latinoamericano*. Mexico City: Universidad Nacional Autónoma de Méjico.

Polanyi, Karl (1957) *The Great Transformation*. Boston, MA: Beacon Press. (Orig. pub. 1944.)

Prigogine, Ilya (1996) *La Fin des certitudes*. Paris: Odile Jacob.

Retamar, Roberto (1989) *Caliban and Other Essays*. Minneapolis: University of Minnesota Press.

Ribeiro, Darcy (1979) *Ensaios insólitos*. Porto Alegre: L & PM Editores.

Ribeiro, Darcy (1996) *Mestiço é que é bom*. With the collaboration of Oscar Niemeyer et al. Rio de Janeiro: Editora Revan.

Ritzer, George (1996) *The McDonaldization of Society*, revised edn. Thousand Oaks, CA: Pine Forge.

Robertson, Roland (1992) *Globalization*. London: Sage.

Santos, Boaventura de Sousa (1995) *Towards a New Common Sense: Law, Science and Politics in the Paradigmatic Transition*. New York: Routledge.

Santos, Boaventura de Sousa (1998a) *Reinventar a democracia*. Lisboa: Gradiva.

Santos, Boaventura de Sousa (1998b) 'Oppositional Postmodernism and Globalization', *Law and Social Inquiry* 23(1): 121–39.

Santos, Boaventura de Sousa (1998c) 'Participatory Budgeting in Porto Alegre: Toward a Redistributive Democracy', *Politics & Society* 26(4): 416–510.

Santos, Boaventura de Sousa (1999a) 'Towards a Multicultural Conception of Human Rights', pp. 214–29 in M. Featherstone and S. Lash (eds) *Spaces of Culture: City–Nation–World*. London: Sage.

Santos, Boaventura de Sousa (1999b) 'On Oppositional Postmodernism', in Ronald Munck and Denis O'Hearn (eds) *Critical Development Theory*. London: Zed Books.

Sarmiento, Domingo (1966) *Facundo, civilización y barbarie*. Mexico: Editorial Porrúa.

Schumpeter, Joseph (1962) *Capitalism, Socialism and Democracy*, 3rd edn. New York: Harper and Row. (Orig. pub. 1942.)

Tapié, Victor (1988) *Barroco e classicismo*, 2 vols. Lisboa: Presença.

Tarrow, Sidney (1999) *Power in Movement: Social Movements and Contention Politics*. Cambridge: Cambridge University Press.

Toulmin, Stephen (1990) *Cosmopolis: The Hidden Agenda of Modernity*. New York: Free University Press.

Wölfflin, Heinrich (1979) *Renaissance and Baroque*. Ithaca, NY: Cornell University Press.

Hybridity, So What?
The Anti-hybridity Backlash and the Riddles of Recognition

Jan Nederveen Pieterse

O PENING UP to identity politics and politics of difference is one of
the changes of recent times, and recognition further widens this
frame. As the goalposts are shifted towards recognition and difference
new problems arise. As identity politics comes to the fore, does interest
politics fade into the background? What is the relationship between identity
and class, between recognition and social justice? What about recognition
of the steepest difference of all, which is the world's development gap? These
questions are explored elsewhere in this volume. This inquiry probes a
different set of questions. If we recognize 'others', according to which boundaries do we identify 'others'? If we recognize difference, what about 'difference within'? What about those who straddle or are in between categories
and combine identities?

To what extent is recognition a function of the available categories of
knowledge and cognitive frames in which self and others are identifiable and
recognizable? Can it be that recognition is an exercise in reproduction, re-
cycling the categories in which existing social relations have been coded
while stretching their meaning? Recognition, then, stretches or revalues
social boundaries but does not transgress them. To what extent is the politics
of recognition a politics of musical chairs – as one more identity is acknowledged, another is left behind? As the spotlight turns to one identity, does
another fade into the shadow? To what extent does the politics of recognition
chase the social horizon which ever recedes as one comes closer? To what
extent is 'progress' (such a difficult word) measured not simply in attainment
(because any attainment is partial and entails a price) but in process and
motion? And then what would such acknowledgement of process entail?

■ *Theory, Culture & Society* 2001 (SAGE, London, Thousand Oaks and New Delhi),
   Vol. 18(2–3): 219–245
   [0263-2764(200104/06)18:2–3;219–245;017488]

'Recognition' refers to the willingness to socially or publicly validate or affirm differences as they are perceived, but what about differences that are not being perceived? Recognition and difference are a function of the existing identities and boundaries that are available on the social and cultural maps. Recognition is part of a process of struggle over cognition. Hybridity is a journey into the riddles of recognition. Take any exercise in social mapping and it is the hybrids that are missing. Take most models and arrangements of multiculturalism and it is hybrids that are not counted, not accommodated. So what? This article addresses this question. The 2000 Census in the United States is the first that permits multiple identification: for the first time one can identify as Caucasian, African American, Hispanic, etc., and as all of those. This public recognition of multiple identity has been controversial particularly for minorities whose entitlements depend on recognition of their numbers.

The first section of this article discusses the varieties of hybridity and the widening range of phenomena to which the term now applies. According to anti-hybridity arguments hybridity is inauthentic and is a kind of 'multiculturalism lite'. Examining the current anti-hybridity backlash provides an opportunity to deepen and fine-tune our perspective on hybridity. Part of what is missing in these arguments is historical depth; the third section in this article deals with the *longue durée* and proposes multiple historical layers of hybridity. The fourth section concerns the politics of boundaries, for in the end the real problem is not hybridity – which is common throughout history – but boundaries and the social proclivity to boundary fetishism. Hybridity is unremarkable and is noteworthy only from the point of view of boundaries that have been essentialized. What hybridity means varies not only over time but also in different cultures, and this informs different patterns of hybridity. Then we come back to the original question: so what? The importance of hybridity is that it problematizes boundaries.

Varieties of Hybridity

Fairly recent on the horizon, after Latino rock, is Mandarin pop, a Cantonese and Pacific American combination of styles. One of its original inspirations is Hong Kong crooners doing Mandarin cover versions of Japanese popular ballads. The Japanese ballads were already a mixture of Japanese and American styles that featured, for instance, saxophone backgrounds. Mandarin pop (or Mandopop) is part of the soundscape of the Pacific Chinese diaspora. Its audience ranges from youngsters in China, Hong Kong and Taiwan to prosperous second-generation Chinese immigrants in the United States (Tam, 2000).

Many have these kind of cultural phenomena in mind when they think of hybridity. We could call it the world music model of hybridity. Its general features are that it concerns cultural expressions, which are new and recent, a recombination of existing combinations, and involve a limited range in expression and a distinctive audience, particularly an urban, newly prosperous audience. And while they are significant because they reflect and cater to a new class or stratum, their meaning is clearly restricted.

New hybrid forms are significant indicators of profound changes that are taking place as a consequence of mobility, migration and multiculturalism. However, hybridity thinking also concerns existing or, so to speak, old hybridity, and thus involves different ways of looking at historical and existing cultural and institutional arrangements. This is a more radical and penetrating angle that suggests not only that things are no longer the way they used to be, but were never really the way they used to be, or used to be viewed.

For some time hybridity has been a prominent theme in cultural studies.[1] It follows older themes of syncretism in anthropology and creolization in linguistics. In cultural studies hybridity denotes a wide register of multiple identity, cross-over, pick-'n'-mix, boundary-crossing experiences and styles, matching a world of growing migration and diaspora lives, intensive intercultural communication, everyday multiculturalism and erosion of boundaries. In optimistic takes on hybridity, 'hybrids were conceived as lubricants in the clashes of culture; they were the negotiators who would secure a future free of xenophobia' (Papastergiadis, 1997: 261). This angle, which is both instrumental and celebratory, may overlook that hybridity is also significant in its own right, as the experience of hybrids. An Afro-German writes:

> I always liked being a 'mulatto', even in the terrible times of National Socialism. I have been able to manage the black and white in me very well. I remember when a colleague once asked me during the terrible 1940s whether I was very unhappy having to live as mulatto. I said, 'No, you know, what I have experienced in my life because of my ethnic origin, you will never in your entire life experience.' (quoted in Beck, 1998: 125)

Hybridity thinking has been criticized for being a 'dependent' thinking that makes sense only on the assumption of purity (Young, 1995). In addition, of late there has been a polemical backlash against hybridity thinking. Hybridity, it is argued, is inauthentic, without roots, for the elite only, does not reflect social realities on the ground. It is multiculturalism lite, highlights superficial confetti culture and glosses over deep cleavages that exist on the ground. The downside of this anti-hybridity backlash is that it recycles the 19th-century parochialism of an ethnically and culturally compartmentalized world, whose present revival and re-articulation are baffling. In my understanding, hybridity is deeply rooted in history and quite ordinary. Indeed, what is problematic is not hybridity but the fetishism of boundaries that has marked so much of history. That history should not be seen this way and hybridity somehow viewed as extraordinary or unusual is baffling. Besides I'm hybrid myself.[2] However, engaging the anti-hybridity backlash offers an opportunity to enter more deeply into and thus develop the hybridity perspective.

Table 1   Varieties of Hybridity

New hybridity: Recent combinations of cultural and/or institutional forms. Dynamics: migration, trade, ICT, multiculturalism, globalization. Analytics: new modernities. Examples: Punjabi pop, Mandarin pop, Islamic fashion shows.	Existing or old hybridity: existing cultural and institutional forms are translocal and crosscultural combinations already. Dynamics: crosscultural trade, conquest and contact. Analytics: history as collage. Examples: too many.
Objective: as observed by outsiders.	Subjective: as experience and self consciousness.
As process: hybridization. As outcome: hybrid phenomena.	As discourse and perspective: hybridity consciousness.

The first point to consider is the varieties of hybridity, as phenomena and as perspective (a schema is in Table 1).

Hybridization as a process is as old as history, but the pace of mixing accelerates and its scope widens in the wake of major structural changes, such as new technologies that enable new phases of intercultural contact. Contemporary accelerated globalization is such a new phase. A major terrain of newly emerging mixtures is the new middle classes and their cultural and social practices arising in the context of migration and diaspora and the new modernities of the 'emerging markets'. For almost two decades the growth rates of the Asian Tiger economies and other emerging markets have been twice as high as those of Western countries. This entails vast applications of new technologies and the emergence of new social mores and consumption patterns. They are typically fusion cultures that combine new technologies and existing social practices and cultural values (cf. Robison and Goodman, 1996; Nederveen Pieterse, 1998a).

Nilufer Göle discusses changes in Islam in Turkey in terms of 'hybridization between Islamists and modernity' (2000: 112).

> As can be observed in the Turkish context, not only are Islamists using the latest model of Macintosh computers, writing best-selling books, becoming part of the political and cultural elite, winning elections, and establishing private universities, but they are also carving out new public spaces, affirming new public visibilities, and inventing new Muslim lifestyles and subjectivities. . . . An Islamic service sector offers luxury hotels that advertise facilities for an Islamic way of vacationing; they feature separate beaches and nonalcoholic beverages. Islamic dress and fashion shows, Islamic civil society associations, Islamic pious foundations, associations of Islamic entrepreneurs, and Islamic women's platforms all attest to a vibrant and rigorous social presence. (Göle, 2000: 94)

If practices of mixing are as old as the hills, the *thematization* of mixing as a discourse and perspective is fairly new. In one sense it dates from the

1980s. In a wider sense it concerns the general theme of *bricolage* and improvisation. Its lineages include psychoanalysis and its bringing together of widely diverse phenomena – such as dreams, jokes, Freudian slips and symbols – under new headings relevant to psychological diagnosis.[3] Psychoanalysis synthesized sensibilities ranging from Nietzsche to 19th-century novels and art. Dada made mixing objects and perspectives its hallmark, which inspired the technique of collage. Marcel Duchamp hybridized art itself. Surrealism moved further along these lines and so did conceptual and installation art.

The domains in which hybridity plays a part have proliferated over time:

- The term hybridity originates in pastoralism, agriculture and horticulture.[4] Hybridization refers to developing new combinations by grafting one plant or fruit to another.
- A further application is genetics. When belief in 'race' played a dominant part, miscegenation and 'race mixture' were prominent notions.
- Previously hybridity referred to combinations of different animals, such as the griffin, or animals and humans, such as the centaur and satyr; now it also refers to cyborgs (cybernetic organisms), combinations of humans or animals and technology (pets carrying chips for identification, biogenetic engineering).
- Hybridity first entered social science via the anthropology of religion, through the theme of syncretism. Roger Bastide defined syncretism as 'uniting pieces of the mythical history of two different traditions in one that continued to be ordered by a single system' (1970: 101).
- Creole languages and creolization in linguistics were the next field to engage social science interest. Bakhtin's work on polyphony is a related strand. In time, creolization became a wider metaphor beyond language (e.g. Richards, 1996; Siebers, 1996).
- Presently, the main thrust of hybridity thinking concerns cultural hybridity, including art (e.g. Harvey, 1996).
- Other strands concern structural and institutional hybridization, including governance (de Ruijter, 1996).[5]
- Organizational hybridity (Oliver and Montgomery, 2000) and diverse cultural influences in management techniques are other common themes (e.g. Beale, 1999).
- Interdisciplinarity in science has given rise to 'new hybrids' such as ecological economics (McNeill, 1999: 322).
- 'Menus have increasingly become monuments to cultural hybridity' (Warde, 2000: 303).
- Most common of all is everyday hybridity in identities, consumer behaviour, lifestyle, etc.

International relations, education, the 'hybrid car' (combining petrol and electricity) and so forth: nowadays there's no end to the travel and spread of hybridity. The current polemic on hybridity, however, only considers cultural hybridity, which captures but a small slice of the domains indicated above. The world music model of hybridity is narrower still and only concerns recent cultural blends. Besides short-changing the varieties of hybridity, other fundamental considerations are oddly missing in the current anti-hybridity backlash. One concerns the historical depth of hybridity viewed in the *longue durée*. The second is the circumstance that boundaries and borders can be matters of life or death and the failure to acknowledge hybridity is a political point whose ramifications can be measured in lives.

In the end the anti-hybridity backlash is a minor debate. The issue is not whether to be for or against hybridity; the debate concerns another question: hybridity so what? What is the significance of hybridity? To take this further means to unpack hybridity in its varieties and to distinguish patterns of hybridity. Meanwhile the other side of this question is: boundaries so what?

The Anti-hybridity Backlash

Criticisms of particular versions of hybridity arguments and quirks in hybridity thinking are familiar. The most conspicuous shortcoming is that hybridity skips over questions of power and inequality: 'hybridity is not parity'.[6] Some arguments make no distinction between different levels: 'The triumph of the hybrid is in fact a triumph of neo-liberal multiculturalism, a part of the triumph of global capitalism' (Araeen, 2000: 15). These whole-sale repudiations of hybridity thinking belong in a different category: this is the anti-hybridity backlash, which this article takes on. In the discussion below most arguments against hybridity thinking have been taken from Friedman (1997, 1999) as representative of a wider view.[7] A précis of anti-hybridity arguments and rejoinders is in Table 2.

'Hybridity is Meaningful only as a Critique of Essentialism'

There is plenty of essentialism to go round. Boundary fetishism has long been, and in many circles continues to be, the norm. After the nation, one of the latest forms of boundary fetishism is 'ethnicity'. Another reification is the 'local'. Friedman cites the statement above (Nederveen Pieterse, 1995: 63) and then concludes that 'hybridization is a political and normative discourse' (1999: 242). Indeed, but so of course is essentialism and boundary fetishism. 'In a world of multiplying diasporas, one of the things that is not happening is that boundaries are disappearing' (1999: 241). That, on the other hand, is much too sweeping a statement to be meaningful. On the whole, cross-boundary and cross-border activities have been on the increase, as a wide body of work in international relations and international political economy testifies, where the erosion of boundaries is one of the most common accounts of contemporary times and globalization.

Were Colonial Times Really so Essentialist?

This is a question raised by Young (1995). Here we can distinguish multiple levels: actual social relations, in which there was plenty of border-crossing,

Table 2 Arguments for and against Hybridity

Contra hybridity	Pro hybridity
Hybridity is meaningful only as a critique of essentialism.	There is plenty of essentialism around.
Were colonial times really so essentialist?	Enough for hybrids to be despised.
Hybridity is a dependent notion.	So are boundaries.
Asserting that all cultures and languages are mixed is trivial.	Claims of purity have long been dominant.
Hybridity matters to the extent that it is a self-identification.	Hybrid self-identification is hindered by classification boundaries.
Hybridity talk is a function of the decline of Western hegemony.	It also destabilizes other hegemonies.
Hybridity talk is carried by a new cultural class of cosmopolitans.	Would this qualify an old cultural class of boundary police?
'The lumpenproletariat real border-crossers live in constant fear of the border'	Crossborder knowledge is survival knowledge.
'Hybridity is not parity'	Boundaries don't usually help either.

and discourse, which is differentiated between mainstream and marginal discourses. Discourse and representation were also complex and multi-layered, witness for instance the mélange of motifs in Orientalism (e.g. Mackenzie, 1995; Clarke, 1997). While history, then, is a history of ambivalence, attraction and repulsion, double takes and zigzag moves, nevertheless the 19th and early 20th-century colonial world was steeped in a Eurocentric pathos of difference, *dédain*, distinction.[8] All the numerous countermoves in the interstices of history do not annul the *overall* pathos of the White Man's Burden and the *mission civilisatrice*, nor its consequences.

> But the imperial frontiers are not only geographical frontiers, where the 'civilized' and the 'barbarians' confront and contact one another; they are also frontiers of status and ethnicity which run through imperialized societies, as in the form of the colonial 'colour bar'. Here colonizers and colonized are segregated and meet, here slave masters and slaves face one another and here, where imperial posturing is at its most pompous and hatred is most intense, the imperial house of cards folds and paradox takes over. For this frontier is also the locus of a *genetic dialectic*, a dialectic which, in the midst of the most strenuous contradictions, gives rise to that strangest of cultural and genetic

syntheses – the *mulatto, mestizo*, half-caste. The mestizo is the personification of the dialectics of empire and emancipation. No wonder that in the age of empire the mestizo was dreaded as a monster, an infertile hybrid, an impossibility: subversive of the foundations of empire and race. The mestizo is the living testimony of an attraction that is being repressed on both sides of the frontier. The mestizo is proof that East and West *did* meet and that there is humanity on either side. (Nederveen Pieterse, 1989: 360–1)

Hybridity is a Dependent Notion

'In the struggle against the racism of purity, hybridity invokes the dependent, not converse, notion of the mongrel. Instead of combating essentialism, it merely hybridizes it' (Friedman, 1999: 236). The mongrel, half-caste, mixed race, *métis, mestizo* was a taboo figure in the colonial world. When so much pathos was invested in boundaries, boundary crossing involved dangerous liaisons. In an era of thinking in biological terms, boundaries were biologized ('race'), and by extension so was boundary crossing. Status, class, race, nation were all thought of as *biological* entities in the lineage from Comte de Boulainvilliers and Gobineau to Houston Stewart Chamberlain and Hitler (cf. Nederveen Pieterse, 1989: Ch. 11).

By the turn of the century, genetics had gone through a paradigm shift from a dominant view that gene mixing was weakening and debilitating (decadence) to the view in Mendelian genetics that gene mixing is invigorating and that combining diverse strains creates '*hybrid vigour*'. This principle still guides plant-breeding companies now. Social and cultural hybridity thinking takes this further and revalorizes the half-castes. The gradual emergence of hybrid awareness (in 19th-century novels, psychoanalysis, modernism, bricolage) and its articulation in the late 20th century can be sociologically situated in the rapid succession of waning aristocracy (as represented in the theme of *décadence*), bourgeois hegemony and its supersession and reworking from the second half of the 20th century.

Hybridity as a point of view is meaningless *without* the prior assumption of difference, purity, fixed boundaries. Meaningless not in the sense that it would be inaccurate or untrue as a description, but that, without an existing regard for boundaries, it would not be a point worth making. Without reference to a prior cult of purity and boundaries, a pathos of hierarchy and gradient of difference, the point of hybridity would be moot.

Asserting that all Cultures and Languages are Mixed is Trivial (Friedman, 1999: 249)

Trivial? When since time immemorial the dominant idea has been that of pure origins, pure lineages? As in perspectives on language, nation, race, culture, status, class, gender. The hieratic view was preoccupied with divine or sacred origins. The patriarchal view posited strong gender boundaries. The aristocratic view cultivated blue blood. The philological view saw language as the repository of the genius of peoples, as with Herder and the subsequent 'Aryan' thesis. The racial view involved a hierarchy of races. The

Westphalian system locked sovereignty within territorial borders. Next came the nation and chauvinism. All these views share a preoccupation with pure origins, strong boundaries, firm borders. The contemporary acknowledgement of mixture in origins and lineages indicates a sea change in subjectivities and consciousness that correlates, of course, with sea changes in social structures and practices. It indicates a different ethos that in time will translate into different institutions. To regard this as trivial is to misread history profoundly.

Hybridity Matters to the Extent that it is Self-identification

> Hybridity only exists as a social phenomenon when it is identified as such by those involved in social interaction. This implies that where people do not so identify, the fact of cultural mixture is without social significance ... hybridity is in the eyes of the beholder, or more precisely in the practice of the beholder. (Friedman, 1999: 249, 251)

Hybrid self-identification *is* in fact common: obvious instances are second-generation immigrants and indeed hyphenated identities. Tiger Woods, the champion golfer, describes himself as 'Cablinasian': 'a blend of Caucasian, black, Indian and Asian' (Fletcher, 1997). Donald Yee, who is part black, part Asian and part Native American, can sympathize. 'When Mr Yee fills out racial questionnaires, he frequently checks "multiracial". If that is not an option, he goes with either black or Asian. "Nothing bothers me", he said. "It is just that it doesn't capture all of me"' (Fletcher, 1997).

Creolization in the Caribbean, *mestizaje* in Latin America and fusion in Asia are common self-definitions. In some countries national identity is overtly hybrid. Zanzibar is a classic instance (Gurnah, 1997). Mexico and Brazil identify themselves as hybrid cultures. Nepal is a mélange of Tibetan, Chinese and Indian culture of the Gangetic plains (Bista, 1994) and the same applies to Bhutan. Singapore's identity is often referred to as Anglo-Chinese (Wee, 1997).

Even so, the view that, in relation to hybridity, only self-identification matters presents several problems. (1) The obvious problem is how to monitor hybrid self-identification since most systems of classification and instruments of measurement do not permit multiple or in-between identification. In the United States, 'Until 1967 states were constitutionally permitted to ban mixed-race marriages. More than half the states had anti-miscegenation statutes in 1945; 19 still had them in 1966' (Fletcher, 1997). The US census is a case in point. The 2000 census is the first that, after much resistance and amid ample controversy, permits multiple self-identification, i.e. as being white as well as African American, Hispanic, etc. (2) What about the in-betweens? The point of hybridity thinking is that the in-betweens have been numerous all along and because of structural changes have been growing in number. (3) Only the eye of the beholder counts? Going native as epistemological principle? Because most people in the Middle Ages thought the earth is flat, it was flat? Because between 1840 and 1950 many people were racist, there are races? Or, there were as long as most people thought so? Jews were bad when most Germans under National Socialism thought so? *Vox populi, vox dei* – since when? This is unacceptable in principle and untenable in practice.

Hybridity Talk is a Function of the Decline of Western Hegemony

This is true in that the world of Eurocentric colonialism, imperialism and racism is past. It is only partially true because hybridity talk can refer just as much to the passing of other centrisms and hegemonies, such as China the middle kingdom, Japan and the myth of the pure Japanese race (Yoshino, 1995: 24–7), Brahmins in India, Sinhala Buddhists in Sri Lanka and their claim to 'Aryan' origins, Israel the Jewish state, Kemalist Turkism centred on Anatolia, Greekness among the Greeks. For all hegemonies, the claim to purity has served as part of a claim to power. This applies to all status boundaries, not just those of nation, ethnicity or race. The Church clamped down on heresies; the aristocracy and then the bourgeoisie despised mésalliance. Status requires boundaries and with boundaries come boundary police.

Hybridity Talk is Carried by a New Cultural Class of Cosmopolitans who Seek to Establish Hegemony

Hybridity represents 'a new "elite" gaze', 'a new cosmopolitan elite' (Friedman, 1999: 236; cf. Ahmad, 1992; Dirlik, 1992). Here innuendo comes in. *Ad hominem* reasoning, casting aspersions on the motives of the advocates of an idea, rather than debating the idea, is not the most elevated mode of debate. Then, should we discuss the motives of those who talk homogeneity? Of those who talk of boundaries allegedly on behalf of the working class and 'redneck' virtues? Of those who create a false opposition between working-class locals and cosmopolitan airheads? According to Friedman, 'Cosmopolitans are a product of modernity, individuals whose shared experience is based on a certain loss of rootedness. . . . Cosmopolitans identify with the urban, with the "modern". . . . They are the sworn enemies of national and ethnic identities' (1999: 237).

   Aversion to cosmopolitanism and the decadence of city life was part of Hitler's outlook and the Nazi ideology of blood and soil. With it came the Nazi idealization of the German peasant and, on the other hand, anti-Semitism. According to a German source in 1935: 'Dangers threaten the nation when it migrates to the cities. It withers away in a few generations, because it lacks the vital connection with the earth. The German must be rooted in the soil, if he wants to remain alive' (quoted in Linke, 1999: 199).

   It is odd to find this combination of elements restated. For one thing, it is an ideological and not an analytical discourse. Brief rejoinders are as follows. (1) The specific discourse of cosmopolitanism does not really belong in this context; there is no necessary relationship. But if it is brought in, one would rather say that humanity is a cosmopolitan species. Adaptability to a variety of ecological settings is inherent in the species. (2) Also if this view is not accepted, cosmopolitanism still pre-dates modernity and goes back to the intercivilizational travel of itinerant craftsmen, traders and pilgrims. (3) The stereotype that is implicitly invoked here echoes another stereotype, that of the wandering Jew. (4) Why or by which yardstick would or should 'rootedness' be the norm? Have nomadism and itineracy not also a long record? (5) Why should affinity with the urban (if it would apply at all) necessarily involve animosity to national and ethnic identities? The Romantics thought otherwise. Cities have been central to national as well as regional identities. (6) According to Friedman, 'Modernist identity as an ideal type is anti-ethnic, anti-cultural and anti-religious' (1999: 237). 'Anti-cultural' in this context simply does not make sense. Apparently this take on modernism excludes Herder and the Romantics and assumes a single ideal-type modernity.

`While Intellectuals May Celebrate Border-crossing, the Lumpenproletariat Real Border-crossers Live in Constant Fear of the Border' (Friedman, 1999: 254)

Experiences with borders and boundaries are too complex and diverse to be captured under simple headings. Even where boundaries are strong and fences high, knowing what is on either side is survival knowledge. This is part of the political economy of mobility. Geographical mobility is an alternative key to social mobility. In negotiating borders, hybrid bicultural knowledge and cultural shape-shifting acquire survival value. 'Passing' in different milieus is a survival technique. This applies to the large and growing transborder informal sector in which migrant grassroots entrepreneurs turn borders to their advantage (cf. Portes, 1995, 1996; Nederveen Pieterse, 2000a).

Friedman sees it otherwise.

> But for whom, one might ask, is such cultural transmigration a reality? In the works of the post-colonial border-crossers, it is always the poet, the artist, the intellectual, who sustains the displacement and objectifies it in the printed word. But who reads the poetry, and what are the other kinds of identification occurring in the lower reaches of social reality? (1997)

(Elsewhere: 'This author, just as all hybrid ideologues, takes refuge in literature', 1999: 247.) This is deeply at odds with common experience. Thus, research in English and German major cities finds that it is precisely lower-class youngsters, second-generation immigrants, who now develop new, mixed lifestyles (Räthzel, 1999: 213).[9] Friedman recognizes this among Turks in Berlin but then neutralizes this finding by arguing that 'the internal dynamics of identification and world-definition aim at coherence' (1999: 248). Why not? Hybridity is an argument against homogeneity, not against coherence. The point is precisely that homogeneity is not a requirement for coherence.

When Friedman does acknowledge hybridity he shifts the goalposts. 'Now this combination of cultural elements might be called hybridization, but it would tell us nothing about the processes involved' (1999: 248). The processes involved indeed may vary widely. And probably there is something like a stereotyping of hybridity – of world music stamp.

Friedman's argument against hybridity is inconsistent, contradictory and at times far-fetched, so it is not worth pursuing far. Friedman argues that all cultures are hybrid but that boundaries are not disappearing: these two statements alone are difficult to put together. He argues that hybridity talk is trivial unless it is self-identification, but if hybridity is part of self-identification it is overruled by coherence, and we should examine the processes involved. However, if all cultures are hybrid all along, then the problem is not hybridity but boundaries: how is it that boundaries are historically and socially so significant? How come that while boundaries continuously change shape in the currents and tides of history, boundary fetishism remains, even among social scientists? If hybridity is real but boundaries are prominent, how *can* hybridity be a self-identification: in a world of boundaries, what room and legitimacy are there for boundary-crossing identities, politically, culturally?

How to situate the anti-hybridity argument? At one level it is another instalment of the critique of 'postmodernism', which in these times recurs with different emphases every 10 years or so. In the present wave, the polemical emphasis is 'Marxism versus cultural studies', which is obviously a broad-stroke target. At another level the argument reflects unease with multiculturalism. When these two lines coincide we get the novel combination of redneck Marxism. In this view multiculturalism is a fad that detracts from, well, class struggle.[10] A positive reading is that this refocuses the attention on political economy, class, social justice and hard politics, which is surely a point worth making in relation to Tinkberbell postmodernism. At the same time, this is an exercise in symbolic politics, unfolding on a narrow canvas, for it mainly concerns positioning within academia. Would this explain why so much is missing from the debate? Among the fundamental considerations that are missing in the anti-hybridity backlash is the historical depth of hybridity viewed in the *longue durée*. More important still is the circumstance that boundaries and borders can be issues of life and death; and the failure to recognize and acknowledge hybridity is then a political point that may be measured in lives.

Hybridity and the *Longue Durée*

Hybridization is common in nature. Carrying spurs between flowers, bees and other insects contribute to the variety of flora. While cross-pollination is inherent in nature, hybridity is common in human history as well. Thousands of years of dividing and policing of space, territorial and symbolic, stand between us and our mixed evolutionary and long-term history, or, more precisely, are interspersed with it. Thanks to boundaries, civilizations have flourished and also suffocated. Boundaries have come and gone. Been erected, fought over and then walked over.

Many contemporary debates take as their point of departure recent history rather than the *longue durée*. According to Friedman, 'The current stage is one in which culture has begun to overflow its boundaries and mingle with other cultures, producing numerous new breeds or hybrids' (1999: 237). A historically more plausible view is that cultures have been overflowing boundaries all along and that boundaries have been provisional and ever contentious superimpositions upon substrata of mingling and traffic. It is not recent times that are the yardstick (or, they would be only from a superficial point of view), but evolutionary times. A distinctive feature of contemporary times is that they are times of *accelerated mixing*. Thus, it is not mixing that is new but the scope and speed of mixing.

Population movements, crosscultural trade, intercultural contact and intermarriage have been common throughout history. Occasionally there have been forced population transfers, diaspora or exile. Sometimes this involved, so to speak, population grafting; in Babylon Alexander compelled 7,000 of his soldiers to marry 7,000 Persian women. At times large public works involved the relocation of thousands of craftsmen.

We can think of hybridity as *layered* in history, including pre-colonial, colonial and postcolonial layers, each with distinct sets of hybridity, as a function of the boundaries that were prominent, and accordingly a different pathos of difference. (For colonizing countries, these are pre-colonial, imperial and post-imperial periods. A précis is in Table 3.)

But we should add prehistory as an earlier phase of mixing. The evolutionary backdrop of our common origins in Africa confirms that humanity is a hybrid species.[11] The species' subsequent 'clustering' in different regions of the world has not precluded large-scale contact and population movements across and between the continents (Gamble, 1993). This mixed heritage is confirmed by the 'cultures' identified by archaeologists, which in Palaeolithic and Neolithic times sprawl widely and do not coincide with the boundaries of much later times. The diffusion of technologies – of pastoralism, agriculture, horse riding, the stirrup, chariot, saddle, bow and arrow, bronze and iron, and so forth – rapidly and over vast distances, is a further indication of long-distance communication early on (McNeill, 1982). Half the world's population speaks languages that derive from a single common root, i.e. an Indo-European root (Mallory, 1991). A further indicator is the spread of the 'world religions'. The spread of diseases and plagues is another marker of episodes of intercultural contact (McNeill, 1977). Besides technologies, language and religions, the travel of symbols is another indicator of crosscultural communication, examined in art history (a fine source is Wittkower, 1989). Anthropologists have studied the travel of customs and foodstuffs. In other words, our foundations are profoundly, structurally, inherently mixed, and it could not be otherwise. Mixing is intrinsic to the evolution of the species. History is a collage.

Superimposed upon the deep strata of mixing in evolutionary time are historical episodes of long-distance cross-cultural trade, conquest and empire, and specific episodes such as trans-Atlantic slavery and the triangular trade. Within and across these levels we can distinguish further types of hybridity.

Table 3   Historical Layers of Hybridity

Colonies	Colonizing countries	Boundaries
	Prehistory	Ecology, geography
	Precolonial	Plus cultural difference (language, religion)
Colonial, dependent	Imperial, metropolitan	'Victorian' hierarchies (modes of production, race, status, class)
Postcolonial	Post-imperial	Development hierarchies (GNP and other indices)

Taking a political economy approach we can identify the following general types of historical hybridity:

- *Hybridity across modes of production.* This gives rise to mixed social formations. It entails combinations between hunting/gathering and cultivation or pastoralism, agriculture and industry, craft and industry, etc. within and across social formations. Semi-feudalism and feudal capitalism are other instances. As the classic debate on the articulation of modes of production demonstrates (Foster-Carter, 1978), modes of production did not simply succeed one another but coexisted.
- *Hybridity before and after industrialization.* The agricultural revolution was the first major break in history and industrialization was the second, introducing a global development gap. The year 1800 is a marker, indicating the first use of fossil fuels (in the steam engine).
- *Hybrid modes of regulation.* The social market, Fordism, market socialism and the Third Way are examples of mixed forms of regulation.[12]

Besides nations with overtly hybrid identities, there are *hybrid regions* or zones, such as the Sudanic belt in Africa, that straddle geographic and cultural areas. Southeast Asia is a region of hybrid Indo-Chinese and Malay features. *Hybrid cities* are typically located at civilizational crossroads, major arteries of trade, or involve significant immigrant populations. Istanbul, Venice and Toledo are classic instances. Baghdad and Cairo, Lahore and Delhi, Calcutta and Bombay are other examples.[13] Also, in nations where hybridity does not form part of national identity, it looms in the background. A caption in a museum in Norway notes that a particular type of jewellery is found 'from Dublin to the Volga'. Regional and folklore museums usually reveal the transborder cultural continuities that national museums militantly ignore; they relate to deeper cultural strata and a different historical awareness.

Against the backdrop of deep time, the current hybridity discussion seems superficial, for it is entirely dominated by the episodes of colonialism and nationalism of the last hundred or couple of hundred years. What is striking is the spell these episodes cast, and the preoccupation with boundaries this involves (cf. Nederveen Pieterse, 2000b).

Boundaries

In the USA, demographers speak of a silent explosion in the number of mixed-race people. Between 1960 and 1990, the number of interracial married couples rose from 150,000 to more than 1.1 million, and the number of interracial children leaps accordingly. 'Since 1970, the number of mixed-race children in the United States has quadrupled. And there are six times as many intermarriages today as there were in 1960' (Etzioni, 1997). No wonder that a commentator observes:

> Look at Tiger Woods and see the face of America's future . . . it was Tiger Woods' *face* that provided the real benchmark – showing how far Americans have come on an unstoppable national journey: the journey from the time-honored myth of racial clarity to the all-mixed-up reality of multiracialism. (Overholser, 2000)

In addition to the choice of 16 racial categories that the Census Bureau used to offer Americans, Etzioni and others proposed a new 'multiracial' category. This idea has been infuriating to some African American leaders, who regard it as undermining black solidarity. 'African-American leaders also object to a multiracial category because race data are used to enforce civil rights legislation in employment, voting rights, housing and mortgage lending, health care services and educational opportunities' (Etzioni, 1997). The proponents argue that this category – and a 'category of "multiethnic"' origin, which most Americans might wish to check' – would help soften the racial and ethnic divisions that now run through American society. This is only an example of the clash between the politics of recognition based on the allocation of collective rights and the idea of fluid group boundaries.

Most of the world population now lives on less than $2 a day while a few hundred billionaires own as much as half the world population. Technical explanations for the world's development gaps are many but insufficient. A superficial impression has it that there is a lack of circulation or flow. On the whole, human capacities are evenly spread and capacitation or empowerment is possible, so presumably what stands in the way are boundaries, barriers or borders of various kinds. Ecology and geography map bio-regions and climate zones. Boundaries are a central theme in social science (cf. Moore and Buchanan, 2001). Economics measures boundaries such as GNP and income; micro-economics examines investment and location strategies; political science studies systems of organization and representation within given boundaries; sociology examines how boundaries such as nation, class, caste, region inform social practices. But, invariably, it is through cultural codes that boundaries are experienced, lived, upheld.

We could follow this with a history of boundaries – boundaries of clan, tribe, language, region, culture, civilization, empire, religion, state, nation, race, ethnicity, and a history of *centrisms*, i.e. hegemonic positions of power and points of view from which social landscapes have been viewed, mapped and defined. These boundaries have at no time precluded cross-border contact, but attempts have been made to control it. We could then follow with a history of boundary and border-crossing, smuggling, piracy, crosscultural traffic, migration, travel, diaspora, pilgrimage, trade: the hybridity angle on history unsettles the boundaries as well as the codes that sustain them.

Boundary Fetishism and Life and Death

According to Zbigniew Brzezinski, in the 20th century 167,000,000 to 175,000,000 lives have been deliberately extinguished through politically motivated carnage (quoted in Hirsch, 1995: xii). If we consider this death toll, a major and perhaps a greater part of ethnonationalist and ethnic killing involves internecine strife, i.e. political factions eliminating competitors within their own camp. The targets include crossover factions who threaten to blur the lines of conflict, rivals for leadership, forces that defy the political and military hegemony of the leading faction, and many of those who would wage peace rather than war. Episodes of 'ethnic cleansing', genocide, communal violence and civil war involve the militant suppression of the in-between, the elimination of hybridity. This refers to political as well as cultural in-betweens.

In Bosnia, about a third of the population was hybrid – intermarried or of mixed parentage – but none of the wartime counts of Bosnian Moslems, Bosnian Croats, Bosnian Serbs acknowledged this.

> No provisions are made for the more than 26 percent of the population that is intermarried, for the substantial numbers of urban dwellers who refused to describe themselves as either Serbs, Muslims, or Croats in the last census; or for the Serbs and Croats who support and have fought for the Bosnian government against their ethnic fellow nations that are trying to destroy Bosnia. All of that has been buried under the assumption that the *only* civic links that remain in Bosnia are those of the ethnic community. (Denitch, 1994: 7; cf. Nederveen Pieterse, 1998b)

The opportunistic and political character of the markers of 'ethnicity' has also been apparent in Bosnia:

> . . . each side will alternately emphasize their common roots when it indeed suits its purposes. Before the war, for example, when the Serbs still hoped to keep Bosnia in Yugoslavia, the media frequently highlighted similarities with the Muslims, while Croats often stressed that Bosnia had been part of historical Croatia and that most Bosnian Muslims were originally of Croatian descent. (Bell-Fialkoff, 1993: 121)

In Vojvodina, the region of former Yugoslavia where cultural mixing, measured by rate of intermarriage, was highest, conflict was absent (Botev,

1994). In the region where intermarriage was lowest, at 0.2 per cent in Kosovo, conflict was sparked off.

Different Cultural Takes on Hybridity

Hybridity involves different meanings not only across time but also across cultural contexts. In 'high' and classical cultural settings, the gatekeepers of 'standards' easily repudiate hybridity as infringement of the classical canon (without awareness or acknowledgement of the 'mixed' character of the canon itself). In popular culture, mixing of elements and styles may pass unnoticed, be taken for granted or welcomed (Frow, 1992). Creativity and innovation often turn on unlikely combinations, so in art and sciences hybridity is common and at times more readily acknowledged than in other domains.

Hybridity carries different meanings in different cultures, among different strata within cultures and at different times. Radhakrishnan (1996) distinguishes between metropolitan and peripheral hybridity; but the meaning of hybridity is not the same in all peripheries. The meaning of hybridity or in-between space differs according to the way it has come about.

In Asia on the whole it carries a different ring than in Latin America. In Asia the general feeling has been upbeat, as in East–West fusion culture. Hybridity tends to be experienced as chosen, willed (although there are plenty of sites of conflict). In Latin America the feeling has long been one of fracture, fragmentation, *tiempos mixtos*. Hybridity used to be experienced as a fateful condition that was inflicted rather than willed. An example is the Mexican 'Malinche complex' discussed by Octavio Paz (1967; Papastergiadis, 1997). This goes back to the original duality at the foundation of the Latin American experience: the experience of conquest and the divide between *criollos* and *indigenes*, which has led to Latin American societies being characterized as 'dual societies'. (A diagnosis that ignores other identities such as descendants of African slaves, Asian immigrants, and again the in-betweens, the Ladinos.) However, in recent Latin American accounts, the notion of hybridity as an affliction has changed, along with growing recognition of popular creativity (e.g. Canclini, 1995, 2000; Ortiz, 2000). 'Latinity' as bricolage is now a common perception.

A common theme in Asia is Western technology/Eastern values. In everyday discourse one often hears of the negative consequences of rapid modernization, for instance in Indonesia: 'Just how successful has the government been at developing the spiritual and cultural sectors in order to counter the negative impacts of rapid modernization?' (*Jakarta Post*, 9 March 1995). Modernization has never been universally embraced and there has been a wide spectrum of interests and positions which, however, have typically been *interpreted* through the lens of modernity, with modernity as a yardstick, from 'traditionalists' to 'modernizers', anti- or pro-modernization stances, and notions of conservative or defensive modernization.

In sub-Saharan Africa, key themes in relation to modernity have been traditional social institutions and values – as in négritude, African socialism and *ujamaa*. Slavery, the gun–slave cycle and European colonialism have been important episodes in interrupting, side-tracking the development of African societies. Here colonialism has been closer and more destructive than anywhere else and decolonization has been most recent. Revisionist history informs Afrocentric readings of Egyptian civilization and the ancients, and indigenization informs language politics and Afrocentric ethno-sociology. At the same time, 'reworking modernity' is also a prominent strand in African societies (Pred and Watts, 1992).

It would not be difficult to make a *general* case for modernization and development in the South as processes of hybridization. To an extent this terminology is already being used. Bayart (1992) refers to social and political 'hybridation' to characterize African modernities. Hybridity is a common terminology in Latin America, and in Asia terms such as fusion are common. Neotraditionalism is common and another example is neopatriarchy in the Arab world (Sharabi, 1988). Everywhere there is a language of combinations, articulations and improvisations to describe the various changes in the wake of anticolonialism, decolonization and development.

In the West, hybridity thinking is *à la mode* but borders persist – witness the issues of migration, racism and illegal aliens, the class divisions of the ghettos and the 'two-thirds society', and the vagaries of international development discourse. Still, it makes a huge difference whether the argument is that there is too much multiculturalism or not enough, and this remains unclear in the anti-hybridity argument.

Patterns of Hybridity

In cultural, literary and postcolonial studies, hybridity, syncretism, cre-olization, *métissage* have become common tropes. Usually the reference is to cultural rather than institutional or structural hybridity. Hybridity is fast becoming a routine, almost trite point of reference in studies of global culture that speak of the 'mongrel world' and the 'hybridity factor' (Zachary, 2000; cf. Iyer, 2000). Yet, as hybridity becomes a ubiquitous attribute or quality, by the same token it becomes increasingly meaningless, a universal soup: if everything is hybrid, what does hybridity mean? Hence the next question to come up is what kind of hybridity? Radhakrishnan (1996) distinguishes between metropolitan (ludic) and postcolonial (critical) hybridity, Bhavnani (1999) between situational and organic hybridity. Patterns of hybridity in relation to modes of production and regulation are explored above. A major objection to hybridity is that it sidesteps power differences: 'hybridity is not parity'.[14] So the critical variable is power.

Thus, in assessing varieties of multiculturalism, pertinent criteria are power and equality, or degrees of symmetry and the extent to which culture is centred on a standard or canon. *Mestizaje* in Latin America has a cultural centre of gravity; it is an ideology of whitening, Europeanization, parallel to modernization (Klor de Alva, 1995). Creolization in the Caribbean is more fluid, although it remains centred on 'browning' (Thompson, 1999). A précis of two patterns of hybridity is in Table 4.

Table 4   Patterns of Hybridity

Axes	Implications
Asymmetric/symmetric	The relative power and status of elements in the mixture. E.g. colonial society is asymmetric. These are polarities of a continuum, of which the perfectly symmetric extreme may be difficult to give an example of.
With/ without centre	Hybridities with or without a centre are polarities of a continuum. Again it is difficult to think of an example of completely free-floating mixture, for even at a carnival the components are always charged with different values, polarities.

So What?

It is not obvious why the term 'hybridity' has stuck as the general heading for these phenomena. As a word it came of age in the 19th century (Young, 1995: 6). In French '*bricolage*' has long been a common term. Mixing, blending, melding and merging are other terms and nuances with longer lineages than the quasi-scientific term 'hybridity'. Mixing plays a part in agriculture (mixing crops), cooking (ingredients), weaving (tissues, motifs), healing (herbs, methods), art (genres, materials), fashion (styles), etc. The amalgamation and fusion of different substances are fundamental processes in alchemy, producing transubstantiation or decay. This returns in chemistry, metallurgy (alloys) and the pharmaceutical industry. Osmosis plays a part in cell biology and chemistry. Why of all terms hybridity has stuck is probably because of the preoccupation with biological and 'racial' differences and the intellectual imprint of genetics, which are essentially 18th- and 19th-century problematics.[15]

Now let's come back to the original question, 'Hybridity, so what?' In an earlier discussion I asked, 'How do we come to terms with phenomena such as Thai boxing by Moroccan girls in Amsterdam, Asian rap in London, Irish bagels, Chinese tacos . . . ?' etc. (Nederveen Pieterse, 1995: 53). Friedman cites this and asks 'What is it that we must come to terms with here?' (1999: 236). What we must come to terms with is the circumstance that nowadays we are *all* 'Moroccan girls doing Thai boxing in Amsterdam', that is we are all mixing cultural elements and traces *across* places and identities.[16] This is not simply an issue of classification or of elite cosmopolitan experience; rather, the point is that this has become an *ordinary* experience. A Greek restaurant called 'Ipanema' serving Italian food in Brighton: these crossovers are now common in all spheres of life.

This is only the tip of the iceberg. Boundaries themselves are tricky. Thus, the *meanings* of boundaries are by no means constant. For instance, Fiona Wilson (2000) discusses the radically changing meanings of the categories of Indian and mestizo over time and by class in Andean Peru. More revealing still is that boundaries are often bricolage improvisations themselves. Thus, the claims of racial, ethnic and religious 'fundamental-isms' are often pieced together from diverse and hybrid sources. For instance, Stephen Howe (1998) shows how Afrocentrism derives several of its claims and methods from European sources. All this does not mean that boundaries fade or vanish; they probably never will because boundaries are a function of social life. It does not mean that the emotions associated with boundaries wane, or their consequences, such as racist murder.[17] Then, does this mean that 'hybridity', as so many argue, is merely a plaything of a bour-geois elite? Rather the point is that the flux of our times is such that, across classes, the *contingency* of boundaries is now a more common experience than ever before.

Hybridity is a terminology and sensibility of our time in that boundary and border-crossing mark our times. Thus, with regard to national borders these are times of post-nationalism (the high tide of nationalism was between 1840 and 1960). Sovereignty changes meaning and is now increasingly being pooled in regional and international arrangements and covenants; neomedievalism is one of the accounts for current political conditions (Kobrin, 1998). Class and gender boundaries are less strict than before. Aesthetic boundaries are increasingly permeable, with high and low cultures mingling. In the sciences, disciplinary boundaries are increasingly old-fashioned. And so on.

As a perspective, hybridity entails three different sets of claims: empirical (hybridization happens), theoretical (acknowledging hybridity as an analytical tool) and normative (a critique of boundaries and valorization of mixtures, under certain conditions, in particular relations of power). Hybridity is to culture what deconstruction is to discourse: transcending binary categories. Another account of hybridity is 'in-betweenness'. Recog-nizing the *in-between* and the *interstices* means going beyond dualism, binary thinking and Aristotelian logic. Methodologically this is the hallmark of post-structuralism and deconstruction; it represents an epistemological shift outside the boxes of Cartesian epistemology. Postmodernism has been a general heading for this change in outlook. In its constructive sense this involves a profound moment of collective reflexivity that includes the aware-ness that boundaries are historical and social constructions; they are also cognitive barriers whose validity depends on epistemic orders, which are ultimately of an arbitrary or at least contingent nature. This awareness in itself is not new; what is new is its expansion among broader strata of the population and its widening scope in relation to phenomena. Thomas Kuhn on paradigm shifts in science, the emergence of 'new science' beyond New-tonian science, Foucault on epistemic orders, Derrida on deconstruction, Deleuze and Guattari on nomadism, feminist boundary crossings (e.g. Caine et al., 1988), Lyotard on the space in between language games, Bhabha on 'third space', etc. – these are all different moments and ways of stepping out of the Cartesian box of knowledge and order.[18]

This overall movement has so many ramifications that its significance is difficult to map – as if any mapping exercise in the process validates maps, while the point is to recognize the limited and contingent status of any kind of map. One account is that the space across and between boundaries is a liminal space and current changes involve *liminality* of a kind becoming a collective awareness.[19] This awareness may be described as a kind of Trickster knowledge, in which the Trickster is the joker in the pack, the jester, the fool, the shape-shifter who does not take seriously what all society around regards as sacred rules. Along the Mexican–US border, people smugglers are nicknamed 'coyotes'. Among Native Americans, Coyote is a Trickster figure, like Anansi the spider and Brer Rabbit elsewhere. In this sense, hybridity consciousness represents a return of the Trickster, now at a collective scale.

This does not mean that boundary-crossing is a free-for-all. There is free cheese only in the mousetrap. As some boundaries wane others remain or are introduced. Thus, as national borders and governmental authority erode, ethnic or religious boundaries, or boundaries of consumption patterns and brand names emerge in their place. NGOs carve out new spaces of power. Or, as some boundaries fade, people's differential capacities for border-crossing and mobility come to foreground. In virtual space, cognitive boundaries and cyberwars emerge. Another complex issue is the relationship between hybridity and ecological biodiversity. Acknowledging the contingency of boundaries and the significance and limitations of hybridity as a theme and approach means engaging hybridity politics. This is where critical hybridity comes in, which involves a new awareness of and new take on the dynamics of group formation and social inequality. This critical awareness is furthered by acknowledging rather than by suppressing hybridity.

Notes

This article was originally prepared for the panel 'Whatever Happened to Hybridity?' organized by Kobena Mercer at the Vera List Center for Art and Politics of the New School for Social Research, New York, April 2000. Cordial thanks to Kobena Mercer and Alev Cinar for comments on an earlier version.

1. For example in the work of Hall, Bhabha, Gilroy, Hannerz, Hebdige, Appadurai, Rushdie, García Canclini.

2. Of course this makes sense only as a contextual statement. But I weary of such identity proclamations.

3. An interesting discussion of this period is Hughes (1958).

4. 'In Latin *hybrida* originally meant the offspring of a tame sow and a wild boar' (Cashmore, 1996: 165).

5. Nederveen Pieterse (1995) mentions structural hybridization such as 'cities of peasants' and 'agro-industry'.

6. Criticisms along these lines include Young (1995), McLaren (1997), McLaren and Farahmandpur (2000), Shohat and Stam (1994), Fusco (1995). McLaren reviews

objections to hybridity thinking (1997: 10–11) and then gives a different take on 'critical reflexivity and posthybridity as narrative engagement' (76–114).

7. Benita Parry (1987) argued against the hybridity view as privileging discourse which ignores the material realities of colonialism, a line of thinking that was taken further by Ahmad (1992). Other sources are Žižek (1997) and Meera (2001).

8. I have argued that this pathos only dates from after 1800 (Nederveen Pieterse, 1994).

9. Hybridity and multiple identity among second- and third-generation immigrants are abundantly discussed. For example, on Asian Americans see Lowe (1991), Liu (1998), Tamayo Lott (1997), Yang et al. (1997), and on Korean Americans, Hyun (1995). A different theme is Japanese influence in the United States (e.g. Conor, 1991; Feinberg, 1995) and vice versa, changes in Japan (e.g. Kosuka, 1989).

10. This kind of angle is apparent in Friedman's work and in Žižek (1997). That Marxism and anti-multiculturalism need not coincide is illustrated by the work of McLaren.

11. Besides confirming the evolutionary 'out of Africa' thesis, Luigi Cavalli-Sforza (2000) documents a tree of human evolution: a branching diagram of relations among different populations. He shows that the European population is the most genetically mixed-up on earth, quite contrary to Comte de Gobineau who ascribed European genius to their being the most genetically pure and the least weakened by racial mixture. This matches the current findings of human genome research: there is only one race – the human race; 99.9 per cent of the human genome is the same in everyone. So-called racial differences are genetically only skin-deep (Angier, 2000).

12. Considering that all forms of regulation (in the sense of the French regulation school) are historically developed, arguably there are no 'pure' forms of regulation.

13. Now cities generally are characterized as hybrid: 'cities are essentially culturally hybrid' (Amin et al., 2000: vi).

14. Fusco (1995, quoted in McLaren, 1997: 10). Cf. Shohat and Stam (1994) and discussion in Nederveen Pieterse (1995, 1996, 1998b).

15. Ayse Caglar (personal communication) notes that cross-class mixtures are rarely referred to as hybrid (cf. the old terminology of mésalliance). It would apply to phenomena such as the newly rich; but cf. Robison and Goodman (1996).

16. What is globalization? In answer to this question a Pakistani colleague recounts: 'An English Princess (Princess Diana) with an Egyptian boyfriend, uses a Norwegian mobile telephone, crashes in a French tunnel in a German car with a Dutch engine, driven by a Belgian driver, who was high on Scottish whiskey, followed closely by Italian Paparazzi, on Japanese motorcycles, treated by an American doctor, assisted by Filipino para-medical staff, using Brazilian medicines, dies!'.

17. Thus, Niru Ratnam asks 'Can hybridity even begin to deal with issues such as the Lawrence murder?' and observes 'hybridity is simply not the language of Eltham, South London' (1999: 156, 158). Yet Britain today has a high rate of inter-racial relationships (cf. Alibhai-Brown, 2001).

18. Cf. Nederveen Pieterse (2001: Ch. 9, 'Critical Holism and the Tao of Development').

19. In anthropology liminality refers to Arnold van Gennep's rites of passage between different states and Victor Turner's 'liminal space' as a space of transformation. In postcolonial studies, Bhabha refers to the liminal as an interstitial

passage between fixed identifications. *Limen,* a new journal for the theory and practice of liminal phenomena published in Croatia (2001), seeks to address the 'liminal generation in-between industrial and post-industrial, socialism and capitalism, etc.'.

References

Ahmad, Ajjaz (1992) *In Theory: Classes, Nations, Literatures.* London: Verso.

Alibhai-Brown, Yasmin (2001) *Mixed Feelings: The Complex Lives of Mixed-Race Britons,* London: The Women's Press.

Amin, A., D. Massey and N. Thrift (2000) *Cities for the Many, not the Few.* Bristol: Policy Press.

Angier, N. (2000) 'Do Races Differ? Not Really, Genes Show', *New York Times* 22 August.

Araeen, R. (2000) 'A New Beginning: Beyond Postcolonial Cultural Theory and Identity Politics', *Third Text* 50: 3–20.

Bastide, R. (1970) 'Mémoire collective et sociologie du bricolage', *L'Année Sociologique* 21.

Bayart, F. (1992) *L'État en Afrique: la politique du ventre.* Paris: Fayard.

Beale, D. (1999) *Driven by Nissan? A Critical Guide to New Management Techniques.* London: Lawrence and Wishart.

Beck, U. (1998) *Democracy without Enemies.* London: Sage.

Bell-Fialkoff, A. (1993) 'A Brief History of Ethnic Cleansing', *Foreign Affairs* 72(3): 110–21.

Bhavnani, K.K. (1999) 'Rassismen entgegnen: Querverbindungen und Hybridität', pp. 186–203 in B. Kossek (ed.) *Gegen-Rassismen.* Hamburg: Argument Verlag.

Bista, D.B. (1994) *Fatalism and Development: Nepal's Struggle for Modernization.* Calcutta: Orient Longman.

Botev, N. (1994) 'Where East Meets West: Ethnic Intermarriage in the Former Yugoslavia, 1962 to 1989', *American Sociological Review* June: 461–80.

Caine, B., E.A. Grosz and M. de Lepervanche (eds) (1988) *Crossing Boundaries: Feminisms and the Critique of Knowledges.* Sydney: Allen and Unwin.

Canclini, N.G. (1995) *Hybrid Cultures.* Minneapolis, MN: University of Minnesota Press.

Canclini, N.G. (2000) 'A Re-imagined Public Art on the Border', in N.G. Canclini and J.M.V. Arce *Intromisiones compartidas: arte y sociedad en la frontera Mexico/ Estados Unidos.* San Diego, Tijuana: Conaculta, Fonca.

Cashmore, E. (1996) *Dictionary of Race and Ethnic Relations,* 4th edn. London: Routledge.

Cavalli-Sforza, L.L. (2000) *Genes, Peoples, and Languages.* New York: North Point Press and Farrar Straus and Giroux.

Clarke, J.J. (1997) *Oriental Enlightenment: The Encounter between Asian and Western Thought.* London: Routledge.

Conor, B. (1991) *Japan's New Colony – America.* Greenwich, CT: Perkins Press.

de Ruijter, A. (1996) *Hybridization and Governance.* The Hague: Institute of Social Studies.

Denitch, Bogdan (1994) *Ethnic Nationalism: The Tragic Death of Yugoslavia.* Minneapolis, MN: University of Minnesota Press.

Dirlik, A. (1992) 'The Postcolonial Aura: Third World Criticism in the Age of Global Capitalism', *Critical Inquiry* Winter: 328–56.

Etzioni, A. (1997) ' "Other" Americans Help Break Down Racial Barriers', *International Herald Tribune* 10 May.

Feinberg, W. (1995) *Japan and the Pursuit of a New American Identity: Work and Education in a Multicultural Age*. New York: Routledge.

Fletcher, M.A. (1997) 'Tiger Woods and the Melting Pot: New Categories Break the Mold', *International Herald Tribune* 24 April.

Foster-Carter, A. (1978) 'The Modes of Production Controversy', *New Left Review* 107: 47–77.

Friedman, J. (1997) 'Global Crises, the Struggle for Cultural Identity and Intellectual Porkbarrelling: Cosmopolitans versus Locals, Ethnics and Nationals in an era of De-hegemonisation', pp. 70–89 in P. Werbner and T. Modood (eds) *Debating Cultural Hybridity*. London: Zed.

Friedman, J. (1999) 'The Hybridization of Roots and the Abhorrence of the Bush', pp. 230–55 in M. Featherstone and S. Lash (eds) *Spaces of Culture: City–Nation–World*. London: Sage.

Frow, J. (1992) 'The Concept of the Popular', *New Formations* 18: 25–38.

Fusco, C. (1995) *English is Broken Here: Notes on Cultural Fusion in the Americas*. New York: New Press.

Gamble, C. (1993) *Timewalkers: The Prehistory of Global Colonization*. London: Penguin.

Göle, Nilufer (2000) 'Snapshots of Islamic Modernities', *Daedalus* 129(1): 91–117.

Gurnah, Ahmed (1997) 'Elvis in Zanzibar', pp. 116–41 in A. Scott (ed.) *The Limits of Globalization*. London: Routledge.

Harvey, Penelope (1996) *Hybrids of Modernity: Anthropology, the Nation State and the Universal Exhibition*. London: Routledge.

Hirsch, H. (1995) *Genocide and the Politics of Memory: Studying Death to Preserve Life*. Chapel Hill: University of North Carolina Press.

Howe, Stephen (1998) *Afrocentrism: Mythical Pasts and Imagined Homes*. London: Verso.

Hughes, H.S. (1958) *Consciousness and Society: The Reorientation of European Social Thought 1890–1913*. New York: Vintage.

Hyun, Peter (1995) *In the New World: The Making of a Korean American*. Honolulu: University of Hawai'i Press.

Iyer, Pico (2000) *The Global Soul: Jet Lag, Shopping Malls and the Search for Home*. New York: Knopf.

Klor de Alva, J. Jorge de (1995) 'The Postcolonization of the (Latin) American Experience: A Reconsideration of "Colonialism", "Postcolonialism", and "Mestizaje"', pp. 241–75 in G. Prakash (ed.) *After Colonialism: Imperial Histories and Postcolonial Displacements*. Princeton, NJ: Princeton University Press.

Kobrin, S.J. (1998) 'Back to the Future: Neomedievalism and the Postmodern Digital World Economy', *Journal of International Affairs* 51(2): 361–86.

Kosuka, Masataka (ed.) (1989) *Japan's Choice: New Globalism and Cultural Orientation in an Industrial State*. London: Pinter.

Linke, Uli (1999) *Blood and Nation: The European Aesthetics of Race*. Philadelphia: University of Pennsylvania Press.

Liu, Hong (1998) 'Old Linkages, New Networks: The Globalization of Overseas Chinese Voluntary Associations and its Implications', *China Quarterly* 155: 582–609.

Lowe, L. (1991) 'Heterogeneity, Hybridity, Multiplicity: Marking Asian American Differences', *Diaspora* 1(1): 24–44.

Mackenzie, J. (1995) *Orientalism: History, Theory and the Arts*. Manchester: Manchester University Press.

McLaren, P. (1997) *Revolutionary Multiculturalism: Pedagogies of Dissent for the New Millennium*. Boulder, CO: Westview Press.

McLaren, P. and R. Farahmandpur (2000) 'Reconsidering Marx in Post-Marxist Times: A Requiem for Postmodernism?', *Educational Researcher* April: 25–33.

McNeill, D. (1999) 'On Interdisciplinary Research: With Particular Reference to the Field of Environment and Development', *Higher Education Quarterly* 53(4): 312–32.

McNeill, W. (1977) *Plagues and Peoples*. Oxford: Basil Blackwell.

McNeill, W. (1982) *The Pursuit of Power*. Chicago, IL: University of Chicago Press.

Mallory, J.P. (1991) *In Search of the Indo-Europeans: Language, Archaeology and Myth*. London: Thames and Hudson.

Meera, Nanda (2001) 'We are all Hybrids Now: the Dangerous Epistemology of Post-colonial Populism', *The Journal of Peasant Studies* 28(2).

Moore, M. and A. Buchanan (eds) (2001) *The Making and Unmaking of Boundaries*. Princeton, NJ: Princeton University Press.

Nederveen Pieterse, J. (1989) *Empire and Emancipation: Power and Liberation on a World Scale*. New York: Praeger.

Nederveen Pieterse, J. (1994) 'Unpacking the West: How European is Europe?', pp. 129–49 in A. Rattansi and S. Westwood (eds) *Racism, Modernity, Identity: On the Western Front*. Cambridge: Polity Press.

Nederveen Pieterse, J. (1995) 'Globalization as Hybridization', pp. 45–68 in M. Featherstone, S. Lash and R. Robertson (eds) *Global Modernities*. London: Sage.

Nederveen Pieterse, J. (1996) 'Globalization and Culture: Three Paradigms', *Economic and Political Weekly* 31(23): 1389–93.

Nederveen Pieterse, J. (1998a) 'Hybrid Modernities: Mélange Modernities in Asia', *Sociological Analysis* 1(3): 75–86.

Nederveen Pieterse, J. (1998b) 'Sociology of Humanitarian Intervention: Bosnia, Rwanda and Somalia Compared', pp. 230–65 in J. Nederveen Pieterse (ed.) *World Orders in the Making: Humanitarian Intervention and Beyond*. London and New York: Macmillan and St Martin's Press.

Nederveen Pieterse, J. (2000a) 'Globalization and Human Integration: We are All Migrants', *Futures* 32(5): 385–98.

Nederveen Pieterse, J. (2000b) *Social Capital, Migration and Cultural Difference: Beyond Ethnic Economies*. The Hague: Institute of Social Studies Working Paper 327.

Nederveen Pieterse, J. (2001) *Development Theory: Deconstructions/Reconstructions*. London: Sage.

Oliver, A. and K. Montgomery (2000) 'Creating a Hybrid Organizational Form from Parental Blueprints: The Emergence and Evolution of Knowledge Firms', *Human Relations* 53(1).

Ortiz, R. (2000) 'From Incomplete Modernity to World Modernity', *Daedalus* 129(1): 249–59.

Overholser, G. (2000) 'Look at Tiger Woods and See the Face of America's Future', *International Herald Tribune* 22 June: 9.

Papastergiadis, N. (1997) 'Tracing Hybridity in Theory', pp. 257–81 in P. Werbner and T. Modood (eds) *Debating Cultural Hybridity*. London: Zed.

Parry, B. (1987) 'Problems in Current Theories of Colonial Discourse', *Oxford Literary Review* 9.

Paz, O. (1967) *The Labyrinth of Solitude*. London: Allen Lane.

Portes, A. (ed.) (1995) *The Economic Sociology of Immigration*. New York: Russell Sage Foundation.

Portes, A. (1996) 'Transnational Communities: Their Emergence and Significance in the Contemporary World-System', pp. 151–68 in R.P. Korzeniewicz and W.C. Smith (eds) *Latin America in the World Economy*. Westport, CT: Greenwood Press.

Pred, A. and M.J. Watts (1992) *Reworking Modernity: Capitalisms and Symbolic Discontent*. New Brunswick, NJ: Rutgers University Press.

Radhakrishnan, R. (1996) *Diasporic Mediations*. Minneapolis, MN: University of Minnesota Press.

Räthzel, N. (1999) 'Hybridität ist die Antwort, aber was war noch mal die Frage?', pp. 204–19 in B. Kossek (ed.) *Gegen-Rassismen*. Hamburg: Argument Verlag.

Ratnam, Niru (1999) 'Chris Ofili and the Limits of Hybridity', *New Left Review* 224: 153–9.

Richards, P. (1996) 'Agrarian Creolization: The Ethnobiology, History, Culture and Politics of West African Rice', pp. 291–318 in R. Ellen and K. Fukui (eds) *Redefining Nature: Ecology, Culture and Domestication*. Oxford: Berg.

Robison, R. and D.S.G. Goodman (1996) *The New Rich in Asia*. London: Routledge.

Sharabi, H. (1988) *Neopatriarchy: A Theory of Distorted Change in Arab Society*. New York: Oxford University Press.

Shohat, Ella and Robert Stam (1994) *Unthinking Eurocentrism: Multiculturalism and the Media*. New York: Routledge.

Siebers, H. (1996) 'Creolization and Modernization at the Periphery: The Case of the Q'eqchi'es of Guatemala', PhD dissertation, Catholic University Nijmegen.

Tam, Pui-Wing (2000) 'Mandarin Pop Swings into US', *Wall Street Journal Europe* 3 April: 31.

Tamayo Lott, J. (1997) *Asian Americans: From Racial Category to Multiple Identities*. London: Sage and AltaMira Press.

Thompson, Denise P. (1999) 'Skin Deep: Citizenship, Inclusion and Entitlements for the "Dark"-skinned Woman in Jamaica', MA Thesis, The Hague: Institute of Social Studies.

Warde, A. (2000) 'Eating Globally: Cultural Flows and the Spread of Ethnic Restaurants', pp. 299–316 in D. Kalb, M. van der Land, R. Staring, B. van Steenbergen and N. Wilterdink (eds) *The Ends of Globalization: Bringing Society Back In*. Lanham, MD: Rowman and Littlefield.

Wee, C.W.-L. (1997) 'Framing the "New" East Asia: Anti-imperialist Discourse and Global Capitalism', pp. 75–97 in S. Rashid (ed.) *'The Clash of Civilizations'? Asian Responses*. Karachi: Oxford University Press.

Wilson, Fiona (2000) 'Indians and Mestizos: Identity and Urban Popular Culture in Andean Peru', *Journal of Southern African Studies* 26(2): 239–53.

Wittkower, R. (1989) *The Impact of Non-European Civilizations on the Art of the West*, ed. D.M. Reynolds. Cambridge: Cambridge University Press.

Yang, Jeff, D. Gan, T. Hong and staff of *A Magazine* (1997) *Eastern Standard Time: A Guide to Asian Influence on American Culture*. Boston, MA: Houghton Mifflin.

Yoshino, Kosaku (1995) *Cultural Nationalism in Contemporary Japan*. London: Routledge.

Young, R.C. (1995) *Colonial Desire: Hybridity in Theory, Culture, and Race*. London: Routledge.

Zachary, G.P. (2000) *The Global Me*. New York: Barnes and Noble.

Žižek, S. (1997) 'Multiculturalism, or The Cultural Logic of Multinational Capitalism', *New Left Review* 225.

Jan Nederveen Pieterse is Professor at the Department of Sociology of University of Illinois at Urbana-Champaign. His research interests include globalization, development studies and cultural studies. He is the author of several books, co-editor of *Review of International Political Economy* and advisory editor of several journals. Further information is on the web site [www.noparking.demon.nl].

Complex Choreography
Politics and Regimes of Recognition

Sallie Westwood

T HIS ARTICLE is an exploration of the politics of recognition and the
ways in which the conditions of existence of this politics may be
revisioned and elaborated as 'regimes of recognition'. The excavation
of these themes begins with an all too brief account of the politics of recognition in Ecuador, concentrating attention upon the ways in which political
subjects are called forth and negotiate in myriad ways with elected politicians
and the military within the contestations of the nation. One way in which to
understand this complex choreography, which also constitutes a politics of
belonging, is through the use of a decentred account of political and social
formations. However, in elaborating the 'regimes of recognition' three specific
sites are foregrounded: democracy, citizenship and the nation, but these, too,
are understood as non-unitary and as sites of contestations. Democracy,
citizenship and the nation are not finished products or merely institutional
arrangements, but sites of contention and possibilities. It is these sites that
are central to the development of a politics of recognition that goes beyond
the debate between equality and difference to further a new agonistic politics.
In part this might be encompassed by the idea of 'stakeholders', currently part
of the reinvention of welfare and the relationships between government and
citizens. On the other hand, writers have suggested alternative ways in which
the politics of recognition may be understood, excavating the philosophical
basis of the idea from Hegel's dialectic and more recently from the writings
of Levinas, Fanon and Lacan. This work is enormously important and assists
us in developing our understanding of recognition and the ways in which we
can foster mutuality and trust against otherization. It is also helpful in uncov-
ering the ways in which mutuality may not be achieved and how we secure a
basis for non-recognition as a political act. This article seeks an alternative
route to understanding which draws upon both of those outlined.

■ *Theory, Culture & Society* 2001 (SAGE, London, Thousand Oaks and New Delhi),
   Vol. 18(2–3): 247–264
   [0263-2764(200104/06)18:2–3;247–264;017490]

I want to suggest that one way forward is to accept that difference and community are not irreconcilable everywhere and all the time. Similarly, recognition is not for all the time and everywhere, but there are key sites for the politics of recognition which, as emblematic moments, move us toward the kind of 'planetary humanism' suggested by Paul Gilroy (2000) or the cosmopolitan future suggested by Beck (2000) among others. Neither am I reinventing the forms of 'strategic essentialism' favoured by some writers as a way of reconciling the politics of difference with the philosophical basis of post-structuralism and the need to act within a political arena designed around representational politics. Given this context, it was often difficult to make claims that did not call up a community of identities homogenized into a unitary political subject. Political subjects are a key moment in the understanding of recognition but not the only way in which a new politics will be forged. It is clear from the literature of the social movements that the identities which can be forged into political subjects is much wider than the notion of parties or conventional constituencies and the political practices of liberal democracy. One example of this is provided by the indigenous movement in Ecuador explored in this article. Equally, new constituencies have been forged in the interface between cyberspace and the world of capital and nations. This was evidenced in the November 1999 demonstrations against the World Trade Organization in Seattle. This was, in part, a moment of recognition, where a very diverse collectivity came together to demonstrate against the power of corporate capitalism and in the name of the poor and the dispossessed. Since that time the websites and activists have continued to train and prepare, and to track the globalization of capital; and they gathered again at the September 2000 Prague meeting of the major players, the IMF and the World Bank. This form of organizing is multiplex and shifting, with a constituency that is called forth in relation to an enemy, global capitalism in the guise of the World Trade Organization, the IMF, the World Bank, a rights discourse and the desire for a voice in relation to decisions that bear upon the lives of people throughout the world. This is not a 'party', a permanent structure with cadres in the conventional sense, but an ongoing party in the sense of a celebration of the people. The populism is clearly evident in the slogans and the style of politics which is permeable and fleeting but which has disproportionate effects because it presents a spectacle for the media. The coordinators understand this and work towards this. The point is not only to counter the IMF or the WTO but to shame the WTO and to demonstrate world-wide that it can be disrupted and that 'the people' can have an impact.

The spectacle of politics used so effectively against the WTO and the May 1999 anti-capitalism protests in London have been conducted within the terrain of liberal democracy while demonstrating the limits of tolerance. However, there are huge differences around the world in relation to the costs of political activism and the constraints under which people organize. The terrain within which people work means that political activism may assume a clandestine role within a clandestine culture which uses popular cultures like song and dance, festivals and the Church in which to embroider the song of protest. Many of these practices were crucial to the survival of civil society in Latin America in the 1970s and into the 1980s. These are nation-states where civil wars, like that in Colombia, continue year after year with abuses on both sides and, despite attempts at peace talks, go on claiming lives, terrifying villages and disrupting every aspect of society. Globally, these are troubled times in which the prospect of recognition seems often to be further away than during the era of the Cold War, where one side at least shared a discourse and set of precepts about what was worth fighting for and who were our enemies and who were our friends. These forms of politics are moments of recognition drawing upon a series of complementary and contradictory discourses to call forth political subjects. The more recent global concerns invoke the sense of a common humanity against the deep divide between the powerful and the exploited. This suggests a variety of sites and ways in which recognition can be thought and practised. I will explore this suggestion in the discussion that follows.

The Politics of Recognition

Latin America is important to our understanding of the regimes of recognition, democracy, citizenship and the nation as sites for the production of the politics of recognition, allowing us to explore this in ways that have hitherto eluded us. In Mexico, the Zapatista uprising received world-wide media coverage through the astute use of the Internet and the global press by Comrade Marcos. The Zapatista struggle globalized a local issue in which poverty and land claims were allied with state abuses towards people who are not recognized as citizens or nationals, who are not part of the imaginary of the Mexican nation and who are therefore excluded and denied in relation to citizenship rights, individually and collectively. The Zapatista struggle is one of many current significant struggles in Latin America, which also include the contestations around indigenous rights in Amazonia. In order to explore this further I want to focus upon the nation-state of Ecuador.

Ecuador, a small nation with powerful neighbours like Colombia and Peru, is a country in which the military has had a major role in making the nation, using its power to forge a national army, and to claim the title *Nacional* for the military football team. While the military in Ecuador have engaged in Human Rights training since 1993, in a previous era it was General Pinochet who advised on strategy and organization. However, the military vision of Ecuador shifted towards inclusivity and the integration of both black and indigenous Ecuadoreans into the Army and through community development schemes, technical schools and interventions in the countryside. This was an important shift in the imaginary of the nation, which had previously marginalized these populations through the reliance on an ideology of *mestizaje*. In strategic terms, the military sought ways in which to pacify the indigenous populations, as many of them occupy lands on the borders; the military thus acted in the interests of territorial integrity. But this is a military within a democracy, facing organized citizens who share an interest in land. Currently, the decentred nation is disassembled and reassembled in a constant dance between the military and the organized indigenous movement, which is both national and transnational.

Even in this small nation of 11 million plus, where there is a national curriculum, national symbols, museums and histories that recount the story of the nation, the nation is not secure, from within or without. It is decentred through globalization, regionalism, the politics of identities and difference, through racisms, ethnicities, class and gender. Thus a politics of difference engages in a perpetual politics of the nation, while government and the military seek to centre the nation by invoking the common enemy on the border, Peru, the Other of Ecuadorean nation-ness, with whom Ecuador has periodic wars and constant battles over territorial integrity (Radcliffe and Westwood, 1996). The ideological investments in nation building are thus woven into the state and institutional structure of the country that takes its name from the Equator. Latterly, for all this ideological work on nation-ness, Ecuador has become a dollar economy and its national assets are no longer national due to debt and the failure to negotiate successfully with the IMF and the World Bank. Now, some would say the American presence in Ecuador looks like a very old story of US intervention in its 'backyard', part of its growing commitment in neighbouring Colombia. This commitment of dollars, military personnel and armaments is prompted, according to the White House, by the war against drugs and drug barons, but some commentators suggest that this is to be the final war against Leftists.

These considerations apart, there are deep internal struggles in Ecuador over democracy, citizenship and nation-ness, sustained by one of the most well-organized and articulate indigenous movements in Latin America, CONAIE (acronym for the Confederation of Indigenous Nationalities in Ecuador),[1] which has transnational links across the border to Bolivia and a website. CONAIE is a moment in the politics of recognition. The organization brings together indigenous peoples who are very diverse in terms of linguistic identifications, customs and religions, and who are widely dispersed over a region stretching from the Andes to Amazonia. CONAIE has produced a collective subject of politics out of diversity in order to step on to the political stage and into the struggles of the democratic arena. This political subject is not uniform and does not claim a unitary identity as '*indigenista*', but is born of the recognition of difference and of the multicultural world which is Ecuador. This is all the more interesting because, of course, national identities in Latin America are organized around a fictive ethnicity which is hybrid-*mestizo/a*, a category which, for all the celebration of hybridity in some texts, does not eradicate racism but, perversely, fine-tunes the valorization of whiteness and the disavowal of blackness. Into this hybrid world of the urban *mestizo/a* has come the indigenous movement, claiming for itself a space in the nation. CONAIE fought for a programme in which indigenous languages should be valued and taught, and won some victories, but these were not sustained in the longer term as a form of state-sponsored multiculturalism. In 1996 CONAIE contested elections and Luis Macas was returned as a deputy in the National Congress on a grassroots platform that, it was hoped, would secure the social movement's intervention in the democratic process. But it was not long before social movement politics was back on the streets, protesting the sale of national assets, rising prices, failing currency and the corruption of politicians. A coup overthrew the government of Ecuador and ousted the president, Jamil Mahoud, on 22 January 2000. Again, it was an alliance between the military and CONAIE which coordinated street protests. The third player in this scenario was the USA and the dollar economy which had arrived a few weeks earlier, wiping out savings and adding to the immiseration of large sections of the population. The USA brokered a return to civilian rule and a new president, Gustavo Noboa, who was immediately called to account by the leader of CONAIE, Antonio Vargas. Thus, the articulation between globalizing forces and the imaginary of the nation as a political space was being enacted in novel ways which continue today.

The central platform on which CONAIE built its organization and its strength was an alternative understanding of the nation as a pluri-nation, a decentred, polycentric nation in which many nations were recognized and had an equal and equivalent part to play, including those of indigenous descent. The notion of the pluri-nation was also important to the tactics CONAIE used and the gains that it wanted in material terms. CONAIE secured a collective subject of politics in part through shared histories, through a community of suffering and through mutual respect; but also, and crucially, through the claim for land. And, of course, a nation's claim for territorial integrity is the first of all claims. Equally, CONAIE sought to change the Constitution in order to accommodate the notion of a pluri-nation. This is a claim more extensive than the call to hybridization and hyphenated identities (see García Canclini, 2000). The successes and twists and turns in the fortunes of CONAIE in relation to its constituency have been, in part, related to the alliances that have been forged with the military against corrupt politicians. Alliances with the military have been forged in relation to democratic claims and the role of the citizenry in relation to the nation. The military stood alongside trade unions and CONAIE on the streets in 1996 and 1997 in defence of the nation and national integrity, against the selling of national assets and the incursions of foreign capital into Amazonia, plundering the land for oil. The military, trade unions and CONAIE again cooperated in 1999 and 2000, claiming democracy for the people against the corruption and incompetence of politicians. However, this should not be read as a story of harmonious relations between CONAIE and the Ecuadorean military. Many indigenous and rural peoples still see the army as colonizing their villages and their land. Nevertheless, relations between CONAIE and the military against corrupt politicians begin to disturb an account of radical democracy and radical citizenship without the national and offer, instead, a different view of the nation from below, in struggles that have become globalized through the legal claims against

Texaco in the oil fields, use of the Internet and the cross-border organization of CONAIE.

Mindful of this all too brief encounter with Ecuador and CONAIE, I now wish to turn to the work of developing, in an equally schematic way, an understanding of 'regimes of recognition' in which the sites of nation and citizen play a major role. I begin with a previous attempt, by Michael Walzer, to produce 'regimes of toleration' which provide an albeit contested model of tolerance and, again, raise the issue of the nation-state.

On Tolerance

Michael Walzer's 1997 book, *On Toleration*, sought to provide a discussion and case studies for 'five regimes of toleration'. His defence of toleration is based on the understanding that: 'Toleration makes difference possible; difference makes toleration necessary' (1997: xii) This might prove a useful way in which to consider the dance of recognition, and one whereby it is possible to articulate a series of regimes of recognition, drawing upon a variety of sites and discourses. For Walzer the five regimes and the ways in which tolerance was discursively organized were: multinational empires where, despite the abuses of imperial power, tolerance was a necessary component of peace. But, as Walzer notes, it was a tolerance that 'tended to push people into groups' and while the structures and codes of these groups were tolerated, transgressions beyond and between the borders were not. Second, international society promotes tolerance on the basis of nation-state organization and the principle of sovereignty; but this has boundaries, as recent events in Kosova have shown. The third regime of recognition is consociation, i.e. the bi-national or tri-national state, for example, Switzerland or Belgium. Walzer also cites Lebanon, where tolerance existed over a period of time before the degeneration of relations between groups. Generally, consociations exist on the basis of a system of equality before the law in which quotas and the practice of specific customs and languages are upheld. As Walzer (1997: 24) notes: 'Toleration is not out of the question once nationalism and religion are in play, and consociation may still be its morally preferred form.'

However, the most common form is now the nation-state, the fourth regime of tolerance, which is organized around the notion of the citizen with rights and responsibilities. Minority rights, though protected in laws relating to citizenship, become the preserve of what Walzer calls the 'private collective', whether this is related to cultural and educational concerns or religious practices. Similarly, difference is a problem for the nation-state which has worked on a universalistic basis for rights and demands forms of assimilation not always appropriate. Thus minorities, especially national minorities at times of war, become the objects of intense scrutiny and modes of surveillance, as has been all too evident in relation to Ecuador. The fifth regime of tolerance is the immigrant society, where collectivities are bound to the new land through a notion of tolerance overseen by a neutral state. Immigrants become citizens and can adopt hyphenated identities, a practice which is consistent with both group identifications and the celebration of individual freedoms that may, or may not, be consistent with the practices of the state.

These regimes of tolerance are a heuristic device, a sort of Weberian set of 'ideal types' which assist in our understanding of the defining features of tolerance. But they may present more problems than they allow us to solve. Walzer follows his description of the regimes with case studies of societies and nation-states that are hybrid, or in a number of ways upset the five regimes he has elaborated. The reader can invent myriad special cases and point to the difficulties of the regimes, drawing upon the Ecuadorean material elaborated above. Walzer is aware of the shortcomings in this approach and proceeds by introducing issues of power, class, gender, education and religion but not race, which is so crucial to the argument with which we are concerned in this article. This sociologizing of the issues does not necessarily benefit the argument because of the generality within which the regimes are framed. Instead, I want to suggest that Walzer's analysis is useful in another way. Walzer aggregates the forms of tolerance into the modern and the postmodern. The modern is conventionally understood to be marked by the rise of nation-states and the development of citizenship within the unversalizing discourse of the individual and freedoms for the individual. It is when he approaches the postmodern that tolerance begins to connect with recognition.

Walzer (1997: 87) suggests that:

> In immigrant societies (and also now in nation-states under immigrant pressure), people have begun to experience what we might think of as a life without clear boundaries and without secure or singular identities. Difference is, as it were, dispersed, so that it is encountered everywhere, everyday.

This, suggests Walzer, means that community ties are loosened but that the work of tolerance is now located in the home (the home, of course, being so much the motor of national identifications and community ties). With some assistance from Kristeva, Walzer considers the notion that we are all now strangers in a strange land. But he is unsettled by this because, he maintains, strangers are, at best, connected in transitory ways, and the recognition of difference and the tolerance of otherness requires a sense of similarity and community against which the other is recognized. Thus, Walzer concludes with a plea for the politics of difference in which we both enjoy the freedom of being strangers and our encounters with strangers while, within the public sphere, we develop a model of tolerance. As he notes:

> we need at the same time to shape the regimes of toleration in ways that fortify the different groups and perhaps even encourage individuals to identify strongly with one or more of them. . . . Radical freedom is thin stuff unless it exists within a world that offers it significant resistance. (1997: 91–2)

Thus Walzer draws together in his discourse on toleration the many tensions that this volume seeks to explore and it is from these tensions that a way of debating difference and recognition may be framed. As Touraine (2000:174) writes: 'The spirit of tolerance, which was so powerful when it was fighting hegemonic ambitions, does not have any real answer to the question raised by the relations between the particular and the universal.' Following Walzer, it is important to ask: what would the regimes of recognition be as models? It is to this that I now turn.

Regimes of Recognition

Is it possible or even useful to try to elaborate regimes such as Walzer used in relation to tolerance? The answer is, of course, yes and no. Yes, because it alerts us to the conditions of existence of recognition and no because, as Charles Taylor (1994) pointed out, there has to be a politics of recognition. It is not a series of models but a set of practices outside the state which invoke solidarity and difference as a basis for political subjects immersed in cultural forms, rather than citizens. However, the usefulness of describing a series of regimes is that this is one way in which we can articulate, or bring together, a series of sites with the modalities of recognition as we understand them. The regimes are a grammar from which many creations of language may flow, like the CONAIE example given in this article, where citizenship articulated with cultural forms is definitely on the agenda. These sketches are intended to be suggestive rather than exhaustive.

Democracy

The first regime of recognition is the regime of democracy which incorporates a number of sites and a series of modalities with which we are familiar. Thus, democracy is decentred, used and abused in its representative and participatory modes. As David Held's work suggests, there are 'models of democracy' with histories relating to an interpretation of the past in which Athens is seen as the classical model. Held (1987) elaborates nine models from the classical Athenian case to 'Democratic Autonomy' in which civil society and the state are the axes within which democratic rights and obligations are exercised. The suggestion here is that citizens share in government and disputes relate to the ways in which this share is realized. This model provides a foundation for the notion of a 'stakeholder society' in which citizens are free and equal in relation to their claims and have the right to organize around their claims, contributing to a democracy of difference. This is a politics beyond left and right and in which the mainstay of representative democracy, the mass parties, become disembedded from their class and regional base, producing instead modes of convergence and attention to limited goals and programmes. Beck (1997) argues that these developments are a consequence of risk society and the development of reflexive modernity.

This suggests an alternative way of thinking democracy. As Sheldin S. Wolin (1996: 43) writes:

Democracy needs to be reconceived as something other than a form of government: as a mode of being that is conditioned by bitter experience, doomed to succeed only temporarily, but as a recurrent possibility as long as the memory of the political survives.

Nowhere is this better understood than in the Latin American nation-states forged from anti-colonial, republican histories, but histories in which the military have figured so strongly. Yet the memory of democracy was kept alive through the *juntas* and the state abuses of the 1970s period through the power of a civil society gone underground. The return of democracy in the 1980s brought into the political arena an array of claims located with the politics of difference but crucially also with the politics of recognition. Democracy is a crucial site in the regime of recognition, but it is, as Chantal Mouffe (1996) and others have made clear, more than a finished product which can be defended by rationalist claims. Rather:

> Modern democractic politics, linked as it is to the declaration of human rights, does indeed imply a reference to universality. But, this universality is conceived as a horizon that can never be reached. Every pretension to occupy the place of the universal, to fix its final meaning through rationality must be rejected since the recognition of undecidability is the condition of existence of democratic politics. (Mouffe, 1996: 254)

This is, in effect, what allows the possibility of recognition; endings are not determinate and conditions of struggle cannot be read off from the form of governance.

Democracy, about which much more could be written, is the first of the sites in which a regime of recognition is produced. But, democracy requires more than philosophical justifications and ruminations upon Kant or Rousseau as the inspiration for models of democracy. Post-structuralist understandings have made possible the insight that living with undecidability is a necessary precondition to 21st-century democratic forms. The second site is equally important and introduces, however understood, the subjects of democratic politics, both individual and collective, conceived as citizens with rights and claims in relation to the modern state.

Citizenship

Authors writing on citizenship often return to the incremental model of T.H. Marshall and his gender-blind account of the development of modern citizenship within liberal democracy. But the notion that the idea of citizenship incrementally becomes more and more inclusive has been challenged by numerous authors who have sought a deeper critique, beginning with the abstracted notion of the rational actor of politics enabled by citizenship rights to engage with democratic forms (see Phillips, 1991, for example). Certainly, any understanding of a politics of recognition requires the deconstruction of the abstracted individual and the insertion of the embodied and the muliplicity of difference that this sustains. Such a view is also consistent with the notion of the political not as an arena in which politics take place but as 'a discursive surface and not an empirical referent' (Mouffe, 1993: 81). Chantal Mouffe continues, 'Therefore citizenship as a form of political identity cannot be neutral, but will have a variety of forms' (1993: 83). This understanding of citizenship is power-filled and relates to the formation of collective political subjects out of diversity. However, this is not just a set of competing demands with the state as referee. Rather:

> ... a sense of 'we' is created by a recognition that the demands of these various movements can form a chain of democratic equivalence. It must be stressed that such a relation of *equivalence* does not eliminate *difference* – that would be simple identity. (Mouffe, 1993: 83)

Simple identity would reproduce the errors of the abstracted 'representative' citizen and a denial of difference, equivalence and recognition. Or, as Iris Marion Young (1993) suggests, it would present a series of antagonistic groups locked into their own exclusivity, the negative outcome of which has been most recently witnessed in Kosova or Rwanda. Cyberspace, too, has proved a terrain of difference, in which claims to authenticity and essentialist identities grow at an ever increasing pace; from White Pride World Wide to Jew Watch, these hate sites are proliferating at a time when our multiple, hybrid selves contemplate a cosmopolitan future. Instead, like the politics of CONAIE, difference needs to be read heterogeneously and as encompassing 'both similarity and dissimilarity that can be reduced neither to coextensive identity nor overlapping otherness' (Young, 1993: 130).

Thus, citizenship is not fixed by law and citizens cannot be viewed as simply representing a specific constituency, although they often are, as 'the black vote' or 'the elderly', for example, located with an empirically distorted category and then as political subjects made to stand in for that category. This is a form of closure and erasure which is contested by an account of radical democracy and radical citizenship. Radical citizenship is premised upon the politics of recognition in which, to quote Iris Marion Young, political subjects can be 'together in difference' and solidarities of contingency with degrees of permeability can be forged as a politics in process, thereby creating the conditions of radical democracy.

Citizenships, I want to suggest, are not conferred simply by the process of law which offers voting rights to individuals not incarcerated and of sound mind at the age of majority. There are social citizenships, cultural citizenships and sexual citizenships, to name but a few, that are always going to be the stuff of politics because they are so contested and operate within a constant process of boundary making, unmaking and remaking. Thus there is no 'sovereign citizen' against which claims are judged. Instead, as Engin Isin and Patricia Wood (1999:152) note, in relation to cultural citizenship, for example:

> Cultural citizenship is not only about rights to produce and consume symbolic goods and services but also an intervention in this identity work. It is not only

about redistributive justice concerning cultural capital but also about the recognition and valorization of a plurality of meanings and representations.

This latter point is underlined by Isin and Wood as a counter to the notion of fragmentation aligned with disintegration. Multiplicity and plurality are not conceived here as an endgame but rather as a beginning, a generative and productive process in which citizenships are constituted in relation to time and space now more contested and compressed in an increasingly global order. It is within the myriad ways of being citizens that a cosmo-politan citizenship can be forged and cosmopolitan sensibilities are a crucial element of recognition. Curiously, and unfashionably, this brings me to the third site in the regime of recognition – the nation and nation-ness.

The Nation

Much has been written about our post-national world and the dissassembling of the nation and yet, as Castells (1998) points out, the era of the nation-state as sovereign territory organizing its own affairs may well be ending but supra-national organizations are just that – supra-national – and, in order to be part of the global game, a national flag is still important. While the European Union brings together nation-states in one market and this is mirrored in MERCOSUR in Latin America, it is also the era of national claims and ruptures organized around nation-ness. In part, just as the anti-colonial struggles were claims within the discourse of nationhood for rights, citizen-ship and justice against colonial dominance, so, too, are the claims of the Palestinians or the Kurds, relating national time and the desire for a homeland to national space and territorial integrity. As Appadurai (1996) explores and current politics attests, however, there are as many ruptures within nation-states that contribute to the disassembling of nations in a post-national world. Many of these struggles are fuelled by the rhetoric of nation-ness.

These are contradictory times when urban spaces are diasporic spaces and the life of the migrant is the symbol of the postmodern world. But, as Bauman (1998) is at pains to point out, there are 'tourists ' and 'vagabonds' within the world of global mobilities. One group, the tourists, move from one hermetically sealed hotel to the next and are part of a growing global elite who travel more and more, at faster and faster speeds, but somehow always occupy the same 'international' ambience, sanitized, familiar and commit-ted to standardization with a local flourish. While the vagabonds know only too well that there are nation-states with borders and guards to keep them out, jail them, send them back across the river or the ocean. The migrants are vilified as vagabonds whether they are in search of work or a safe place or both. When did travelling to be safe in the world, to make some money or seek a better life become the object of such derision and so dangerous? The answer lies in part in the institution of the nation, in boundaries and borders and the racialized spaces of nation-ness. Thus, the nation becomes a crucial site for the politics of recognition and part of the regime of recognition, not

a hollowed-out category as some would argue. The nation may be transformed by diasporas and migrations, by devolutions and supra-national ties.
Nevertheless, as an 'imagined community' and a political focus, the nation
remains a site in the regime of recognition precisely because it is so contested, from the racist abuse of the fascists throughout the European nation-
states to disassembled and cosmopolitan city identities that have come into
being through the global cities of the 20th century. These are contradictory
times for 'the nation'. Or, as Anderson (1991: 141) wrote:

> In an age when it is so common for progressive, cosmopolitan intellectuals
> (particularly in Europe?) to insist on the near pathological character of
> nationalism, its roots in fear and hatred of the Other, and its affinities with
> racism, it is useful to remind ourselves that nations inspire love, and often
> profoundly self-sacrificing love.

Anderson terms this 'political love', and allies these sentiments and attach-
ments with the ways in which the nation is also 'home' and family in both
official and popular discourses that induct nationals into nation-ness. This
sense of belonging is invoked by the notion of La Patria throughout Latin
America, for example, imbricated in folkloric elements and the symbols of
nationhood. But, as CONAIE in Ecuador demonstrates, a sense of belonging is also a creative struggle in which the politics of recognition is crucial
to the production of belonging (Westwood and Phizacklea, 2000).

Not Yet Concluded

The regimes of recognition outlined above provide a sketch of the main sites
in which we should examine the ways in which a politics of recognition could
be framed and developed. The issues we may be able to predict but the main
players, as the discussion of Ecuador suggests, may surprise us. In concluding it is instructive to return to the writings of Charles Taylor and his
discussion of the politics of recognition, and subsequently to a more recent
intervention by Alain Touraine as a way of further exploring the regimes and
politics of recognition.

Charles Taylor's account of the politics of recognition raises the issues
reproduced as a basis for this volume and is drawn from philosophical
sources, most especially the work of Rousseau as the architect of a politics
of equal dignity and liberalism as an account of competing forces within the
neutrality of debate. Taylor (1994) is correct in pointing to the assumption
of neutrality as one of the great problems for a politics of recognition. The
politics of recognition has been allied with the politics of multiculturalism
in which equal claims are made not by individuals but by collectivities
calling up specific ethnic, cultural and religious histories and identities.
Multiculturalism has been a state-sponsored project in many of the liberal
democracies, using the notion of a neutral space and the state as neutral
arbiter as the axes for the progress of the multicultural agenda. The
difficulties have been all too apparent but they have been a response to an

understanding that misrecognition does enormous harm to individuals as citizens and as members of specific collectivities. This point has been most forcefully expressed in the work of Frantz Fanon (1986), where he explores the ways in which misrecognition, imposed by the colonizers, becomes part of the self-identification of the colonized. The answers to this invoke, both from Fanon and later writers like Richard Wright, a cathartic need to expunge the colonizer through violent means.

Taylor denies any contribution from the post-structuralist writings of Nietzsche or Foucault, but this article is trying to suggest ways in which the understanding of a decentred social can develop the argument for a politics of recognition and provide spaces for its practice. Taylor uses the example of Canada and Quebec and the claims for autonomy, nation-ness and cultural difference that have inflamed relations between Canada and Quebec. I think my previous discussion suggests some of the ways in which it is possible to re-write these relations using the sites suggested as ways in which the relations between 'imaginary communities' can be disaggregated.

This concern is also part of Anthony Appiah's debate with Taylor, in which he also wishes to acknowledge, especially in relation to claims of authenticity and the rise of an African-American black nationalism, that the white America against which it is organized is no more hermetically sealed off than the lives of black Americans. The two have grown up together and made a deep impact on each other, which has created the specificities of black cultures in the USA. The binaries created in the calls for authenticities produce a series of further misrecognitions which disallow the ways in which identities are changing over time and are, in part, self-productions not essential fixed attributes. As Anthony Appiah (1994: 161) notes:

> And if one is Black in a society that is racist then one has to deal constantly with assaults on one's dignity. In this context, insisting on the right to live a dignified life will not be enough. It will not even be enough to require being treated with equal dignity despite being Black, for that will require a concession that being Black counts naturally or to some degree against one's dignity. And so one will end up asking to be respected *as a Black*.

To ask, to demand, this is precisely what black and minority populations continue to do, as the CONAIE organization has made clear for the plurality of identities from which it is formed. The demand may be constituted in the realm of the political but it is not confined to those spaces of political action. Crucially, the demand is an everyday demand integral to life in the diasporic, multi-racial worlds within which we live.

For Touraine (2000) the task is to bring politics and the subject together with an understanding of democracy as 'the politics of the Subject'. Only with this understanding, he argues, can we move towards a democracy that invokes, 'the recognition of cultural diversity, the rejection of exclusion, and the right of every individual to have a life story in which he or she can realize, at least to some extent, a personal and collective project' (Touraine, 2000: 250). Rather than a collapse into individualist and identity claims, Touraine seeks ways in which to ally the pursuit of individual and collective strategies with forms of collective action and mobilization that ignite the social movements that produce change in the political and cultural spheres. These movements are essential as an intervention in the crisis of modernity. Touraine (2000: 304) concludes that: 'Our new battles will be battles for diversity rather than unity, for freedom rather than participation. Our greatest passions will be aroused by the domain of culture rather than economics.' While I am sympathetic to Touraine's project overall, the final ralllying cry seems to reiterate familiar binaries, diversity/unity and economics/culture and, as this article has suggested, the politics that we are trying to encourage is beyond binaries. Why can we not struggle for unity and diversity and how is it possible to separate cultures from economics? Neither CONAIE nor the protesters in Seattle and Prague use this as a premise for political intervention.

Currently, the answer to Touraine's question, 'Can we live together?', appears to be yes and no, and much of the affirmative relates not to the structures and debates over democracy but the lived reality of everyday lives in multi-racial urban spaces. At the global level, the call to strengthen the human rights agenda and ensure that it passes into law at the national level is an important corrective to liberal democracy and nation-state abuses. The pressure to enshrine the human rights agenda in law is premised upon an older discourse of humanism in which individuals and their rights must be protected in relation to the state. Respect and dignity for all are the key themes, now extended to the rights of children, of minorities, religious rights and freedom of assembly and trade union membership. But it is interesting that, in the European Human Rights Act of 1998, Article 9 'Freedom of Thought, Conscience and Religion', freedom of religious practice is clearly circumscribed. The article states:

> Freedom to manifest one's religion or beliefs shall be subject only to such limitations as are prescribed by law and are necessary in a democratic society in the interests of public safety, for the protection of public order, health or morals, or for the protection of the rights and freedoms of others.

Clearly this is also a warning to fascists, racists, homophobic and other anti-democratic groups that there are limits to rights and tolerance. The basis for this limitation lies in the politics of recognition and the protection of the rights of democratic discourse and minorities. By bringing 'religion' and 'beliefs' into the same frame, the Act is ackowledging the interface between religion and politics. But the Act does not prevent the existence of hate sites in cyberspace, nor the sale of goods and services through a multitude of organizations with hate at their core. The Christian Coalition is matched by the Hindu variant of an essentialist identity and many more organizations have recognized the power of the Web in 'going global' as a defence against hybridization and a cosmopolitan future. In part, this is a call to the diasporas to remain within an essentialist notion of the religious and/or national subject.

The cosmopolitan future has been the source of considerable interest among intellectuals of late. The attempt is to use cosmopolitan as a travelling concept which can in this time of increasing globalization and hybridization offer a way of naming the world we would wish to produce. The discussions have been interesting in terms of the separation of cosmopolitanism from internationalism which, of course, invokes something different from the 'planetary humanism' suggested by Paul Gilroy (2000). The spectre of socialism haunts the notion of internationalism and its organization through the now defunct communist parties. But I do think it is worth raising this spectre in a world now so determined on versions of Third Way politics and capitalist triumphalism. Internationalism may be tainted but it did produce global reciprocities like the interventions by Cuba at home and abroad in the production of doctors as well as guerrillas. It also produced a sense of unity across diversity in the common call to the masculinist brotherhood, and allowed a nation-state once called Yugoslavia to live with difference. This required, above all, a politics of recognition constructed through the socialist subject interpellated into a dominant discourse. This is problematic for the politics of recognition and the issue with which Levinas struggled in trying to understand and provide a philosophical basis for recognition.

Levinas (1969, 1987), hampered by a philosophical language that constantly fails him, seeks an ethical basis for recognition in the life-world but actually produces a politics of recognition. He does this because his basic premise is the unknowability of the Other and the importance of this premise is expressed by Davis (1996: 3) when he writes: 'Levinas's endeavour is to protect the Other from the aggressions of the Same, to analyse the possibilities and conditions of its appearance in our lives, and to formulate the ethical significance of the encounter with it.' The importance is 'the encounter' which cannot be simply iterated through language. All familiarity is suspended and the outcome is unpredictable, unscripted and thereby creative. This is the very basis of social life, not mutual intelligibility but as Seán Hand (1989: 55), paraphrasing Levinas, wrote 'It is alterity, then, not shared attributes, that is the key to social life.'

If this is the case, then the importance of the human rights agenda is underlined, and the debates on cosmopolitanism. These debates have sought ways in which to integrate models of democracy with supra-national organizations in an increasingly globalized world. But, as both Stuart Hall (2000) and Ulrich Beck (2000) have attempted to elaborate, it is to the local level that we need to look in order to see prototype cosmopolitan worlds being made on a daily basis. Given the hybridization of cultures and the multiracial populations of cities, the constant encounters between strangers is producing, for Hall, forms of 'vernacular cosmopolitanism', while Beck uses the term 'banal cosmopolitanism' for the myriad of daily encounters that now constitute the social in the city (see Ang, 2000, for example). This is consistent with a notion of a decentred social, in which racism has not disappeared but in which there are spaces of recognition produced through the creative encounters where there are no scripts. Instead, the cultural moment has provided axes, especially for young people to share, exchange and enjoy 'cross-over' music alongside dance, film and style. Black people have had a major impact on urban style throughout the 20th century, from dance to language, and this continues. These moments are the multilingual appropriations of the cosmopolitan city in which the modalities of recognition, previously explored, are woven together into new forms of the cultural and, of course, the national, helping to re-shape the imaginary of the nation. Such a revisioning is at the heart of the CONAIE project in Ecuador. CONAIE is promoting a conception of a pluri-nation with pluri-nationalities consistent with an inclusivist account of national identities and premised upon a lack of fixity, available for redefinition in ways that we cannot yet know. This is the politics of recognition in action both at the local level and at the state level where the legal apparatus itself can change in order to constitute the nation and the citizen in plurality.

There are many ways to explore the politics of recognition and literature has created complex and subtle languages which aid our understanding. I would like to close this discussion with one such exploration by the Australian writer David Malouf. Malouf's 1994 novel *Remembering Babylon* explores the limits and porousness of settler society in Australia and the encounter between Self and Other, nature and the social, through the story of Gemmy. Shipwrecked and survivor of the outback Gemmy stumbles into a settlement to be met with a gun. His response is telling: 'Do not shoot. . . . I am a B. . . b. . . british object', and the community into which he has tumbled continue to treat him as an object. Malouf (1994: 31) comments, 'It was the mixture of monstrous strangeness and unwelcome likeness that made Gemmy Fairley so disturbing to them, since at any moment he could show either one face or the other; as if he was always standing there at one of those meetings, but in this case willingly, and the encounter was an embrace.'

Note

1. CONAIE - Confederación de Nacionalidades Indígenas de Ecuador.

References

Anderson, B. (1991) *Imagined Communities: Reflections on the Origins and Spread of Nationalism.* London: Verso.

Ang, Ien (2000) 'Identity Blues', in P. Gilroy, L. Grossberg and A. McRobbie (eds) *Without Guarantees: In Honour of Stuart Hall.* London: Verso.

Appadurai, Arjun (1996) *Modernity at Large: Cultural Dimensions of Globalization.* Minneapolis: University of Minnesota Press.

Appiah, Anthony K. (1994) 'Identity, Authenticity, Survival: Multicultural Societies and Social Reproduction', in A. Gutman (ed.) *Multiculturalism: Examining the Politics of Recognition*. Princeton, NJ: Princeton University Press.

Bauman, Z. (1998) *Globalization: The Human Consequences*. Cambridge: Polity Press.

Beck, Ulrich (1997) *Democracy without Enemies*. Cambridge: Polity Press.

Beck, Ulrich (2000) 'Cosmopolitanism', Keynote Address at the *Theory, Culture & Society* Cosmopolis conference, Helsinki.

Castells, Manuel (1998) *The Information Age, Vol. II: The Power of Identity*. Oxford: Blackwell.

Davis, Colin (1996) *Levinas: An Introduction*. Cambridge: Polity Press.

Fanon, Frantz (1986) *Black Skin, White Masks*. London: Pluto Press.

García Canclini, Néstor (2000) 'The State of War and the State of Hybridization', in P. Gilroy, L. Grossberg and A. McRobbie (eds) *Without Guarantees: In Honour of Stuart Hall*. London: Verso.

Gilroy, Paul (2000) *Between Camps: Nations, Cultures and the Allure of Race*. London: Penguin, Allen Lane.

Hall, S. (2000) 'Keynote Address', Conceiving Cosmopolitanism Conference, University of Warwick, 27–9 April.

Hand, Seán (ed.) (1989) *The Levinas Reader*. Oxford: Blackwell.

Held, David (1987) *Models of Democracy*. Cambridge: Polity Press.

Isin, Engin F. and Patricia K. Wood (1999) *Citizenship and Identity*. London: Sage.

Levinas, Emmanuel (1969) *Totality and Infinity*, trans. Alphonso Lingis. Pittsburgh, PA: Duquesne University Press.

Levinas, Emmanuel (1987) *Collected Philosophical Papers*, trans. Alphonso Lingis. Dordrecht: Martinus Nijhoff.

Malouf, David (1994) *Remembering Babylon*. London: Vintage.

Mouffe, Chantal (1993) 'Liberal Socialism and Pluralism: Which Citizenship?', in J. Squire (ed.) *Principled Positions: Postmodernism and the Rediscovery of Value*. London: Lawrence and Wishart.

Mouffe, Chantal (1996) 'Democracy, Power and the "Political"', in S. Benhabib (ed.) *Democracy and Difference: Contesting the Boundaries of the Political*. Princeton, NJ: Princeton University Press.

Phillips, Anne (1991) *Engendering Democracy*. Cambridge: Polity Press.

Radcliffe, Sarah and Sallie Westwood (1996) *Remaking the Nation: Place, Identity and Politics in Latin America*. London: Routledge.

Taylor, Charles (1994) 'The Politics of Recognition', in A. Gutman (ed.) *Multiculturalism: Examining the Politics of Recognition*. Princeton, NJ: Princeton University Press.

Touraine, Alain (2000) *Can We Live Together? Equality and Difference*. Cambridge: Polity Press.

Walzer, Michael (1997) *On Toleration*. New Haven, CT and London: Yale University Press.

Westwood, Sallie and Annie Phizacklea (2000) *Transnationalism and the Politics of Belonging*. London: Routledge.

Wolin, Sheldin S. (1996) 'Fugitive Democracy', in S. Benhabib (ed.) *Democracy and*

Difference: Contesting the Boundaries of the Political. Princeton, NJ: Princeton University Press.

Young, Iris Marion (1993) 'Together in Difference: Transforming the Logic of Group Political Conflict', in J. Squires (ed.) *Principled Positions: Postmodernism and the Rediscovery of Value*. London: Lawrence and Wishart.

Sallie Westwood is Professor of Sociology at the University of Manchester and has broad interests in globalization and development, nations and national identities and the theorization of trust and risk in the global diamond trade.

Dyscivilization, Mass Extermination and the State

Abram de Swaan

T HE DISCUSSION of political culture in the West, implicitly or in so many words, is haunted by the spectre of the transformation from democracy into tyranny, from civilization towards barbarism. Such transitions have happened before. Can it happen again, and if so, how?

At least since the First World War two views opposed each other in this debate. On the one hand, tyranny and barbarism are seen as a reversal of progress and rationalization. On the other hand, they were seen as the very culmination of rationality and modernity.

Although these oppositions are simplistic and one-sided, they are hard to transcend. In recent years, Norbert Elias and Zygmunt Bauman have written on Nazi genocide in much more subtle and nuanced terms, while nevertheless each siding predominantly with one of the opposing sides. This is not the place to analyse their respective positions at length, nor to compare and evaluate them. Here, the questions raised by Bauman, and by many authors who preceded him, are taken up in a discussion of civilization theory, as proposed by Norbert Elias and his students.[1]

At the very core of the civilizing process, sometimes a contrary current manifests itself: while the state continues to monopolize the exercise of violence, and promotes and protects civilized modes of behaviour and expression in society, at the same time it perpetrates massive and organized acts of extreme violence towards specific categories of its citizens. The paradigm of such a counter-current in the civilizing process is Nazi Germany, but similar phenomena have occurred elsewhere.

Elias himself and a number of his students have presented and clarified their sociological concept of 'civilization' on numerous occasions, and if nevertheless it remains hard to grasp this is not just due to a lack of clarity in the argument, or to a scarcity of empirical referents, but above all to the

■ *Theory, Culture & Society* 2001 (SAGE, London, Thousand Oaks and New Delhi),
 Vol. 18(2–3): 265–276
 [0263-2764(200104/06)18:2–3;265–276;017487]

complexity and subtlety of the concept itself. Elias opted for a multi-dimensional and highly intricate definition that evolved over more than half a century as his publications succeeded one another (Goudsblom, 1994).

In later years Elias came to prefer the plural 'civilizing processes' to denote the multi-tiered development that he had observed in Western Europe. He adopted Cas Wouters's expression 'informalization' to convey the idea that a civilizing process might evolve towards less rigid, that is, more varied, subtle and flexible modes of interaction as he himself had already suggested in his 'Project for a Theory of the Civilizing Process'.[2] He wrote at length about the precarious course of the civilizing process among the Germans, and even entitled a chapter in that book 'Der Zusammenbruch der Zivilisation' or 'the breakdown of civilization'.[3]

In recent years a number of Elias's students have taken up this thread where Elias left it and written about 'decivilization' and 'decivilizing processes' (e.g. Fletcher, 1997; Goudsblom, 1994; Mennell, 1990; Szakolczai, 1997; Van Krieken, 1999; Wacquant, 1999; Zwaan, 1996).

Both expressions, 'decivilization' and 'breakdown of civilization', refer to constellations of widespread and violent destruction that succeed earlier periods when civilization prevailed to a greater degree, with more restrained modes of interaction and more tempered self-constraints. The very terms suggest that something that once existed has since disappeared, that it was lost or destroyed. This sense of loss and decay is vividly evoked by such expressions as: 'regression to barbarism', 'vulnerability of civilization', 'breakdown', 'decay' (explicitly versus 'growth') and 'the open relapse of the National Socialists into barbarism'. All these terms have been taken from a single page (Elias, 1996: 308) in the essay in which Elias directly confronts the extermination of the Jews in the Second World War.[4]

In this study, Elias immediately sets out to argue that 'civilization' is not a permanent state but rather a precarious process, that may very well reverse itself. 'How was it possible', he asks, 'that people could plan and execute in a rational, indeed scientific way, an undertaking which appears to be a throwback to the barbarism and savagery of earlier times . . .?' (Elias, 1996: 302). Elias concludes that no *'raison d'état'*, no war-objectives, no goals of internal politics were served by the murder of the Jews, rather to the contrary. And although many profited from the crime, these material gains can hardly explain the enormity of the massacre. In other words, it was a deeply irrational enterprise, that can only be explained in terms of the Nazi ideology itself.

But in the same context, Elias (1996: 307) expressly mentions another aspect: 'the killings in the gas chambers'. And he comments: 'Compared with pogroms, and with military procedures, this new form of extermination meant an advance of rationalization and bureaucratization.' And, no doubt, many of the preceding stages in the extermination of the Jews, their registration, concentration, deportation, exploitation, proceeded in a thoroughly planned, systematic, bureaucratic manner.

At the heart of Elias's thinking is the twofold movement of rationalization and bureaucratization on the one hand, *and* regression, breakdown, increasing barbarism on the other. Most accounts of the Nazi genocide and other episodes of mass extermination proceed in terms of either the one or the other perspective, either rationality, bureaucracy and modernity *or* barbarism, regression, breakdown. But the main momentum of Elias's theoretical work veers towards an interpretation of the extermination of the Jews in terms of a 'breakdown of civilization'. Thus, Elias has stressed that the German state was a weak state that failed at the task of pacifying and civilizing the Germans and therefore allowed a reversal to barbarism to occur.[5]

A clear example of the contrary approach, one that considers the extermination of the Jews, and genocide in general, as the very core of modernity is provided by the writings of Zygmunt Bauman, in his *Modernity and the Holocaust* (1989), and even more explicitly in his *Postmodern Ethics*: 'The modern era has been founded on genocide, and has proceeded through more genocide' (1993: 227).

One must grant that Elias and Bauman, in their better moments, discern both aspects concurrently in National Socialism: order *and* barbarism, design *and* impulse, organization *and* wildness. Framed in these opposing terms, the discussion dates back to the aftermath of the First World War when, after a century of relative peace and widespread faith in progress, the mutual mass destruction of trench warfare had to be accounted for somehow.[6]

In a brief and lucid account, Arpád Szakolczai (1997) addresses precisely this issue. At the first level of explanation, he argues, impulsive behaviour can be understood as a relaxation, an escape, one might say, a *Ventilsitte*, among civilized persons in a civilized society. On the second level, there are historical 'inflection points' where impulses and tendencies that before had to be warded off now become acceptable and are even cultivated: e.g. the profit motive (Weber), or sexuality (Foucault), or – Szakolczai's own example – bellicosity during the crusades. And Szakolczai (1997; italics added) continues:

> There is, however, an even more important third level of explanation. This concerns the conditions under which the civilising process can turn against itself, where the question is no longer simply a paradoxical compromise between the civilising process and its opposite, the impulses set loose by a previous dissolution of order, but *where the fundamental mechanisms of the civilising process are effectively, purposefully and explicitly undermined. It is at that level that the totalitarian movements of the twentieth century can be located*, with the important caveat that they are very closely related to the previously mentioned inflections of the civilising process, therefore they cannot be fully externalised and exorcised, restricted to the cases of Nazism and Bolshevism.

It appears that Szakolczai is on the verge of transcending the opposition between modernity and barbarism, and is ready to identify the dialectics between them. In fact, the civilizing process may indeed be 'undermined' or 'inflected'. The assumption in Elias's theory of civilization is that state formation, i.e. the monopolization of violence (and taxation) will lead to more civilized modes of intercourse and expression, i.e. a lessening of all forms of violent behaviour, state violence included. And implicitly it is assumed that the state will treat *all* law abiding citizens more or less equally, i.e. that there will be some measure of *equality before the law*. But this need not occur.

The monopolization of violence by the state may result in the overall civilization of society and yet, in certain cases, these civilized canons may nevertheless exclude certain categories of citizens from protection who will then be exposed to all the violent resources of the state monopoly. The regime may mobilize the entire machinery of the state to persecute and annihilate this target group, and this more thoroughly than could have been achieved in societies where the state apparatus has not succeeded in monopolizing the means of violence so effectively. In the process of bringing about this destruction, the intended victims must first be identified, they must be registered, they must be isolated and made the object of a persistent campaign of vilification and dehumanization; hatred and loathing must be evoked against them among the population at large. This is what I have called elsewhere the social work of 'disidentification', which goes together with a campaign to strengthen positive identifications among the rest of the population (De Swaan, 1997). In the next phase special units must be recruited and trained to round up, isolate and destroy the target population, and for this task specific locations must be screened off from the uninitiated so that the torturing and killing may proceed unnoticed (but not unbeknownst to them) in reservations of destruction. Thus, in a psychological, a social and a spatial sense, this process occurs as one of *compartmentalization*.

All the while, the rest of society maintains its pacified ways, and the vast majority of citizens continues to be protected by law, custom and etiquette. Just as it would not occur to the butcher to use his knife outside his shop or on anything but animal flesh, the guards and henchmen would not dream of attacking anyone beyond the designated category, or brutalizing their victims outside the spaces marked off for the purpose. Obviously, what occurs under these conditions is the *bureaucratization of barbarism*. The most barbarous acts are perpetrated, sometimes in a calculated and detached manner, sometimes wildly, with passion, lust and abandon. What matters is that the barbarism occurs in demarcated spaces, in delineated episodes, well separated from the rest of society, from the everyday existence of the other citizens. The barbarity is compartmentalized. This compartmentalization refers at once to the categorization of a target population, the physical isolation of the sites of destruction, the institutional identification of the authorized agents, the censoring of all information and opinion on the subject, the social demarcation of brutalization from other forms of interaction, and for the perpetrators the psychological separation of their psychic experiences from all other mental processes or social encounters. Mark Danner (1997: 59) quotes observers of the 'Bosnia Genocide':

> Western and his colleagues were struck not only by the cruelty of these abuses but by their *systematic* nature; they very rapidly came to understand that though the Serb soldiers and, especially, the 'paramilitary' troops responsible for 'mopping up' were committing wildly sadistic acts of brutality under the influence of alcohol, their officers were making rational, systematic use of terror as a method of war. Rather than being a regrettable but unavoidable concomitant of combat, rapes and mass executions and mutilations here served as an essential part of it . . .

Here, the wildness and brutality are let loose, or maybe even instilled, and at the same time instrumentalized, for specific purposes, within demarcated spaces at an appointed time: an archipelago of enclaves where cruelty reigns while being reined in all the while.

The term 'compartmentalization' refers to a 'defence mechanism', in this case one that operates through the strict isolation (Freud, 1966) of certain, especially problematic emotions and impressions. But the notion (like 'repression' for example) immediately evokes social correlates, at every level of social life. Both at the personal and the group level this compartmentalization proceeds through *disidentification* from the designated victim population, the withdrawal of identificatory affect, the denial that the target population might be similar to oneself and the repression of emotions that result from identification, such as sympathy, pity, concern, jealousy, etc. (De Swaan, 1997).

Under these conditions of state-monopolized violence, a high level of civilization is maintained in almost all respects and for the vast majority of the population; however, the regime creates and maintains compartments of destruction and barbarism, in meticulous isolation, almost invisible and well-nigh unmentionable. It is as if the civilizing process continues with the same means, but with a different turn: in one word, it has become a *dyscivilizing process*.

Within the confines of these compartments the civilizing process has been suspended; under carefully controlled conditions decivilization is allowed to proceed, barbarism is expressly provoked and unleashed against the target population that has been exempt from all state protection. If decivilization may be described at the psychological and social level as 'regression' (into a prior, a more primitive, more disorganized stage) then this dyscivilization may be described in terms of 'regression in the service of the state'.[7]

Civilization has not broken down, the social order has not fallen to pieces, barbarism has not spread all over, decivilization has occurred only in well-defined episodes and spaces. What takes place is dyscivilization: the totalitarian state continues to function in a bureaucratic, planned, 'modern' and even 'rational' manner. The ruling elites have mobilized barbarism for their own purposes and carefully encapsulated it into special compartments of local decivilization, where even wild destructiveness has been made instrumental, functional in the regime's campaign against its designated enemies.

Compartmentalization is the social arrangement and the psychic defence mechanism *par excellence* in a dyscivilizing society. To maintain it requires both rigid separations and carefully staged passages between the different emotional and interactional domains. As a consequence, the transition to a more flexible, more varied repertoire of relational and emotional modes, as Elias observed it in the contemporary civilizing process, cannot occur under conditions of dyscivilization. What Cas Wouters (1986) has described as a process of 'informalization' is much akin to what I have characterized elsewhere (De Swaan, 1990) as a 'shift from relational and emotional management through command to a management through negotiation'. Such a transition is incompatible with the defence mechanism of compartmentalization. Dyscivilizing societies will develop quite strong, but also quite rigid types of social control and self-control. Very elaborate codes of conduct and expression will be maintained to the smallest detail, until the moment that one steps over the threshold and into the compartment of barbarity, where all cruelty and wildness are permitted, until one leaves this reservation again and resumes one's controlled demeanour, *as if nothing had ever happened*: that is dyscivilized behaviour.

The student of civilizing and dyscivilizing processes will be especially interested in these transitions, these recurrent 'rites de passage' from 'civil' to 'dyscivil' conduct and experience: how after a day's work the guard gets ready to leave and go home (washes up, changes clothes, forgets all about it, remains silent about it all at home, denies everything, lies about it, or recounts the day's events in vivid, lurid detail). Is there a precise schedule and calendar or do personnel simply slip in and out of their roles in a haphazard, irregular fashion? Are the venues hidden, inaccessible, isolated by deserts, woods, screened off by walls and fences, or rather visible to passers by, who may even enter and watch at will? How do the guards, the torturers, the militiamen think about themselves? We almost always get to know them in a defensive stance, forced to speak in front of their judges, little do we know about them when they were in full action, on the offensive and may have had to prove precisely the opposite: their zeal and zest and gusto, their loyalty and commitment to the task. But again, how during one phase do they think of themselves in the other phase: are they 'a different person', do they 'turn off all emotions', 'try not to think' or are they proud and pleased with themselves in their other capacity? These are all questions about the nature of personal and social compartmentalization.

The *modus operandi* of compartmentalization need not be so extreme, it may occur under comparatively innocuous conditions. Thus, in contemporary consumer societies, butchery is equally relegated to special compartments: not only abattoirs, but even pig and chicken farms are hidden from the public's view, and once out of sight they are effectively out of mind.

Somehow, when enjoying their meat, consumers manage to forget that they are actually eating an animal and to ignore the way it was raised and killed, even though they know these facts very well.

In most societies prostitution is effectively shielded off from the rest of social life: there are spatial enclosures, 'zones of tolerance', 'red light districts', 'closed houses', there are temporal separations ('darkness', 'girls of the night'), and both the prostitutes and their clients usually succeed in slipping in and out of these prostitutional reserves without being noticed. Similar observations can be made about prisons, insanity wards and Michel Foucault's other favourite haunts.[8]

The spatial isolation and social exclusion of a designated category of people were taken a momentous step further in the 'ghettoization' of American inner cities, as Loïc Wacquant (1993, 1999) has described it. What adds much interest to his detailed account is Wacquant's explicit analysis in terms of 'decivilization': as the state withdraws from the inner-city areas, chains of interdependence break down, self-restraints disintegrate, 'depacification' proceeds as violence proliferates without the police intervening anymore, social differentiation is reversed as only informal economic activities remain, and so on. Islands of 'decivilization' have emerged in the very midst of a relatively civilized society without affecting it very much in its entirety. Again, it is effective compartmentalization that maintains this precarious separation of 'civilized' and 'decivilized' spheres. Wacquant stresses the necessary disidentification that keeps the 'underclass' as a separate category, outside the bounds of normal citizenship. Outside these 'ghettos' life proceeds 'as usual'.[9] Wacquant is especially interested in the decivilizing process that occurs within the inner city ghettos. What matters here is how these pockets of decivilization are effectively shielded off from surrounding society, warded off from consciousness, exempted from affective or moral identification. No doubt, the onset of a dyscivilizing process already exists. The transition from almost lethal neglect to actual extermination, however, would require many further momentous steps.[10]

At the core of Elias's ideas on the civilizing process is an implicit assumption of minimal equality, of some measure of equal treatment and equal esteem. Such a modicum of equality means that people identify with all others in their society as beings that are more or less the same as they themselves are.[11] It implies, moreover, a degree of equality before the law, and even some equalization in living standards. When one category of people is completely excluded from this minimal equality, the civilizing process may take a different turn and proceed along a different track. It takes a radical and annihilationist regime to complete the shift in the direction of a dyscivilizing process.

Subsequent stages of compartmentalization are increasingly incompatible with a free press, or with legal guarantees such as freedom of movement or freedom of speech – all of which by their very nature tend to transgress, to transcend the very borders that are essential to maintain compartments. Unless, of course, the target population is exempted from these rights and there is a consensus among all others to ignore whatever is done to it (somewhat like the situation that prevailed in the slaveholding society of the antebellum South of the US or in the early 20th century on the plantations of the Netherlands Indies under Dutch colonial rule).

Even a rather generous welfare state could exist in a dyscivilizing society, pried loose from its universal-egalitarian foundations, if only the targeted victims are excluded from its benefits (somewhat like the welfare policies that prevailed in Nazi Germany).

In terms of Elias's theory of civilization, the twin processes of the monopolization of the means of violence and the overall civilization of society have been pried apart in the present argument: even when monopolization of violence prevails, the overall civilization of society may or may not occur. In the first case we have the 'normal' civilizing process in the sense of Elias's theory. But in the second case, the state has achieved the monopolization of the resources of violent coercion, and yet civilized relations do not prevail in society in its entirety. Certain spaces, certain groups are excluded and have become the target of the full destructive apparatus of the state: this second trajectory I have termed the 'dyscivilizing' process.

Once this separation of the monopolization of violence on the one hand and the civilization of society on the other has been conceptualized, two more possibilities follow from the theoretical construct. Both refer to conditions of an incomplete or receding monopolization of violence by the state. First, as concerns the incomplete monopolization of the means of violence: since no monopoly of violence has yet been brought about, less civilized behaviour is to be expected in terms of the theory. When an effective monopoly of violence has been established at some point, but has begun to disintegrate since then, the theory suggests that human relations and modes of expression will regress and that a process of 'decivilization' will occur throughout society.

Civilizing theory as it stands excludes another possibility: that the monopolization of violence has not yet been accomplished or that it has broken down again and that nevertheless civilized modes of behaviour and expression are prevalent throughout society. In terms of civilization theory, this would be an 'abnormal' state of affairs. And yet this is clearly the situation that prevails among a Maroon community of Surinam, according to Bonno Thoden van Velzen (1982) who ascribes a high degree of self-control to the Djuka, without a monopoly of violence having been achieved in their society.

A more rigorous empirical and historical discussion of these matters would have to establish the degree of monopolization of violence in different societies[12] on the one hand and, on the other hand, assess the degree and distribution of civilized modes of behaviour and experience within these societies. Apparently, relatively civilized modes of conduct and expression may exist in the absence of effective monopolization of violence, and, conversely, when a strong monopoly of violence has been achieved, more

Table 1   The state, mass extermination and the breakdown of civilization

---

Monopolization of violence (state formation)
   *De*creasing levels of domestic violence
      'Normal' civilizing processes:
   [NB externalization of violence: world wars, colonial wars]

Monopolization of violence (state formation)
   *In*creasing levels of compartmentalized domestic violence
      'Dyscivilizing' processes:
      categorical disidentification; compartmentalization (with encapsulated local
      decivilizing processes)
   [NB externalization of violence: idem]

Demonopolization of violence
   *In*creasing levels of domestic violence
      'Normal' decivilizing processes
      pervasive deinstitutionalization, anomie, regression – 'breakdown'
   [NB external invasions, 'peace keeping missions' etc.]

Demonopolization of violence
   *De*creasing levels of internal violence
      'Civilizing' processes 'without a state'?
      low-level, local balances of power
   [NB external indifference, oblivion]

---

civilized forms of interaction and experience may spread, or society may follow a different trajectory: while overall a degree of civilization prevails, the full violence of the state is unleashed against specific categories in well-demarcated local, temporal, social and mental compartments – the trajectory of dyscivilization.

Notes

1. For a combined discussion of Elias's and Bauman's views, see Fletcher (1997: 148–75) and Watts (1998).

2. This is a quite literal rendering of the German title of the last part of the original German edition (Elias, 1978–9) ('Entwurf zu einer Theorie der Zivilisation', pp. 312–454). It was abandoned for the heading 'Towards a Theory of Civilizing Process*es*' (my emphasis) in the English editions (Elias, 1982, 2000).

3. Quotations are from the English edition (Elias, 1996).

4. Elias adds that this was not the only regression into barbarism in the civilized societies of the 20th century.

5. For a thoughtful account of the 'ethnic cleansing' in the former Yugoslavia in terms of a 'fragmentation' and 'disintegration' of the state and a subsequent

'decivilizing process', see Zwaan (1996). For a discussion of a variety of 20th-century developments in terms of civilization theory see also Mennell (1990).

6. It is worthwhile to note that to this very day the massacres of hundreds of thousands, maybe millions of Africans, e.g. in the conquest of the Congo (cf. Hochschild, 1998) merit hardly any mention in the literature on the overall evaluation of the 19th century.

7. This is a variation on the expression 'regression in service of the ego', which goes back to Ernst Kris (1952: 312): 'the ego may use the primary process and not only be overwhelmed by it . . . under certain conditions the ego regulates regression . . .'. This refers to an ego-controlled regression in order to accomplish certain ego-syntonic tasks, as may occur for example during the creative process or in the course of the patient's psychoanalysis. In the case of dyscivilization, barbaric episodes occur under conditions of full control by the state apparatus in order better to accomplish certain objectives the regime has set itself.

8. It would be most worthwhile to pursue the themes in Foucault's *oeuvre* that anticipate the present line of argument.

9. It takes 'only one wrong turn' for people to inadvertently become enmeshed in the inferno of decivilization: this is of course what happened to the hero of Tom Wolfe's *Bonfire of the Vanities* (1987), from the moment he took the wrong highway exit.

10. Robert van Krieken (1999) describes one step along that road when he relates how the Australian authorities took children of (mixed) aboriginal descent away from their parents, precisely in the name of 'civilization'.

11. Cf. Fletcher (1997: 286), who defines civilization a.o. as 'an expansion in the scope of mutual identification within and between groups'.

12. Such an effort might find support in the literature that has emerged around the concept of 'strong' and 'weak' states, e.g. Badie and Birnbaum (1983), Migdal (1988).

References

Badie, Bertrand and Pierre Birnbaum (1983) *The Sociology of the State*. Chicago, IL and London: University of Chicago Press.

Bauman, Zygmunt (1989) *Modernity and the Holocaust*. Cambridge: Polity Press.

Bauman, Zygmunt (1993) *Postmodern Ethics*. Oxford: Blackwell.

Danner, Mark (1997) 'America and the Bosnia Genocide', *New York Review of Books* 4 December.

De Swaan, Abram (1990) *The Management of Normality: Critical Essays in Health and Welfare*. London/New York: Routledge.

De Swaan, Abram (1997) 'Widening Circles of Disidentification: On the Psycho- and Sociogenesis of the Hatred of Distant Strangers – Reflections on Rwanda', *Theory, Culture & Society* 14(2): 105–22.

Dunning, Eric and Stephen Mennell (1995) 'Elias on Germany, Nazism, and the Holocaust: On the Balance Between "Civilising" and "De-civilising" Trends in the Social Development of Western Europe', *British Journal of Sociology* 45(3): 339–57.

Elias, Norbert (1978–9) *Über den Prozeß der Zivilisation: soziogenetische und psycho- genetische Untersuchungen;1. Bd.: Wandlungen des Verhaltens in den weltlichen Oberschichten des Abendlandes; 2. Bd.: Wandlungen der Gesellschaft: Entwurf zu einer Theorie der Zivilisation*. Frankfurt am Main: Suhrkamp (reprint). (Orig. pub. 1939, rev. edn, Bern: Francke, 1969.)

Elias, Norbert (1982) *The Civilizing Process: State Formation and Civilization*, trans. Edmund Jephcott. Oxford: Blackwell.

Elias, Norbert (1996) *The Germans; Power Struggles and the Development of Habitus in the Nineteenth and Twentieth Centuries*, ed. Michael Schröter, trans. and with a Preface by Eric Dunning and Stephen Mennell. Cambridge: Polity Press.

Elias, Norbert (2000) *The Civilizing Process: Sociogenetic and Psychogenetic Investigations*, revised trans., eds Eric Dunning and Johan Goudsblom. Oxford: Blackwell.

Fletcher, Jonathan (1997) *Violence and Civilization: An Introduction to the Work of Norbert Elias*. Cambridge: Polity Press.

Freud, Anna (1966) *The Ego and the Mechanisms of Defense*, rev. edn. New York: International Universities Press. (Orig. pub. 1936.)

Goudsblom, Johan (1994) 'The Theory of the Civilizing Process and its Discontents', 13th International Sociological Association Congress (session on figurational sociology), Bielefeld, 18–23 July, Amsterdam School of Social Science Research, *Papers in Progress*.

Hochschild, Adam (1998) *King Leopold's Ghost: A Story of Greed, Terror, and Heroism in Colonial Africa*. Boston, MA: Houghton Mifflin.

Kris, Ernst (1952) *Psychoanalytic Explorations in Art*. New York: International Universities Press.

Mennell, Steven (1990) 'Decivilising Processes: Theoretical Significance and Some Lines of Research', *International Sociology* 5(2): 205–23.

Migdal, Joel S. (1988) *Strong Societies and Weak States: State–Society Relations and State Capabilities in the Third World*. Princeton, NJ: Princeton University Press.

Szakolczai, Arpád (1997) 'Decivilizing Processes and the Dissolution of Order, with Reference to the Case of East Europe', paper delivered at the Norbert Elias centenary conference, Bielefeld, 2–22 June.

Thoden van Velzen, B. (1982) 'The Djuka Civilization', *Netherlands Journal of Sociology* 20: 85–97.

Van Krieken, Robert (1999) 'The Barbarism of Civilization: Cultural Genocide and the "Stolen Generations"', *British Journal of Sociology* 50(2): 297–315.

Wacquant, Loïc J.D. (1993) 'Dé-civilisation et diabolisation: la mutation du ghetto noir américain', pp. 103–25 in Christine Fauré and Tom Bishop (eds) *L'Amérique des Français*. Paris: François Bourin.

Wacquant, Loïc J.D. (1999) 'Elias in the Dark Ghetto', *Amsterdams Sociologisch Tijdschrift* 24(3–4): 340–8.

Watts, Rob (1998) 'Something Happened: An Essay in Genocide, Sociology and Modernity', paper presented at the 14th Congress of the International Sociology Association, 25 July–1 August, Montreal.

Wolfe, Tom (1987) *The Bonfire of the Vanities*. New York: Farrar, Straus and Giroux.

Wouters, Cas (1986) 'Formalization and Informalization: Changing Tension and Balances in Civilizing Processes', *Theory, Culture & Society* 3: 1–19.

Zwaan, Ton (1996) 'Staatsdesintegratie, Geweld en Decivilisering; Joegoslavië in het Perspectief van de Civilisatietheorie', *Amsterdams Sociologisch Tijdschrift* 23(3): 425–53.

Abram de Swaan is University Professor at the University of Amsterdam and chairman of the Amsterdam School for Social Science Research. He occupied the European chair at the Collège de France in Paris 1997–8. His books include *In Care of the State* (Polity Press, 1988), *The Management of Normality* (Routledge, 1990) and, *Human Societies: An Introduction to Sociology* (Polity Press, 2000) and, most recently, *Words of the World: The Dynamics of the Global Language System* (Polity Press, 2001) is in press.

Index